THE LAW OF PSYCHIC PHENOMENA

THE LAW

OF

PSYCHIC PHENOMENA

A Working Hypothesis

FOR THE

SYSTEMATIC STUDY OF HYPNOTISM, SPIRITISM, MENTAL THERA-PEUTICS, ETC.

BY

THOMSON JAY HUDSON, Ph.D., LL.D.

AUTHOR OF "A SCIENTIFIC DEMONSTRATION OF THE FUTURE LIFE," "THE DIVINE PEDIGREE OF MAN," ETC.

THIRTY-FIRST EDITION

CHICAGO

A. C. McCLURG & CO.

1908

UNIVERSITY PRESS, JOHN WILSON
AND SON · CAMBRIDGE, U. S. A.

TO THE

Honorable Lester L. Bond,

THE COMPANION OF MY YOUTH, THE STEADFAST FRIEND OF
MY MANHOOD, MY MENTOR ALWAYS,

THIS VOLUME IS AFFECTIONATELY DEDICATED BY

THE AUTHOR.

PREFACE.

I DO not expect this book to stand upon its literary merits; for if it is unsound in principle, felicity of diction cannot save it, and if sound, homeliness of expression cannot destroy it. My primary object in offering it to the public is to assist in bringing Psychology within the domain of the exact sciences. That this has never been accomplished is owing to the fact that no successful attempt has been made to formulate a working hypothesis sufficiently comprehensive to embrace all psychic phenomena. It has, however, long been felt by the ablest thinkers of our time that all psychic manifestations of the human intellect, normal or abnormal, whether designated by the name of mesmerism, hypnotism, somnambulism, trance, spiritism, demonology, miracle, mental therapeutics, genius, or insanity, are in some way related; and consequently, that they are to be referred to some general principle or law, which, once understood, will simplify and correlate the whole subject-matter, and possibly remove it from the domain of the supernatural. The London Society for Psychical Research, whose ramifications extend all over the civilized world, was organized for the purpose of making a systematic search for that law. The Society numbers among its membership many of the ablest scientists now living. Its methods of investigation are purely scientific, and painstaking to the last degree, and its field embraces all psychic phenomena. It has already accumulated and verified a vast array of facts of the most transcendent interest and importance. In the mean time a large number of the ablest scientists of Europe and America have been pursuing independent investigations in the phenomena of hypnotism. They too have accumulated facts and discovered principles of vast importance, especially in the field of mental therapeutics, — principles which also throw a flood of light upon the general subject of Psychology.

This vast array of facts, thus accumulated and verified, and awaiting scientific classification and analysis, would seem to justify at least a tentative effort to apply to them the processes of induction, to the end that the fundamental law of psychic phenomena may be discovered.

In the following pages I have attempted such a classification of verified phenomena, accounts of which I find in the literature current on the subject; and I have tentatively formulated a working hypothesis for the systematic study of all classes of psychic phenomena. It will be observed that I have availed myself largely of the labors of others, instead of confining myself to experimental researches of my own. I have done this for two reasons : *first,* that I might avoid the accusation of having conducted a series of experiments for the purpose of sustaining a pet theory of my own; and *second,* because I hold that substantial progress cannot be made in science until one is ready to accord due credit to human integrity, and to give due weight to human testimony.

In conclusion, I desire to say that I claim no credit for this work, save that which is due to an honest desire to promote the truth for its own sake. Sincerely believing in the correctness of my hypothesis, I have not hesitated to follow it to its legitimate conclusion in every field which I have entered. If at the close of the book I have seemed to trespass upon the forbidden field of theological discussion, it was not for the purpose of sustaining any preconceived opinions of my own; far from it. It was because I was irresistibly led to my conclusions by the terms of my hypothesis and the inflexible logic of its application. I cannot but be aware that my conclusions sometimes oppose the preconceived opinions of others. But no one who accepts my hypothesis as the true one will be compelled more frequently than I have been to renounce his former convictions.

T. J. H.

WASHINGTON, D. C.
    October 21, 1892.

CONTENTS.

CHAPTER I.

INTRODUCTORY.

CHAPTER II.

DUALITY AND SUGGESTION.

CHAPTER III.

REASONING POWERS OF THE TWO MINDS DIFFERENTIATED.

CHAPTER VII.

EFFECTS OF ADVERSE SUGGESTION.

CHAPTER VIII.

HYPNOTISM AND MESMERISM.

CHAPTER IX.

HYPNOTISM AND MESMERISM *(continued)*.

CHAPTER X.

HYPNOTISM AND CRIME.

CHAPTER XI.

PSYCHO-THERAPEUTICS.

CHAPTER XII.

PSYCHO-THERAPEUTICS (*continued*).

CHAPTER XIII.

A NEW SYSTEM OF MENTAL THERAPEUTICS.

CHAPTER XIV.

A NEW SYSTEM OF MENTAL THERAPEUTICS (*continued*).

CHAPTER XV.

THE PHENOMENA OF SPIRITISM.

CHAPTER XVI.

THE PHENOMENA OF SPIRITISM (*continued*).

CHAPTER XVII.

THE PHENOMENA OF SPIRITISM (*continued*).

CHAPTER XVIII.

THE PHENOMENA OF SPIRITISM (*continued*).

CHAPTER XIX.

THE PHYSICAL PHENOMENA OF SPIRITISM.

CHAPTER XXV.

THE SPIRITUAL PHILOSOPHY OF CHRIST.

CHAPTER XXVI.

THE MISSION OF CHRIST. FUTURE REWARDS AND PUNISHMENTS.

CHAPTER XXVII.

DEDUCTIONS FROM VARIOUS ATTRIBUTES OF THE SOUL.

THE

LAW OF PSYCHIC PHENOMENA.

CHAPTER I.

INTRODUCTORY.

Necessity of a Working Hypothesis. — The Newtonian Hypothesis. — The Atomic Theory. — A Psychological Hypothesis necessary. — Theories of Hypnotism and Mesmerism. — Spiritism. — Mental Therapeutics. — Liébault's Law of Suggestion. — Duality of Mind. — A Working Hypothesis for Psychology formulated. — Its Three Terms.

SUBSTANTIAL progress in any science is impossible in the absence of a working hypothesis which is universal in its application to the phenomena pertaining to the subject-matter. Indeed, until such an hypothesis is discovered and formulated, no subject of human investigation can properly be said to be within the domain of the exact sciences. Thus, astronomy, previous to the promulgation of Kepler's Laws and the formulation of the Newtonian hypothesis of gravitation, was in a state of chaos, and its votaries were hopelessly divided by conflicting theories. But the moment Newton promulgated his theorem a revolution began which eventually involved the whole scientific world. Astronomy was rescued from the domain of empiricism, and became an exact science. What the Newtonian hypothesis did for astronomy, the atomic theory has done for chemistry. It enables one skilled in that science to practise it with a certainty of re-sults in exact proportion to his knowledge of its principles and his skill in applying them to the work in hand. He knows that if he can combine hydrogen and oxygen, in the proportion of two atoms of the former to one of the latter, water will be the result. He knows that one atom, or part, of oxygen and one of carbon combined under heat will produce carbonic oxide,—a poisonous gas; that the addition of another atom, or part, of oxygen will produce carbonic anhydride (dioxide),—a harmless gas; and so on throughout the vast realm of chemical combinations.

The fact that the literal correctness of a given hypothesis is not demonstrable except by results, in no wise militates against its value in the domain to which it belongs. Indeed, it would cease to be a hypothesis the moment it were demonstrated. Newton's theorem is undemonstrable except from its results. Its correspondence, however, with every known fact, the facility with which astronomical calculations can be made, and the precision with which every result can be predicted, constitute a sufficient demonstration of its substantial correctness to inspire the absolute confidence of the scientific world. No one would hesitate to act in the most important concerns of life — nay, to stake his very existence — upon calculations based upon Newton's hypothesis. Yet there are not found wanting men who deny or doubt its abstract correctness. Volumes have been written to disprove it. But as no one has yet discovered a fact or witnessed a phenomenon outside of its domain, the world refuses to surrender its convictions. When such a fact is discovered, then, and not till then, will there arise a necessity for revising the "Principia." It is a trite and true saying that one antagonistic fact will destroy the value of the finest theory ever evolved.

It is equally impossible to demonstrate the abstract correctness of the atomic theory. An appeal to the evidence found in uniform results is all that is possible to one who would give a reason for the faith that is in him. No one ever saw, felt, tasted, or smelled an atom. It is beyond the reach of the senses; nor is it at all probable that science or skill will ever be able to furnish instrumental aids capable of enabling man to take cognizance of the ultimate unit of matter. It exists for man only in hypothesis. Nevertheless, the fact remains, that in all the wide range of human investigation there is not a more magnificent generalization, nor one more useful to mankind in its practical results, than the atomic theory. Yet there are those who doubt its abstract correctness, and labor to disprove the existence of the atom. If the ultimate object of chemical science were to demonstrate the existence of the atom, or to seize it and harness it to the uses of mankind, it might be worth while to set the chemical fraternity right by demonstrating its non-existence. If the practice of chemistry on the basis of the theory were defective in its practical results, or failed in universal application, it would then be the duty of scientists to discard it entirely, and to seek a better working hypothesis.

The most that can be said of any scientific hypothesis is, that whether true in the abstract or not, everything happens just as though it were true. When this test of universality is applied, when no known fact remains that is unexplained by it, the world is justified in assuming it to be true, and in deducing from it even the most momentous conclusions. If, on the contrary, there is one fact pertaining to the subject-matter under investigation which remains outside the domain of the hypothesis, or which is unexplained by it, it is indubitable evidence that the hypothesis is unsafe, untrue, and consequently worthless for all practical purposes of sound reasoning. Thus, Sir Isaac Newton, after having formulated his theorem, threw it aside as worthless, for a time, upon making the discovery that the moon, in its relations with the earth, apparently did not come within the terms of his hypothesis. His calculations were based upon the then accepted estimate of the length of a degree of latitude. This estimate having been corrected by the careful measurements of Picard, Newton revised his figures, and found that the supposed discrepancy did not exist. The last doubt in his mind having been thus set at rest, he gave to the world a theorem which rendered possible substantial progress in astronomical science.

In the field of psychological investigation a satisfactory working hypothesis has never been formulated. That is to say, no theory has been advanced which embraces all psychological phenomena. Many theories have been advanced, it is true, to account for the various classes of phenomena which have been observed. Some of them are very plausible and satisfactory — to their authors — when applied to a particular class of facts, but utterly fail when confronted with another class.

Thus, the students of the science of hypnotism are, and since the days of Mesmer have been, hopelessly divided into schools which wage war upon each other's theories, and dispute the correctness of each other's observations of facts. Mesmer's theory of fluidic emanations, which he termed "animal magnetism," seemed to account for the facts which he observed, and is still held to be substantially true by many votaries of this science. John Bovee Dods' electrical theory — positive lungs and negative blood — was sufficiently plausible in its day to attract many followers, as it afforded a satisfactory explanation of many phenomena which came under his observation. Braid's physiological explanation of certain classes of the phenomena afforded, in his time, much comfort to those who believe that there is nothing in man which cannot be weighed in a balance or carved with a scalpel. In our own day we find the school of the Salpêtrière, which holds that hypnotism is a disease of the nervous system, that its phenomena are explicable on physiological principles, that the suggestions of the operator play but a secondary *rôle* in their production, and that they can be produced, or successfully studied, only in diseased persons. On the other hand, the Nancy school of hypnotists holds that the science can be studied with profit only in perfectly healthy persons, and from a purely psychological standpoint, and that suggestion is the all-potent factor in the production of all hypnotic phenomena. All three of the last-mentioned schools agree in ignoring the possibility of producing the higher phenomena of hypnotism, known as clairvoyance and thought-transference, or mind-reading; whilst the earlier hypnotists demonstrated both beyond the possibility of a reasonable doubt. Indeed, a committee of the ablest scientists of the Royal Academy of Medicine of France, after an investigation extending over a period of six years, reported that it had demonstrated the existence of such powers in the human mind.

Another large class of psychological phenomena, which has been productive of more conflicting theories than any other, and which from time immemorial has puzzled and appalled mankind, is by a large class of persons referred to the direct agency of the spirits of the dead. It would require a volume to catalogue the various theories which have been advanced to account for this class of phenomena, and when done it would serve no useful purpose. It is safe to say, however, that no two individuals, whether believers or unbelievers in the generic doctrine of spiritism, exactly agree as to the ultimate cause of the phenomena. The obvious reason is that no two persons have had exactly the same experience, or have observed exactly the same phenomena. In the absence of a working hypothesis applicable to all the infinite variety of facts observed, it follows that each investigator must draw his own conclusions from the limited field of his own experience. And when we take into consideration the important *rôle* which passion and prejudice ever play in the minds of men when the solution of an undemonstrable problem is attempted, it is easy to see that a bewildering hodge-podge of heterogeneous opinions is inevitable.

Another class of phenomena, about which an infinite variety of opinions prevails, may be mentioned under the general head of mental therapeutics. Under this generic title may be grouped the invocations of the gods by the Egyptian priests; the magic formulas of the disciples of Esculapius; the sympathetic powder of Paracelsus; the king's touch for the cure of goitre; the wonderful cures at the tomb of Deacon Paris and at Lourdes; the miraculous power supposed to reside in the relics of the saints; the equally miraculous cures of such men as Greatrakes, of Gassner, and of the Abbot Prince of Hohenlohe; and the no less wonderful healing power displayed by the modern systems known as mind cure, faith cure, Christian science, animal magnetism, and suggestive therapeutics.

One fact, pregnant with importance, pertains to all these systems; and that is that marvellous cures are constantly effected through their agencies. To the casual observer it would seem to be almost self-evident that, underlying all, there must be some one principle which, once understood, would show them to be identical as to cause and mode of operation. Yet we find as many conflicting theories as there are systems, and as many private opinions as there are individuals who accept the facts. Some of the hypotheses gravely put forth in books are so bizarre as to excite only the pity or the ridicule of the judicious. One notable example is found in that system, the basic theory of which is that matter has no existence, that nothing is real but mind, and that, consequently, disease and pain, suffering and death, are mere hallucinations of morbid intellects. Other theories there are, which, if not equally absurd, are probably equally remote from the truth; and each treats the persons as well as the opinions of the others with that virulent contumely which is the ever-present resort of him who would force upon his neighbor the acceptance of his own undemonstrable article of faith. Nevertheless, as before remarked, the fact remains that each of these systems effects some most wonderful results in the way of curing certain diseases.

What is true of the phenomena embraced under the general head of mental therapeutics is also true of the whole range of psychological phenomena; namely, the want of a working hypothesis which shall apply to all the facts that have been observed and authenticated.

No successful attempt has heretofore been made to supply this want; nor has success been possible until within a very recent period, for the simple reason that previous to the discovery of certain facts in pyschological science, the scientific world was without the necessary data from which a correct hypothesis could be formulated. The researches of Professor Liébault in the domain of hypnotism, seconded by those of his pupil, Professor Bernheim, have resulted in discoveries which throw a flood of light upon the whole field of psychological investigation. Their field of observation being confined to hypnotism, and chiefly to its employment as a therapeutic agent, it is not probable that either of those eminent scientists realized the transcendent importance of their principal discovery, or perceived that it is applicable to psychological phenomena outside the domain of their special studies. The discovery is this : *that hypnotic subjects are constantly amenable to the power of suggestion ; that suggestion is the all-potent factor in the production of all hypnotic phenomena.* This proposition has been demonstrated to be true beyond the possibility of a reasonable doubt. In subsequent chapters of this book it will be shown that this fact supplies the missing link in the chain of propositions necessary for a complete working hypothesis for the subject under consideration.

The general propositions applicable to all phases of psychological phenomena are here only briefly stated, leaving the minor, or subsidiary, propositions necessary for the elucidation of particular classes and sub-classes of phenomena to be stated under their appropriate heads.

The first proposition relates to the dual character of man's mental organization. That is to say, man has, or appears to have, two minds, each endowed with separate and distinct attributes and powers; each capable, under certain conditions, of independent action. It should be clearly understood at the outset that for the purpose of arriving at a correct conclusion it is a matter of indifference whether we consider that man is endowed with two distinct minds, or that his one mind possesses certain attributes and powers under some conditions, and certain other attributes and powers under other conditions. It is sufficient to know that everything happens just as though he were endowed with a dual mental organization.

Under the rules of correct reasoning, therefore, I have a right to assume that MAN HAS TWO MINDS; and the assumption is so stated, in its broadest terms, as the first proposition of my hypothesis. For convenience I shall designate the one as the *objective* mind, and the other as the *subjective* mind. These terms will be more fully explained at the proper time.

The second proposition is, that THE SUBJECTIVE MIND IS CONSTANTLY AMENABLE TO CONTROL BY SUGGESTION.

The third, or subsidiary, proposition is, that THE SUBJECTIVE MIND IS INCAPABLE OF INDUCTIVE REASONING.

CHAPTER II.

DUALITY AND SUGGESTION.

The Doctrine of the Trinity of Man. — The Greek Philosophy. — The Early Christian Fathers. — Hermetic Philosophy. — Swedenborg. — Duality in Modern Philosophy. — "Objective" and "Subjective" Minds. — Their Distinctive Differences and Modes of Operation. — The Subjective Mind a Distinct Entity. — Illustrations from Hypnotism. — Suggestion. — Auto-Suggestion. — Universality of the Law of Suggestion.

THE broad idea that man is endowed with a dual mental organization is far from being new. The essential truth of the proposition has been recognized by philosophers of all ages and nations of the civilized world. That man is a trinity, made up of " body, soul, and spirit," was a cardinal tenet in the faith of many ancient Greek philosophers, who thus clearly recognized the dual character of man's mental or spiritual organization. Plato's idea of terrestrial man was that he is a " trinity of soul, soul-body, and earth-body." The mystic jargon of the Hermetic philosophers discloses the same general idea. The " salt, sulphur, and mercury " of the ancient alchemists doubtless refers to man as being composed of a trinity of elements. The early Christian Fathers confidently proclaimed the same doctrine, as is shown in the writings of Clement, Origen, Tatian, and other early exponents of Christian doctrine.

Indeed, it may be safely assumed that the conception of this fundamental truth was more or less clearly defined in the minds of all ancient philosophers, both Christian and pagan. It is the basis of their conception of God as a Trinity in his personality, modes of existence, and manifestations, — a conception of which Schelling says : " The philosophy of mythology proves that a trinity of divine potentialities is the root from which have grown the religious ideas of all nations of any importance that are known to us."

In later times, Swedenborg, believing himself to be divinely inspired, declared that " There appertain to every man an internal man, a rational man, and an external man, which is properly called the natural man." Again, he tells us that there are three natures, or degrees of life, in man, — " the natural, the spiritual, and the celestial."

Of modern writers who accept the dual theory, Professor Wigan, Dr. Brown-Séquard, and Professor Proctor are notable examples. Numerous facts are cited by these writers, demonstrating the broad fact of duality of mind, although their theory of causation, based on cerebral anatomy, will not bear a moment's examination in the light of the facts of hypnotic science.

In more recent years [1] the doctrine of duality of mind is beginning to be more clearly defined, and it may now be said to constitute a cardinal principle in the philosophy of many of the ablest exponents of the new psychology.

Thousands of examples might be cited to show that in all the ages the truth has been dimly recognized by men of all civilized races and in all conditions of life. Indeed, it may be safely predicated of every man of intelligence and refinement that he has often felt within himself an intelligence not the result of education, a perception of truth independent of the testimony of his bodily senses.

It is natural to suppose that a proposition, the substantial correctness of which has been so widely recognized, must not only possess a solid basis of truth, but must, if clearly understood, possess a veritable significance of the utmost importance to mankind.

Hitherto, however, no successful attempt has been made

---

[1] Since the above was written, Du Prel's able and interesting work, entitled "The Philosophy of Mysticism," has appeared, in which the dual theory is demonstrated beyond question by reference to the phenomena of dreams.

to define clearly the nature of the two elements which con stitute the dual mind; nor has the fact been recognized that the two minds possess distinctive characteristics. It is a fact, nevertheless, that the line of demarcation between the two is clearly defined; that their functions are essentially unlike; that each is endowed with separate and distinct attributes and powers; and that each is capable, under certain conditions and limitations, of independent action.

For want of a better nomenclature, I shall distinguish the two by designating the one as *objective*, and the other as *subjective*. In doing so the commonly received definitions of the two words will be slightly modified and extended; but inasmuch as they more nearly express my exact meaning than any others that occur to me, I prefer to use them rather than attempt to coin new ones.

In general terms the difference between man's two minds may be stated as follows: —

The objective mind takes cognizance of the objective world. Its media of observation are the five physical senses. It is the outgrowth of man's physical necessities. It is his guide in his struggle with his material environment. Its highest function is that of reasoning.

The subjective mind takes cognizance of its environment by means independent of the physical senses. It perceives by intuition. It is the seat of the emotions, and the storehouse of memory. It performs its highest functions when the objective senses are in abeyance. In a word, it is that intelligence which makes itself manifest in a hypnotic subject when he is in a state of somnambulism.

In this state many of the most wonderful feats of the subjective mind are performed. It sees without the use of the natural organs of vision; and in this, as in many other grades, or degrees, of the hypnotic state, it can be made, apparently, to leave the body, and travel to distant lands and bring back intelligence, oftentimes of the most exact and truthful character. It also has the power to read the thoughts of others, even to the minutest details; to read the contents of sealed envelopes and of closed books. In short, it is the subjective mind that possesses what is popularly

designated as clairvoyant power, and the ability to apprehend the thoughts of others without the aid of the ordinary,
objective means of communication.

In point of fact, that which, for convenience, I have
chosen to designate as the subjective mind, appears to be a
separate and distinct entity; and the real distinctive difference between the two minds seems to consist in the fact
that the " objective mind " is merely the function of the physical brain, while the " subjective mind " is a distinct entity,
possessing independent powers and functions, having a
mental organization of its own, and being capable of sustaining an existence independently of the body. In other
words, it is the soul. The reader would do well to bear
this distinction clearly in mind as we proceed.

One of the most important, as well as one of the most
striking, points of difference between the two minds, relates
to the subject of suggestion. It is in this that the researches of the modern hypnotists give us the most important aid. Whether we agree with the Paris school in giving
to suggestion a secondary place among the causes of hypnotic phenomena, or with the Nancy school in ascribing
all the phenomena to the potentiality of suggestion, there
can be no doubt of the fact that when suggestion is actively
and intelligently employed, it is always effective. The following propositions, therefore, will not be disputed by any
intelligent student of hypnotism : —

1. That the objective mind, or, let us say, man in his
normal condition, is not controllable, against reason, positive knowledge, or the evidence of his senses, by the suggestions of another.

2. That the subjective mind, or man in the hypnotic
state, is unqualifiedly and constantly amenable to the power
of suggestion.

That is to say, the subjective mind accepts, without
hesitation or doubt, every statement that is made to it,
no matter how absurd or incongruous or contrary to the
objective experience of the individual. If a subject is
told that he is a dog, he will instantly accept the suggestion, and, to the limit of physical possibility, act the part

suggested. If he is told that he is the President of the United States, he will act the part with wonderful fidelity to life. If he is told that he is in the presence of angels, he will be profoundly moved to acts of devotion. If the presence of devils is suggested, his terror will be instant, and painful to behold. He may be thrown into a state of intoxication by being caused to drink a glass of water under the impression that it is brandy; or he may be restored to sobriety by the administration of brandy, under the guise of an antidote to drunkenness. If told that he is in a high fever, his pulse will become rapid, his face flushed, and his temperature increased. In short, he may be made to see, hear, feel, smell, or taste anything, in obedience to suggestion. He may be raised to the highest degree of mental or physical exaltation by the same power, or be plunged by it into the lethargic or cataleptic condition, simulating death.

These are fundamental facts, known and acknowledged by every student of the science of hypnotism. There is another principle, however, which must be mentioned in this connection, which is apparently not so well understood by hypnotists generally. I refer to the phenomenon of auto-suggestion. Professor Bernheim and others have recognized its existence, and its power to modify the results of experiments in one class of hypnotic phenomena, but apparently have failed to appreciate its full significance. It is, in fact, of coextensive importance with the general principle, or law, of suggestion, and is an essential part of it. It modifies every phenomenon, and sometimes seems to form an exception to the general law. Properly understood, however, it will be seen, not only to emphasize that law, but to harmonize all the facts which form apparent exceptions to it.

The two minds being possessed of independent powers and functions, it follows as a necessary corollary that the subjective mind of an individual is as amenable to the control of his own objective mind as to the objective mind of another. This we find to be true in a thousand ways. For instance, it is well known that a person cannot be hypnotized against his will. As the hypnotic condition is usually induced by the suggestion of the operator, his failure is due to the contrary auto-suggestion of the subject. Again, if the subject submits to be hypnotized, but resolves beforehand that he will not submit to certain anticipated experiments, the experiments are sure to fail. One of the finest hypnotic subjects known to the writer would never allow himself to be placed in a position before a company which he would shrink from in his normal condition. He was possessed of a remarkable dignity of character, and was highly sensitive to ridicule; and this sensitiveness stepped in to his defence, and rendered abortive every attempt to cause him to place himself in a ridiculous attitude. Again, if a hypnotic subject is conscientiously opposed to the use of strong drink, no amount of persuasion on the part of the operator can induce him to violate his settled principles. And so on, through all the varying phases of hypnotic phenomena, auto-suggestion plays its subtle *rôle*, often confounding the operator by resistance where he expected passive obedience. It does not militate against the force of the rule that suggestion is the all-controlling power which moves the subjective mind. On the contrary, it confirms it, demonstrates its never-failing accuracy. It shows, however, that the stronger suggestion must always prevail. It demonstrates, moreover, that the hypnotic subject is not the passive, unreasoning, and irresponsible automaton which hypnotists, ancient and modern, have believed him to be.

As this is one of the most important branches of the whole subject of psychological phenomena, it will be more fully treated when the various divisions of the subject to which the principle is applicable are reached. In the mean time, the student should not for a moment lose sight of this one fundamental fact, that the subjective mind is always amenable to the power of suggestion by the objective mind, either that of the individual himself, or that of another who has, for the time being, assumed control.

CHAPTER III.

REASONING POWERS OF THE TWO MINDS DIFFERENTIATED.

The Subjective Mind incapable of Inductive Reasoning. — Its Processes always Deductive or Syllogistic. — Its Premises the Result of Suggestion. — Illustrations by Hypnotism. — Hypnotic Interview with Socrates. — Reasons from an Assumed Major Premise. — Interview with a Philosophic Pig. — The Pig affirms the Doctrine of Reincarnation. — Dogmatism of Subjective Intelligence. — Incapable of Controversial Argument. — Persistency in following a Suggested Line of Thought.

ONE of the most important distinctions between the objective and subjective minds pertains to the function of reason. That there is a radical difference in their powers and methods of reasoning is a fact which has not been noted by any psychologist who has written on the subject. It is, nevertheless, a proposition which will be readily conceded to be essentially true by every observer when his attention is once called to it. The propositions may be briefly stated as follows : —

1. The objective mind is capable of reasoning by all methods, — inductive and deductive, analytic and synthetic.

2. The subjective mind is incapable of inductive reasoning.

Let it here be understood that this proposition refers to the powers and functions of the purely subjective mind, as exhibited in the mental operations of persons in a state of profound hypnotism, or trance. The prodigious intellectual feats of persons in that condition have been a source of amazement in all the ages ; but the striking peculiarity noted above appears to have been lost sight of in admiration of the other qualities exhibited. In other words, it has never been noted that their reasoning is always deductive, or syllogistic. The subjective mind never classifies a series of known facts, and reasons from them up to general principles; but, given a general principle to start with, it will reason deductively from that down to all legitimate inferences, with a marvellous cogency and power. Place a man of intelligence and cultivation in the hypnotic state, and give him a premise, say in the form of a statement of a general principle of philosophy, and no matter what may have been his opinions in his normal condition, he will unhesitatingly, in obedience to the power of suggestion, assume the correctness of the proposition; and if given an opportunity to discuss the question, will proceed to deduce therefrom the details of a whole system of philosophy. Every conclusion will be so clearly and logically deducible from the major premise, and withal so plausible and consistent, that the listener will almost forget that the premise was assumed. To illustrate : —

The writer once saw Professor Carpenter, of Boston, place a young gentleman in the hypnotic state at a private gathering in the city of Washington. The company was composed of highly cultivated ladies and gentlemen of all shades of religious belief; and the young man himself — who will be designated as C — was a cultured gentleman, possessed a decided taste for philosophical studies, and was a graduate of a leading college. In his normal condition he was liberal in his views on religious subjects, and, though always unprejudiced and open to conviction, was a decided unbeliever in modern spiritism. Knowing his love of the classics and his familiarity with the works of the Greek philosophers, the professor asked him how he should like to have a personal interview with Socrates.

"I should esteem it a great privilege, if Socrates were alive," answered C.

"It is true that Socrates is dead," replied the professor; "but I can invoke his spirit and introduce you to him. There he stands now," exclaimed the professor, pointing towards a corner of the room.

C looked in the direction indicated, and at once arose, with a look of the most reverential awe depicted on his countenance. The professor went through the ceremonial of a formal presentation, and C, almost speechless with embarrassment, bowed with the most profound reverence, and offered the supposed spirit a chair. Upon being assured by the professor that Socrates was willing and anxious to answer any question that might be put to him, C at once began a series of questions, hesitatingly and with evident embarrassment at first; but, gathering courage as he proceeded, he catechised the Greek philosopher for over two hours, interpreting the answers to the professor as he received them. His questions embraced the whole cosmogony of the universe and a wide range of spiritual philosophy. They were remarkable for their pertinency, and the answers were no less remarkable for their clear-cut and sententious character, and were couched in the most elegant and lofty diction, such as Socrates himself might be supposed to employ. But the most remarkable of all was the wonderful system of spiritual philosophy evolved. It was so clear, so plausible, and so perfectly consistent with itself and the known laws of Nature that the company sat spell-bound through it all, each one almost persuaded, for the time being, that he was listening to a voice from the other world. Indeed, so profound was the impression that some of them — not spiritists, but members of the Christian Church — then and there announced their conviction that C was actually conversing either with the spirit of Socrates or with some equally high intelligence.

At subsequent gatherings other pretended spirits were called up, among them some of the more modern philosophers, and one or two who could not be dignified with that title. When a modern spirit was invoked, the whole manner of C changed. He was more at his ease, and the conversation on both sides assumed a purely nineteenth-century tone. But the philosophy was the same; there was never a lapse or an inconsistency. With the introduction of every new spirit there was a decided change of diction and character and general style of conversation, and each one was always the same, whenever reintroduced. If the persons themselves had been present, their distinctive peculiarities could not have been more marked; but if all that was said could have been printed in a book *verbatim*, it would have formed one of the grandest and most coherent systems of spiritual philosophy ever conceived by the brain of man, and its only blemish would have been the frequent change of the style of diction.

It must not be forgotten that C was not a spiritist, and that the whole bent of his mind inclined to materialism. He frequently expressed the most profound astonishment at the replies he received. This was held to be an evidence that the replies were not evolved from his own inner consciousness. Indeed, it was strenuously urged by some of the company present that he must have been talking with an independent intelligence, else his answers would have coincided with his own belief while in his normal condition. The conclusive answer to that proposition is this: He was in the subjective state. He had been told that he was talking face to face with a disembodied spirit of superior intelligence. He believed the statement implicitly, in obedience to the law of suggestion. He saw, or thought he saw, a disembodied spirit. The inference, for him, was irresistible that this was a demonstration of the truth of spiritism; that being assumed, the rest followed as a natural inference. He was, then, simply reasoning deductively from an assumed major premise, thrust upon him, as it were, by the irresistible force of a positive suggestion. His reasoning was perfect of its kind, there was not a flaw in it; but it was purely syllogistic, from general principles to particular facts.

It will doubtless be said that this does not prove that he was not in actual converse with a spirit. True; and if the conversation had been confined to purely philosophical subjects, its exalted character would have furnished plausible grounds for a belief that he was actually in communion with the inhabitants of a world where pure intelligence reigns supreme. But test questions were put to one of the supposed spirits, with a view of determining this point. One of them was asked where he died. His reply was, " In a little town near Boston." The fact is that he had lived in a little town near Boston, and the somnambulist knew it. But he died in a foreign land, — a fact which the somnambulist did not know. C was subsequently, when in his normal condition, informed of the failure of this test question, and was told at the same time what the facts were concerning the circumstances of the death of the gentleman whose spirit was invoked. He was amused at the failure, as well as at the credulity of those who had believed that he had been in conversation with spirits ; but at a subsequent sitting he was again informed that the same spirit was present, and he at once manifested the most profound indignation because of the deception which had been practised upon him by the said spirit, and demanded an explanation of the falsehood which he had told concerning the place of his death. Then was exhibited one of the most curious phases of subjective intelligence. The spirit launched out into a philosophical disquisition on the subject of spirit communion, and defined the limitations of spiritual intercourse with the inhabitants of this earth in such a philosophical and plausible manner that not only was the young man mollified, but the spiritists present felt that they had scored a triumph, and had at last heard an authoritative explanation of the fact that spirits are limited in their knowledge of their own antecedents by that of the medium through whom they communicate.

For the benefit of those who will say that there is, after all, no proof that C was not in actual communication with a superior intelligence, it must be stated that at a subsequent séance he was introduced to a very learned and very philosophical pig, who spoke all the modern languages with which C was acquainted, and appeared to know as much about spiritual philosophy as did the ancient Greek. C had been told that the pig was a reincarnation of a Hindoo priest whose " karma " had been a little off color, but who retained a perfect recollection of his former incarnation, and had not forgotten his learning. It is perhaps unnecessary to say that the pig was able to, and did, give a very learned

and eminently satisfactory exposition of the doctrine of reincarnation and of Hindoo philosophy in general. As C
was then fresh from his reading of some modern theosophi-
cal works, he was apparently much gratified to find that they
were in substantial accord with the views of the pig.

The inference to be drawn from these facts is obvious and
irresistible : the subjective mind of the young man accepted
the suggestion of the operator as an absolute verity. The
deductions from the premises thus given were evolved from
his own inner consciousness. But that he believed them to
have been imparted to him by a spirit, is as certain as that
believed that he saw a spirit.

It must not be understood from the statement of the general proposition regarding the subjective processes of reasoning that persons in the subjective state necessarily go
through the forms of syllogistic reasoning. On the contrary,
they seldom, if ever, employ the forms of the syllogism, and
it is rare that their discourses are argumentative. They
are generally, in fact, dogmatic to the last degree. It never
seems to occur to them that what they state to be a fact can
possibly be, in the slightest degree, doubtful. A doubt,
expressed or implied, of their perfect integrity, of the
correctness of their statements, or of the genuineness of the
phenomena which is being exhibited through them, invariably results in confusion and distress of mind. Hence they
are incapable of controversial argument, — a fact which constitutes another important distinction between the objective
and subjective minds. To traverse openly the statements
of a person in the subjective state, is certain to restore him
to the normal condition, often with a severe nervous shock.
The explanation of these facts is easy to find in the constant
amenability of the subjective mind to the power of suggestion. They are speaking or acting from the standpoint of
one suggestion, and to controvert it is to offer a counter
suggestion which is equally potent with the first. The
result is, and must necessarily be, utter confusion of mind
and nervous excitement on the part of the subject. These
facts have an important bearing upon many psychological
phenomena, and will be adverted to more at length in future

chapters, my present purpose being merely to impress upon the reader's mind the general principles governing subjective mental phenomena.

It will be seen from the foregoing that when it is stated that the subjective mind reasons deductively, the results of its reasoning processes are referred to rather than its forms. That is to say, whilst it may not employ the forms of the syllogism, its conclusions are syllogistically correct, — are logically deducible from the premises imparted to it by suggestion. This peculiarity seems to arise from, or to be the necessary result of, the persistency with which the subjective mir   "l follow every idea suggested.   It is well known to hyp... is that when an idea is suggested to a subject, no matter of how trivial a character, he will persist in following that idea to its ultimate conclusion, or until the operator releases him from the impression.   For instance, if a hypnotist suggests to one of his subjects that his back itches, to another that his nose bleeds, to another that he is a marble statue, to another that he is an animal, etc., each one will follow out the line of his particular impression, regardless of the presence of others, and totally oblivious to all his surroundings which do not pertain to his idea ; and he will persist in doing so until the impression is removed by the same power by which it was created.   The same principle prevails when a thought is suggested and the subject is invited to deliver a discourse thereon.   He will accept the suggestion as his major premise ; and whatever there is within the range of his own knowledge or experience, whatever he has seen, heard, or read, which confirms or illustrates that idea, he has at his command and effectually uses it, but is apparently totally oblivious to all facts or ideas which do not confirm, and are not in accord with, the one central idea.   It is obvious that inductive reasoning, under such conditions, is out of the question.

CHAPTER IV.

PERFECT MEMORY. OF THE SUBJECTIVE MIND.

Confirmed by Hypnotic Phenomena. — Opinions of Psychologists. — Sir William Hamilton's Views. — Observations of Dr. Rush. — Talent for Poetry and Music developed by Abnormal Conditions. — Talent for Drawing evolved by Madness. — Resuscitation of Knowledge in the Insane. — Extraordinary Feats of Memory during Illness. — A Forgotten Language recovered. — Whole Pages of Greek and Hebrew remembered by an Illiterate Servant Girl. — Speaking in Unknown Tongues explained. — The Result of the Operations of Natural Law.

ONE of the most striking and important peculiarities of the subjective mind as distinguished from the objective, consists in its prodigious memory. It would perhaps be hazardous to say that the memory of the subjective mind is perfect, but there is good ground for believing that such a proposition would be substantially true. It must be understood that this remark applies only to the most profoundly subjective state and to the most favorable conditions. In all degrees of hypnotic sleep, however, the exaltation of the memory is one of the most pronounced of the attendant phenomena. This has been observed by all hypnotists, especially by those who make their experiments with a view of studying the mental action of the subject. Psychologists of all shades of belief have recognized the phenomena, and many have declared their conviction that the minutest details of acquired knowledge are recorded upon the tablets of the mind, and that they only require favorable conditions to reveal their treasures.

Sir William Hamilton, in his " Lectures on Metaphysics," page 236, designates the phenomenon as "latent memory." He says : —

" The evidence on this point shows that the mind frequently contains whole systems of knowledge, which, though in our normal state they have faded into absolute oblivion, may, in certain abnormal states — as madness, febrile delirium, somnambulism, catalepsy, etc. — flash out into luminous consciousness, and even throw into the shade of unconsciousness those other systems by which they had, for a long period, been eclipsed, and even extinguished. For example, there are cases in which the extinct memory of whole languages was suddenly restored ; and, what is even still more remarkable, in which the faculty was exhibited of accurately repeating, in known or unknown tongues, passages which were never within the grasp of conscious memory in the normal state."

Sir William then proceeds to quote, with approval, a few cases which illustrate the general principle. The first is on the authority of Dr. Rush, a celebrated American physician :

" The records of the wit and cunning of madmen," says the doctor, " are numerous in every country. Talents for eloquence, poetry, music, and painting, and uncommon ingenuity in several of the mechanical arts, are often evolved in this state of madness. A gentleman whom I attended in an hospital in the year 1810, often delighted as well as astonished the patients and officers of our hospital by his displays of oratory in preaching from a table in the hospital yard every Sunday. A female patient of mine who became insane, after parturition, in the year 1807, sang hymns and songs of her own composition during the latter stage of her illness, with a tone of voice so soft and pleasant that I hung upon it with delight every time I visited her. She had never discovered a talent for poetry or music in any previous part of her life. Two instances of a talent for drawing, evolved by madness, have occurred within my knowledge. And where is the hospital for mad people in which elegant and completely rigged ships and curious pieces of machinery have not been exhibited by persons who never discovered the least turn for a mechanical art previous to their derangement?

" Sometimes we observe in mad people an unexpected resuscitation of knowledge ; hence we hear them describe past events, and speak in ancient or modern languages, or repeat long and interesting passages from books, none of which, we are sure, they were capable of recollecting in the natural and healthy state of their mind." [1]

It must be remembered that when these events occurred, the profession knew little of the phenomena of hypnotism. In the light of present knowledge on that subject it is easy to understand that the phenomena here recorded are referable to one common origin, whatever may have been the proximate cause of their manifestation. There are many ways by which the subjective mind may be caused to become active and dominant besides deliberately producing hypnotic sleep. Diseases of various kinds, particularly those of the brain or nervous system, and intense febrile excitement, are frequently causes of the total or partial suspension of the functions of the objective mind, and of exciting the subjective mind to intense activity.

The next case quoted by Sir William is from "Recollections of the Valley of the Mississippi," by an American clergyman named Flint : —

"I am aware," he remarks, "that every sufferer in this way is apt to think his own case extraordinary. My physicians agreed with all who saw me that my case was so. As very few live to record the issue of a sickness like mine, and as you have requested me, and as I have promised, to be particular, I will relate some of the circumstances of this disease. And it is in my view desirable, in the bitter agony of such diseases, that more of the symptoms, sensations, and sufferings should have been recorded than have been; and that others in similar predicaments may know that some before them have had sufferings like theirs, and have survived them. I had had a fever before, and had risen, and been dressed every day. But in this, with the first day I was prostrated to infantine weakness, and felt, with its first attack, that it was a thing very different from what I had yet experienced.

"Paroxysms of derangement occurred the third day, and this was to me a new state of mind. That state of disease in which partial derangement is mixed with a consciousness generally sound, and sensibility preternaturally excited, I should suppose the most distressing of all its forms. At the same time that I

[1] Beasley on the Mind, p. 474.

was unable to recognize my friends, I was informed that my memory was more than ordinarily exact and retentive, and that I repeated whole passages in the different languages which I knew, with entire accuracy. I recited, without losing or misplacing a word, a passage of poetry which I could not so repeat after I recovered my health."

The following more curious case is given by Lord Monboddo in his "Ancient Metaphysics": [1]—

"It was communicated in a letter from the late Mr. Hans Stanley, a gentleman well known both to the learned and political world, who did me the honor to correspond with me upon the subject of my first volume of Metaphysics. I will give it in the words of that gentleman. He introduces it by saying that it is an extraordinary fact in the history of mind, which he believes stands single, and for which he does not pretend to account; then he goes on to narrate it: 'About six-and-twenty years ago, when I was in France, I had an intimacy in the family of the late Maréchal de Montmorenci de Laval. His son, the Comte de Laval, was married to Mademoiselle de Manpeaux, the daughter of a lieutenant-general of that name, and the niece of the late chancellor. This gentleman was killed at the battle of Hastenbeck. His widow survived him some years, but is since dead.

"'The following fact comes from her own mouth; she has told it me repeatedly. She was a woman of perfect veracity and very good sense. She appealed to her servants and family for the truth. Nor did she, indeed, seem to be sensible that the matter was so extraordinary as it appeared to me. I wrote it down at the time, and I have the memorandum among some of my papers.

"'The Comtesse de Laval had been observed, by servants who sat up with her on account of some indisposition, to talk in her sleep a language that none of them understood; nor were they sure, or, indeed, herself able to guess, upon the sounds being repeated to her, whether it was or was not gibberish.

"'Upon her lying-in of one of her children she was attended by a nurse who was of the province of Brittany, and who immediately knew the meaning of what she said, it being in the idiom of the natives of that country; but she herself when awake did not understand a single syllable of what she had uttered in her sleep, upon its being retold her.

[1] Vol. ii. p. 217.

"'She was born in that province, and had been nursed in a family where nothing but that language was spoken; so that in her first infancy she had known it, and no other; but when she returned to her parents, she had no opportunity of keeping up the use of it; and, as I have before said, she did not understand a word of Breton when awake, though she spoke it in her sleep.

"'I need not say that the Comtesse de Laval never said or imagined that she used any words of the Breton idiom, more than were necessary to express those ideas that are within the compass of a child's knowledge of objects.'"

A highly interesting case is given by Mr. Coleridge in his "Biographia Literaria."[1]

"It occurred," says Mr. Coleridge, "in a Roman Catholic town in Germany, a year or two before my arrival at Göttingen, and had not then ceased to be a frequent subject of conversation. A young woman of four or five and twenty, who could neither read nor write, was seized with a nervous fever, during which, according to the asseverations of all the priests and monks of the neighborhood, she became possessed, and as it appeared, by a very learned devil. She continued incessantly talking Latin, Greek, and Hebrew, in very pompous tones, and with most distinct enunciation. This possession was rendered more probable by the known fact that she was, or had been, a heretic. Voltaire humorously advises the devil to decline all acquaintance with medical men; and it would have been more to his reputation if he had taken this advice in the present instance. The case had attracted the particular attention of a young physician, and by his statement many eminent physiologists and psychologists visited the town and cross-examined the case on the spot. Sheets full of her ravings were taken down from her own mouth, and were found to consist of sentences, coherent and intelligible each for itself, but with little or no connection with each other. Of the Hebrew, a small portion only could be traced to the Bible; the remainder seemed to be in the Rabbinical dialect. All trick or conspiracy was out of the question. Not only had the young woman ever been a harmless, simple creature, but she was evidently laboring under a nervous fever. In the town in which she had been resident for many years as a servant in different families, no solution

[1] Vol. i. p. 117 (edit. 1847).

presented itself. The young physician, however, determined to trace her past life step by step; for the patient herself was incapable of returning a rational answer. He at length succeeded in discovering the place where her parents had lived; travelled thither, found them dead, but an uncle surviving; and from him learned that the patient had been charitably taken by an old Protestant pastor at nine years old, and had remained with him some years, even till the old man's death. Of this pastor the uncle knew nothing, but that he was a very good man. With great difficulty, and after much search, our young medical philosopher discovered a niece of the pastor's who had lived with him as his housekeeper, and had inherited his effects. She remembered the girl; related that her venerable uncle had been too indulgent, and could not bear to hear the girl scolded; that she was willing to have kept her, but that, after her parent's death, the girl herself refused to stay. Anxious inquiries were then, of course, made concerning the pastor's habits; and the solution of the phenomenon was soon obtained. For it appeared that it had been the old man's custom for years to walk up and down a passage of his house into which the kitchen-door opened, and to read to himself, with a loud voice, out of his favorite books. A considerable number of these were still in the niece's possession. She added that he was a very learned man and a great Hebraist. Among the books were found a collection of Rabbinical writings, together with several of the Greek and Latin Fathers; and the physician succeeded in identifying so many passages with those taken down at the young woman's bedside that no doubt could remain in any rational mind concerning the true origin of the impressions made on her nervous system."

The reader will not fail to observe that in all these cases the subjects reproduced simply what they had seen, heard, or read. The impressions upon the objective mind, particularly in the case related by Coleridge, must have been superficial to the last degree; but the result demonstrated that the record upon the tablets of the subjective mind was ineffaceable.

These are not isolated cases. Thousands of similar phenomena have been recorded by the most trustworthy of observers. Their significance cannot be mistaken. In their light the wonderful mental feats of trance-speakers are easily explicable, without invoking the aid of a supernatural agency.   Speaking "in unknown tongues " is seen to be merely a feat of subjective memory.

When we consider what a prodigy of learning the average man would be if he could have at his command all that he had ever seen, heard, or read ; when we remember that the subjective mind does record, and does have at its command, all the experiences of the individual, and that, under certain abnormal conditions, in obedience to the initial impulse of suggestion, all its treasures are instantly available, — we may marvel at the wonderful gifts with which the human mind is endowed ; but we may rest assured that the phenomena displayed are the results of the operations of natural law.

The reader should distinctly bear in mind that there is a wide distinction between objective and subjective memory. The former is one of the functions of the brain, and, as has been shown by recent investigations, has an absolute localization in the cerebral cortex ; and the different varieties of memory, such as visual memory, auditory memory, memory of speech, etc., can be destroyed by localized disease or by a surgical operation.   Subjective memory, on the other hand, appears to be an inherent power, and free from anatomical relations ; or at least it does not appear to depend upon the healthy condition of the brain for its power of manifestation.   On the contrary, the foregoing facts demonstrate the proposition that abnormal conditions of the brain are often productive of the most striking exhibitions of subjective memory.   The late Dr. George M. Beard of New York, who was the first American scientist clearly to recognize the scientific importance of the phenomena of hypnotism, who was the formulator of the "Six Sources of Error " which beset the pathway of the investigator of that science, and the one who did more than any other American of his time to place the study of hypnotic phenomena on a scientific basis, evinces a clear recognition of this distinction when he says : —

" To attempt to build up a theory of trance [hypnotic phenomena] on a basis of cerebral anatomy is to attempt the impossible.

All theories of trance based on cerebral anatomy or physiology — such as suspension of the activity of the cortex, or half the brain — break down at once when brought face to face with the facts." [1]

All the facts of hypnotism show that the more quiescent the objective faculties become, or, in other words, the more perfectly the functions of the brain are suspended, the more exalted are the manifestations of the subjective mind. Indeed, the whole history of subjective phenomena goes to show that the nearer the body approaches the condition of death, the stronger become the demonstrations of the powers of the soul. The irresistible inference is that when the soul is freed entirely from its trammels of flesh, its powers will attain perfection, its memory will be absolute. Of this more will be said in its proper place. In the mean time, it may be proper here to remark that subjective memory appears to be the only kind or quality of memory which deserves that appellation; it is the only memory which is absolute. The memory of the objective mind, comparatively speaking, is more properly designated as recollection. The distinction here sought to be made can be formulated in no better language than that employed by Locke in defining the scope and meaning of the two words : " When an idea again recurs without the operation of the like object on the external sensory, it is *remembrance;* if it be sought after by the mind, and with pain and endeavor found, and brought again into view, it is *recollection*." [2]

[1] Nature and Phenomena of Trance (" Hypnotism " or " Somnambulism "), p. 6.

[2] Essays Concerning Human Understanding, vol. i. p. 213.

CHAPTER V.

SUBJECTIVE MEMORY (*continued*).

IT is thought that the facts related in the preceding chapter are sufficient to demonstrate the substantial correctness of the proposition that the memory of the subjective mind is practically perfect. Before leaving this branch of the subject, however, and proceeding to detail other peculiarities which distinguish the two minds, it is deemed proper to offer a few practical illustrations of the principles involved, drawn from common observation, and incidentally to apply those principles to the solution of various problems of every-day experience. It will be remembered that thus far we have confined our observations to the operations of the subjective mind when the subject is in a diseased or in a deeply hypnotic condition, with the objective senses in complete abeyance. This has been done for the purpose of more clearly illustrating the fundamental propositions. The phenomena of purely subjective mental action, are, however, of little practical importance to mankind when compared with the action of the subjective mind modified by the co-ordinate power of the objective intelligence.

It is not to be supposed that an All-wise Providence has placed within the human frame a separate entity, endowed with such wonderful powers as we have seen that it possesses, and hedged about by the limitations with which we know it to be environed, without so ordaining its relations with man's objective intelligence as to render it of practical value to the human race in its struggle with its physical environment. It might at first glance seem incongruous to suppose that the subjective mind could be at once the storehouse of memory and the source of inspiration, limited as to its methods and powers of reasoning, and at the same time subject to the imperial control of the objective mind. A moment's reflection, however, will show that in the very nature of things it must necessarily be true. " A house divided against itself cannot stand." There must be a controlling power in every well-regulated household, municipality, nation, or organism. There is a positive and a negative force in the greatest physical power known to mankind. There is a male and a female element in every race and order of created organisms; and those philosophers who hold that there appertain to every man a male and a female element have dimly recognized the duality of man's mental organization.

Why it is that the objective mind has been invested with the controlling influence, limited as are its resources and feeble as are its powers, is a question upon which it would be idle to speculate. It profits us only to know the fact and to study its practical significance, without wasting our energies in seeking to know the ultimate cause. We may rest assured that in this, as in all other laws of Nature, we shall find infinite wisdom.

If any one doubts the wisdom of investing the objective mind with the controlling power in the dual organization, let him visit a madhouse. There he will see all shades and degrees of subjective control. There he will see men whose objective minds have completely abdicated the throne, and whose subjective minds are in pursuit of one idea, — controlled by one dominant impression, which subordinates all others. These are the monomaniacs, — the victims of false suggestions. These suggestions may be given from without, in a thousand different ways which will be readily recognized by the student of insanity, or by auto-suggestion. Long and intense concentration of mind upon one subject, and inordinate egotism, will be readily recognized as striking illustrations of the power of auto-suggestion as a factor in monomania. The maniac is one whose objective mind is disorganized by disease of its organ, the brain; the result being distortion of objective impressions, and consequent false suggestions to the subjective mind.

Those who study the subject from this standpoint will find an easy solution to many an obscure problem. The subject is here adverted to merely to show the consequences arising from allowing the subjective mind to usurp complete control of the mental organization. It will be readily seen that human society, outside of lunatic asylums, constantly furnishes numerous examples of abnormal subjective control. So generally is this fact recognized that it has passed into a proverb that " every man is insane on some subject."

The question arises, What part does the subjective mind play in the normal operation of the human intellect? This question may be answered in a general way by saying that the most perfect exhibition of intellectual power is the result of the synchronous action of the objective and subjective minds. When this is seen in its perfection the world names it *genius*. In this condition the individual has the benefit of all the reasoning powers of the objective mind, combined with the perfect memory of the subjective mind and its marvellous power of syllogistic arrangement of its resources. In short, all the elements of intellectual power are then in a state of intense and harmonious activity. This condition may be perfectly normal, though it is rarely seen in its perfection. Probably the most striking examples which history affords were Napoleon Bonaparte and Shakspeare. The intelligent student of the history of their lives and work will not fail to recall a thousand incidents which illustrate the truth of this proposition. True genius is undoubtedly the result of the synchronous action of the two minds, neither unduly predominating or usurping the powers and functions of the other. When the subjective is allowed to dominate, the resultant acts of the individual are denominated "the eccentricities of genius." When the subjective usurps complete control, the individual goes insane.

There are certain classes of persons whose intellectual labors are characterized by subjective activity in a very marked degree. Poets and artists are the most conspicuous examples. So marked is the peculiarity of the poetic mind in this respect that it has become almost proverbial. Lord Macaulay, in his Essay on Milton, uses language which shows that he clearly recognized the subjective element in all true poetry. He says : —

"Perhaps no man can be a poet, or can even enjoy poetry, without a certain unsoundness of mind, — if anything which gives so much pleasure ought to be called unsoundness. By poetry we mean not, of course, all writing in verse, nor even all good writing in verse. Our definition excludes many metrical compositions which on other grounds deserve the highest praise. By poetry we mean the art of employing words in such a manner as to produce an illusion on the imagination ; the art of doing by means of words what the painter does by means of colors. Thus the greatest of poets has described it, in lines universally admired for the vigor and felicity of their diction, and still more valuable on account of the just notion which they convey of the art in which he excelled.

> "' As imagination bodies forth
> The forms of things unknown, the poet's pen
> Turns them to shapes, and gives to airy nothing
> A local habitation and a name.'

" These are the fruits of the 'fine frenzy' which he ascribes to the poet, — a fine frenzy doubtless, but still a frenzy. Truth, indeed, is essential to poetry, but it is the truth of madness. The reasonings are just, but the premises are false. After the first suppositions have been made, everything ought to be consistent; but those first suppositions require a degree of credulity which almost amounts to a partial and temporary derangement of the intellect. Hence, of all people, children are the most imaginative. They abandon themselves without reserve to every illusion. Every image which is strongly presented to their mental eye produces on them the effect of reality. No man, whatever his sensibility may be, is ever affected by Hamlet or Lear as a little girl is affected by the story of poor Red-Riding-Hood. She knows that it is all false, that wolves cannot speak, that there are no wolves in England. Yet in spite of her knowledge she believes; she weeps; she trembles; she dares not go into a dark room, lest she should feel the teeth of the monster at her throat. Such is the despotism of the imagination over uncivilized minds."

In other words, such is the despotism of suggestion over the subjective mind. No truer statement of the methods of subjective mental action could be written. " The reasonings are just, but the premises are false," says Macaulay. True, the deductive reasonings of the subjective mind are always just, logical, syllogistically perfect, and are equally so whether the premises are false or true.

Macaulay's remark concerning children is eminently philosophical and true to nature. Children are almost purely subjective; and no one needs to be told how completely a suggestion, true or false, will take control of their minds. This is seen in perfection when children are playing games in which one of them is supposed to be a wild beast. The others will flee in affected terror from the beast; but the affectation often becomes a real emotion, and tears, and sometimes convulsions, result from their fright.

The remark elsewhere made regarding the eccentricities of genius applies in a marked degree to poets. It is probable that in all the greater poets the subjective mind often predominates. Certainly the subjective element is dominant in their works. The career of Lord Byron is at once a splendid illustration of the marvellous powers and the inexhaustible resources of the subjective mind in a man of learning and cultivation, and a sad commentary on the folly and danger of allowing the subjective mind to usurp control of the dual mental organization.

Many of the poems of Coleridge furnish striking examples of the dominance of the subjective in poetry. His readers will readily recall the celebrated fragment entitled "Kubla Khan; or, a Vision in a Dream," beginning as follows: —

> "In Xanadu did Kubla Khan
> A stately pleasure-dome decree, —
> Where Alph, the sacred river, ran
> Through caverns measureless to man
> Down to a sunless sea."

It is unfortunately true that the subjective condition in his case was often brought about by artificial means; and it is expressly stated in a prefatory note to "Kubla Khan" that this fragment was written while under the influence of an anodyne. As an illustration of the principle under consideration it is, however, none the less valuable; while the career of the gifted but unfortunate poet should serve as a warning against the practices in which he indulged.

Macaulay further remarks: —

" In an enlightened age there will be much intelligence, much science, much philosophy, abundance of just classification and subtle analysis, abundance of wit and eloquence, abundance of verses, — and even of good ones, — but little poetry. Men will judge and compare; but they will not create." [1]

In other words, this is an age of purely objective cultivation. All our powers of inductive reasoning are strained to their highest tension in an effort to penetrate the secrets of physical Nature, and to harness her dynamic forces. Meantime, the normal exercise of that co-ordinate power in our mental structure is fast falling into desuetude, and its

[1] Scott's poems are good illustrations. They are not ranked as first class for the sole reason that they are too objective.

manifestations, not being understood, are relegated to the domain of superstition.

Socrates, in his Apology to the Athenians, seems to have entertained opinions in regard to poets similar to those of Lord Macaulay. In his search for wiser men than himself he went first to the politicians. Failing there, he went to the poets, with the following result : —

" Taking up, therefore, some of their poems, which appeared to me most elaborately finished, I questioned them as to their meaning, that at the same time I might learn something from them. I am ashamed, O Athenians, to tell you the truth; however, it must be told. For, in a word, almost all who were present could have given a better account of them than those by whom they had been composed. I soon discovered this, therefore, with regard to the poets, that they do not effect their object by wisdom, but by a certain natural inspiration, and under the influence of enthusiasm, like prophets and seers; for these also say many fine things, but they understand nothing that they say."

Words could not express more clearly the recognition of the subjective element in poetic composition; and it exactly accords with Macaulay's idea regarding the poets and the poetry of the ancient days.

The subjective mind once recognized as a factor in the mental powers of the poet, it follows that its resources are all at his command. Its perfect memory, its instant command of all the acquired knowledge of the individual, however superficially attained or imperfectly remembered, objectively, is a source of stupendous power. But, like all other gifts of nature, it is liable at times to be a source of inconvenience ; for it sometimes happens that in ordinary composition a person will unconsciously reproduce, *verbatim*, some long-forgotten expressions, perhaps a whole stanza, or even an entire poem. It may, perchance, be of his own composition; but it is just as likely to be something that he has read years before and forgotten, objectively, as soon as read. In this way many persons have subjected themselves to the charge of plagiarism, when they were totally unconscious of guilt. Many of the great poets have been accused of minor plagiarisms, and much inconsiderate criticism has been the result. Oliver Wendell Holmes mentions unconscious reproduction as one of the besetting annoyances of a poet's experience. "It is impossible to tell," he says, "in many cases, whether a comparison which suddenly suggests itself is a 'new conception or a recollection. I told you the other day that I never wrote a line of verse that seemed to me comparatively good, but it appeared old at once, and often as if it had been borrowed." [1]

A certain class of trance-speaking mediums, so called, are often called upon to improvise poems, the subject being suggested by some one in the audience. Often a very creditable performance is the result; but it more frequently happens that they reproduce something that they have read.

Sometimes whole poems are thus reproduced by persons in an apparently normal condition. This accounts for the frequent disputes concerning the authorship of popular verses. Instances of this kind are fresh in the minds of most readers, as, for example, a recent controversy between two well-known writers relative to the authorship of the poem beginning, "Laugh, and the world laughs with you." The circumstances of such coincidences often preclude the possibility of either claimant deliberately plagiarizing the work, or telling a falsehood concerning its authorship. Yet nothing is more certain than that one of them is not its author. Possibly neither is entitled to that credit. When, in the nature of things, it is impossible for either to prove the fact of authorship, and when the evidence on both sides is about equally balanced, we may never know the exact truth; but as the theory of unconscious subjective reproduction is consistent with the literary honesty of both, it may well be accepted as the true one, aside from the inherent probability of its correctness.

[1] Autocrat of the Breakfast-Table.

The solution of the great question as to the authorship of Shakspeare's works may be found in this hypothesis. The advocates of the Baconian theory tell us that Shakspeare was an unlearned man. This is true so far as high scholastic attainments are concerned ; but it is also known that he was a man of extensive reading, and was the companion of many of the great men of his time, among whom were Bacon, Ben Jonson, Drayton, Beaumont, Fletcher, and others. It is in evidence that the Mermaid Tavern was the scene of many an encounter of wit and learning between these worthies. In this way he was brought into constant contact with the brightest minds of the Elizabethan age. He was not only familiar with their works, but he had also the benefit of their conversation, — which familiarized him with their thoughts and modes of expression, — and of close personal relations with them in their convivial moods, when wit and eloquence, learning and philosophy, flowed as freely as their wine.

The internal evidence of his works shows that Shakspeare's mind, compared with that of any other poet whose writings are known, was the most harmoniously developed. In other words, his objective and subjective faculties were exquisitely balanced. When this fact is considered in the light of what has been said of the marvellous powers of subjective memory, and in connection with his intellectual environment, the source of his power and inspiration becomes apparent. In his moments of inspiration — and he seems always to have been inspired when writing — he had the benefit of a perfect memory and a logical comprehension of all that had been imparted by the brightest minds of the most marvellous literary and philosophical age in the history of mankind. Is it any wonder that he was able to strike a responsive chord in every human breast, to run the gamut of every human emotion, to portray every shade of human character, and to embellish his work with all the wit and learning of his day and generation?

Artists constitute another class in whom the subjective faculties are largely cultivated, and are often predominant.

Indeed, no man can become a true artist whose subjective mind is not cultivated to a high degree of activity. One may become a good draughtsman, or learn to delineate a figure with accuracy, or to draw a landscape with photographic fidelity to objective nature, and in faultless perspective, by the cultivation of the objective faculties alone; but his work will lack that subtle something, that nameless charm, which causes a canvas to glow with beauty, and each particular figure to become instinct with life and action. No artist can successfully compose a picture who cannot see " in his mind's eye " the perfected picture before he touches his pencil to canvas; and just in proportion to his cultivation of the subjective faculties will he be able thus to see his picture. Of course these remarks will be understood to presuppose an objective art education. No man, by the mere cultivation or exercise of his subjective faculties, can become a great artist, any more than an ignoramus, by going into a hypnotic trance, can speak the language of a Webster. All statements to the contrary are merely the exaggerations of inaccurate observers. Genius in art, as in everything else, is the result of the harmonious cultivation and synchronous action of both characteristics of the dual mind.

In art, as in poetry, the undue predominance of the subjective mind is apt to work disastrously. No better illustration of this is now recalled than is furnished by the works of Fuseli or of Blake : —

" Look," says Dendy,[1] " on those splendid illustrations of the Gothic poets by the eccentric, the half-mad Fuseli. Look on the wild pencillings of Blake, another poet-painter, and you will be assured that they were ghost-seers. An intimate friend of Blake has told me the strangest tales of his visions. In one of his reveries he witnessed the whole ceremony of a fairy's funeral, which he peopled with mourners and mutes, and described with high poetic beauty. He was engaged, in one of these moods, in painting King Edward I., who was sitting to him for his picture. While they were conversing, Wallace sud-

[1] Philosophy of Mystery, p. 93.

denly presented himself on the field, and by this uncourteous in-
trusion marred the studies of the painter for that day. . . . Blake
was a visionary," continues our author, " and thought his fancies real; he was mad."

The writer once knew an artist who had the power to
enter the subjective condition at will; and in this state he
could cause his visions to be projected upon the canvas
before him. He declared that his mental pictures thus
formed were perfect in detail and color, and all that he had
to do to fix them was to paint the corresponding colors over
the subjective picture. He, too, thought his fancies real;
he believed that spirits projected the pictures upon the
canvas.

The foregoing cases represent a class of artists whose subjective faculties are uncontrolled by the objective mind, —
an abnormal condition, which, if it found expression in
words instead of pigments, would stamp the subject as a
candidate for the lunatic asylum.

Fortunately, most artists have their fancies more under
control; or, more properly speaking, they are aware that their
visions are evoked by their own volition. This power varies with different individuals, but all true artists possess it
in a greater or less degree. An extraordinary manifestation
of this power is reported by Combe. The artist was noted
for the rapidity of his work, and was extremely popular on
account of the fidelity of his portraits, and especially because he never required more than one sitting of his patron.
His method, as divulged by himself, was as follows : —

" When a sitter came, I looked attentively on him for half
an hour, sketching from time to time on the canvas. I did not
require a longer sitting. I removed the canvas and passed to
another person. When I wished to continue the first portrait, I
recalled the man to my mind. I placed him on the chair, where
I perceived him as distinctly as though really there, and, I may
add, in form and color more decidedly brilliant. I looked from
time to time at the imaginary figure, and went on painting, occasionally stopping to examine the picture exactly as though
the original were before me; whenever I looked towards the
chair I saw the man."

In this way he was enabled to paint over three hundred portraits in one year.

It is seldom that subjective power is manifested in this particular manner. It may be added, however, that, given an artist for a subject, the same phenomena can be reproduced at will by the ordinary processes of hypnotism. The most common manifestations of the power are not so easily recognized or distinguished from ordinary mental activity; but every artist will bear witness that there are times when he works with extraordinary ease and rapidity, when the work almost seems to do itself, when there seems to be a force outside of himself which impels him on, when, to use the common expression to define the mental condition, he feels that he is "inspired." It is then that the artist does his best work. It is under these mental conditions that his work is characterized by that subtle, indefinite charm vaguely expressed by the word "feeling."

Another class of persons who possess the faculty of evoking at will the powers of the subjective mind are the great orators, such as Patrick Henry, Charles Phillips the Irish orator, Henry Clay, Daniel Webster, and many others, to say nothing of that numerous class of purely subjective orators known to spiritists as trance, or inspirational, speakers. The student of the life of Patrick Henry will not fail to see that his whole history is an illustration of the pertinency of these remarks. It is related of Clay that on one occasion he was unexpectedly called upon to answer an opponent who had addressed the Senate on a question in which Clay was deeply interested. The latter felt too unwell to reply at length. It seemed imperative, however, that he should say something; and he exacted a promise from a friend, who sat behind him, that he would stop him at the end of ten minutes. Accordingly, at the expiration of the prescribed time the friend gently pulled the skirts of Mr. Clay's coat. No attention was paid to the hint, and after a brief time it was repeated a little more emphatically. Still Clay paid no attention, and it was again repeated. Then a pin was brought into requisition; but Clay was by that time thoroughly aroused, and was pouring forth a tor·rent of eloquence. The pin was inserted deeper and deeper into the orator's leg without eliciting any response, until his friend gave it up in despair. Finally Mr. Clay happened to glance at the clock, and saw that he had been speaking two hours; whereupon he fell back into his friend's arms, completely overcome by exhaustion, up-braiding his friend severely for not stopping him at the time prescribed.

The fact that Mr. Clay, on that occasion, made one of the ablest speeches of his life, two hours in length, at a time when he felt almost too ill to rise to his feet, and that his body at the time was in a condition of perfect anesthesia, is a splendid illustration of the synchronous action of the two minds, and also of the perfect control exercised by the subjective mind over the functions and sensations of the body.

There is, perhaps, no better description on record of the sensations of a speaker, when the synchronous action of the two minds is perfect, than that given by Daniel Webster. A friend had asked him how it happened that he was able, without preparation, to make such a magnificent effort when he replied to Hayne. The reply was (quoting from memory) substantially as follows: "In the first place, I have made the Constitution of the United States the study of my life; and on that occasion it seemed to me that all that I had ever heard or read on the subject under discus-sion was passing like a panorama before me, arranged in perfectly logical order and sequence, and that all I had to do was to cull a thunderbolt and hurl it at him."

Two important conclusions are deducible from the premi-ses here laid down. The first is that it is essential to the highest mental development that the objective and subjec-tive faculties be cultivated harmoniously, if the latter are cultivated at all.

The second conclusion is of the most transcendent inter-est and importance. It is that the subjective mind should never be allowed to usurp control of the dual mental organization. Important as are its functions and transcendent as are its powers, it is hedged about with such limitations that it must be subjected to the imperial control of the objective mind, which alone is endowed with the power to reason by all methods.

To sum up in a few words : To believe in the reality of subjective visions is to give the subjective mind control of the dual mental organization ; and to give the subjective mind such control is for Reason to abdicate her throne. The suggestions of the subjective mind then become the controlling power. The result, in its mildest form of manifestation, is a mind filled with the grossest superstitions, — a mind which, like the untutored mind of the savage, "sees God in clouds, and hears him in the wind." Its ultimate form of manifestation is insanity.

CHAPTER VI.

PERCEPTION OF THE FIXED LAWS OF NATURE.

Three Sub-classes of Mental Phenomena. — Mathematical Prodigies. — Musical Prodigies. — Measurement of Time. — Distinction between Results of Objective Education and Intuitive Perception. — Zerah Colburn, the Mathematical Prodigy. — The Lightning Calculator. — Blind Tom, the Musical Prodigy. — The Origin and Uses of Music. — East Indian Fakirs. — Measurement of Time. — The Power possessed by Animals. — Illustrative Incidents. — Hypnotic Subjects. — Jouffroy's Testimony. — Bernheim's Views. — Practical Observations. — The Normal Functions of Objective Intelligence. — The Limitations of Subjective Intelligence pertain to its Earthly State only. — Its Kinship to God demonstrated by its Limitations. — Omniscience cannot reason inductively. — Induction is Inquiry. — Perception the Attribute of Omniscience. — Conclusions regarding the Power of the Soul.

THERE are three other sub-classes of subjective mental phenomena which must be grouped by themselves, inasmuch as they are governed by a law which does not pertain to the classes mentioned in the preceding chapter, although there are some characteristics which are common to them all. The first of these classes of phenomena is manifested in mathematical prodigies; the second in musical prodigies; and the third pertains to the measurement of time.

The important distinction to be observed between the phenomena described in the preceding chapter and those pertaining to mathematics, music, and the measurement of time, consists in the fact that in the former everything depends upon objective education, whilst the latter are apparently produced by the exercise of inherent powers of the subjective mind.

In order not to be misunderstood it must be here stated that on all subjects of human knowledge not governed by fixed laws, the subjective mind is dependent for its information upon objective education. In other words, it knows only what has been imparted to it by and through the objective senses or the operations of the objective mind. Thus, its knowledge of the contents of books can only be acquired by objective methods of education. Its wonderful powers of acquiring and assimilating such knowledge are due to its perfect memory of all that has been imparted to it by objective education, aided by its powers of memory and of logical arrangement of the subject-matter. Leaving clairvoyance and thought-transference out of consideration for the present, the principle may be stated thus: The subjective mind cannot know, by intuition, the name of a person, or a geographical location, or a fact in human history. But it does know, by intuition, that two and two make four.

No one without an objective education can, by the development of the subjective faculties alone, become a great poet, or a great artist, or a great orator, or a great statesman. But he may be a great mathematician or a great musician, independently of objective education or training, by the development of the subjective faculties alone. Many facts are on record which demonstrate this proposition. Hundreds of instances might be cited showing to what a prodigious extent the mathematical and musical faculties can be developed in persons, not only without objective training, but, in some instances, without a brain capable of receiving any considerable objective education.

Mathematical prodigies of the character mentioned are numerous; one of the most remarkable was the famous Zerah Colburn. The following account of his early career, published when he was yet under eight years of age, is taken from the "Annual Register" of 1812, an English publication, and will serve to illustrate the proposition:

"The attention of the philosophical world has been lately at-tracted by the most singular phenomenon in the history of human mind that perhaps ever existed. It is the case of a child, under eight years of age, who, without any previous knowledge of the common rules of arithmetic, or even of the use and power of the Arabic numerals, and without having given any attention to the subject, possesses, as if by intuition, the singular faculty of solving a great variety of arithmetical questions by the mere operation of the mind, and without the usual assistance of any visible symbol or contrivance.

"The name of the child is Zerah Colburn, who was born at Cabut (a town lying at the head of the Onion River, in Vermont, in the United States of America), on the 1st of September, 1804. About two years ago, — August, 1810, — although at that time not six years of age, he first began to show these wonderful powers of calculation which have since so much attracted the attention and excited the astonishment of every person who has witnessed his extraordinary abilities. The discovery was made by accident. His father, who had not given him any other instruction than such as was to be obtained at a small school established in that unfrequented and remote part of the country, and which did not include either writing or ciphering, was much surprised one day to hear him repeating the products of several numbers. Struck with amazement at the circum-stance, he proposed a variety of arithmetical questions to him, all of which the child solved with remarkable facility and cor-rectness. The news of the infant prodigy was soon circulated through the neighborhood, and many persons came from dis-tant parts to witness so singular a circumstance. The father, encouraged by the unanimous opinion of all who came to see him, was induced to undertake with this child the tour of the United States. They were everywhere received with the most flattering expressions, and in several towns which they visited, various plans were suggested to educate and bring up the child free from all expense to his family. Yielding, however, to the pressing solicitations of his friends, and urged by the most re-spectable and powerful recommendations, as well as by a view to his son's more complete education, the father has brought the child to this country, where they arrived on the 12th of May last; and the inhabitants of this metropolis have for the last three months had an opportunity of seeing and examining this wonderful phenomenon, and verifying the reports that have been circulated respecting him. Many persons of the first eminence for their knowledge in mathematics, and well known for their philosophical inquiries, have made a point of seeing and conversing with him, and they have all been struck with astonishment at his extraordinary powers. It is correctly true, as stated of him, that he will not only determine with the greatest facility and despatch the exact number of minutes or seconds in any given period of time, but will also solve any other question of a similar kind. He will tell the exact product arising from the multiplication of any number consisting of two, three, or four figures by any other number consisting of the like number of figures; or any number consisting of six or seven places of figures being proposed, he will determine with equal expedition and ease all the factors of which it is composed. This singular faculty consequently extends not only to the raising of powers, but to the extraction of the square and cube roots of the number proposed, and likewise to the means of determining whether it is a prime number (or a number incapable of division by any other number); for which case there does not exist at present any general rule amongst mathematicians. All these and a variety of other questions connected therewith are answered by this child with such promptness and accuracy (and in the midst of his juvenile pursuits) as to astonish every person who has visited him.

" At a meeting of his friends, which was held for the purpose of concerting the best methods of promoting the views of the father, this child undertook and completely succeeded in raising the number 8 progressively up to the sixteenth power. And in naming the last result, viz., 281,474,976,710,656! he was right in every figure. He was then tried as to other numbers consisting of one figure, all of which he raised (by actual multiplication, and not by memory) as high as the tenth power, with so much facility and despatch that the person appointed to take down the results was obliged to enjoin him not to be so rapid. With respect to numbers consisting of two figures, he would raise some of them to the sixth, seventh, and eighth power, but not always with equal facility; for the larger the products became, the more difficult he found it to proceed. He was asked the square root of 106,929; and before the number could be written down, he immediately answered, 327. He was then required to name the cube root of 268,336,125; and with equal facility and promptness he replied, 645. Various other questions of a similar nature, respecting the roots and powers of very high numbers, were proposed by several of the gentlemen present, to all of which he answered in a similar manner. One of the party requested him to name the factors which pro-

duced the number 247,483 : this he immediately did by mentioning the numbers 941 and 263, — which, indeed, are the only two
numbers that will produce it. Another of them proposed 171,395,
and he named the following factors as the only ones, viz., 5 ×
34,279, 7 × 24,485, 59 × 2,905, 83 × 2,065, 35 × 4,897, 295 ×
581, and 413 × 415. He was then asked to give the factors of
36,083 ; but he immediately replied that it had none, — which in
fact was the case, as 36,083 is a prime number. Other numbers
were indiscriminately proposed to him, and he always succeeded
in giving the correct factors, except in the case of prime numbers,
which he discovered almost as soon as proposed. One of the
gentlemen asked him how many minutes there were in forty-
eight years ; and before the question could be written down he
replied, 25,228,800 ; and instantly added that the number of
seconds in the same period was 1,513,728,000. Various questions
of the like kind were put to him, and to all of them he answered
with equal facility and promptitude, so as to astonish every one
present, and to excite a desire that so extraordinary a faculty
should, if possible, be rendered more extensive and useful. It
was the wish of the gentlemen present to obtain a knowledge of
the method by which the child was enabled to answer with so
much facility and correctness the questions thus put to him ;
but to all their inquiries on the subject (and he was closely examined on this point) he was unable to give them any information. He persistently declared (and every observation that was
made seemed to justify the assertion) that he did not know how
the answer came into his mind. In the act of multiplying two
numbers together, and in the raising of powers, it was evident,
not only from the motion of his lips, but also from some
singular facts which will be hereafter mentioned, that some
operations were going forward in his mind ; yet that operation
could not, from the readiness with which the answers were furnished, be at all allied to the usual mode of proceeding with such
subjects ; and moreover he is entirely ignorant of the common
rules of arithmetic, and cannot perform upon paper a simple
sum in multiplication or division. But in the extraction of
roots and in mentioning the factors of high numbers, it does
not appear that any operation can take place, since he will give
the answer immediately, or in a very few seconds, where it
would require, according to the ordinary method of solution, a
very difficult and laborious calculation ; and, moreover, the
knowledge of a prime number cannot be obtained by any
known rule.

   " It must be evident, from what has here been stated, that
the singular faculty which this child possesses is not altogether

dependent on his memory. In the multiplication of numbers and in the raising of powers, he is doubtless considerably assisted by that remarkable quality of the mind; and in this respect he might be considered as bearing some resemblance (if the difference of age did not prevent the justness of the comparison) to the celebrated Jedidiah Buxton, and other persons of similar note. But in the extraction of the roots of numbers and in determining their factors (if any), it is clear to all those who have witnessed the astonishing quickness and accuracy of this child that the memory has nothing to do with the process. And in this particular point consists the remarkable difference between the present and all former instances of an apparently similar kind."

The latter remark above quoted would not apply to the present day, for many parallel cases have been reported within the present decade.

It was hoped that the powers of this child would develop by education; and for this purpose he was placed in school and trained in objective methods of mathematical calculation. It was believed that when his mind became mature he would be able to impart to others the process by which his calculations were made. But his friends were doomed to disappointment. His powers did not improve by objective training. On the contrary, they deteriorated just in proportion to his efforts in that direction, and his pupils derived no benefit from the extraordinary faculties with which he was endowed. This has been the invariable rule in such cases.

A few years ago a gentleman travelled through this country teaching arithmetic. He was known as the "lightning calculator." His powers were indeed marvellous. He could add a column of as many numbers as could be written on a sheet of legal cap, by casting an instantaneous glance upon the page; but he succeeded no better as a teacher than thousands of others who could not add a column of numbers without reading every figure by the usual laborious, objective process. He could give no explanation of his powers other than that he possessed extraordinary quickness of vision. But any one who is sufficiently

acquainted with the elements of optical laws to be aware
that in the light of a flash of lightning a drop of falling rain
appears to be suspended motionless in the air, knows that
objective vision is not capable of such rapid transition as
to enable one to see at a glance each particular figure in a
column of a hundred numbers.   When to this is added the
labor of calculating the relation and aggregate values of
the numbers, the conclusion is inevitable that such powers
are not given to our objective senses, but must be inherent
in the human soul, and beyond the range of objective
explanation or comprehension.

Musical prodigies furnish further illustrations of the principle involved.   Of these the most remarkable is the negro
idiot, known as Blind Tom.   This person was not only blind
from birth, but was little above the brute creation in point
of objective intelligence or capacity to receive objective instruction.   Yet his musical capacity was prodigious.   Almost
in his infancy it was discovered that he could reproduce on
the piano any piece of music that he had ever heard.   A
piece of music, however long or difficult, once heard, seemed
to be fixed indelibly in his memory, and usually could be reproduced with a surprising degree of accuracy.   His capacity for improvisation was equally great, and a discordant
note rarely, if ever, marred the harmony of his measures.

These well known facts of Blind Tom's history furnish
complete illustrations, — first of the perfection of subjective
memory; and second, of the inherent power of the subjective mind to grasp the laws of harmony of sounds; and
that, too, independently of objective education.

Music belongs to the realm of the subjective; it is a
passion of the human soul, and it may be safely affirmed
that all really good music is the direct product of the subjective mind.   It is true that there is much so-called music
to be heard which is the product of the objective intelligence.   But no one can fail to recognize its origin, from its
hard, mechanical, soulless character and quality.   It bears
the same relation to the product of the subjective mind that
mere rhyme does to the poetry of a Milton.   Music is at

once the legitimate offspring of the subjective mind and one of the most potent means of inducing the subjective condition. It is a well-known practice of so-called "spiritual mediums" to have music at their séances, for the ostensible purpose of securing the "harmonious conditions" necessary to insure a successful performance. Their theory is that the music harmonizes the audience, and that by a reflex action the medium is favorably affected. It is probable that such would be the effect to a limited extent, but the greatest effect is direct and positive upon the medium.

The East Indian fakirs invariably invoke the aid of music to enable them to enter the subjective state when they are about to give an exhibition of occult power. In fact, the power of music over the subjective mind is practically unlimited. It speaks the universal language of the soul, and is comprehended alike by prince and by peasant. It is the most powerful auxiliary of love, of religion, and of war. It nerves the soldier to deeds of heroism, and soothes his dying moments. It inspires alike the devotee of pleasure and the worshipper of God. But whilst it interprets every human emotion and embodies the inward feelings of which all other arts can but exhibit the outward effect, its laws are as fixed and immutable as the laws of mathematics.

The next subdivision or branch of the subject pertains to the faculty of measuring the lapse of time. This power is inherent in the subjective mind, and in that alone ; the objective mind, *per se,* does not possess it. The only means by which the objective mind can measure time is by the exercise of the physical senses, either in the observation of the motions of the heavenly bodies, or of some other physical object or phenomenon which objective experience has shown to be a safe criterion upon which to base an estimate.

The subjective mind, on the other hand, possesses an inherent power in that direction, independent of objective aids or the exercise of reason. It is possessed by man in common with many of the brute creation. It is strikingly exhibited in dogs, horses, and other domestic animals accustomed to regular hours of employment.

A friend of the writer once owned a large plantation in one of the Southwestern States, upon which he worked a large number of mules. They were regularly employed on week-days, but on Sundays they were turned into a corral and allowed to rest. On regular work-days they were tractable and easily handled; but if one was wanted for a Sunday excursion it was with the greatest difficulty that he could be caught or made to perform any labor whatever.

An English gentleman, well known to the writer, relates a curious anecdote of a dog which was raised in his family. After the dog had come to maturity, one of the sons married and set up an establishment about three miles from the parental mansion. It was the habit of the family to see that the dog was fed regularly, immediately after each meal, with the scraps from the table. At the home mansion the Sunday dinner-hour was the same as on week-days, but was just two hours earlier than that adopted at the son's establishment. This fact the dog by some means became acquainted with, and he never failed to take advantage of the information. Every Sunday he would wait patiently for the home dinner; and having finished it, he would promptly take his departure, and never failed to put in an appearance at the son's house on time for dinner, where he was sure to be welcomed and entertained as an honored guest. On week-days the dinner-hour at the two houses was the same, and consequently he never made a pilgrimage in search of an extra meal on any day but Sunday.

A favorite mastiff in the family of the writer has taken upon himself the regulation of the household affairs. He awakens the family in the morning at a certain hour, and insists upon promptitude in rising. At precisely twelve o'clock he notifies the family that it is time to feed the horse, and will give no one any peace until his friend's wants are supplied. His own meal seems to be a secondary consideration. At three o'clock he notifies his mistress that it is time to visit the kitchen and give directions for preparing dinner. It is not because he expects to be fed at that time, for he is never fed until the family have dined, two hours later. At nine o'clock he rises from his rug on the library floor, and insists upon a visit to the kitchen for a lunch. It is rare that he varies five minutes from the regular hours above noted, but is generally within a minute.

This power is exhibited in its perfection in hypnotic subjects and in ordinary sleep. It is that faculty which enables one to awake at an appointed hour in the night, when, before going to sleep, he has made a firm resolution to do so. M. Jouffroy, one of the most celebrated philoso-phers of France, in speaking of this subject says : —

"I have this power in perfection, but I notice that I lose it if I depend on any one calling me. In this latter case my mind does not take the trouble of reasoning the time or of listening to the clock. But in the former it is necessary that it do so, other-wise the phenomenon is inexplicable. Every one has made or can make this experiment."

M. Jouffroy is doubtless mistaken in supposing that the mind is necessarily employed in watching the clock ; for the experiment is just as successful in the absence of any timepiece. Besides, the fact that animals possess the faculty shows that it is an inherent attribute of the sub-jective mind. It is the lapse of time that is noted by men as well as by animals, and is wholly independent of arti-ficial methods or instruments for marking the divisions of time. Every one possesses this faculty in a greater or less degree, and the subject need not, therefore, be enlarged upon.

As before intimated, hypnotic subjects possess in a very remarkable degree the faculty of noting the lapse of time. On this subject Professor Bernheim [1] says : —

"If a somnambulist is made to promise during his sleep that he will come back on such and such a day, at such and such an

---

[1] *Suggestive Therapeutics,* p. 37.

hour, he will almost surely return on the day and at the hour, although he has no remembrance of his promise when he wakes up. I made A say that he would come back to me in thirteen days, at ten o'clock in the morning. He remembered nothing when he waked. On the thirteenth day, at ten o'clock in the morning, he appeared, having come three kilometres from his house to the hospital. He had been working in the foundries all night, went to bed at six in the morning, and woke up at nine with the idea that he had to come to the hospital to see me. He told me that he had had no such idea on the preceding days, and did not know that he had to come to see me. It came into his head just at the time when he ought to carry it out."

It is also well known to all hypnotists that subjects in a hypnotic sleep will awaken at any hour prescribed to them by the operator, seldom varying more than five minutes from the time set, even when the sleep is prolonged for hours. If the subject is commanded to sleep, say, ten or fifteen minutes, he will generally awaken exactly on time. This fact also is universally recognized by those familiar with hypnotic phenomena, and the subject need not be further illustrated.

In concluding this chapter, it is impossible to refrain from indulging in a few general observations regarding the conclusions derivable from the peculiar characteristics of the subjective intelligence thus far noted. We have seen that certain phenomena depend for their perfect development upon objective education, and that certain other phenomena are exhibited in perfection independent of objective education. In other words, certain powers are inherent in the subjective intelligence. These powers appear to pertain to the comprehension of the laws of Nature. We have seen that, under certain conditions, the subjective mind comprehends by intuition the laws of mathematics. It comprehends the laws of harmony of sounds, independently of objective education. By true artists the laws of the harmony of colors are also perceived intuitively.[1] These

[1] It must be here remarked that although the laws pertaining to the harmony of colors may be comprehended by intuition, yet an

facts have been again and again demonstrated. It would seem, therefore, to be a just conclusion that the subjective mind, untrammelled by its objective environment, will be enabled to comprehend all the laws of Nature, to perceive, to know all truth, independent of the slow, laborious process of induction.

We are so accustomed to boast of the " god-like reason " with which man is endowed, that the proposition that the subjective mind — the soul — of man is incapable of exercising that function, in what we regard as the highest form of reasoning, seems, at first glance, to be a limitation of the intellectual power of the soul, and inconsistent with what we have been accustomed to regard as the highest attributes of human intelligence. But a moment's reflection will develop the fact that this apparent limitation of intellectual power is, in reality, a god-like attribute of mind. God himself cannot reason inductively. Inductive reasoning presupposes an inquiry, a search after knowledge, an effort to arrive at correct conclusions regarding something of which we are ignorant. To suppose God to be an inquirer, a seeker after knowledge, by finite processes of reasoning, is a conception of the Deity which negatives his omniscience, and measures Infinite Intelligence by purely finite standards. For our boasted " god-like reason " is of the earth, earthy. It is the noblest attribute of the finite mind, it is true, but it is essentially finite. It is the outgrowth of our objective existence. It is our safest guide in the walks of earthly life. It is our faithful monitor and guardian in our daily struggle with our physical environment. It is our most reliable auxiliary in our efforts to penetrate the secrets of Nature, and wrest from her the means of subsistence. But its functions cease with the necessities which called it into existence ; for it will be no longer useful when

objective education is necessary to enable the artist to combine the necessary pigments to produce the colors on canvas, and to perform the other mechanical labor necessary to place the paints upon the canvas in such relations as to produce a picture. When this is acquired, intuition will do the rest.

the physical form has perished, and the veil is lifted which hides from mortal eyes that world where all truth is revealed. Then it is that the soul — the subjective mind — will perform its normal functions, untrammelled by the physical form which imprisons it and binds it to earth, and in its native realm of truth, unimpeded by the laborious processes of finite reasoning, it will imbibe all truth from its Eternal Source.

CHAPTER VII.

EFFECTS OF ADVERSE SUGGESTION.

The Subjective Mind Incapable of Controversial Argument. — A Sceptical Audience demoralizes it. — The Presence of an Avowed Sceptic prevents Successful Exhibition of Subjective Phenomena. — Labouchere and Bishop. — The Royal Academy of Medicine. — Its Offer to Clairvoyants. — Failure to earn Reward. — Harmonious Conditions required by Spiritists. — The Seybert Commission. — Trance-Speaking Mediums. — How demoralized. — Adverse Suggestion the Cause of Failure in All Cases. — Possible Lack of Telepathic Conditions in Bishop's Case. — General Conclusions. — Failure Consistent with Honesty of Mediums.

ANOTHER important peculiarity of the subjective mind is that it is incapable of controversial argument. This subject has been briefly alluded to in a former chapter; but it is of so much importance that a more extended consideration of it is demanded, inasmuch as it affords a clear explanation of various phenomena which have never yet been satisfactorily accounted for. It is well known among hypnotists that it is very difficult, if not impossible, to make satisfactory experiments with a subject in the presence of a sceptical audience. Especially is this true if the scepticism is open, avowed, and aggressive. It is also well known that, when a subject is in a state of lucid somnambulism, no satisfactory results can be obtained if any one disputes him, or attempts an argument, or accuses him of shamming, or of a want of good faith. Such a course always results in great distress of mind on the part of the subject, and generally in restoring him to normal consciousness. In the higher phases of hypnotic phenomena this peculiarity is still more marked. In exhibiting the phenomena of clairvoyance and thought-transference, or mind-reading, it is next to impossible to obtain good results in the presence of an avowed sceptic. The controversy between Washington Irving Bishop and Mr. Labouchere is fresh in the minds of most readers. Mr. Bishop was giving successful exhibitions of his wonderful powers in public assemblies and in private circles in London. He had demonstrated again and again his power to read the thoughts of others and to decipher the contents of sealed envelopes under the strictest test conditions, in the presence of many competent and trustworthy observers. In the height of his success Mr. Labouchere came out in his paper and denounced the whole thing as a humbug. To prove his sincerity he placed a Bank of England note for a large amount in a sealed envelope, and offered to give it to Mr. Bishop if he should correctly read the number. Repeated trials to do so ended in dismal failure. It was a feat that he had successfully performed a thousand times before, and many times afterwards. But the number on that particular bank-note he never could decipher.

In 1831 the Royal Academy of Medicine of France appointed a commission to investigate the subject of animal magnetism. The commission was composed of some of the ablest scientists of the Academy, and it prosecuted its investigations until 1837, when it made its report. Amongst other things it announced that it had demonstrated the fact that some mesmeric subjects possessed clairvoyant power; that such subjects could, with their eyes "exactly closed by the fingers," distinguish objects, tell the color and number of cards, and read lines of a book opened at a chance page. Without entering into the details of the controversy that followed this report, it is sufficient to say that a standing offer of a large sum of money was made to any one who should demonstrate the reality of clairvoyant power in the presence of a committee appointed for the purpose. It is said that many attempts have been made by good clairvoyants to earn this money, but every attempt has ended in total failure. Volumes might be written detailing such tests and such failures.

Exhibitions of the phenomena of spiritism are constantly liable to utter failure in the presence of avowed sceptics. Every one who has attended a " spiritual " séance is aware of the strict regard paid to securing " harmonious conditions ; " and all know how dismal is the failure when such conditions cannot be obtained. It frequently happens that some one will inadvertently remark that " spirits never come when I am around ; " and in nine such cases out of ten the séance will end in failure when such a remark is made. Any argument against spiritism, especially if addressed to the medium, or any controversy on the subject in his presence, will destroy all chance of a successful exhibition. Investigating committees nearly always fail to observe the promised phenomena when the character and objects of the committee are known to the medium. Thus, the Seybert Commission, a majority of whose members were pronounced sceptics, utterly failed to witness any phenomena which might not be produced by legerdemain. In their report they take occasion to say : —

" Our experience has been . . . that as soon as an investigation, worthy of the name, begins, all manifestations of spiritist power cease. . . . Even the very spirit of investigation, or of incredulity, seems to exercise a chilling effect and prevents a successful manifestation." [1]

It will be observed that the last sentence betrays the fact that the writer regards " the spirit of investigation " and " the spirit of incredulity " as synonymous terms. It is certain that the Seybert Commission as a body did so regard them, and made no effort to conceal the fact from the mediums who submitted to be examined. Every medium

[1] Seybert Commission, Report, p. 15.

whom they examined was made fully aware of the incredulity of the majority of the Commission, and thus every effort to produce the phenomena failed.

The same peculiarity is observed in trance-speaking mediums, especially in those who speak in a purely subjective condition. No matter how great is their flow of eloquence, or how perfect their command of their subject, they utterly break down when confronted by an adverse argument. So well is this peculiarity known that their friends never suffer them to be interrupted.

It would be useless to multiply instances of this character. It is sufficiently evident from what has been said that one invariable result follows the one condition. In the investigation of physical phenomena the scientific observer would not hesitate to concede that where a marked result invariably follows a given condition, the two must sustain towards each other the relation of cause and effect. It will not be difficult to establish that relation in this case; and that, too, on principles consistent with the supposition of the absolute integrity of all concerned.

It is, in fact, but another striking illustration of the fundamental principles laid down in preceding chapters of this book. It demonstrates more completely than almost any other phenomenon the absolute amenability of the subjective mind to the power of suggestion. It will not be gainsaid that all the phenomena mentioned — clairvoyance, thought-transference, hypnotism, and mediumship — are embraced under the one generic title, subjective or hypnotic; they are therefore governed by the same general laws.

The hypnotic subject who is in the presence of an openly sceptical audience, and who hears some one declare that the subject is shamming, instantly seizes upon the declaration; and it is to him a suggestion that is as potent as the one which induced the hypnotic condition. The suggestion of the operator is thus neutralized, so to speak, by a counter-suggestion, which reduces the subject at once to his normal condition. In such a case the subject cannot be again hypnotized so long as the sceptic is present; his very presence is a standing suggestion of the unreality of the hypnotic condition which cannot be overcome by the operator.

In the case of Bishop, the mind-reader, the same principle applies with equal force. The mental state which enabled him to read the contents of a sealed envelope was self-induced. It was a partially hypnotic condition, induced by auto-suggestion. When Labouchere's envelope was presented to him, the very manner of presenting it — the offer of its contents as a gift if he would read the number of the bank-note within — was a defiance of his power. It was a suggestion of the most emphatic character and potency that, do what he would, he could not read the contents of that envelope. Again, the anxiety engendered in the mind of the clairvoyant was another factor which added force to the suggestion. The offer was not only defiant, it was even public. The whole civilized world was apprised of the controversy. The professional reputation of the man was at stake. His future career depended upon his success; and every dollar of value in that note not only added to his anxiety to win the prize, but contributed its force to the suggestion that he could not succeed.

There is, however, another factor which should be considered in Bishop's case, and which may account for his failure on other grounds than adverse suggestion. Bishop was a professional mind-reader, and, as I understand it, did not profess to have independent clairvoyant powers. If, therefore, no one knew the number of the bank-note, it is obvious that failure was inevitable, for the reason that the fundamental conditions of success were absent. There was no mind in possession of the number, and there was no mind to read. It was, therefore, not a fair test of his professed powers in any view of the case. But if Labouchere did know the number of the note, the failure was easily accounted for, as before remarked, on the principle of adverse suggestion.

It is obvious that the principle of adverse suggestion

applies to all phases and conditions of subjective mental
activity; and the necessity for harmonious conditions, so
constantly insisted upon by spiritists as a condition precedent to the production of their peculiar forms of hypnotic
phenomena, is seen to be a scientific fact of immense value
and significance, and not a mere subterfuge to enable them
to practice a fraud and impose on the credulity of their
auditors.

CHAPTER VIII.

HYPNOTISM AND MESMERISM.

Warfare of the Schools. — History of the Science. — Mesmer's Career. — The Academicians. — The Successors of Mesmer. — The Royal Academy of Medicine. — Its Idiotic Prejudices. — Dr. Braid's Discovery. — Re-baptism of the Science. — Effects of Braid's Discoveries. — Liebault's Theory of Suggestion. — The Nancy School and the Paris School compared. — The Fluidic Theory. — The Law of Suggestion the Greatest Discovery in Psychic Science. — The Significance of Braid's Discoveries not Appreciated. — Hypnotism of Animals. — The Charcot School. — The Sources of its Errors. — Reform in Terminology suggested. — The Mesmeric Theory. — Braid's Processes not productive of Higher Phenomena· — Mesmerization of Animals. — Recapitulation of Points.

THUS far little has been said regarding the light which has been shed upon the subject under consideration by the discoveries of modern science. The more important of these discoveries having resulted from investigations of the subject of hypnotism, it will be necessary briefly to review the more salient features of that science, and to trace its progress from the time of Mesmer down to the present day.

Since the time when Mesmer first brought his discoveries to the attention of the scientific world the students of the phenomena which he evoked have been hopelessly at variance. That they should entertain diverse theories regarding the cause of phenomena so strange and full of mystery is natural. That they should, in the absence of knowledge of the subject, abuse and vilify each other because of their differences of opinion, was to be expected. Hatred of our neighbor because his problematical theories do not agree with our undemonstrable hypotheses is, unfortunately, one of the salient weaknesses of human nature.

It is, however, comparatively rare that scientific investigators disagree regarding the demonstrable facts pertaining to a subject under investigation. Yet this is the condition in which we find the science of hypnotism after more than a century of research by some of the ablest scientists of the world. They are divided into schools, to-day, as they were in the infancy of the science. Indeed, the science is still in its infancy. Facts have accumulated, it is true; and they will be found to be of infinite advantage to some future investigator whose mind is capable of rising above the prejudices which characterize the different schools, and of assimilating and harmonizing their demonstrated facts into one comprehensive system.

Thus far the different schools have distrusted or denied each other's facts, and waged war upon each other's theories. The most carefully conducted experiments of one school will, in the hands of the other, produce opposite results. Hence each experimenter is irresistibly led to distrust the scientific accuracy of the methods employed by others, or to admit their integrity only at the expense of their intelligence. In the mean time each school has conducted its experiments seemingly by the most rigid scientific methods and with conscientious fidelity to truth; but the results of each apparently disprove the conclusions of all the others. Hence it is that, in the bibliography of hypnotism, we find an immense mass of well-authenticated facts which, tried by the standards of any one of the different schools, appears like an appalling hodge-podge of falsehood and delusion, chicanery and superstition. Indeed, no other science, since the dawn of creation, has suffered so much at the hands of ignorance and superstition as the science under discussion. Its ancient history is the record of the supernatural in all the nations of the earth. Its phenomena have been the foundation of all the religions and all the superstitions of ancient times. Its modern history has also been largely a record of superstitious belief, fostered by chicanery and ignorance ; the nature of the phenomena being such that in the hands alike of honest ignorance and conscious fraud they may be made to sanction every belief, confirm every dogma, and foster every superstition. It was these facts which drove scientific men from the field of investigation in the early modern history of the science. Mesmer himself, in the light of modern knowledge of the subject, is apt to be accused of charlatanism ; but, as we shall see further on, he is entitled, in common with all investigators, to the largest measure of charity.

As before remarked, the facts of hypnotism obtained by the experimenters of the different schools appear to contradict each other. This, however, is obviously only an apparent contradiction, for it is axiomatic that no one fact in Nature is inconsistent with any other fact. It follows that there must be some underlying principle or principles, heretofore overlooked, which will harmonize the facts. It is the purpose of this chapter to outline a few fundamental principles which, properly understood, will enable the student of hypnotism to reconcile many seeming inconsistencies. An understanding of the salient points of difference between the various schools can best be conveyed by briefly outlining the modern history of the science.

Mesmer is entitled to the credit of having first brought the subject to the attention of the scientific world, although probably his attention was attracted to it by the writings of Paracelsus and Van Helmont. In the early part of his career he was deeply interested in the study of astrology, and he fancied that the planets somehow exerted an influence on the health of human beings. He at first thought that this influence was electrical, but afterwards referred it to magnetism. At that time his cures were effected by stroking the diseased bodies with artificial magnets. He achieved considerable success by such means, and published a work in 1766 entitled " De Planetarum Influxa." In 1776, however, he met Gassner, a Catholic priest who had achieved great notoriety by curing disease by manipulation, without the use of any other means Mesmer then threw away his magnets, and evolved the theory of "animal magnetism." This he held to be a fluid which pervades the universe, but is most active in the human nervous organization, and enables one man, charged with the fluid, to exert a powerful influence over another.

Two years after meeting Gassner he went to Paris, and at once threw that capital into the wildest excitement by the marvellous effects of his manipulations. He was treated with contumely by the medical profession; but the people flocked to him, and many wonderful cures were effected. His methods, in the light of present knowledge, smack of charlatanism; but that he believed in himself was demonstrated by his earnest demand for an investigation. This the Government consented to, and a commission, composed of physicians and members of the Academy of Sciences, was appointed, of which Benjamin Franklin was a member. The report admitted the leading facts claimed by Mesmer, but held that there was no evidence to prove the correctness of his magnetic fluid theory, and referred the wonderful effects witnessed to the "imagination" of the patients. Their conclusion was that the subject was not worthy of further scientific investigation.

It is difficult at this day to conceive by what process of reasoning that learned body could arrive at such a conclusion. They admitted the existence of a motive force capable of controlling man's physical organization, that this force is amenable to control by man, and that this control is capable of being reduced to an art. Then they proceed to announce a discovery of their own, — a discovery, by the way, which turns out to be the most important which modern science had, at that time, contributed to the solution of the great problem. They discovered that the phenomena were purely subjective, thereby demonstrating the power of mind over matter. If they had stopped there, or if they had concluded that this wonderful force was worthy of the most searching scientific investigation, they would have been entitled to the gratitude of all mankind, and the science would have been at once wrested from the hands of ignorance and empiricism. That they should content themselves with disproving Mesmer's theory of causation, and, after having themselves made a discovery of the true cause, should announce that their own discovery was not worth the trouble of further investigation, is inexplicable.

Soon after this, Mesmer was driven into exile, followed by the execrations of a majority of the medical profession, and died in 1815. He left many disciples, a majority of whom were shallow empirics, and mesmerism was brought still further into disrepute. There were a few able and scientific men, however, who still pursued the investigation, among whom were the Marquis de Puységur, Deleuze, and others. These gentlemen revolutionized the art by first causing their subjects to sleep by means of gentle manipulation, instead of surrounding them with mysticism in dimly lighted apartments filled with sweet odors and the strains of soft and mysterious music, as was the practice of Mesmer. They developed in their subjects the power of clairvoyance, and demonstrated it in a thousand ways. They caused them to obey mental orders as readily as if the orders were spoken. They healed the sick, caused the lame to walk, and the blind to see. In short, they so far revived the interest in the subject that the Royal Academy of Medicine, in France, felt compelled to order a new investigation. This was done in 1825. A committee was appointed, composed of the ablest and most cautious scientists in their body. For nearly six years that committee pursued its investigations, and in 1831 it submitted its report. It would be tedious to enumerate all the conclusions at which it arrived. Its principal efforts were directed to the determination of the therapeutic value of mesmerism. It confirmed much that had been claimed for it in that respect, and demonstrated the power of clairvoyance, by indubitable tests. It also confirmed the claim that persons could be magnetized at a distance as well as by contact, although

there is nothing in the report which shows how far the possibilities of suggestion were removed in that class of experiments. Indeed, in deference to truth it must be here
remarked that mesmerists at that time had but a faint and
undefined notion of the subtle *rôle* which suggestion plays
in all psychological phenomena. Hence it follows that in
examining the record of experiments in the higher phenomena of hypnotism we must make due allowance for
possible error in all cases where the nature of the experiments does not preclude the possibility of suggestion having
influenced the result, or where the possibilities of suggestion
have not been intelligently eliminated.

The effect of this report was instantaneous and remarkable. The advocates of magnetism as a therapeutic agent,
and the believers in the occult features of the phenomena,
such as clairvoyance and thought-transference, had scored
a triumph. But it served only to exasperate the average
scientist and to intensify his prejudices. The Academy
refused to dignify the report by printing it, and it rests
to-day in silent oblivion in the manuscript archives of the
institution. Another committee was soon after appointed,
headed by a member who had openly sworn hostility to the
doctrine. The result was what might have been expected.
After the examination of two subjects under circumstances
which, in the light of what is now known, rendered failure
inevitable, the committee made a very undignified report,
announcing the failure to produce the occult phenomena
promised, and impugning the intelligence of the former
committee. Strange and illogical as it may seem, the later
report, which proved nothing, which was confined to an
announcement of merely negative results, which simply
showed that the committee did not witness certain promised phenomena, was accepted by the average scientist as
containing the gospel of hypnotism, as against the report
of the earlier committee, which, after five years of laborious
research, announced that it had witnessed the phenomena
in question and demonstrated their reality.

For some years subsequent to this the investigation of

the subject was confined to its psychological and therapeutic features ; but every scientist who dabbled in it was
tabooed by the majority of his associates. Many able
works were produced on the subject, but none of them
attracted the attention of the academicians until Dr. Braid,
of Manchester, undertook to demonstrate the theory that
the hypothetical magnetic fluid had nothing to do with the
production of the phenomena. Braid discovered that by
placing a bright object before the eyes of the subject, and
causing him to gaze upon it with persistent attention, he
could be thrown into the hypnotic sleep, during which
many of the well-known phenomena ascribed to magnetism
could be produced. This seemed to point to the possibility of a physiological explanation of the subject-matter.
It attracted the attention of the scientists, and thus to
Braid belongs the credit of causing the subject to be at
last acknowledged as being within the domain of the exact
sciences. The academicians were now mollified. The pet
theory of the mesmerists appeared to have been demol-
ished. The method was simple and easily applied. The
phenomena of thought-transference could not be produced
by its methods. It promised a physiological explanation ;
and, best of all, it had been given a new name. It had
received many names before Braid undertook the task of
rechristening it ; but, with the exception of " mesmerism,"
each was objectionable, because it implied a theory of
causation. The name " mesmerism " was obviously im-
proper, because Mesmer was neither the discoverer of the
force, nor the inventor of the practical method of evoking
it. " Animal magnetism " implied Mesmer's theory of
magnetic currents. " Mental or animal electricity " implied practically the same theory. " Neurology " indicated
the science of the nervous system. " Patheism " (from
the Greek radical signifying disease or suffering) and
" etherology " (which means the science of the refined
part of the atmosphere) were equally meaningless as applied to the subject. " Psycodunamy " signified the power
of the soul ; and " electro-biology " was American, and not

to be tolerated. But when Braid denominated it " hypnotism," — from the Greek word signifying sleep, — it was
hailed as a compromise sufficiently noncommittal to entitle
it to recognition, and " hypnotism " it will be called until
some academician drags to light the ultimate cause of all
things.

Braid has been accorded a great deal of credit for his
original researches and discoveries, but it is questionable
whether he has not been the indirect means of retarding the
true progress of the science. It is a remarkable fact that
since his method of hypnotizing has been generally adopted,
the higher phenomena, such as clairvoyance and thought-
transference, have fallen into disrepute, and are now rarely
produced. Indeed, it may be said to be practically a lost
art, considered as a result of hypnotic processes. The cause
of this will receive attention hereafter. Braid could not
cause his subjects to obey his mental orders, and he disbelieved in the power of clairvoyance. He acknowledged
that some of his subjects could tell the shape of what was
" held at an inch and a half from the skin, on the back
of the neck, crown of the head, arm, or hand, or other
parts of the body," but held that " it is from feeling they
do so." [1] He demonstrated the extreme sensitiveness of
one subject by causing her to obey the motion of a glass
funnel held in his hand, at a distance of fifteen feet.[2] Truly,
a remarkable case of " feeling."

Braid is entitled to great credit for the discovery that the
hypnotic state can be induced independently of the presence or co-operation of another person. Further than that,
his work is practically valueless, for the reason that he
never understood the power or influence of suggestion. It
is therefore manifestly impossible to determine the value of
any experiment of his, except in cases the nature of which
precludes the possibility of suggestion being employed, or
in cases where it was expressly eliminated.

Two facts, however, seem to have been demonstrated by his
experiments, both of which are of the utmost importance :

[1] Braid on Hypnotism, p. 37, *note*.   [2] Ibid.

1. That the hypnotic sleep can be induced independently of personal contact with, or the personal influence of, another.

2. That the sleep can be induced by his method without the aid of suggestion.

The mistake which his followers have made is in jumping to the conclusion that because one of the primary conditions of hypnotic phenomena can be induced without the aid of the magnetic hypothesis, therefore the magnetic hypothesis is necessarily incorrect. The same logic would induce a man who for the first time sees a railroad train in motion to conclude that any other method of locomotion is impracticable. Braid himself was not so illogical; for he expressly says that he does not consider the methods identical, but does "consider the condition of the nervous system induced by both modes to be analogous."

Another mistake, shared in common by both the modern schools of hypnotists, is the failure to appreciate the significance of the fact that by Braid's method the hypnotic condition can be induced without the aid of suggestion. One school ignores the fact altogether, or considers it of doubtful verity, and the other regards it merely as an evidence that suggestion plays a secondary *rôle* in hypnotic phenomena. That both are to some extent wrong will appear at the proper time, as will also the fact of the failure of all the schools to grasp its real significance.

For some years after the appearance of Braid's book there was but little, if any, progress made in the science. His methods, however, were generally adopted, but the value of his discovery was not appreciated by his own countrymen; and it was not until the Continental scientists extended his researches that he obtained substantial recognition. Liébault was the first to confirm his experiments, and in 1866 he published a work, in which he advanced much that was new in fact and theory. He was, in fact, the founder of what is now known as the Nancy school of hypnotism. Many prominent scientists have followed him, and many able works have been produced, prominent among which may be mentioned " Suggestive Therapeutics," by Professor Bernheim, and " Hypnotism," by Albert Moll, of Berlin.

Professor Charcot, of the Paris Salpêtrière, is also the founder of a school of hypnotism, which is generally known as the Paris school, or school of the Salpêtrière. Charcot's great reputation as a scientist obtained for him many followers at first, prominent among whom are Binet and Féré, whose joint work, entitled " Animal Magnetism," has been widely read both in Europe and America.

These schools differ widely both in theory and practice, their only point of union being their utter contempt for the theory and practice of what must still be known, for want of a better term, as the mesmeric school.

These three schools represent the grand divisions which it will be necessary to recognize in the discussion of the subject under consideration.

The leading points of difference between the three schools may be briefly stated as follows : —

1. The theory of the Nancy school is that the different physiological conditions characterizing the hypnotic state are determined by mental action alone ; that the phenomena can best be produced in persons of sound physical health and perfect mental balance ; and that this mental action and the consequent physical and psychological phenomena are the result, in all cases, of some form of suggestion.

2. The Paris school holds that hypnotism is the result of an abnormal or diseased condition of the nerves ; that a great number of the phenomena can be produced independently of suggestion in any form ; that the true hypnotic condition can be produced only in persons whose nerves are diseased ; and that the whole subject is explicable on the basis of cerebral anatomy or physiology.

3. The mesmerists hold to the fluidic theory of Mesmer : that the hypnotic condition is induced, independent of suggestion, by passes made by the operator over the subject, accompanied by intense concentration of mind and will on the part of the former ; that from him flows a subtle fluid which impinges upon the subject wherever it is directed,

and produces therapeutic or other effects in obedience to the will of the operator ; that these effects can best be produced by personal contact ; but that they can be produced at a distance and without the knowledge of the subject, and independently of suggestion.

In discussing the merits of these several schools, it is perhaps superfluous to say that it is self-evident that neither school can be entirely right. Each presents an array of facts which seems to support its theory ; but as the theories are irreconcilable, and the facts apparently contradict each other, it follows that some fundamental principle underlying the whole subject-matter has been overlooked. It is the purpose of this book to suggest a possible way to the discovery of the principle, — the missing link which will unite the chain and bind the facts of psychological science into one harmonious whole.

The Nancy school of hypnotism is entitled to the credit of having made the most important discovery in psychological science. The fact that the subjective mind is constantly amenable to control by the power of suggestion, constitutes the grand principle in psychological science, which, when properly appreciated and applied, will solve every problem and illuminate every obscurity in the labyrinthian science of the human soul, so far as it will ever be possible for finite intelligence to penetrate it. It is safe to say that in all the broad realm of psychological science there is not a phenomenon upon which it will not shed light. It is no discredit to that school to say that its leaders and teachers do not yet seem to comprehend the profound significance of their discovery, and that in one direction they have extended it too far. It is the latter proposition which will first receive attention.

They hold, very correctly, that all the phenomena of hypnotism, subsequent to the induction of the hypnotic condition, are due to the power of suggestion in some form. That this is true, admits of no possible doubt. They also find by experiment that the hypnotic condition can be induced simply by the power of suggestion. Their conclu-

sion is that suggestion is a necessary factor in the induction
of the hypnotic condition. That this is not true can be
very readily demonstrated by reference to a few well-known
and admitted facts. One of the first discoveries made by
Braid was that by his methods the hypnotic condition
could be induced in persons who had never seen or heard
of hypnotic phenomena.

The following passage from that learned author seems to
have been overlooked by those of his commentators who
seek for evidence in his experiments to prove that suggestion is a necessary factor in the induction of the hypnotic
condition : —

" In order to prove my position still more clearly, I called up
one of my men-servants, who knew nothing of mesmerism, and
gave him such directions as were calculated to impress his mind
with the idea that his fixed attention was merely for the purpose
of watching a chemical experiment in the preparation of some
medicine, and being familiar with such, he could feel no alarm.
In two minutes and a half his eyelids closed slowly with a vibra-
ting motion, his chin fell on his breast, he gave a deep sigh, and
instantly was in a profound sleep, breathing loudly. . . . In
about one minute after his profound sleep I aroused him and
pretended to chide him for being so careless, said he ought to
be ashamed of himself for not being able to attend to my instructions for three minutes without falling asleep, and ordered
him downstairs. In a short time I recalled this young man, and
desired him to sit down once more, but to be careful not to go
to sleep again, as on the former occasion. He sat down with
this intention ; but at the expiration of two minutes and a half his
eyelids closed, and exactly the same phenomena as in the former
experiment ensued." [1]

Now, whilst it is true that Braid did not realize the supreme potency of suggestion as it is now understood by the
Nancy school, he did intelligently eliminate it in the experiment above related. It was his purpose to demonstrate his
theory that " the phenomena of mesmerism were to be accounted for on the principle of a derangement of the state
of the cerebro-spinal centres, and of the circulatory and

[1] Neurypnology, p. 18.

respiratory and muscular systems."[1] In other words, he was
seeking to demonstrate his theory that the phenomena of
mesmerism are attributable to a physical rather than a
mental cause. Hence his care to select a subject who
knew nothing of what was expected of him.

Braid relates another circumstance equally demonstrative
of the proposition that suggestion is not a necessary factor
in the induction of the hypnotic state. He says : —

"After my lecture at the Hanover Square Rooms, London,
on the 1st of March, 1842, a gentleman told Mr. Walker, who
was along with me, that he was most anxious to see me, that I
might try whether I could hypnotize him. He said both himself
and friends were anxious he should be affected, but that neither
Lafontaine nor others who had tried him could succeed. Mr.
Walker said, 'If that is what you want, as Mr. Braid is engaged
otherwise, sit down, and I will hypnotize you myself in a minute.'
When I went into the room, I observed what was going on, the
gentleman sitting staring at Mr. Walker's finger, who was standing a little to the right of the patient, with his eyes fixed steadily
on those of the latter. I passed on and attended to something
else ; and when I returned a little after, I found Mr. Walker
standing in the same position, *fast asleep, his arm and finger in
a state of cataleptiform rigidity*, and the patient wide awake
and staring at the finger all the while."[2]

This is a clear case of the induction of the hypnotic condition without the aid of suggestion. Mr. Walker had no
thought of going into the state himself, but was intent on
hypnotizing the patient. The suggestion in his mind was,
therefore, in the opposite direction. He had, however, inadvertently placed himself in the proper attitude, and so
concentrated his gaze as to induce the state, and that
directly contrary to his auto-suggestion.

These two instances have been cited from Braid for the
reason that (1) he was the discoverer of the method of
hypnotizing by causing the subject to gaze steadily upon
an object ; and (2) he was not attempting to prove or disprove the theory of suggestion. His testimony is obviously
all the more reliable for that reason, for one is prone to

[1] Neurypnology, p. 19.   [2] Ibid., p. 39.

distrust the verity of experiments made for the purpose of sustaining a theory. Many facts have been recorded which demonstrate the proposition that by Braid's method the hypnotic state can be induced independently of suggestion. One class only of such facts needs to be cited to convince the most sceptical.

I allude to religious devotees, who are often thrown into the hypnotic state, even to the degree of ecstasy, by gazing upon the crucifix, or upon pictures of the Holy Virgin or of the saints. The Catholic clergy would seem to have a dim perception of the principle involved when they elevate the cross above the eyes of those in whom they wish to excite devotional enthusiasm. Be that as it may, the fact is of scientific value to the investigator of psychological phenomena. The natural attitude of prayer — the eyes raised towards heaven — is certainly not only conducive to devotional feeling, but, in emotional natures, to a state at least cognate to hypnotism, if not identical with it. Hence the subjective hallucinations which often result from the long and earnest prayers of religious enthusiasts.

More conclusive still is the fact that animals can be hypnotized. Albert Moll, who is one of the ablest, and certainly one of the most unprejudiced, of modern scientific writers on the subject of hypnotism, writing from the standpoint of the Nancy school, makes the following observations on the subject of hypnotizing animals : —

"States resembling, or perhaps identical with, hypnosis, are also found in animals, and can easily be experimentally induced. The first experiments of this kind are referred to by the Jesuit Kircher, — the so-called *experimentum mirabile Kircheri*. Kircher described these experiments in 1646; but according to Preyer, the experiment had been made by Schwenter several years earlier. The most striking of these experiments, which are being continued in the present day, is as follows: A hen is held down on the ground; the head in particular is pressed down. A chalk line is then drawn on the ground, starting from the bird's beak. The hen will remain motionless. Kircher ascribes this to the animal's imagination; he said that it imagined that it was fastened, and consequently did not try to move. Czermak repeated the experiment on different animals, and an nounced in 1872 that a hypnotic state could be induced in other animals besides the hen. Preyer shortly after began to interest himself in the question, and made a series of experiments like Czermak's. Preyer, however, distinguishes two states in animals, — catalepsy, which is the effect of fear; and the hypnotic state. Heubel, Richet, Danilewsky, and Rieger, besides the authors mentioned above, have occupied themselves with the question.

" Most of the experiments have been made with frogs, crayfish, guinea-pigs, and birds. I have made many with frogs. This much is certain : many animals will remain motionless in any position in which they have been held by force for a time. There are various opinions as to the meaning of this. Preyer thinks many of these states are paralyses from fright, or catalepsy, produced by a sudden peripheral stimulus. In any case they vividly recall the catalepsy of the Salpêtrière, also caused by a strong external stimulus."[1]

The experiments of Kircher, above mentioned, were undertaken with a view of demonstrating his theory that animals possessed great powers of imagination. The chalk mark, he held, represented to the imagination of the hen a string with which she supposed herself to be bound. In his day, of course, nothing was known of hypnotism. It has since been demonstrated that the chalk mark has nothing to do with the production of the phenomenon. The same result follows when the chalk mark is omitted. The writer has hypnotized a pet rooster by Braid's method without using any violence whatever, or even touching the fowl. He was exceedingly tame, and it was only necessary to hold a small object directly before his eyes ; when his attention was attracted, he would gaze steadily upon it, and in a very few minutes would go fast asleep. This could not have been a catalepsy caused by fright, nor could it have been the result of a belief in his inability to move, nor a peripheral stimulus caused by friction against the skin, nor could it have been suggestion. In fact, there is no legitimate conclusion apparent except that it was a true hypnosis, identical with that produced on human beings by Braid's methods.

[1] Moll on Hypnotism, p. 213.

This branch of the subject has been dwelt upon some-what at length, not merely for the purpose of showing that the adherents of the Nancy school carry the doctrine of suggestion too far, but because it is an important point in the study of the subject, and throws a flood of light upon many important and perplexing problems, as will be seen hereafter. The principle to be borne in mind is this: hypnosis can be produced by Braid's method either with or without the aid of suggestion.

This does not militate in the slightest degree against the doctrine of suggestion when its powers and limitations are properly understood. It still remains true that all hypnotic phenomena subsequent to the induction of the condition are the result of suggestion in some form. This is the grand discovery of the Nancy school; and when it is once appreciated and understood, it will be found to constitute the master-key which will unlock the secrets of every psy-chological mystery. That it is unqualifiedly true no longer admits of serious doubt; it is acknowledged by nearly every scientist in the civilized world who has given the sub-ject intelligent attention. It is true that the great name of Charcot has commanded a following; but however valuable may have been his observations in the infancy of the sci-ence, it has become obvious to most of his former followers that his fundamental hypothesis is defective, and that his conclusions are therefore necessarily unreliable.

The discussion of the merits of the Paris school will be brief, and will be chiefly confined to a statement of the reasons for considering its experiments and conclusions unreliable, and to pointing out a few of the more obvious sources of its errors.

The first source of error lies in the fact that the experi-ments of this school are made almost exclusively upon hysterical women. The assumption is that hypnotism is a nervous disease, and that the disease is found in its most pronounced form in hysterical subjects. That this propo-sition is unqualifiedly wrong is positively known to every student of hypnotism outside the Paris school. and needs no further refutation than the bare statement that the experience of all other schools goes to demonstrate the fact that the best hypnotic subjects are perfectly healthy persons.

Another source of error lies in the fact that they ignore suggestion as a necessary factor in the production of hypnotic phenomena. Of course they are aware of the potency of suggestion when purposely and intelligently employed; but they hold that very many of the most important of the phenomena can be produced without its aid. These, however, are principally physical effects, such as causing any muscle of the body to contract by pressing upon the corresponding nerve, and then releasing the tension by exciting the antagonistic muscle. The condition necessary for the production of this phenomenon is called by Charcot, "neuro-muscular hyperexcitability." In the able and interesting work by Binet and Féré, pupils of Charcot, a chapter is devoted to this branch of the subject. They record, with a scientific exactitude that is very edifying, many curious results in the way of causing contracture of various muscles by kneading, pressure, percussion, etc., releasing the tension by exciting the opposing muscles, and transferring the contractures from one muscle to another by the magnet. Then, with an ingenuousness that is truly charming, they add, as a "singular fact," that "contractures can be easily produced in many hysterical patients in their waking state, either by kneading the muscles, by pressure on the nerves, or by striking the tendons. These contractures in the waking state are, indeed, of the same nature as those which occur during lethargy, since they yield to the excitement of the antagonistic muscles, and may be transferred by the magnet."

After this admission it seems superfluous to remark that this class of experiments prove nothing more than that the state of neuro-muscular hyperexcitability is a pathological symptom common to hysterical patients, whether in the waking state or in hypnotic lethargy. They certainly prove nothing which can be construed as characteristic of hypnotism; and the Nancy school wastes its time in demonstrating that the symptoms cannot be reproduced in healthy persons except by the aid of suggestion.

Another serious error into which the Charcot school has fallen in its effort to eliminate the effects of suggestion consists in the assumption that subjects in the lethargic state know nothing of what is passing around them, either objectively or subjectively. No greater mistake is possible. *The subjective mind never sleeps.* No matter how profound the lethargy, it is ever alert, and comprehends instantly, with preternatural acuteness, everything that occurs. Professor Bernheim, in the preface to "Suggestive Therapeutics," makes the same assertion. He says :—

"One should first be aware of the fact that in all degrees of hypnosis the subject hears and understands everything, even though he may appear inert and passive. Sometimes the senses are particularly sharp in this state of special concentration, as if all the nervous activity were accumulated in the organ of which the attention is solicited."

The state of lethargy is that in which Charcot supposes his subjects to be incapable of receiving a suggestion. Acting upon that hypothesis, it is not astonishing that he should deceive himself as well as the students and spectators attending his clinic. He believes that they hear nothing when they hear everything. It is easy to see how every suggested phenomenon is promptly produced under such conditions. But there is one phenomenon of which the learned professor fails to note the significance, and that is, that, no matter how profound the lethargy, his subject promptly awakens at the word of command.

The simple truth regarding the experiments of the Paris school is in a nutshell. Its fundamental error lies in the assumption that hypnosis has a purely physical origin, and that the phenomena are explicable on physiological principles. The phenomena which can be produced independently of suggestion are purely physical, and depend upon the physical condition of neuro-muscular hyperexcitability. That this is true is shown by the fact that the physical phenomena produced by Charcot upon his hysterical patients cannot be produced on healthy subjects without the aid of suggestion. But such experiments do not properly belong to the domain of psychic science proper, but rather to the Bradian system of physical manipulation. This is as much as confessed by Binet and Féré, when they divulge the fact that the physical phenomena in question can be produced on hysterical patients in their waking condition.

Another prolific source of error which besets the pathway of the Paris school consists in its disbelief in, and consequent disregard of, the possibility that its subjects may be possessed of clairvoyant or telepathic powers. That this frequently happens, especially in subjects of the character employed by Charcot and his coadjutors, admits of no possible doubt in the minds of those who have studied the higher phases of hypnotic science. The London Society for Psychical Research has demonstrated beyond all question the fact that telepathy is a power possessed by many; and the early mesmerists have shown conclusively that the hypnotic condition is the one of all others the most favorable for the development and exhibition of that power. This subject will be dwelt upon more at length in its proper place. It is sufficient for present purposes to remark that no line of experiments in hypnotism, in which telepathy and clairvoyance are ignored as possible factors, can be held to be demonstrative of any proposition or theory whatever. But whatever of pathological value or interest may be attached to the physical phenomena evoked by the Paris school, they certainly shed no light upon psychological science, nor do they properly belong to that domain.

And just here I wish to suggest a reform in the nomenclature of the science under consideration. The word "hypnotism" was adopted by Braid at a time when he regarded himself as the discoverer of a principle which embraced the whole science of induced sleep. It is from the Greek word "hypnos," which broadly signifies sleep. But, without some qualifying word, it is too broad, inasmuch as the system to which Braid applied it is now known to be but one of many processes of inducing sleep. He imagined that he had discovered a full explanation of all psychic phenomena of the class then known as mesmeric ; whereas he had only discovered the one fact that the sleep could be induced by producing an abnormal physical condition of certain nerve-centres. It was a very important discovery, for psychic science would be incomplete without it; but it does not constitute the whole science. It does, however, explain many phenomena otherwise inexplicable, and marks a line of distinction which could not otherwise be drawn. The methods of the Charcot school are essentially Braidian, and hence its results are limited largely to physical phenomena, and its conclusions necessarily pertain to physical science.

The Nancy school, on the other hand, produces all its phenomena by oral suggestion, and ignores the fact that the sleep can be induced in the absence of any form of suggestion. It repudiates Braid's method of inducing it as unnecessary, and also as injurious, in that the physical disturbance of the nerve-centres unduly excites the patient.

The mesmeric school differs from both the others in methods and theory, as we shall see further on.

It seems necessary, therefore, that the terminology of the science should be changed so as clearly to define the theoretical differences of the three schools. It is obvious, however, that the terminology cannot be based on results, for they are inextricably intermingled. Thus, the Braidian or Charcot operator might accidentally produce psychic phenomena identical with that produced by the mesmerists, and *vice versa*. And so might the suggestive school. Indeed, the writings of both schools occasionally betray the fact that they sometimes catch glimpses of something in their patients which defies chemical analysis, and cannot be carved with the scalpel.

The terminology must, therefore, refer to the methods of inducing the subjective state. If the word " hypnotism " is to be retained because it embraces all degrees of induced sleep by whatsoever process it may have been induced, it would seem proper to designate the Braidian process as *physical hypnotism*, the Nancy process as *suggestive hypnotism*, and the mesmeric process as *magnetic*, or *fluidic*, *hypnotism*.

I merely throw this out as a suggestion to be considered by future writers on the subject. For my own purposes I shall hereafter employ the word "hypnotism" to define the Braidian and suggestive processes as distinguished from all others when these are contrasted, while the word "mesmerism" will be employed as it is generally understood. When they are not contrasted, "hypnotism" will be used as a generic term.

Last in the order of mention, but really first in importance, is the school of mesmerism. The theory of the mesmerists has undergone little, if any, modification since it was first promulgated by Mesmer himself. It is, as before stated, that there exists in man a subtle fluid, in the nature of magnetism, which, by means of passes over the head and body of the subject, accompanied by intense concentration of mind and will on the part of the operator, can be made to flow from the ends of his fingers and impinge upon the subject, producing sleep and all the varied subsequent phenomena at the will of the operator. In the early days of mesmerism suggestion was ignored as a possible factor in the production of the phenomena, this law not having been discovered previous to the experiments of Liébault. The same is practically true to-day. Mesmerism has made very little progress within the last half century. Its votaries cling to the old theories with a pertinacity proportioned to the opposition encountered at the hands of the hypnotists. On the whole, the progress of mesmeric science, *per se*, has been backward since the discoveries of Braid, — not because Braid disproved the fluidic theory, for he did not disprove it, nor did he claim to have done so, but for reasons which will appear in their proper place.

Suggestion is now, as before the discoveries of Liébault, ignored by mesmerists as a necessary factor either in the induction of the mesmeric condition, or in the production of the subsequent phenomena. In this they are partly right and partly wrong. Suggestion, in the ordinary acceptation of the term, — that is, oral suggestion, — is not an indispensable factor in the induction of the condition. This is shown in a great variety of ways. One fact alone demonstrates the principle, and that is, that subjects who have been often mesmerized by a particular individual can be by him thrown into that state, under certain favorable conditions, even though the two may be many miles apart. Account is not taken in this of the many experiments of the old mesmerists, who previously informed their subjects of the intended experiment. But many instances might be cited where this has been accomplished under test conditions, the element of suggestion being carefully eliminated. The writer has mesmerized a subject at a distance of three hundred miles, and that under conditions which rendered oral or objective suggestion impossible. Particular instances will not be cited here, for the reason that in subsequent chapters of this book the principle involved will be rendered so plain that further proofs would be superfluous. A further demonstration of this principle lies in the fact that children, too young to understand what is expected of them, and animals of various kinds, can be mesmerized. This is abundantly proved by the experiments of Wilson, who, as early as 1839, mesmerized elephants, horses, wolves, and other animals in London. Obersteimer states that in Austria the law requires army horses to be mesmerized for the purpose of shoeing them. This process was introduced by a cavalry officer named Balassa, and hence it has been termed and is now known as " the *Balassiren* of horses " (Moll). This is the secret of the celebrated horse-tamers, Sullivan and Rarey. By their methods the wildest colts and the most vicious horses could be subdued in an hour. Mesmerism is the power exerted by the lion-tamer and the snake-charmer. The power is often exerted unconsciously, — that is, without a knowledge on the part of the operator of the source of his power.

The mesmerists of the present day are not, of course,

*i*gnorant or unmindful of the potency of suggestion in the production of mesmeric phenomena subsequent to the induction of the condition. But, like the Paris school of hypnotists, they hold that suggestion plays a secondary *rôle* in the production of many of the phenomena. That they are wrong in this will more fully appear in subsequent chapters of this book.

The points of difference between the three schools of this science have now been reviewed, and the theories of each briefly stated. It is found, —

1. That the Nancy school attributes all the phenomena, including the induction of the state, to the power of suggestion, and that it is to the psychic powers and attributes of man alone that we must look for an explanation.

2. The Paris school, on the other hand, ignores suggestion as a necessary factor either in the induction of the state or in the production of subsequent phenomena, and seeks an explanation of the subject-matter on the bases of physiology and celebral anatomy.

3. The mesmerists ignore suggestion as a necessary factor at any stage of their experiments, and explain the whole on the magnetic fluid theory.

We also find three distinct methods of inducing the sleep; and as it is of the utmost importance to bear the different methods in mind, they will be here restated : —

The Nancy school, true to its theory, employs suggestion alone to induce the condition. Passes are sometimes made over its subjects after the manner of the mesmerists, but only with a view of giving an air of mystery to the proceedings, and thus adding potency to the suggestion.

The Paris school employs physical means to induce the state almost exclusively. They are practically the same as those employed by Braid, namely, causing the subject to gaze steadily at a bright object, — although many variations of the method have been introduced, such as flashing an electric light in the eyes of the subject, striking a gong without warning close to his ears, or by some peripheral excitation, such as rubbing the scalp, etc.

The mesmeric method proper consists in making passes from the head downwards, gazing fixedly into the subject's eyes, and concentrating the mind upon the work in hand, strongly willing the subject to sleep. It is true that many of the so-called mesmerists now employ Braid's method entirely, and others depend largely upon suggestion. But the true mesmeric method is as has been stated.

CHAPTER IX.

HYPNOTISM AND MESMERISM (*continued*).

Mesmeric Methods. — The Fluidic Theory. — Influence of the Mind of the Operator. — The Early Mesmerists. — Their Methods and their Effects. — Decadence of the Higher Phenomena under Braid's Methods. — The Causes explained. — Telepathic Powers developed by Mesmerism. — Mesmerism as a Therapeutic Agent. — Method of Operation recommended. — How to acquire the Power. — The Necessary Conditions of Success. — Will Power explained. — The Fluidic Theory requires Revision. — Distinction between Mesmerism and Hypnotism sharply drawn. — Mesmerization of Animals distinguished from the Hypnotization of Animals. — Methods employed in Each. — Tamers of Horses and Wild Beasts. — Dog-Trainers. — Primitive Man. — His Powers. — His Immunity from Harm. — Daniel. — The Adepts. — General Conclusions.

THAT the magnetic hypothesis of the mesmerists has many facts to sustain it cannot be denied. The experience of thousands goes to show that when passes are made over them, even at a distance of several feet, a sensation is felt akin to a gentle shock of electricity, which produces a remarkably soothing effect upon the nervous system, and eventually produces the mesmeric sleep. It is also known that when patients are mesmerized for therapeutic purposes, and passes are made over the affected part, the same soothing effect is produced, and pain is relieved. In fact, if we consider mesmerism solely as a therapeutic agent, and study it from that standpoint alone, the fluidic hypothesis is perhaps as good as any. But when we come to study mesmeric phenomena as a part, and only a very small part, of a grand system of psychological science ; when we ex amine it in its relations to other phenomena of a cognate character, — it is found that the fluidic theory should be received with some qualification.

The first thought which strikes the observer is that, admitting the fluidic theory to be substantially correct, the fluid is directed and controlled entirely by the mind of the operator. It is well known that passes effect little or nothing if the attention of the operator is distracted, from any cause whatever. The subject may be put to sleep, it is true, solely by the power of suggestion ; but the peculiar effects of mesmerism, as distinguished from those of hypnotism, will be found wanting. The effects here alluded to consist mainly of the development of the higher phenomena, such as clairvoyance and telepathy.

It is well known that the early mesmerists constantly and habitually developed telepathic powers in their subjects. Causing their subjects to obey mental orders was a common platform experiment half a century ago. These experiments were often made, under test conditions, by the most careful and conscientious scientists, and the results are recorded in the many volumes on the subject written at the time. Many of these works were written by scientists whose methods of investigation were painstaking and accurate to the last degree. In the light of the developments of modern science, in the light of the demonstrations, by the members of the London Society for the Promotion of Psychical Research, of the existence of telepathic power, we cannot read the works of the old mesmerists without having the conviction forced upon us that telepathy was developed by their experiments to a degree almost unknown at the present day. Why it is that the power to develop that phenomenon by mesmerists has been lost or has fallen into desuetude, is a question of the gravest scientific interest and importance. The hostility and ridicule of the academicians undoubtedly had its effect on many minds, and caused many scientific investigators to shrink from publicly avowing their convictions or the results of their investigations. But that does not account for the fact that mesmerists, who believe in the verity of the phenomena, are rarely able to produce it at the present day.

The first question which presents itself is one of dates. When did the higher phenomena show the first signs of decadence? A moment's reflection will fix it at or about the date of the promulgation of the theories of Dr. Braid. It is a historic fact, well known to all who have watched the progress of hypnotic science, that as soon as it was found that the mesmeric or hypnotic sleep could be induced by causing the subject to gaze upon a bright object held before his eyes, all other methods were practically abandoned. It was much easier to hold an object before the subject's eyes for a few minutes, with the mind at rest, than to make passes over him for an indefinite length of time, accompanying the passes by fixity of gaze and intense concentration of mind. The important point to bear in mind right here is the fact that in the old mesmeric method, fixity of gaze and concentration of will on the part of the operator, were considered indispensable to success. It seems clear, then, that it is to this change of methods that we must look for an explanation of the change in results. That being conceded, we must inquire how the conditions were changed by the change of methods. What effects, if any, either in the condition of the subject or of the operator, or in both, are missing when the new methods are applied?

It is now necessary to recall to mind the fact (1) that Braid demonstrated that suggestion is not a necessary factor in the induction of the hypnotic state; and (2) that steadily gazing upon an object will induce the condition in a more or less marked degree, whether the subject is expecting the result or not. The intelligent student will so readily recall thousands of facts demonstrating this proposition that it is safe to set it down as an axiom in hypnotic science that intense gazing upon an object, accompanied by concentration of mind, will displace the threshold of consciousness to a greater or less extent, depending upon the mental characteristics of the individual and the circumstances surrounding him. The subjective powers are thus brought into play. The subjective mind is released, or elevated above the threshold of consciousness, and performs its functions independently of, or synchronously with, the objective mind, just in proportion to the degree of hypnosis induced. It may be only in a slight degree, it may be imperceptible to those surrounding him, or it may reach a state of complete hypnosis, as in the cases mentioned by Braid ; but certain it is that the subjective powers will be evoked in exact proportion to the degree of causation. The conclusion is obvious and irresistible that when a mesmerist employs the old methods of inducing the subjective state, — passes, fixed gazing, and mental concentration, — *he hypnotizes himself by the same act by which he mesmerizes the subject.*

The far-reaching significance of this fact will be instantly apparent to those who are aware that telepathy is the normal means of communication between two subjective minds, and that it is only between subjective minds that telepathy can be employed. The objective mind has no part or lot in telepathy until the threshold of consciousness is displaced so as to enable the objective mind to take cognizance of the message. It will be understood, therefore, that when the subject is mesmerized, and all his objective senses are in complete abeyance, and the operator with whom he is *en rapport* is in a partially subjective state, the conditions exist which render possible the exhibition of telepathic powers.

This is what was meant when it was said in an earlier chapter of this book that the discoveries of Braid had really served to retard the progress of hypnotic science ; not because his discoveries are not of the utmost practical value, but because much of their true significance has been misunderstood. The fact that persons can be hypnotized by his methods, and that many of the phenomena common to mesmerism can be produced by that means, is a fact of vast importance ; but it is only one link in the great chain, and not the whole chain, as his followers would have us believe. The later discovery of the law of suggestion was also of the most transcendent interest and importance ; but it is not the whole law of psychic science. This, too, has helped to retard the progress of the science in its higher branches. When it was discovered that suggestion by itself could induce the hypnotic state, Braid's methods were in turn abandoned by students of the science. This was partly because it was easier than Braid's method, and partly because it produced less physical and mental excitement, and hence, for therapeutic purposes, was less liable to excite the patient unduly. But the fact remains that neither by Braidism nor by the suggestive method can the subject ordinarily be made to respond telepathically. It is true that there might be exceptions to the rule. If, for instance, the operator in employing either of the methods should come in physical contact with the subject, and should at the same time happen to concentrate his gaze upon some object for a length of time, and fix his mind upon the work in hand, he would be very likely to come into telepathic communication with the subject. That this has often happened there can be no doubt ; and it constitutes one of the possible sources of error which lie in the pathway both of the Paris and the Nancy schools. It is perhaps superfluous to remark that the higher phenomena of hypnotism can only be developed with certainty of results by throwing aside our prejudices against the fluidic theory, and employing the old mesmeric methods.

In this connection it is deemed proper to offer a few suggestions as to the best methods to be employed for producing mesmeric effects, either for therapeutic or for any other purposes.

It is recommended, for several reasons, that the mesmeric passes be employed. First, they are so generally believed to be necessary that they greatly assist by way of suggestion. Secondly, they are a great assistance to the operator, as they enable him more effectually to concentrate his mind upon the work in hand, and to fix his attention upon the parts which he desires to affect. Thirdly, they operate as a suggestion to the operator himself, which is as necessary and as potent to effect the object sought as is suggestion to the subject. Fourthly, whether the fluidic theory is correct or not, the power, whatever it is, appears to flow from the fingers; and, inasmuch as it appears to do so, the effect, both upon the mind of the operator and of the subject, is the same as if it were so, — the great *desideratum* being the confidence of both.

The most important point to be gained, however, is self-confidence in the mind of the operator. Without that no greater results can be produced by mesmeric methods than by the process of simple oral suggestion. The latter affects the mind of the subject alone, and all the subsequent effects are due solely to the action of his mind. Mesmeric methods, on the other hand, if properly applied, supplement the effects of oral suggestion by a constant force emanating from the subjective mind of the operator. In order to evoke that force it is necessary for the operator to inspire his own subjective mind with confidence. This can be done by the simple process of auto-suggestion. The power to do this does not depend upon his objective belief. The power to control subjective belief is inherent in the objective mind; and that control can be made absolute, even in direct contradiction to objective belief. If, therefore, the mesmeric operator doubts his power over his subject, he can, nevertheless, exert all the necessary force simply by reiterated affirmation to himself that he possesses that power. This affirmation need not, and perhaps should not, be uttered aloud. But it should be constantly reiterated mentally while the passes are being made; and if in addition to this he concentrates his gaze upon the open or closed eyes of the subject, or upon any part of the head or face, the effect will be all the more powerful. Whatever effect is desired should be formulated in the mind of the operator, and reiterated with persistency until it is produced. The principle involved is obvious, and easily understood. The subject is passive, and receptive of subjective mental impressions. The subjective mind of the operator is charged with faith and confidence by auto-suggestion. That faith is impressed telepathically upon the subjective mind of the patient; and even though his objective belief may not coincide with the subjective impression thus received, the latter obtains control unconsciously to the subject, and the end is accomplished.

The power to mesmerize by this method is within the reach of any one with sufficient intelligence to understand the directions, and sufficient mental balance to follow them with persistency; provided always the subject is willing to be mesmerized, and is possessed of the requisite mental equilibrium to enable him to become passive and receptive.

All mesmerists and all hypnotists agree in holding that self-confidence is a necessary part of the mental equipment of the successful operator. This is true. It is also true that the possession of the requisite confidence is the one thing which distinguishes the successful from the unsuccessful operator. The foregoing remarks show how that confidence can be commanded, in spite of objective unbelief.

Much has been said by mesmerists about the exertion of "will power;" but no one has ever explained just how that power is to be exerted, or in what it consists. Most people seem to imagine that it is exercised by compressing the lips, corrugating the brows, and assuming a fierce, determined, not to say piratical, aspect. It is perhaps needless to remark that the attitude of mind indicated by such an aspect is the farthest possible from that which is required for the successful exercise of so-called will power. It requires no mental or nervous strain to exert that power. On the contrary, a calm serenity of mind is indispensable. When that is acquired, the only other requisites are confidence and an earnest desire to bring about the results sought. That these three requisites can easily be acquired by any one of common intelligence has already been shown.

From what has been said it seems evident that the force developed by mesmeric manipulations has its origin in mental action. That that is the motive power is certain. Whether this mental action creates or develops a fluid akin to magnetism, is a question which may never be solved. Nor is it deemed important that it should be; and it may be as well to class it at once among the many things un- knowable, as to waste valuable time in a vain effort to wrest the secret from Nature. Electricity is known as a great force in physical nature; and it is harnessed and made to perform many services to mankind. Like all the great forces of nature, it is invisible, except through its effects, and it defies analysis. It will never be known to man except as one of the great correlated forces. It is equally impossible to know just what the force is which emanates from the mesmerist and controls his subject. We know that it exists, and that it can be utilized, and that is all. Whether it is a fluid or not is as impossible to know with certainty as it is to know what electricity is made of, if we should determine it to be a substance.

For some purposes, as has been remarked, the fluidic hypothesis is as good as any, and for such purposes it may be provisionally accepted. But the question is, Will that hypothesis apply to all the phenomena? If that question is answered in the negative, it demonstrates its incorrect- ness, and it becomes imperative that it should be aban- doned. When mesmeric passes are made over a patient, a fluid appears to emanate from the hands of the operator. An effluence of some kind certainly does come from that source, and one that is perceptible to the physical senses of the patient. Is it not a fact, nevertheless, that the passes are principally useful as a means of controlling the minds both of the subject and the operator? There are many facts which seem to point unmistakably in that direction. The one fact alone that persons can be mesmerized at a distance, seems conclusive. No passes are then made, and yet all the effects of personal contact are produced. Thou- sands of persons have been healed at a distance, by simple concentration of mind on the part of the operator, the patient knowing absolutely nothing of the proposed experiment. This branch of the subject will be more fully treated in a future chapter on psycho-therapeutics. It is sufficient to remark now that the method of healing here indicated is, when intelligently applied, the most effective of all systems of mental therapeutics. And the significant fact is that in the majority of cases the best results are produced when the patient is kept in absolute ignorance of what is being done for him. The reason for this will more fully appear as we proceed.

Again, the manner of mesmerizing animals is proof positive that the successful exercise of mesmeric power is not dependent upon passes made by the hand of the operator, for the usual method is to gaze steadily into the eyes of the animal.

And this brings us to the discussion of some important . . . pertaining to the mesmerization of animals, which seem not to have been observed by the investigators of that subject, but which show more clearly than almost anything else the line of distinction between hypnotism and mesmerism.

The intelligent reader will not have failed to observe that the effect produced upon hens, frogs, crayfish, guinea-pigs, and birds is purely hypnotic. The methods employed are Braid's. That is to say, they are purely physical, sometimes produced by sudden peripheral stimulus, as in flashing a Drummond light in the eyes of a cock (Richer). But in general the external stimulus used with animals is tactile, as in seizing them (Moll) ; or in causing them to gaze upon an object, as in Kircher's method of hypnotizing a cock ; or in gently stroking the back, as in hypnotizing a frog or a crayfish. Each of these methods may be classified as a hypnotic process, and the full equivalent of the method discovered by Braid. The effect is also purely hypnotic ; that is to say, sleep is induced, varying in degree from a light slumber to a profound lethargy.

On the other hand, such animals as horses, wild beasts, etc., may be mesmerized, but not hypnotized. The processes are purely mesmeric, and generally consist in gazing into the animal's eyes. The effect is simply to render the animal docile, and obedient to the will of the operator. No one was ever able to put an animal to sleep by gazing into its eyes; but the most ferocious of the animal tribe may be tamed and subjected to the dominion of man by that simple process. A celebrated horse-tamer, who travelled through this country a few years ago, was in the habit of astonishing and amusing his audiences by selecting the wildest horse present, walking up to him, gazing into his eyes (apparently) for a few moments, and walking away, when the horse would follow him wherever he went, apparently as perfectly fascinated as any hypnotic or mesmeric subject was ever fascinated by a professional mesmerist. A close observation of the horse-tamer's methods revealed the fact that he simply rolled his eyes upward and inward, precisely as Braid compelled his subjects to do by holding a bright object before their eyes. He did not gaze into the eyes of the horse at all, but simply held himself in that attitude for a few moments, in close proximity to the horse's head, when the object was accomplished, and the horse became obedient to every command that it was capable of comprehending. It is probable that the horse-tamer knew as little of the secret of his power as did the horse. The tamers of wild beasts proceed in the same manner, and probably with as little knowledge of the principles underlying the method.

Now, the question arises, What is the effect thus produced on the animal? It is certainly not hypnotized by being compelled to gaze into the eyes of the operator, for sufficient time is not given to " fatigue the muscles of the eye." Besides, the animal cannot be compelled to gaze at anything. Is not the primary effect — hypnotic or mesmeric — produced, not directly upon the animal, but upon the man himself ? It seems clear that this is the true solution of the problem. Braid has taught us that by steadily gazing at any object a man can hypnotize himself without knowing, or having it suggested to him, that it is possible for him to do so. The man, then, is partially hypnotized by gazing into the animal's eyes. The threshold of his consciousness is thus displaced. His subjective powers are brought into play, and in that condition his subjective mind is *en rapport* with that of the animal. The mind of the animal, being almost purely subjective, is thus dominated by the imperious will of his master, — man. That telepathy is the normal means of communication between animals cannot be doubted by any one who has observed their habits with intelligence. That man has the power, under certain conditions, to enter into telepathic communication with animals, there are thousands of facts to demonstrate. In a recent English work on the training of dogs,[1] this subject is alluded to in the following language : —

"As I before remarked, a man to be a first-rate dog-breaker must have lots of animal magnetism. Now, I do not doubt that in nearly every man who is born into the world this faculty exists to a greater or less extent. It is the force of will that develops it ; and the more it is developed, the stronger it becomes. While, on the other hand, if the will is naturally weak, and no other pains are taken to strengthen it, it falls into abeyance, and in time, I think, is utterly lost, — and that sometimes beyond recall.

"That there is such a power as this, no one who has ever had any experience with animals will attempt to deny. Take the horse, for instance. This is the easiest subject on which to exert the power, simply because the rider, and even the driver, is in closer contact with it than with any other animal.

"As an example, take two somewhat timid, highly bred young horses, and put them side by side at the tail of a flying pack of hounds. Both their riders are equally good men as far as nerve, hands, and seat are concerned ; but the one is a cut-and-thrust, whip-and-spur sort of fellow, while the other is a cool, quiet, deliberate customer, of sweet manners but iron will. As they cross the first half-a-dozen flying fences, side by side, it wants a keen eye to mark any difference in the execution. The difference, as a rule, will consist only in the different ways in which the horses land after their jumps, — the one will pitch a little heavily, a little 'abroad,' a little as if he got there somehow, but did not quite know how ; whilst the other will land lightly,

---

[1] Scientific Education of Dogs. By H. H. London. p. 85.

exactly in the right spot, and precisely as if the two partners were one.

"How comes this? One horse is being steered by physical power and science only; the other by a wonderful force, which joins together in one two minds and two bodies.

"Now, see the test. Yonder waves a line of willows, and both riders know that the biggest and nastiest water jump in the county is ahead of them. Both equally mean to get over; but if they do, it will be in two different fashions : the one will compel his horse to jump it by sheer physical force ; the other will jump it, if it is jumpable at all, as the 'senior partner' of the animal he bestrides. Down they go, sixty yards apart, and each, say, has picked a place which it is only just possible for a horse to cover; neither horse can turn his head ; for, at the last stride, the velvet hands have become grips of iron. Splash goes Number 1; he went as far as he could : but that last two feet wanted just an impetus which was absent. How about Number 2? The rider has fixed his eye, and his mind with it, on yonder grassy spot on the other side of the water, and, sure enough, the fore-feet are simply 'lifted' into it by something inward, not outward; but only the fore-feet. Still, the calculation of the strung-up mind has entered into that, the stirrups have been cast loose in the 'fly,' and the moment the hoofs touch the bank, the rider is over his horse's head, with reins in hand ; a second more, the horse is beside him ; yet another, and they are away forward, without losing more than a minute.

"Assheton Smith expressed in *some* manner — but only in *some* manner — what I mean in his well-known dictum, 'Throw your heart over a fence, and your horse is sure to follow.'

"I could give hundreds of instances and anecdotes of this magnetic power of the rider over the horse, but one will suffice to prove my point.

"I was out for a ride one day with an argumentative friend along the road, and was on a very celebrated old hunter that had been my friend and partner for many a season. We were talking on this subject, and my friend scoffed at the very idea of such a thing as a sort of visionary nonsense. A hundred yards ahead there was an intersecting cross-road, at right angles to that on which we were riding. I pulled up my horse.

"'Now,' I said, 'look here; I will prove my theory to you. Choose and tell me which of these roads my horse shall take. You shall ride three lengths behind me ; I will throw the reins on his neck, and I will bet you a sovereign he goes the way I will him ; and you shall be the judge whether it is possible for me to have influenced him by any word, touch, or sign, — only, you must keep at a walk, and not utter a word or a sound.'

"He made the bet, and fixed on the right hand cross-road as being the one he knew very well the horse had never been before, whilst the two others were both roads to 'meets.'

"I simply fixed my eyes and my will on the road, and when the horse arrived at the spot, he turned down with the same alacrity as if his stable had been in full view.

"I need not say that I have many times tried the same experiment, and that with many variations and many different horses, and hardly ever failed, — indeed, on American prairies I have found the habit once or twice a dangerous nuisance, inasmuch as the then involuntary exercise of the power has, when I have been myself lost, influenced the horse to go the wrong way, because I was thinking it was the right one, whereas, if he had been let alone, he would not have made a mistake.

"Now, this magnetic power can be used with dogs, only in an inferior degree to horses."

The author then goes on to relate numerous instances, some of them truly marvellous, in which he demonstrated his power over dogs. He was evidently intelligently conscious of his power, but did not know the conditions necessary to enable him to exercise it with uniform potency.

The most striking manifestations of the force under consideration are by professional tamers of wild beasts. The reason of this lies in the simple fact that they uniformly employ the means necessary to its development, — namely, fixing their eyes upon those of the beast. This is the traditional method. Its potency has been recognized for ages, although the philosophical principles underlying it have never been understood.

The conditions necessary for the exercise of this power are : first, the subjective, or partially subjective, condition of the operator ; and secondly, his perfect faith and confidence in his power. The first is easily attained by the simple process developed by Braid. The second comes from successful practice, but may be commanded by the power of auto-suggestion, as I have already shown.

History is full of instances going to show that man, in the subjective condition, is always safe from harm by wild

animals. The subjective powers of primitive man were undoubtedly far superior to any now possessed by any one
save, perhaps, the East Indian adepts. Before the development of objective means of communication in the form of
speech, his ideas were conveyed to his fellows by telepathy.
And just in proportion to the development of objective
means of communication did he cease to employ, and finally
lose, his primitive methods and powers. God gave him
dominion over the beasts of the field and the fowls of the
air. In his primitive condition he was destitute of effective
weapons of offence or defence, such as have been evolved
during the long ages of a later civilization. He was surrounded by a monstrous fauna, capable of annihilating the
present race of civilized mankind, could it be suddenly re-
surrected and turned loose in its old numbers and haunts.
In what consisted the power of primitive man to assert and
maintain his God-given dominion over the monsters of his
day and generation? It must have been the same power
which is now exceptionally exercised by the artificial dis-
placement of the threshold of consciousness, thus develop-
ing in a small degree his long dormant subjective powers.
His dominion was then a true one, all-potent, and far more
perfect and effective than it is to-day, with all the appliances of civilization at his command.

Facts of record are not wanting to sustain the proposi
tion that man in a subjective, or partially subjective, condition is safe from the attacks of wild beasts. One of the
first recorded instances, and the one most familiar, is
the story of Daniel. Daniel was a prophet, — a seer. At
this day he would be known in some circles as a spiritual
medium ; in others, as a mind-reader, a clairvoyant, etc.,—
according to the conception of each individual as to the
origin of his powers. In other words, he was a man possessed of great subjective powers. He was naturally and
habitually in that state in which, in modern parlance, the
threshold of his consciousness was displaced, and the powers
of his soul were developed. In this state he was thrown
into the lions' den, with the result recorded. The sceptic

as to the divine authenticity of the Scriptures can readily accept this story as literally true when he recalls the experiments made in Paris a few years ago. In that city a young lady was hypnotized and placed in a den of lions. The object of the experiment is not now recalled; but the result was just the same as that recorded of the ancient prophet. She had no fear of the lions, and the lions paid not the slightest attention to her.

The adepts of India, and even the inferior priests of the Buddhistic faith, often display their power by entering the jungles, so infested by man-eating tigers that an ordinary man would not live an hour, and remain there all night, with no weapons of defence save the God-given powers of the soul.

The power of idiots, and persons afflicted with certain forms of insanity, to tame and subdue animals has often been remarked. In such persons the objective mind is either wholly or partially in abeyance, and the subjective mind is proportionally active. Their immunity from harm by animals, however ferocious, is proverbial.

Volumes might be filled with facts showing the power of the subjective mind of man over animals; but enough has been said to demonstrate the fact that the power exists, and that under certain well-defined conditions it can be exercised by any person of ordinary intelligence.

It is believed that enough has been said to show the source of the power developed by mesmeric processes, as distinguished from the results of hypnotism. It has been seen that the primary source of power is in the mesmerist, that it is developed by processes which place him in the same condition as, or in a condition cognate to, that in which the subject himself is placed, and that when these conditions exist, and just in proportion to the perfection of these conditions, can the phenomena of telepathy, clairvoyance, and all the higher phenomena of subjective activity be produced.

The difference between the effects of mesmerism on man and animals is one of degree only; and the difference of degree is determined only by their difference in intelligence. The laws are the same. When a man is mesmerized, his subjective mind may be stimulated to activity, whether his objective mind is completely in abeyance or not. If it is completely in abeyance, the subjective phenomena will be all the more pronounced and complete. But when an animal is put to sleep, little or no subjective phenomena can be exhibited, for the simple reason that he has not the power of speech, and his intelligence is otherwise limited. The same law also governs the production of hypnotic phenomena in men and animals alike. An animal can be put to sleep by hypnotic processes; but he cannot be made to exhibit subjective phenomena during that sleep, owing solely to the limitations of his intelligence. He is not capable of receiving and understanding a suggestion. Besides, in hypnotism, as has been shown, there is no telepathic rapport existing between the operator and the subject. Consequently the phenomena which may be exhibited through or by means of mesmeric processes, which grow out of telepathic rapport, cannot be exhibited in hypnotism.

It may be thought that the laws governing the production of mesmeric phenomena show that the law of suggestion is, after all, limited in its scope and application. This is not true, except in the sense that suggestion, as has already been shown, is not a necessary element in the induction of the hypnotic state. The proposition that the subjective mind is constantly amenable to control by suggestion is not affected in the slightest degree by mesmeric phenomena. On the contrary, they distinctly prove the universality of that law. Suggestion is not necessarily limited to oral communication. Nor is it necessarily a communication which can be taken cognizance of by means of any of the objective senses. Telepathic communication is just as much a suggestion to the subjective mind as is oral speech. Indeed, telepathic suggestion is often far more effective than objective language, as will be clearly shown in a future chapter on the subject of psycho-therapeutics.

Hence the power to mesmerize at a distance. In such cases, however, it seems to be necessary that the operator and subject should be by some means brought into telepathic rapport. When that has been done, especially when the rapport has been established by the subject having been previously mesmerized by the same operator, it is perfectly easy to mesmerize at a distance. In such a case no previous arrangement is necessary. The suggestion is then purely mental. But it is suggestion, nevertheless, and demonstrates the universality of the law. Numerous instances of the exercise of this power by purely telepathic methods are cited in the able work on Hypnotism by Professor Björnstrom, to which the reader is referred for particulars.

One further remark should be made regarding the power to mesmerize at a distance, and that is, that it depends solely upon the faith and confidence of the operator. Distance, or space, as it is cognized by our objective senses, does not appear to exist for the subjective mind. There is, therefore, nothing in distance, *per se,* to prevent the full effects of mesmeric power from being felt at the antipodes just as plainly and effectively as it is in the same room. We are, however, so in the habit of regarding distance as an adverse element that it is difficult to overcome the adverse suggestion that it conveys. When this principle is once understood and fully realized, there will be nothing to prevent an operator from exercising his power at any distance he may desire.

CHAPTER X.

HYPNOTISM AND CRIME.

Platform Experiments misleading. — Their Utter Inutility as a Test. — So-called "Tests" described and explained. — Sexual Outrages impossible. — Auto-suggestion protects the Virtuous. — A Willing Subject necessary. — Demonstrative Experiments. — Modern Authorities cited against themselves. — Professor Gregory's Views. — The Elevated Moral Tone of Subjects when mesmerized. — Successful Suggestion of Suicide impossible. — The Three Normal Functions of the Subjective Mind. — Self-Preservation. — Propagation. — Preservation of Offspring. — Instinctive Auto-suggestion. — Indifference on Near Approach of Death. — A Universal Law. — Illustrative Incidents. — Suggestive Criminal Abortion impossible. — Premonitions explained. — The Dæmon of Socrates. — Clairaudience. — The Instinct of Death. — Hypnotism in Jurisprudence. — Testimony Valueless. — Vital Secrets impossible to obtain. — Doctors must not monopolize the Forces of Nature. — The Folly of Adverse Legislation.

BEFORE leaving the subject of hypnotism, I deem it proper to say a few words on one of its branches which is just now attracting the attention alike of students of the science and the public at large. The idea is being very generally promulgated among the people that the ability of one man to mesmerize or hypnotize another implies the possession of a very dangerous power, and one which, in the hands of an unscrupulous man, may be used for criminal purposes. It is perhaps not strange that such an idea should prevail among those who have not studied the science except by observation of platform experiments, which are designed rather to amuse than to instruct. There is something so mysterious in the whole subject, viewed from the standpoint of an audience assembled to witness experiments of this character, that it would be strange indeed if the average man were not impressed with an indefinable dread of the power of the hypnotist. He sees him, by means of certain mysterious manipulations, throw his subject into a profound sleep, and awaken him by a snap of the fingers. He sees the subject impressed with all manner of incongruous ideas, — made to believe that he is Diogenes, or a dog, at the will of the operator. He is made to ride an imaginary horse-race, astride a deal table, or to go in swimming on the bare floor. He is made to see angels or devils; to wander in the Elysian fields of paradise, or to scorch in the sulphurous fires of hell; to feel pain or pleasure, joy or sorrow, — all at the caprice of the man in whose power he has placed himself. All this, and much more, can be seen at public exhibitions of hypnotism, and under conditions that leave no doubt in the mind of the observer, of the genuineness of the phenomena. He sees his friends, for whose integrity he can vouch, go upon the platform and become subject to the same mysterious power. Still doubting, he may go upon the stage himself, only to find that he is amenable to the same subtle influence, controllable by some power that is to him agreeable, yet mysterious, indefinable, incomprehensible. At first he perfectly comprehends all his objective surroundings, remembers afterwards all that took place, and very likely fancies that he obeyed the suggestions of the hypnotist merely to please him and to avoid doing anything to mar the harmony of the occasion. Later on he learns that his supposed complacency was really an irresistible impulse to obey the will of the hypnotist. As the experiments proceed he experiences the sensation of double consciousness. He is told that in his hand he holds a delicious fruit, — a strawberry, perhaps. He is still possessed of sufficient objective consciousness to know that there is really no strawberry in his hand, and yet he sees it plainly, feels it, smells it, tastes it, and experiences all the satisfaction incident to having actually eaten the fruit. He

is able to converse rationally on the subject, and to express
his amazement at the vividness and apparent reality of the
subjective sensation.   After a few repetitions of the experiments he loses all consciousness of his objective environment, yields unquestioning obedience to the suggestions of
the hypnotist, and retains no recollection, after he is awakened, of what occurred when he was in the somnambulic
condition.   His friends inform him of the many wonderful
things which occurred, of his ready obedience to all suggestions, — how he made a speech far transcending his natural abilities, under the influence of a suggestion that he was
Daniel Webster; how he flapped his wings and crowed
when told that he was a cock; and so on through the
répertoire of platform experiments.   He is now strongly
impressed with the idea that he was controlled by a power
that he could under no circumstances resist.   But, wishing
to pursue his investigations further, he resolves to test the
question whether this power can be employed for criminal
purposes.   A few friends are called together, a hypnotist is
employed, and a few well-trained subjects are invited to
give a private exhibition for the benefit of " science."   In
order to give the proposed psychological experiment an
undoubted scientific value, a few doctors of physic are invited to be present, — not because they know anything
about psychology or of hypnotism, but because it is well
known that they have heard something about the latter
science, particularly that it has been found to be a great
therapeutic agent, and they are just now deeply interested
in proving that hypnotism, in the hands of any one outside
of the medical profession, must necessarily be employed
for the perpetration of crime.

We will now suppose that the guests are assembled and
the experiments are about to be made.   The question is
freely discussed in the presence of the subjects, each one
of whom is duly impressed with the idea that he is about
to become the instrument of science for the elucidation and
definite settlement of the great problem of the age.   The
subject is now duly hypnotized, and the inevitable paper

dagger is placed in his hands. An imaginary man in a distant part of the room is pointed out, and the subject is informed that the said man is his mortal enemy; and he is duly advised that the best thing he can do under the circumstances is to proceed to slaughter the enemy aforesaid. This he has no hesitation in doing, and he proceeds to do it with great dramatic effect. He sneaks up to his victim in the style of the last heavy villain he has seen on the stage, and plunges the imaginary dagger into the hypothetical man, amidst the applause of the assembled village wisdom.

The next subject is duly hypnotized, and informed that he is a noted pickpocket. The guests are pointed out as a good crowd to work for " wipers," or whatever is thieves' slang for pocket-handkerchiefs. The subject accepts the suggestion at once, and, with much show of cunning, proceeds to relieve the guests of whatever is within his reach.

The next subject is advised that he is an accomplished burglar, and that a neighboring house is overflowing with plunder. He enters into the spirit of the suggestion with great alacrity, and a committee is duly appointed to accompany him to the scene of pillage. The neighbor is, meantime, apprised of the proposed burglary, and every facility is afforded, in the interest of " science." (The reader will remember that actual occurrences are being described.) The burglary is completed with great skill and promptitude, and a miscellaneous collection of valuables is brought away and equitably divided with the hypnotist.

The above are fair samples of the " scientific " experiments which are just now being largely indulged in, and which are believed to demonstrate the possibility of employing hypnotism as an instrument of crime. " If the average subject," it is argued, " in a state of profound hypnotic sleep, is so amenable to the power of suggestion as to plunge a paper dagger into an imaginary enemy at the bidding of a hypnotist, it follows that a criminal hypnotist possesses unlimited power to cause any one of his subjects to plunge a real dagger into any victim whom the hypnotist may select for slaughter." If the conclusions were correct, the power would be indeed formidable, and, in the hands of unscrupulous men, dangerous. Much has been written on the subject of the possibility of sexual outrage by means of hypnotism, and a few cases are reported in the books. None of them, however, bear the unmistakable stamp of genuineness, and most of them bear internal evidence of fraud. The best authorities on the subject are now free to confess to very grave doubts, at least, of the possibility of crime being instigated by this means. Thus, Moll,[1] one of the latest and certainly one of the ablest writers on the subject, has the following : —

"There are important differences of opinion about the offences which hypnotic subjects may be caused to commit. Liégeois, who has discussed the legal side of the question of hypnotism in a scientific manner, thinks this danger very great, while Gilles de la Tourette, Pierre Janet, Benedikt, and others, deny it altogether.

"There is no doubt that subjects may be induced to commit all sorts of imaginary crimes in one's study. I have made hardly any such suggestions, and have small experience on the point. In any case, a repetition of them is superfluous. If the conditions of the experiment are not changed, it is useless to repeat it merely to confirm what we already know. And these criminal suggestions are not altogether pleasant. I certainly do not believe that they injure the moral state of the subject, for the suggestion may be negatived and forgotten. But these laboratory experiments prove nothing, because some trace of consciousness always remains to tell the subject he is playing a comedy (Franck Delbœuf), consequently he will offer a slighter resistance. He will more readily try to commit a murder with a piece of paper than with a real dagger, because, as we have seen, he almost always dimly realizes his real situation. These experiments, carried out by Liégeois, Foreaux, and others in their studies do not, therefore, prove danger."

Such experiments prove nothing, simply because they are experiments. The subject knows that he is among his friends. He has confidence in the integrity of the hypno-

[1] Hypnotism, p 337.

tist. He is most likely aware of the nature of the proposed experiments. He enters into the spirit of the occasion, resolved to accept every suggestion offered, and to carry out his part of the programme in the best style, knowing that no possible harm can befall him. Moreover, he knows that if he performs his part to the satisfaction of his auditors, he will receive their applause; and applause to the subjective mind is as sweet incense. For, be it known, the average hypnotic subject is inordinately vain of his accomplishments.

All those considerations are, however, merely negative evidence against the supposition that the innocent hypnotic subject can be made the instrument of crime, or the victim of criminal assault against his will. These experiments prove nothing, that is all. Nor do they disprove anything. We must, therefore, look elsewhere for positive evidence to demonstrate the impossibility of making the innocent subject the instrument or the victim of crime. This evidence is not difficult to find.

It will be unnecessary to travel outside the domain of admitted, recorded, and demonstrated facts in order to prove the utter impossibility of victimizing virtue and innocence by means of hypnotism. Indeed, it is difficult to understand how any one who recognizes the law of suggestion, and its universal application to psychological phenomena, can believe for one moment that hypnotism can be made the instrument of crime. Yet we find disciples of the Nancy school who seem to imagine that to hold that it cannot be so employed is equivalent to an admission that the law of suggestion is not of universal application. The fact is that just the contrary is true. It is one of the strongest demonstrations of the universality of the law that hypnotism cannot be so employed.

The first proposition in the line of the argument is that when two contrary suggestions are offered to the hypnotic subject, the strongest must prevail. It needs no argument to sustain this proposition; it is self-evident.

The next proposition, almost equally plain, is that auto-suggestion as a factor in hypnotism is equal in potency, other things being equal, with the suggestion of another.

Auto-suggestion is now recognized as a factor in hypnotism by all followers of the Nancy school. Professor Bernheim mentions it as an obstacle in the way of the cure of some of his patients. One case that he mentions was that of a young girl suffering from a tibio-tarsal sprain. " I tried to hypnotize her," says Bernheim ; " she gave herself up to it with bad grace, saying that it would do no good. I succeeded, however, in putting her into a deep enough sleep two or three times. But the painful contracture persisted : she seemed to take a malicious delight in proving to the other patients in the service that it did no good, *that she always felt worse.* . . . The inrooted idea, *the unconscious auto-suggestion,* is such that nothing can pull it up again. When the treatment was begun, she seemed to be convinced that hypnotism could not cure her. Is it this idea, so deeply rooted in her brain, which neutralizes our efforts and her own wish to be cured?"[1]

Moll, more distinctly than Bernheim, recognizes the power of auto-suggestion as a potent factor which must always be taken into account in conducting experiments ; although he, like Bernheim, strangely forgets to take it into account when he discusses hypnotism in its relations to crime. The following passage, for instance, should have been incorporated in his chapter on the Legal Aspects of Hypnotism :

"Expressions of the will which spring from the individual character of the patient are of the deepest psychological interest. The more an action is repulsive to his disposition, the stronger is his resistance (Forel). Habit and education play a large part here; it is generally very difficult successfully to suggest anything that is opposed to the confirmed habits of the subject. For instance, suggestions are made with success to a devout Catholic; but directly the suggestion conflicts with his creed, it will not be accepted. The surroundings play a part also. A subject will frequently decline a suggestion that will make him appear ridiculous. A woman whom I easily put into cataleptic

---

[1] Suggestive Therapeutics, p. 214.

postures, and who made suggested movements, could not be induced to put out her tongue at the spectators. In another such case I succeeded, but only after repeated suggestions. The manner of making the suggestion has an influence. In some cases it must be often repeated before it succeeds; other subjects interpret the repetition of the suggestion as a sign of the experimenter's incapacity, and of their own ability to resist. Thus it is necessary to take character into account. It is often easier to induce some action by suggesting each separate movement than by suggesting the whole action at once (Bleuler). For example, if the subject is to fetch a book from the table, the movements may be suggested in turn: first the lifting, then the steps, etc. (Bleuler.)

"It is interesting to observe the way in which resistance is expressed, both in hypnotic and post-hypnotic suggestion. I myself have observed the interesting phenomenon that subjects have asked to be awakened when a suggestion displeased them.

"Exactly the same resistance is sometimes offered to a post-hypnotic suggestion. It is possible in such a case that the subject, even in the hypnotic state, will decline to accept the suggestion. Many carry out only the suggestions to which they have assented (Pierre Janet).

"Pitres relates an interesting case of a girl who would not allow him to awake her, because he had suggested that on waking she would not be able to speak. She positively declared that she would not wake until he gave up his suggestion. But even when the suggestion is accepted as such, a decided resistance is often expressed during its post-hypnotic execution. This shows itself as often in slow and lingering movements as in a decided refusal to perform the act at all. The more repugnant the acting, the more likely is it to be omitted."[1]

Thousands of experiments are daily being made which demonstrate the impossibility of controlling the hypnotic subject so far as to cause him to do that which he believes or knows to be wrong. A common platform experiment is that of causing subjects to get drunk on water, under the suggestion that it is whiskey. It frequently happens that one or more of the subjects are conscientiously opposed to the use of strong drink as a beverage. Such persons invariably decline, in the most emphatic manner, to indulge in

[1] Hypnotism, p. 171.

the proposed debauch. Like all such experiments on the
stage before a mixed audience, they are passed by as simply
amusing, and no lesson is learned from them. The intelligent student, however, cannot fail to see the far-reaching
significance of the refusal of a subject to violate his tem-
perance principles. Again, every platform experimenter
knows that whilst he can cause a crowd of his subjects to
go in swimming in imaginary waters, he can never induce
them to divest themselves of their clothing beyond the limits of decency. Some cannot even be made to take off their
coats in presence of the audience. Others will decline to
accept any suggestion, the pursuance of which would cause
them to appear ridiculous.

Again, it is well known to hypnotists that an attempt to
contradict or argue with a subject in the hypnotic state invariably distresses him, and persistency in such a course
awakens him, often with a nervous shock. A conflict of
suggestions invariably causes confusion in the subjective
mind, and generally results in restoring the subject to
normal consciousness.

Now, what is an auto-suggestion? In its broad significa-
tion it embraces not only the assertions of the objective
mind of an individual, addressed to his own subjective mind,
but also the habits of thought of the individual, and the settled principles and convictions of his whole life; and the
more deeply rooted are those habits of thought, principles,
and convictions, the stronger and more potent are the auto-
suggestions, and the more difficult they are to overcome by
the contrary suggestions of another. It is, in fact, impossible
for a hypnotist to impress a suggestion so strongly upon a
subject as to cause him actually to perform an act in violation of the settled principles of his life. If this were not
true, suggestion would mean nothing; it would have no
place in psychological science, because it would not be a
law of universal application. The strongest suggestion must
prevail.

It will thus be seen that the question as to whether hypnotism can be successfully employed for criminal purposes,

must be determined in each individual case by the character of the persons engaged in the experiment. If the subject is a criminal character, he might follow the suggestions of a criminal hypnotist, and actually perpetrate a crime. In such a case, a resort to hypnotism for criminal purposes would be unnecessary, and no possible advantage could be gained by its employment.

It is obvious that the same rule applies to sexual crimes; and it may be set down as a maxim in hypnotic science that no virtuous woman ever was, or ever can be, successfully assaulted while in a hypnotic condition. This is a corollary of the demonstrated propositions which precede it; and it admits of no exception or qualification.

A virtuous woman is, indeed, in less danger of successful assault while in that state than she is in her normal condition, for the simple reason that hypnotic subjects are always endowed with a physical strength far superior to that possessed in the normal condition. Besides, it is the observation of every successful hypnotist that the moral tone of the hypnotic subject, while in that condition, is always elevated. On this subject we will let the late Professor Gregory speak : —

"When the sleeper has become fully asleep, so as to answer questions readily without waking, there is almost always observed a remarkable change in the countenance, the manner, and the voice. On falling asleep at first, he looks, perhaps, drowsy and heavy, like a person dozing in church, or at table when overcome by fatigue, or stupefied by excess in wine, or by the foul air of a crowded apartment; but when spoken to, he usually brightens up, and although the eyes be closed, yet the expression becomes highly intelligent, quite as much so as if he saw. His whole manner seems to undergo a refinement which, in the higher stages, reaches a most striking point, insomuch that we see, as it were, before us a person of a much more elevated character than the same sleeper seems to be when awake. It would seem as if the lower, or animal, propensities were laid to rest, while the intellect and higher sentiments shone forth with a lustre that is undiminished by aught that is mean or common. This is particularly seen in women of natural refinement and high sentiments; but it is also seen in men of the same stamp, and more or less in all. In the highest stages of the mesmeric sleep the countenance often acquires the most lovely expression, surpassing all that the great artists have given to the Virgin Mary or to angels, and which may fitly be called heavenly, for it involuntarily suggests to our minds the moral and intellectual beauty which alone seems consistent with our views of heaven. As to the voice, I have never seen one person in the true mesmeric sleep who did not speak in a tone quite distinct from the ordinary voice of the sleeper. It is invariably, so far as I have observed, softer and more gentle, well corresponding to the elevated and mild expression of the face. It has often a plaintive and touching character, especially when the sleeper speaks of departed friends or relations. In the highest stages it has a character quite new, and in perfect accordance with the pure and lovely smile of the countenance, which beams on the observer, in spite of the closed eyes, like a ray of heaven's own light and beauty. I speak here of that which I have often seen, and I would say that, as a general rule, the sleeper, when in his ordinary state and when in the deep mesmeric sleep, appears not like the same, but like two different individuals. And it is not wonderful that it should be so. For the sleeper, in the mesmeric state, has a consciousness quite separate and distinct from his ordinary consciousness; he is, in fact, if not a different individual, yet the same individual in a different and distinct phase of his being, and that phase a higher one." [1]

Professor Gregory's experience and observation have been those of every hypnotist and mesmerist whose works have been examined. There is, indeed, an ineffable and indescribable something which overspreads the countenance of the virtuous woman while she is in the hypnotic state, which disarms passion, and affects the beholder with a feeling that he has something seen of heaven. He knows that the physical senses are asleep, and he feels that the soul is shining forth in all its majesty and purity, untainted by any thought that is gross, any emotion that is impure.

One of the assertions most confidently made by those who hold that crime is the necessary result of hypnotic experiment, outside of the medical profession, is that a hypnotic subject can be made to commit suicide by suggesting to him

[1] Gregory on Animal Magnetism, p. 4.

the propriety of so doing. There is, if possible, even less foundation for this supposition than there is for any other in the whole catalogue. The reason of this will be obvious when we take into consideration some of the distinctive attributes of the subjective mind. It will not be disputed that the attribute of the subjective mind, which is known as intuition when applied to man, corresponds exactly with what we call instinct when applied to animals. Now, there are three primary functions, or, let us say, instincts, of the subjective mind, which are common to men and the whole animal creation. The first pertains to the preservation of the life of the individual, and is called, in common parlance, the instinct of self-preservation. This is admittedly the strongest instinct of animal nature. The second, in the order of strength and of universality, is the instinct of reproduction. The third pertains to the preservation of human life generally, and of one's offspring particularly. Each pertains to the perpetuity of the race. The first and second are universal, and the third is practically so; the only exceptions being in rare cases of individual idiosyncrasy, or in a very low order of animal life. The potency of these instincts is too well known to require comment.

There is one peculiarity, however, pertaining to subjective activity when the life of the individual is in danger, or that of offspring is imperilled, that is not so generally appreciated. In such cases the subjective mind takes prompt possession of the individual, and every act is subjective as long as active exertion is required to preserve the imperilled life. That this is true is shown, first, by the preternatural strength with which the person is endowed under such circumstances; second, by the total absence of fear; and third, by the wonderful presence of mind displayed in the instantaneous adaptation of every means to its proper end, and in doing exactly the right thing at the right time. Comment is often made on the wonderful " presence of mind " displayed by persons in great peril when instantaneous action is required, and there is no time for reflection or reasoning out a plan of action or defence. This presence of mind, so called, is nothing more or less than subjective activity, or, in other words, instinctive action, the objective faculties being in almost complete abeyance for the time being. That this is true is further shown by the fact that a person in imminent and deadly peril will often emerge from the very jaws of death with nerves unshaken, the coolest and most collected person present. This is often mistaken for courage. It has, however, nothing whatever to do with the question of personal bravery. The veriest coward will, under circumstances of unavoidable danger, act with the same coolness, and evince the same presence of mind, as the bravest man. The most timid woman will fight like a demon, and display preternatural strength and courage, for the preservation of her own life or that of her offspring. The action is instinctive. In other words, it is the normal function of the subjective entity.

The condition of the person at such times is akin to, if not identical with, the state of hypnotism or partial hypnotism. It may be that the objective and subjective faculties act at such times in perfect synchronism; but certain it is that every evidence of subjective activity is present, even the phenomenon of anesthesia. This is shown by the fact that at such times the body feels no pain, no matter how severe the injury. The universal testimony of soldiers who have been in battle is to the effect that the time when fear is experienced is just before the action commences. When the first gun is fired, all fear vanishes, and the soldier often performs feats of the most desperate valor and evinces the most reckless courage. If wounded, he feels nothing until the battle is over and all excitement is gone. It is a merciful provision of nature that the nearer we approach death, the less we fear it. This law is universal. It is only in the vigor of youth and manhood that death is looked upon with horror. The aged view its near approach with calm serenity. The convicted murderer, as long as there is hope of pardon, reprieve, escape, or commutation of the death-penalty, evinces the utmost dread of the scaffold; but when the death-penalty is pronounced, and all hope has fled, he often evinces the utmost indifference, welcomes the day of his execution, and marches to the scaffold without a tremor. The newspapers speak with wonder and admiration of his courage, and the universal verdict is that he was a brave man, and " died game." The truth is that the universal law of which we speak, that merciful provision of nature which nerves alike the brave man and the coward, steps in to his defence, his objective senses are benumbed, and he submits to the inevitable change without fear and without pain.

The testimony of Dr. Livingstone is to the same effect. He was once seized by a lion when hunting in the jungles of Africa, and carried some distance, his body between the lion's jaws. When death seemed inevitable, he testifies that all fear left him, and a delicious languor stole over his senses. The grasp of the lion's jaws caused no pain, and he felt fully resigned to his fate. A fortunate shot from the gun of one of his companions released him, and he was rescued.

This, however, is a digression. The main point which it is desired to enforce is, first, that the strongest instinct in mankind is that of self-preservation ; and second, that this instinct, this strong desire to preserve the life of the body, constitutes a subjective, or an instinctive, auto-suggestion of such supreme potency that no suggestion from another, nor any objective auto-suggestion, could possibly overcome it. The inevitable conclusion is that suicide is certainly not a crime which can be successfully instigated by means of hypnotism.

Criminal abortion is another of the crimes which, the people are told, can be performed by means of hypnotic suggestion. The inherent absurdity of this statement is almost as great as that suicide can be successfully instigated by such means. It is here that another strong instinct prevails against a suggestion of that character, namely, the desire inherent in the soul of the mother to preserve her offspring. It is possibly true that conception could be prevented by hypnotic suggestion, and it may be true that barrenness is sometimes caused by unconscious auto-suggestion ; but a very different state of affairs exists after the fœtus is once formed. The instinctive desire to preserve the life that exists, constitutes an instinctive auto-suggestion which no suggestion from another, nor even the objective auto-suggestion of the mother, could prevail against.

It may be safely set down, therefore, as a fundamental truth of hypnotic science that the auto-suggestion most difficult to overcome is that which originates in the normal action of the subjective mind, — otherwise, instinctive auto-suggestion.

The same line of reasoning applies, though with somewhat diminished force, to the commission of other crimes. We will suppose the most favorable condition possible for procuring the commission of a capital crime ; namely, a criminal hypnotist in control of a criminal subject. The disposition of the subject might not stand in the way ; there might be no auto-suggestion against the commission of crime in the habits and principles of the life of the subject ; and yet the instinct of self-preservation would have its weight and influence in suggesting to him that the commission of a murder would imperil his own life. Such a consideration would operate as potently in the hypnotic condition as it would in the normal state. It would be an instinctive auto-suggestion, just the same as in the case of suicide, although it would operate indirectly in one case, and directly in the other. The deductive reasoning of the subjective mind, as we have seen in preceding chapters, is perfect ; and in the case supposed, the subject would instantaneously reason from the proposed crime to its consequences to himself. The same law would operate in preventing the commission of crimes of less magnitude, with a resistance decreased in proportion to the nature of the offence. But it would, in all cases, be a factor of great importance in the prevention of crime ; for the subjective mind is ever alert where the safety and well-being of the individual are concerned. This law is universal, and has often been manifested in the most striking manner. Premonitions of impending danger, so often felt and recorded, are manifestations of the constant solicitude of the subjective entity for the welfare of the individual. It is comparatively rare that these subjective impressions are brought above the threshold of consciousness; but this is largely due to the habits of thought of mankind at the present day. Generally such impressions are disregarded, and in this sceptical and materialistic age are often relegated to the domain of superstition. When they are felt and acted upon, they are generally attributed to a supernatural source. The dæmon of Socrates is a strong case in point. He believed himself to have been constantly attended by a familiar spirit, whose voice he could hear, and whose admonitions were always wise. That he did hear voices there can, in the light of modern science, be little doubt. It is noteworthy, however, that the voice was generally one of warning, and that its strongest manifestations were made when his personal safety or his personal well-being was involved. The explanation, in pursuance of the hypothesis under discussion in this book, is not difficult. He was endowed with that rare faculty which, in one way or another, belongs to all men of true genius, and which enabled him to draw from the storehouse of subjective knowledge. In his case the threshold of consciousness was so easily displaced that his subjective mind was able at will to communicate with his objective mind in words audible to his senses. This phenomenon is known to spiritists as clairaudience. As before remarked, this voice was generally one of warning, and was the direct manifestation of that strongest instinct of the human soul, — the instinct of self-preservation.

To this the classical student will doubtless interpose the objection that the dæmon failed to warn the philosopher in the hour of his direst need; it failed to admonish him against that course of conduct which led to inevitable death. Socrates was accustomed to construe the silence of the dæmon as an approval of his conduct; and when the decisive moment arrived when he could have saved himself had he chosen to do so, the divine voice was silent. Only once did it interpose its warning, and that was to prevent him from preparing a speech which might have saved him from the hemlock.

The explanation of this failure may be found in the experience of all mankind. This instinctive clinging to life weakens with advancing years, and appears to cease altogether the moment a man's career of usefulness in life has ended. This is the experience of every-day life. Men grow rich, and in the full vigor of a green old age retire from business, hoping to enjoy many years of rest. The result is, generally, death in a very short time. An old man thrown out of employment, with nothing to hope for in the future, lies down and dies. Another, losing his aged companion, follows within a few days or weeks. Another lives only to see his children married and settled, and when that is accomplished, cheerfully lets go his hold on life. In fact, it seems to be as much an instinct to die, when one's usefulness is ended, as to cling to life as long as there is something to do to contribute to the general welfare.

Socrates was an old man. He had lived a long and useful life, but his career of usefulness was ended; for the authorities of the State had decided that his teachings were impious, and corrupting to youth. Had he lived, it would have been at the price of dishonor, his compensation a miserable old age. Besides, his doctrine that death is not an evil, together with his lofty sentiments regarding the duty of the citizen to the commonwealth, — a duty which he maintained could be performed in his case only by submitting to its decrees and carrying into execution its judgments, — constituted a potential element of auto-suggestion which must be considered in estimating the psychological features of his case. He felt that the principles of his whole life would be violated by any attempt to escape or evade the penalty which had been decreed against him; and he spent his last hours in an effort to convince his friends that the death of the body is not an evil, when life is purchased at the price of dishonor. He felt that the philosophy which it had been the business of his life to teach, could only be vindicated by his death, at the time and in the manner decreed by the State. The supreme moment had arrived; the instinct of death was upon him; and, in philosophical communion with his followers, he calmly drank the hemlock, and died the death of a philosopher.

The value of testimony in criminal cases, obtained by means of hypnotism, has been very freely discussed by those who have given their attention to the legal aspect of the question. Assuming that a person has been hypnotized, and caused to commit a crime, the question naturally arises, What means are at hand to convict the guilty party? How is evidence to be obtained, and what is its value when obtained? As it has been shown to be a practical impossibility to procure the commission of crime by means of hypnotic suggestion, it will be unnecessary and unprofitable to discuss the question at great length, and it will be dismissed after the presentation of the vital point. It is obvious that when it is demonstrated that evidence is unreliable, and necessarily unworthy of credence, it is useless to discuss the ways and means of obtaining such evidence for use in a court of justice. The intricate maze of metaphysical disquisition in which this question has been so ably obscured by writers on the subject, will not be entered. It is sufficient to know that no testimony obtained from a subject in a state of hypnotism, relating to any vital question which involves the guilt or innocence of himself or his friends, is of any value whatever. It is a popular belief, handed down through the ages, that a somnambulic subject will always tell the truth, and that all the secrets of a sleep-walker can be obtained from him for the asking. This belief has also been held regarding the hypnotic subject; and it is upon this assumption that the hypothetical value of his testimony in criminal jurisprudence depends. It is true that, on ordinary questions, the truth is always uppermost in the subjective mind. A hypnotic subject will often say, during the hypnotic sleep, that which he would not say in his waking moments. Nevertheless, he never betrays a vital secret. The reason is obvious to those who have followed the line of argument in the preceding pages of this chapter. The instinct of self-preservation, always alert to avert any danger which threatens the individual, steps in to his defence. Instinctive auto-suggestion here plays its subtle *rôle*, and no suggestion from another can prevail against it. If the defence involves falsehood, a falsehood will be told, without the slightest hesitation ; and it will be told with preternatural acumen, and with such plausible circumstantiality of detail as to deceive the very elect. Neither will there be any variance or shadow of turning after repeated experiments, for the memory of the subjective mind is perfect.

This rule holds good, not only with regard to secrets which involve the personal safety of the individual, but in all matters pertaining to his material interests, his reputation, or the interests of his friends, whose secrets are confided to his care. That this is true is presumptively proved by the fact that in all the years during which the science of hypnotism has been practised, no one has ever been known to betray the secrets of any society or order. The attempt has often been made, but it has never succeeded. The truth of this assertion can be demonstrated at any time by experiment.

Such an experiment has a greater evidential value in establishing the rule than almost any other laboratory experiment. A subject might plunge a paper dagger into an imaginary man, or he might draw a check, sign a note, a contract, or a deed, in obedience to experimental suggestions, when he would not commit a real crime, or sign away his birthright, in obedience to criminal suggestion. But when a subject is asked to betray the secrets of a society to which he belongs, it is quite a different matter. In the one case a compliance with the suggestion proves nothing, simply because it is a laboratory experiment. In the other case his refusal to comply with the suggestion proves everything, because his betrayal of such a secret in the laboratory is just as vital as to betray it elsewhere.

It is obvious, therefore, that the testimony of a hypnotized subject in a court of justice can possess no evidential value whatever. Not one of the conditions would be present which give weight to human testimony. The subject could not be punished for perjury if he swore falsely. In matters of indifference to him he would be in constant danger of being swayed by the artful or accidental suggestion of another. A false premise suggested to him at the start would color and pervert his whole testimony. A cross-examination would utterly confuse him, and almost inevitably restore him to normal consciousness. On questions of vital interest to himself, auto-suggestion would cause him to resort to falsehood if the truth would militate against him.

It is thought that enough has been said to show that the dangers attending the practice of hypnotism have been grossly exaggerated, and that the sources of danger, which the people are so persistently warned against, have no existence in fact. The premises laid down will not be gainsaid by any who understand the law of suggestion. The conclusions are inevitable. The law of auto-suggestion has been recognized by Continental writers, as has been shown by extracts from their books; but they have failed to carry it to its legitimate conclusion when treating the subject of the legal aspects of hypnotism. It is perhaps not strange that they should fail in this respect, in view of the vital interest which physicians have in hypnotism as a therapeutic agent. But they should remember that the subject is also of vital interest to students of psychology, and that it is only by a study of its psychological aspects that hypnotism can be intelligently applied to the cure of disease. That the phenomena displayed through its agency possess a significance which far transcends that which attaches to it as a substitute for pills, is a proposition which will not be disputed, even by those who seek to monopolize its forces. It is hoped, therefore, that the psychological student will be graciously permitted to pursue his studies at least until it is shown that physicians enjoy such a monopoly of the cardinal virtues that it is unsafe to intrust the forces of nature in the hands of others.

In the mean time the world at large will continue to believe that the laws of hypnotism are no exception to the rule that the forces of nature, when once understood, are designed for the highest good of mankind; and they will continue to demand that those forces shall not be monopolized by any man, or set of men, body politic, or corporation.

From what has been said, the supreme folly of legislation to prohibit experiments in hypnotism is manifest. No one will deny that when a hypnotist permits himself to exercise his art in private he is in possession of opportunities which, under other conditions, might give him an undue advantage over a subject of the opposite sex; but, from the very nature of things, that advantage is infinitely less than that enjoyed by physicians in their habitual intercourse with their patients. Until it is shown that physicians never take advantage of their confidential relations with their patients; until it is shown that physicians are exempt from human passions and frailties; or, at least, until it is shown that physicians are more platonic in their emotions than the ordinary run of human beings, — the world will continue to regard their demand that the study of experimental psychology shall be restricted by legislation to the medical profession, as an exhibition of monumental impudence. It cannot be forgotten that it was the medical profession that drove Mesmer into a dishonored exile and a premature grave for the sole reason that he healed the sick without the use of pills. The faculty ridiculed, proscribed, and ostracized every medical man who dared to conduct an honest investigation of mesmeric phenomena. And now that the scientists of Europe are compelled to admit the therapeutic value of the science, they are instant in demand that no one but physicians shall be permitted to make experiments. It is perhaps natural and right that the treatment of disease by means of drugs should be restricted to those who are educated in the proper use of drugs; but the employment of psychic powers and remedies rests upon an entirely different footing. Their demand that hypnotism be reserved for their exclusive use rests not upon their knowledge of its laws, but is founded upon their wilful ignorance of the fundamental principles which underlie the science.

CHAPTER XI.

PSYCHO-THERAPEUTICS.

Historical Notes. — Mind Cure in Ancient Times. — Bible Accounts. — Miracles of the Church. — Healing by the King's Touch. — Views of Paracelsus and Pomponazzi. — Bernheim's Experiments. — The Modern Schools. — Their Theories. — The True Hypothesis applicable to all Systems. — Illustrations of the Theory. — Producing a Blister by Suggestion. — Bloody Stigmata. — Letters of Blood. — Objective Control of Subjective Mind. — Subjective Control of Bodily Functions. — The Necessary Mental Conditions. — The Precepts and Example of Christ. — Subjective Faith alone required. — Discussion of Various Systems. — Christian Science, etc. — General Conclusions.

IN the whole range of psychological research there is no branch of the study of such transcendent practical interest and importance to the world as that which pertains to its application to the cure of disease. That there resides in mankind a psychic power over the functions and sensations of the body, and that that power can be invoked at will, under certain conditions, and applied to the alleviation of human suffering, no longer admits of a rational doubt. The history of all nations presents an unbroken line of testimony in support of the truth of this proposition. In the infancy of the world the power of secretly influencing men for good or evil, including the healing of the sick, was possessed by the priests and saints of all nations. Healing of the sick was supposed to be a power derived directly from God, and it was exerted by means of prayers and ceremonies, laying on of hands and incantations, amulets and talismans, rings, relics, and images, and the knowledge of it was transmitted with the sacred mysteries.

Numerous examples of the practice of healing by the touch and by the laying on of hands are related in the Old Testament. Moses was directed by the Lord to transmit his power and honor to Joshua by the laying on of hands. Elijah healed the dead child by stretching himself upon the body and calling upon the name of the Lord, and Elisha raised the dead son of the Shunammite woman by the same means. It was even supposed that the power survived his death. The New Testament is full of examples of the most striking character, and the promise of the Master to those who believe, — " In my name shall they cast out devils ; they shall speak with new tongues ; they shall take up serpents ; and if they drink any deadly thing, it shall not hurt them ; they shall lay their hands on the sick, and they shall recover," — applies to all mankind to-day as well as to his followers upon whom he had conferred his power in person. That this power was transmitted to future generations, and that the saints and others regarded it as the heritage of the Church and employed it with humble faith, in imitation of the Master, for the good of mankind, is shown by numerous examples. While the chroniclers have undoubtedly embellished many actual cures and recited many fictitious ones, the fact that the saints and others possessed healing powers cannot be questioned. Thus, Saint Patrick, the Irish apostle, healed the blind by laying on his hands.

" Saint Bernard," says Ennemoser, " is said to have restored eleven blind persons to sight, and eighteen lame persons to the use of their limbs in one day at Constance. At Cologne he healed twelve lame, caused three dumb persons to speak, ten who were deaf to hear, and, when he himself was ill, Saint Lawrence and Saint Benedict appeared to him, and cured him by touching the affected part. Even his plates and dishes are said to have cured sickness after his death ! The miracles of Saints Margaret, Katherine, Hildegarde, and especially the miraculous cures of the two holy martyrs, Cosmos and Damianus, belong to this class. Among others, they freed the Emperor Justinian from an incurable sickness. Saint Odilia embraced in her arms a leper who was shunned by all men, warmed him, and restored him to health.

" Remarkable above all others are those cases where persons who were at the point of death have recovered by holy baptism or extreme unction. The Emperor Constantine is one of the most singular examples. Pyrrhus, king of Epirus, had the power of assuaging colic and affections of the spleen by laying the patients on their backs and passing his great toe over them. The Emperor Vespasian cured nervous affections, lameness, and blindness, solely by the laying on of his hands. According to Cœlius Spartianus, Hadrian cured those afflicted with dropsy by touching them with the points of his fingers, and recovered himself from a violent fever by similar treatment. King Olaf healed Egill on the spot by merely laying his hands upon him and singing proverbs. The kings of England and France cured diseases of the throat by touch. It is said that the pious Edward the Confessor, and, in France, that Philip the First were the first who possessed this power. In England the disease was therefore called 'king's evil.' In France this power was retained till within a recent period. Among German princes this curative power was ascribed to the Counts of Hapsburg, and also that they were able to cure stammering by a kiss. Pliny says, 'There are men whose whole bodies possess medicinal properties, — as the Marsi, the Psyli, and others, who cure the bite of serpents merely by the touch.' This he remarks especially of the island of Cyprus, and later travellers confirm these cures by the touch. In later times the Salmadores and Ensalmadores of Spain became very celebrated, who healed almost all diseases by prayer, laying on of the hands, and by the breath. In Ireland, Valentine Greatrakes cured at first king's evil by his hands; later, fever, wounds, tumors, gout, and at length all diseases. In the seventeenth century the gardener Levret and the notorious Streeper performed cures in London by stroking with the hand. In a similar manner cures were performed by Michael Medina and the Child of Salamanca; also Marcellus Empiricus. Richter, an innkeeper at Royen, in Silicia, cured, in the years 1817, 1818, many thousands of sick persons in the open fields by touching them with his hands. Under the popes, laying on of the hands was called 'chirothesy.'"

Again, Ennemoser says : —

" As regards the resemblance which the science bears to magnetism, it is certain that not only were the ancients acquainted with an artificial method of treating disease, but also with somnambulism itself. Among others, Agrippa von Net-

tesheim speaks of this plainly when he says, in his 'Occulta Philosophia' (page 451): 'There is a science, known to but very few, of illuminating and instructing the mind, so that at one step it is raised from the darkness of ignorance to the light of wisdom. This is produced principally by a species of artificial sleep, in which a man forgets the present, and, as it were, perceives the future through divine inspiration. Unbelieving and wicked persons can also be deprived of this power by secret means."

Coming down to more recent times, we find that cures, seemingly miraculous, are as common to-day as at any period of the world's history. In fact, one unbroken line of such phenomena is presented to the student of psycho-therapeutics, which extends from the earliest period of recorded history to the present time. At no time in the world's history has there been such a widespread interest in the subject as now; and the hopeful feature is that the subject is no longer relegated to the domain of superstition, but is being studied by all classes of people, from the ablest scientists down to the humblest peasant. The result is that theories almost innumerable have been advanced to account for what all admit to be a fact, namely, that there exists a power to alleviate human suffering, which lies not within the domain of material science, but which can be invoked at the will of man and controlled by human intelligence.

It would be tedious and unprofitable to discuss at length the numerous theories advanced by the different sects and schools which have an existence to-day. It is sufficient to know that all these schools effect cures of the most wonderful character, many of them taking rank with the miracles of the Master. This one fact stands out prominent and significant, namely, that the theories advanced to account for the phenomena seem to have no effect upon the power invoked.

Paracelsus stated what is now an obvious scientific fact when he uttered these words: —

"Whether the object of your faith be real or false, you will nevertheless obtain the same effects. Thus, if I believe in

Saint Peter's statue as I should have believed in Saint Peter himself, I shall obtain the same effects that I should have obtained from Saint Peter. But that is superstition. Faith, however, produces miracles; and whether it is a true or a false faith, it will always produce the same wonders."

Much to the same effect are the words uttered in the six-teenth century by Pomponazzi : —

" We can easily conceive the marvellous effects which confidence and imagination can produce, particularly when both qualities are reciprocated between the subjects and the person who influences them. The cures attributed to the influence of certain relics are the effect of this imagination and confidence. Quacks and philosophers know that if the bones of any skeleton were put in place of the saint's bones, the sick would none the less experience beneficial effects, if they believed that they were near veritable relics."

Bernheim,[1] quoting the foregoing passages, follows with a story, related by Sobernheim, of a man with a paralysis of the tongue which had yielded to no form of treatment, who put himself under a certain doctor's care. The doctor wished to try an instrument of his own invention, with which he promised himself to get excellent results. Before performing the operation, he introduced a pocket thermometer into the patient's mouth. The patient imagined it to be the instrument which was to save him. In a few minutes he cried out joyfully that he could once more move his tongue freely.

" Among our cases," continues Bernheim, " facts of the same sort will be found. A young girl came into my service, having suffered from complete nervous aphonia for nearly four weeks. After making sure of the diagnosis, I told my students that nervous aphonia sometimes yielded instantly to electricity, which might act simply by its suggestive influence. I sent for the induction apparatus. Before using it I wanted to try simple suggestion by affirmation. I applied my hand over the larynx and moved it a little, and said, ' Now you can speak aloud.' In an

[1] Suggestive Therapeutics, p. 197.

instant I made her say 'a,' then 'b,' then 'Maria.' She continued to speak distinctly; the aphonia had disappeared.

" ' The " Bibliothèque choisie de Médicine," ' says Hack Tuke,
'gives a typical example of the influence exercised by the imagination over intestinal action during sleep. The daughter of
the consul at Hanover, aged eighteen, intended to use rhubarb,
for which she had a particular dislike, on a following day. She
dreamed that she had taken the abhorred dose. Influenced by
this imaginary rhubarb, she waked up, and had five or six easy
evacuations.'

" The same result is seen in a case reported by Demangeon.[1]
' A monk intended to purge himself on a certain morning. On
the night previous he dreamed that he had taken the medicine,
and consequently waked up to yield to nature's demands. He
had eight movements.'

" But among all the moral causes which, appealing to the
imagination, set the cerebral mechanism of possible causes at
work, none is so efficacious as religious faith. Numbers of au-
thentic cures have certainly been due to it.

" The Princess of Schwartzenburg had suffered for eight
years from a paraplegia for which the most celebrated doctors
in Germany and France had been consulted. In 1821 the Prince
of Hohenlohe, who had been a priest since 1815, brought a
peasant to the princess, who had convinced the young prince of
the power of prayer in curing disease. The mechanical apparatus, which had been used by Dr. Heine for several months
to overcome the contracture of the limbs, was removed. The
prince asked the paralytic to join her faith both to his and the
peasant's. ' Do you believe you are already helped?' 'Oh,
yes, I believe so most sincerely!' 'Well, rise and walk.' At
these words the princess rose and walked around the room several times, and tried going up and down stairs. The next day
she went to church, and from this time on she had the use of
her limbs."[2]

Bernheim then proceeds to give a *résumé* of some of the
histories of cures which took place at Lourdes, where thousands flock annually to partake of the healing waters of the
famous grotto. The history of that wonderful place is too
well known to need repetition here. It is sufficient to say
that thousands of cures have been effected there through

---

[1] De l'Imagination, 1879. [2] Charpignon.

prayer and religious faith, and the cures are as well authen-ticated as any fact in history or science.

The most prominent and important methods of healing the sick now in vogue may be briefly summarized as follows:

1. *Prayer and religious faith,* as exemplified in the cures performed at Lourdes and at other holy shrines. To this class also belong the cures effected by prayer alone, the sys-tem being properly known in this country as the Faith Cure and the Prayer Cure.

2. *The Mind Cure,* — "a professed method of healing which rests upon the suppositions that all diseased states or the body are due to abnormal conditions of the mind, and that the latter (and thus the former) can be cured by the direct action of the mind of the healer upon the mind of the patient." [1]

3. *Christian Science.* — This method of healing rests upon the assumption of the unreality of matter. This assumed as a major premise, it follows that our bodies are unreal, and, consequently, there is no such thing as disease, the latter existing only in the mind, which is the only real thing in existence.

4. *Spiritism,* which is a system of healing based on the supposed interposition of spirits of the dead, operating di-rectly, or indirectly through a medium, upon the patient.

5. *Mesmerism.* — This includes all the systems of healing founded on the supposition that there exists in man a fluid which can be projected upon another, at the will of the operator, with the effect of healing disease by the thera-peutic action of the fluid upon the diseased organism.

6. *Suggestive Hypnotism.* — This method of healing rests upon the law that persons in the hypnotic condition are constantly controllable by the power of suggestion, and that by this means pain is suppressed, function modified, fever calmed, secretion and excretion encouraged, etc., and thus nature, the healer, is permitted to do the work of restoration.

Each of these schools is subdivided into sects, entertain-ing modified theories of causation, and employing modified

[1] Century Dictionary.

processes of applying the force at their command. There is but one thing common to them all, and that is that they all cure diseases.

We have, then, six different systems of psycho-therapeutics, based upon as many different theories, differing as widely as the poles, and each presenting indubitable evidence of being able to perform cures which in any age but the present would have been called miraculous.

The most obvious conclusion which strikes the scientific mind is that there must be some underlying principle which is common to them all. It is the task of science to discover that principle.

It will now be in order to recall to the mind of the reader, once more, the fundamental propositions of the hypothesis under consideration. They are, —

First, that man is possessed of two minds, which we have distinguished by designating one as the objective mind, and the other as the subjective mind.

Secondly, that the subjective mind is constantly amenable to control by the power of suggestion.

These propositions having been established, at least provisionally, by the facts shown in the foregoing chapters, it now remains to present a subsidiary proposition, which pertains to the subject of psycho-therapeutics, namely : —

The subjective mind has absolute control of the functions, conditions, and sensations of the body.

This proposition seems almost self-evident, and will receive the instant assent of all who are familiar with the simplest phenomena of hypnotism. It is well known, and no one at all acquainted with hypnotic phenomena now disputes the fact, that perfect anesthesia can be produced at the will of the operator simply by suggestion. Hundreds of cases are recorded where the most severe surgical operations have been performed without pain upon patients in the hypnotic condition. The fact can be verified at any time by experiment on almost any hypnotic subject, and in case of particularly sensitive subjects the phenomena can be produced in the waking condition. How the subjective mind controls the functions and sensations of the body, mortal man may never know. It is certain that the problem cannot be solved by reference to physiology or cerebral anatomy. It is simply a scientific fact which we must accept because it is susceptible of demonstration, and not because its ultimate cause can be explained.

The three foregoing fundamental propositions cover the whole domain of psycho-therapeutics, and constitute the basis of explanation of all phenomena pertaining thereto.

It seems almost superfluous to adduce facts to illustrate the wonderful power which the subjective mind possesses over the functions of the body, beyond reminding the reader of the well-known facts above mentioned regarding the production of the phenomena of anesthesia by suggestion. Nevertheless, it must not be forgotten that the production of anesthesia in a healthy subject is a demonstration of subjective power which implies far more than appears upon the surface. The normal condition of the body is that of perfect health, with all the senses performing their legitimate functions. The production of anesthesia in a normal organism is, therefore, the production of an abnormal condition. On the other hand, the production of anesthesia in a diseased organism implies the restoration of the normal condition, that is, a condition of freedom from pain. In this, all the forces of nature unite to assist. And as every force in nature follows the lines of least resistance, it follows that it is much easier to cure diseases by mental processes than it is to create them; provided always that we understand the *modus operandi*.

It is well known that the symptoms of almost any disease can be induced in hypnotic subjects by suggestion. Thus, partial or total paralysis can be produced; fever can be brought on, with all the attendant symptoms, such as rapid pulse and high temperature, flushed face, etc.; or chills, accompanied by a temperature abnormally low; or the most severe pains can be produced in any part of the body or limbs. All these facts are well known, and still more wonderful facts are stated in all the recent scientific works on hypnotism. For instance, Bernheim states that he has been able to produce a blister on the back of a patient by applying a postage-stamp and suggesting to the patient that it was a fly-plaster. This is confirmed by the experiments of Moll and many others, leaving no doubt of the fact that structural changes are a possible result of oral suggestion. On this subject Bernheim makes the following observations : —

"Finally, hemorrhages and bloody stigmata may be induced in certain subjects by means of suggestion.

"MM. Bourru and Burot of Rochefort have experimented on this subject with a young marine, a case of hystero-epilepsy. M. Bourru put him into the somnambulistic condition, and gave him the following suggestion : 'At four o'clock this afternoon, after the hypnosis, you will come into my office, sit down in the arm-chair, cross your arms upon your breast, and your nose will begin to bleed.' At the hour appointed the young man did as directed. Several drops of blood came from the left nostril.

"On another occasion the same investigator traced the patient's name on both his forearms with the dull point of an instrument. Then, when the patient was in the somnambulistic condition, he said, 'At four o'clock this afternoon you will go to sleep, and your arms will bleed along the lines which I have traced, and your name will appear written on your arms in letters of blood.' He was watched at four o'clock and seen to fall asleep. On the left arm the letters stood out in bright red relief, and in several places there were drops of blood. The letters were still visible three months afterwards, although they had grown gradually faint.

"Dr. Mabille, director of the Insane Asylum at Lafond, near Rochelle, a former pupil of excellent standing, repeated the experiment made upon the subject at Rochefort, after he was removed to the asylum, and confirmed it. He obtained instant hemorrhage over a determined region of the body. He also induced an attack of spontaneous somnambulism, in which the patient, doubting his personality, so to speak, suggested to himself the hemorrhagic stigmata on the arm, thus repeating the marvellous phenomena of the famous stigmatized auto-suggestionist, Louis Lateau.

"These facts, then, seem to prove that suggestion may act upon the cardiac function and upon the vaso-motor system. Phenomena of this order, however, rarely occur. They are exceptional, and are obtained in certain subjects only.   I have in vain tried to reproduce them in many cases.   These facts are sufficient to prove, however, that when in a condition of special psychical concentration, the brain can influence even the organic functions, which in the normal state seem but slightly amenable to the will." [1]

These facts demonstrate at once the correctness of two of the fundamental propositions before stated ; namely, the constant amenability of the subjective mind to the power of suggestion, and the perfect control which the subjective mind exercises over the functions, sensations, and conditions of the body.   All the foregoing phenomena represent abnormal conditions induced by suggestion, and are, as before stated, all the more conclusive proofs of the potency of the force invoked.

If, therefore, there exists in man a power which, in obedience to the suggestion of another, is capable of producing abnormal conditions in defiance of the natural instincts and desires of all animal creation, how much more potent must be a suggestion which operates in harmony with the natural instinctive desire of the patient for the restoration of normal conditions, and with the constant effort of nature to bring about that result !   At the risk of repetition, the self-evident proposition will be restated, that the instinct of self-preservation is the strongest instinct of our nature, and constitutes a most potent, ever-present, and constantly operative auto-suggestion, inherent in our very nature.   It is obvious that any outside suggestion must operate with all the greater potentiality when it is directed on lines in harmony with instinctive auto-suggestion.   It follows that normal conditions can be restored with greater ease and certainty, other things being equal, than abnormal conditions can be induced.   And thus it is that by the practice of each of the various systems of psycho-therapeutics we find that the most marvellous cures are effected, and are again reminded of the words of Paracelsus : " Whether

[1] Suggestive Therapeutics, pp. 36, 37.

the object of your faith be real or false, you will never-theless obtain the same effects."

This brings us to the discussion of the essential mental condition prerequisite to the success of every experiment in psycho-therapeutics, — faith.

That faith is the essential prerequisite to the successful exercise of psychic power is a proposition which has re-ceived the sanction of the concurrent experience of all the ages. Christ himself did not hesitate to acknowledge his inability to heal the sick in the absence of that condition precedent, which he held to be essential, not only to the enjoyment of the blessings which he so freely bestowed in this world, but to the attainment of eternal life. "Oh, ye of little faith," was his reproof to his followers when they returned to him and announced the decrease of their powers to heal the sick; thus proving that he regarded faith as an essential element of success, not only in the patient, but in the healer. also.

If the Great Healer thus acknowledged a limitation of his powers, how can we, his humble followers, hope to transcend the immutable law by which he was governed?

"Why is it that our belief has anything to do with the exercise of the healing power?" is a question often asked. To this the obvious and only reply is that the healing power, being a mental, or psychic, force, is necessarily gov-erned by mental conditions. Just why faith is the neces-sary mental attitude of the patient can never be answered until we are able to fathom the ultimate cause of all things. The experience of all the ages shows it to be a fact, and we must accept it as such, and content ourselves with an effort to ascertain its relations to other facts, and, if pos-sible, to define its limitations and ascertain the means of commanding it at will.

It is safe to say that the statement of the fact under con-sideration has done more to retard the progress of the sci-ence of psychic healing than all other things combined. The sceptic at once concludes that, whatever good the sys-tem may do to credulous people, it can never be of benefit

to him, because he "does not believe in such things."
And it is just here that the mistake is made, — a mistake
that is most natural in the present state of psychic knowledge, and one that is all but universal. It consists in the
assumption that the faith of the objective mind has anything to do with the requisite mental attitude. The reader
is again requested to call to mind the fundamental propositions of the hypothesis under discussion, namely, the dual
personality and the power of suggestion.

It follows from the propositions of our hypothesis, which
need not be here repeated at length, that the subjective
mind of an individual is as amenable to control by the suggestions of his own objective mind as it is by the suggestions of another. The law is the same. It follows that,
whatever may be the objective belief of the patient, if he will
assume to have faith, actively or passively, the subjective
mind will be controlled by the suggestion, and the desired
result will follow.

*The faith required for therapeutic purposes is a purely
subjective faith, and is attainable upon the cessation of active
opposition on the part of the objective mind.* And this is
why it is that, under all systems of mental therapeutics, the
perfect passivity of the patient is insisted upon as the first
essential condition. Of course, it is desirable to secure
the concurrent faith both of the objective and subjective
minds; but it is not essential, if the patient will in good
faith make the necessary auto-suggestion, as above mentioned, either in words, or by submitting passively to the
suggestions of the healer.

It is foreign to the purpose of this book to discuss at
length the various systems of mental therapeutics further
than is necessary for the elucidation of our hypothesis.
The theories upon which the several systems are founded
will not, therefore, be commented upon, *pro* or *con*, except
where they furnish striking illustrations of the principles
herein advanced.

Christian science, so called, furnishes a very striking
example of the principle involved in the proposition that

the requisite subjective faith may be acquired without the concurrence of objective belief, and even in defiance of objective reason. That system is based upon the assumption that matter has no real existence ; consequently we have no bodies, and hence no disease of the body is possible. It is not known whether the worthy lady founder of the school ever stopped to reduce her foundation principles to the form of a syllogism. It is presumed not, for otherwise their intense, monumental, and aggressive absurdity would have become as apparent to her as it is to others. Let us see how they look in the form of a syllogism : —

Matter has no existence. Our bodies are composed of matter. Therefore our bodies have no existence.

It follows, of course, that disease cannot exist in a non-existent body.

That the above embraces the basis of the system called Christian science no one who has read the works of its founder will deny. Of course, no serious argument can be adduced against such a self-evident absurdity. Nevertheless, there are two facts connected with this system which stand out in bold relief : One is that it numbers its followers by the hundred thousand ; and the other is that the cures effected by its practitioners are of daily occurrence and of the most marvellous character.

The first of these facts demonstrates the truth of the trite saying that any system of belief, if earnestly advocated, will find plenty of followers. The second shows in the most conclusive manner that the faith of the objective mind is not a necessary factor in the cure of disease by psychic processes.

It seems obvious that no greater demand could be made upon the resources of our credulity than to tell us that all that is visible or tangible to our objective senses has no real existence. And yet that is what the patient of Christian science is invited to believe as a condition precedent to his recovery. Of course he feels at first that his intelligence is insulted, and he protests against such a palpable absurdity. But he is quieted by soothing words,

and is told to get himself into a perfectly passive condition, to say nothing and to think of nothing for the time
being. In some cases patients are advised to hold themselves in the mental attitude of denying the possible existence of disease. The essential condition of passivity being
acquired by the patient, the healer also becomes passive,
and assumes the mental attitude of denying the existence
of disease in the patient, — or elsewhere, for that matter, —
and affirms with constant iteration the condition of perfect
healthfulness. After a séance of this kind, lasting perhaps
half-an-hour, the patient almost inevitably finds immense
relief, and often feels himself completely restored to health.
To say that the patient is surprised, is but feebly to convey
his impressions; he is confounded. The healer triumphantly asks, " What do you think of my theory now? " It
is of little use for him to reply that he does not see that the
theory is necessarily correct because he was healed. Most
likely he fails to think of that, in his gratitude for restored
health. But if he does, he is met by the triumphant response, " By their fruits ye shall know them." To the
average mind, untrained to habits of logical reasoning, that
settles the question; and Christian science has scored a
triumph and secured a follower. He may not be able to
see quite clearly the logical sequences involved, he may be
even doubtful whether the theory is necessarily correct;
but not being able to formulate his objections, he contents
himself with the thought that he is not yet far enough advanced in " science " to understand that which seems so
clear to the mind of his teacher. In any event, he ceases
to antagonize the theory by any process of reasoning, and
eventually believes, objectively as well as subjectively, in
the substantial correctness of the fundamental theory. In
the mean time it is easy to see that his subjective faith has
been made perfect by his passivity under treatment, and
that his objective faith has been confirmed by his restoration to health.

In all systems of healing, the processes, or rather the conditions, are essentially the same, the first essential condition,

as before stated, being the perfect passivity and receptivity of the patient. That is always insisted upon, and it is the essential prerequisite, be the theory and method of operation what they may. The rest is accomplished by suggestion. Thus, the whole science of mental healing may be expressed in two words, — passivity, and suggestion.

By passivity the patient becomes receptive of subjective impressions. He becomes partially hypnotic, and sometimes wholly so. The more perfectly he is hypnotized, the surer the favorable result. But, in any case, perfect passivity is sure to bring about a good result. In the Christian science methods the healer also becomes passive, and partially self-hypnotized. And this constitutes the difference between individual healers by that method. The more easily the healer can hypnotize himself, and the more perfect that condition, the more powerful will be the effect on the patient. The reason is this : the suggestions to the subjective mind of the patient are conveyed telepathically from the subjective mind of the healer. In order to produce that effect in perfection, it becomes necessary both for patient and healer to be in a partially hypnotic condition. The two subjective minds are then *en rapport.* The subjective mind of the healer, being properly instructed beforehand, then conveys the necessary suggestions to the subjective mind of the patient. The latter, being necessarily controlled by such suggestion, exercises its functions in accordance therewith ; and having absolute control of the sensations, functions, and conditions of the body, it exercises that control; and the result is that pain is relieved, and the normal condition of health is restored.

It is not, however, always necessary that either the patient or the healer should become even partially hypnotized, provided the requisite faith or confidence is established in the subjective mind of the patient. In such a case, however, it requires a concurrence both of objective and subjective faith to produce the best results.

It has been claimed by some mental healers that faith on the part of the patient is not an essential prerequisite to

successful healing.   Doubtless some of the more ignorant
ones believe that statement.   But an observation of the
methods of treatment employed by some who make this
claim leads one to suppose that the statement often made
to their patients that faith is unnecessary is rather a cunning
evasion of the truth for the very purpose of inspiring faith.
Thus, a patient enters the sanctum of a mental healer, and
begins by saying, " I understand that it is necessary that
your patients have faith before they can be healed.   If that
is the case, I never can be healed by mental treatment, for
I am utterly sceptical on the subject."   To which the ready
reply is, " Faith is unnecessary under my system.   I do not
care what you believe, for I can heal you, however sceptical
you may be."   This is generally satisfactory to the sceptic.
He brightens with hope, and submits to the treatment, full
of the faith that he is to be healed without faith.   It is
superfluous to add that by this stroke of policy the healer
has inspired the patient with all the faith required, namely,
the faith of his subjective mind.   I will not animadvert
upon the propriety of this course, though I cannot help but
contrast it with that of the Great Healer, who never de-
scended to falsehood, even to the end that good might come.
He always told his followers frankly that faith was essential ;
and his words are as true to-day as they were when he proclaimed to mankind that great secret of occult power.   Jesus
was the first to proclaim the great law of faith ; and when
he uttered that one word, he epitomized the whole science
of psycho-therapeutics.

CHAPTER XII.

PSYCHO-THERAPEUTICS (*continued*).

Methods classified in Two Divisions. — Mental and Oral Suggestions. — Absent Treatment. — Christian Scientists handicapped by Absurd Theories. — They claim too much. — The Use of Drugs. — Dangers arising from too Radical Change. — Importance of Favorable Mental Environment. — Mental Healing requires Mental Conditions. — Treatment by Hypnotism. — Bernheim's Methods. — Illustrative Cases. — The Practical Value of the System. — The Illogical Limitations of the Theory. — Potency of Telepathic Suggestion. — Researches of the Society for Psychical Research. — Mr. Gurney's Experiments. — They demonstrate the Theory of Effluent Emanations. — Diagnosis by Intuition. — Potency of Mesmerism. — Permanency of Cures. — Conditions necessary. — The Example of Jesus. — Self-healing by Auto-suggestion.

THE science of mental therapeutics may be classed in two general divisions, which are distinguished by the different methods of operation. The same general principle underlies both, but the results are attained by different modes of procedure.

The first method is by passivity on the part of the patient, and mental suggestion by the healer.

The second is by passivity on the part of the patient, and oral suggestion by the healer.

In ordinary practice both methods are used; that is to say, the oral suggestionist often unconsciously telepaths a mental suggestion to the subjective mind of the patient. If he thoroughly believes the truth of his own suggestions, the telepathic effect is sure to follow, and always to the manifest advantage of the patient. This is why it is that in all works on hypnotism and mesmerism the value and im portance of self-confidence on the part of the healer, or, in other words, belief in his own suggestions, is so strenuously insisted upon. Practice and experience have demonstrated the fact, but no writer on the subject attempts to give a scientific explanation of it. But when it is known that telepathy is the normal method of communication between subjective minds, and that in healing by mental processes it is constantly employed, consciously or unconsciously to the persons, the explanation is obvious.

Again, where mental suggestion is chiefly relied upon, the healer usually begins operations by making oral suggestions. Thus, the Christian scientist begins by carefully educating his patient in the fundamental doctrines of the school, and explaining the effects which are expected to follow the treatment. The mind is thus prepared by oral suggestions to receive the necessary mental impressions when the treatment proper begins. The most effective method of healing employed by that school consists in what it denominates " absent treatment." This is effected by purely telepathic means. The patient is absent, and often knows nothing, objectively, of what is being done for him. The healer sits alone and becomes passive ; or, in other words, becomes partially self-hypnotized, and addresses the patient mentally, and proceeds to argue the question with him. The condition of health is strongly asserted and insisted upon, and the possibility of disease as strenuously denied. The advantages of this means of treatment are obvious. The telepathic suggestions are made solely to the subjective mind of the patient, and do not rise above the threshold of his consciousness. The subjective mind, being constantly amenable to control by the power of suggestion, accepts the suggestions offered, and, having in its turn perfect control of the functions and conditions of the body, it proceeds to re-establish the condition of health. In other words, it abandons the abnormal idea of disease ; and, in obedience to the telepathic suggestions of the healer, it seizes upon the normal idea of health. It will readily be seen that by this method of treatment the patient is placed in the best possible condition for the reception of healthful suggestions. He is necessarily in a passive condition. That is, being unconscious, objectively, of the mental suggestions which are being made to his subjective mind, he is not handicapped by antagonistic auto-suggestions arising from objective doubt of the power of the healer, or of the correctness of his theories. The latter is the most serious obstacle which the Christian scientist has to contend with ; and it is safe to say that if his school had not been handicapped by a theory which shocks the common-sense of the average man, its sphere of usefulness would have been much larger than it is now. The school is doing a great and noble work as it is, but it is chiefly among those who are credulous enough to disbelieve the evidence of their own senses. There is, however, a large and growing class of people, calling themselves Christian scientists, who ignore the fundamental absurdities of the theory of the founder of the sect, and content themselves with the knowledge that the practice produces good results. Each one of these formulates a theory of his own, and each one finds that, measured by the standard of results, his theory is correct. The obvious conclusion is that one theory is as good as another, provided always that the mode of operation under it does not depart, in any essential particular, from the standard, and that the operator has the requisite faith in his own theory and practice.

Another circumstance which handicaps the enthusiastic votaries of each of the schools consists in the tendency of all reformers to claim too much for their systems. Forgetting that they have to deal with a generation of people with a hereditary belief in the power of medicines to cure disease, a people whose habits of life and thought are materialistic to the last degree, they expect to change that belief instantaneously, and cause the new method to take the place of the old in all cases and under all circumstances. In other words, they expect to cure all diseases by mental methods alone, and they seek to prohibit their patients from employing any other physician or using any medicines whatever. This is wrong in theory and often dangerous in practice. It may be true, and doubtless is, that one great source of the power of drugs to heal disease is attributable to the mental impression created upon the mind of the patient at the time the drug is administered. This being true, it follows that when a patient believes in drugs, drugs should be administered. If Christian science or any other mental method of healing can then be made available as an auxiliary, it should be employed. But this is just what the ultra-reformers refuse to do. They insist upon the discharge of the family physician, and the destruction of all the medicines in the house, before they will undertake to effect a cure by mental processes. It frequently happens that the patient is not sufficiently well grounded in the new faith, or is afflicted with some disease not readily reached by mental processes, and dies on their hands, when perhaps he might have been saved by the combined efforts of the family doctor and the Christian scientist. Be that as it may, when the patient dies under such circumstances, the Christian scientist must needs bear the brunt of popular condemnation. It goes without saying that one such case does more to retard the progress of mental therapeutics in popular estimation than a thousand miraculous cures can do to promote it. Again, much harm is done to the cause of mental healing by claiming for it too wide a field of usefulness. Theoretically, all the diseases which flesh is heir to are curable by mental processes. Practically, the range of its usefulness is comparatively limited. The lines of its field are not clearly defined, however, for the reason that so much depends on the idiosyncrasies of each individual patient. A disease which can be cured in one case refuses to yield in another, the mental attitudes of the patients not being the same. Besides, the mental environment of the patient has much to do with his amenability to control by mental processes. In an atmosphere of incredulity, doubt, and prejudice, a patient stands little chance of being benefited, however strong may be his own faith in mental therapeutics. Every doubt existing in the minds of those surrounding him is inevitably conveyed telepathically to his subjective mind, and operates as an adverse suggestion of irresistible potentiality. It requires a very strong will, perfect faith, and constant affirmative auto-suggestion on the part of the patient to overcome the adverse influence of an environment of incredulity and doubt, even though no word of that doubt is expressed in presence of the patient. It goes without saying that it is next to impossible for a sick person to possess the necessary mental force to overcome such adverse conditions. Obviously, the mental healer who undertakes a case under such circumstances, procures the discharge of the family physician, and prohibits the patient from using medicines, assumes a very grave responsibility, and does so at the risk of the patient's life and his own reputation.

Success in mental healing depends upon proper mental conditions, just as success in healing by physical agencies depends upon proper physical conditions. This is a self-evident proposition, which the average mental healer is slow to understand and appreciate.

The success of the physician depends as largely upon his knowledge of the idiosyncrasies of his patient, his personal habits, his mode of living, his susceptibility to the influence of medicines, etc., as upon a correct diagnosis and medicinal treatment of the disease. In like manner the success of the mental healer depends largely upon his knowledge of his patient's habits of thought, his beliefs, his prejudices, and, above all, his mental environment.

These remarks apply to all methods of mental healing; and, for the purposes of this book, Christian science may be taken as a representative of all systems of healing by mental suggestion, as distinguished from oral suggestion.

Hypnotism, as practised by the Nancy school, may stand as the representative of mental treatment of disease by purely oral suggestion. The following extract from Professor Bernheim's able work on "Suggestive Therapeutics" (chapter i.) embraces the essential features of the methods of inducing sleep practised by that school:

"I begin by saying to the patient that I believe benefit is to be derived from the use of suggestive therapeutics; that it is possible to cure or to relieve him by hypnotism; that there is nothing either hurtful or strange about it; that it is an *ordinary sleep*, or torpor, which can be induced in every one, and that this quiet, beneficial condition restores the equilibrium of the nervous system, etc. If necessary, I hypnotize one or two subjects in his presence, in order to show him that there is nothing painful in this condition, and that it is not accompanied with any unusual sensation. When I have thus banished from his mind the idea of magnetism and the somewhat mysterious fear that attaches to that unknown condition, above all when he has seen patients cured or benefited by the means in question, he is no longer suspicious, but gives himself up. Then I say, 'Look at me, and think of nothing but sleep. Your eyelids begin to feel heavy, your eyes tired. They begin to wink, they are getting moist, you cannot see distinctly. They are closed.' Some patients close their eyes and are asleep immediately. With others, I have to repeat, lay more stress on what I say, and even make gestures. It makes little difference what sort of gesture is made. I hold two fingers of my right hand before the patient's eyes and ask him to look at them, or pass both hands several times before his eyes, or persuade him to fix his eyes upon mine, endeavoring, at the same time, to concentrate his attention upon the idea of sleep. I say, 'Your lids are closing, you cannot open them again. Your arms feel heavy, so do your legs. You cannot feel anything. Your hands are motionless. You see nothing, you are going to sleep.' And I add, in a commanding tone, 'Sleep.' This word often turns the balance. The eyes close, and the patient sleeps, or is at least influenced. I use the word 'sleep,' in order to obtain as far as possible over the patients a suggestive influence which shall bring about sleep, or a state closely approaching it; for sleep, properly so called, does not always occur. If the patients have no inclination to sleep, and show no drowsiness, I take care to say that sleep is not essential; that the hypnotic influence, whence comes the benefit, may exist without sleep; that many patients are hypnotized, although they do not sleep.

"If the patient does not shut his eyes or keep them shut, I do not require them to be fixed on mine, or on my fingers, for any length of time, for it sometimes happens that they remain wide open indefinitely, and instead of the idea of sleep being conceived, only a rigid fixation of the eyes results. In this case, closure of the eyes by the operator succeeds better. After keeping them fixed one or two minutes, I push the eyelids down, or stretch them slowly over the eyes, gradually closing them more and more, and so imitating the process of natural sleep. Finally, I keep them closed, repeating the suggestion, 'Your lids are stuck together, you cannot open them. The need of sleep becomes greater and greater, you can no longer resist.' I lower my voice gradually, repeating the command, 'Sleep,' and it is very seldom that more than three minutes pass before sleep or some degree of hypnotic influence is obtained. It is sleep by suggestion, — a type of sleep which I insinuate into the brain.

"Passes or gazing at the eyes or fingers of the operator are only useful in concentrating the attention; they are not absolutely essential.

"As soon as they are able to pay attention and understand, children are, as a rule, very quickly and very easily hypnotized. It often suffices to close their eyes, to hold them shut a few moments, to tell them to sleep, and then to state that they are asleep.

"Some adults go to sleep just as readily by simple closure of the eyes. I often proceed immediately, without making use of passes or fixation, by shutting the eyelids, gently holding them closed, asking the patient to keep them together, and suggesting at the same time the phenomena of sleep. Some of them fall rapidly into a more or less deep sleep. Others offer more resistance. I sometimes succeed by keeping the eyes closed for some time, commanding silence and quiet, talking continuously, and repeating the same formulas : 'You feel a sort of drowsiness, a torpor; your arms and legs are motionless. Your eyelids are warm. Your nervous system is quiet; you have no will. Your eyes remain closed. Sleep is coming.' etc. After keeping up this auditory suggestion for several minutes, I remove my fingers. The eyes remain closed. I raise the patient's arms; they remain uplifted. We have induced cataleptic sleep."

Having succeeded in inducing sleep, or getting the patient in a passive and receptive condition, the operator then proceeds to suggest the idea of recovery from the disease with which he is afflicted. On this subject the author speaks as follows : —

"*The patient is put to sleep by means of suggestion;* that is, by making the idea of sleep penetrate the mind. He is *treated by means of suggestion ;* that is, by making the idea of cure penetrate the mind. The subject being hypnotized, M. Liébault's method consists in *affirming in a loud voice the disappearance of his symptoms.*

"We try to make him believe that these symptoms no longer exist, or that they will disappear, the pain will vanish; that the feeling will come back to his limbs ; that the muscular strength will increase; and that his appetite will come back. We profit by the special psychical receptivity created by the hypnosis, by the cerebral docility, by the exalted ideo-motor, ideo-sensitive, ideo-sensorial reflex activity, in order to provoke useful reflexes, to persuade the brain to do what it can to transform the accepted idea into reality.

"Such is the method of therapeutic-suggestion of which M. Liébault is the founder. He was the first clearly to establish that the cures obtained by the old magnetizers, and even by Braid's hypnotic operations, are not the work either of a mysterious fluid or of physiological modifications due to special manipulations, but the work of suggestion alone. The whole system of magnetic medicine is only the medicine of the imagination ; the imagination is put into such a condition by the hypnosis that it cannot escape from the suggestion.

"M. Liébault's method was ignored a long time, even by the physicians at Nancy. In 1884 Charles Richet was satisfied to say that magnetism often has advantages, that it calms nervous agitation, and that it may cure or benefit certain insomnias.

"Since 1882 I have experimented with the suggestive method which I have seen used by M. Liébault, though timidly at first, and without any confidence. To-day it is daily used in my clinic; I practise it before my students ; perhaps no day passes in which I do not show them some functional trouble, pain, paresis, uneasiness, insomnia, either moderated or instantly suppressed by suggestion.

"For example: a child is brought to me with a pain like muscular rheumatism in its arm, dating back four or five days. The arm is painful to pressure; the child cannot lift it to its head. I say to him, 'Shut your eyes, my child, and go to sleep.' I hold his eyelids closed, and go on talking to him. 'You are asleep, and you will keep on sleeping until I tell you to wake up. You are sleeping very well, as if you were in your bed. You are perfectly well and comfortable; your arms and legs and your whole body are asleep, and you cannot move.' I take my fingers off his eyelids, and they remain closed; I put his arms up, and they remain so. Then, touching the painful arm, I say,

'The pain has gone away. You have no more pain anywhere; you can move your arm without any pain; and when you wake up you will not feel any more pain. It will not come back any more.' In order to increase the force of the suggestion by em. bodying it, so to speak, in a material sensation, following M. Liébault's example I suggest a feeling of warmth *loco dolente*. The heat takes the place of the pain. I say to the child, 'You feel that your arm is warm; the warmth increases, and you have no more pain.'

"I wake the child in a few minutes; he remembers nothing; the sleep has been profound. The pain has almost completely disappeared; the child lifts the arm easily to his head. I see the father on the days following: he is the postman who brings my letters. He tells me that the pain has disappeared completely, and there has been no return of it.

"Here, again, is a man twenty-six years old, a workman in the foundries. For a year he has experienced a painful feeling of constriction over the epigastrium, also a pain in the corresponding region of the back, which was the result of an effort made in bending an iron bar. The sensation is continuous, and increases when he has worked for some hours. For six months he has been able to sleep only by pressing his epigastrium with his hand. I hypnotize him. In the first séance I can induce only simple drowsiness; he wakes spontaneously; the pain continues. I hypnotize him a second time, telling him that he will sleep more deeply, and that he will remember nothing when he wakes. Catalepsy is not present. I wake him in a few minutes; he does not remember that I spoke to him, that I assured him that the pain had disappeared. It has completely disappeared; he no longer feels any constriction. I do not know whether it has reappeared."[1]

The foregoing extracts present the gist of the methods employed by the Nancy school of hypnotism. The hypnotic condition is induced solely by oral suggestion, and the disease is removed by the same means. There can be no doubt of the efficacy of the method, thousands of successful experiments having been made by the author and his colleagues. These experiments have demonstrated the existence of a power in man to control by purely mental processes, — the functions and conditions of the human

[1] Suggestive Therapeutics, p. 206.

body. They have thus laid the foundation of a system of
mental therapeutics which must eventually prove of great
value to mankind. But they have done more. They have
demonstrated a principle which reaches out far beyond the
realm of therapeutics, and covers all the vast field of psychological research. They have demonstrated the constant
amenability of the subjective mind to control by the power
of suggestion. It is not surprising that those who have
discovered this great principle should insist upon its applicability to every phenomenon within the range of their
investigations; but it is strange that they should fail to
recognize a co-ordinate power governed by the same law,
within the same field of operations. Yet this is true of the
modern scientific school of hypnotism to-day. The Nancy
school believes in the power of suggestion, but confines its
faith to oral suggestion. Having demonstrated that *oral*
suggestion is efficacious in the production of psychic phenomena, they hold that *mental* suggestion has no power
in the same direction. Having demonstrated that certain
phenomena can be induced independently of any so-called
fluidic emanation or effluence from the hypnotist, they hold
that no fluidic emanation is possible. These conclusions
are not only illogical, they are demonstrably incorrect. The
Christian scientists are constantly demonstrating the potency
of purely telepathic suggestion by what they denominate
"absent treatment;" *i. e.*, treatment of sick persons without the knowledge of the patients. That there is a power
emanating from the operator who hypnotizes by means of
mesmeric passes, seems to be very well authenticated by
the experiments recorded by the old mesmerists. It must
be admitted, however, that many of their experiments do
not conclusively prove anything, for the reason that they
were made before suggestion as a constant factor in hypnotism had been demonstrated. Recent experiments by
members of the London Society for Psychical Research
have, however, now placed that question beyond a doubt.
Their methods of investigation are purely scientific, and
were made with a full knowledge and appreciation of the

principle of suggestion, and of the distinction between mesmerism and hypnotism.

In an account of some experiments in mesmerism, written by Mr. Edmund Gurney, and recorded in vol. ii. pp. 201–205, of the Proceedings of the Society referred to, a very interesting experiment is mentioned, which demonstrates the fact that there is an effluence emanating from the mesmerizer which is capable of producing very marked physical effects upon the subject. In this case the subject was blindfolded and allowed to remain in his normal condition during the whole of the experiment. His hands were then spread out upon a table before him, his fingers wide apart. The mesmerizer then made passes over one of the fingers, taking care not to move his hand near enough to the subject's finger to cause a perceptible movement of the atmosphere, or to give any indication in any other way which finger was being mesmerized. The result was, in every instance, the production of local anæsthesia in the finger operated upon, and in no other.

Oral suggestion, or any other form of physical suggestion, was here out of the question ; and telepathic suggestion was extremely improbable, in view of the fact that the subject was in his normal condition, and consequently not in subjective rapport with the operator. A further experiment was then tried, with a view of ascertaining whether it was necessary for the mesmerist to know which finger he was operating upon. To that end, the operator's hand was guided by the hand of a third party while the passes were being made ; and it was found that the selected finger was unaffected, when the operator did not know which one it was.

The first of these experiments demonstrates the fact that there is an effluence emanating from the mesmerist ; and the second demonstrates the fact that this effluence is directed by his will.

What this effluence is, man may never know. That it is a vital fact in psychic phenomena is certain. Like many other subtle forces of nature, it defies analysis. That it exists, and that under certain conditions not yet very clearly defined it can be controlled by the conscious intelligence of man, is as certain as the existence of electricity. Its source is undoubtedly the subjective mind, and it is identical with that force which, under other conditions, reappears in the form of so-called spirit-rappings, table-tipping, etc.

Space will not permit the reproduction of further account of the experiments of the Society for Psychical Research and the reader is referred to their Proceedings for fuller information. It must suffice to say that the experiments referred to are completely demonstrative, not only of the fact that an effluence does emanate from the mesmeric operator, but that under mesmeric conditions telepathic suggestion is as potent as are the oral suggestions of the hypnotists.

These facts are beginning to be recognized even by the scientists of Europe, thanks to the carefully conducted experiments of the Society for Psychical Research. Professor Liébault himself, the discoverer of the law of suggestion, now freely admits the fact that a specific influence is sometimes exerted by the mesmerizer upon his subject, which does not arise from oral suggestion. In fact, this doctrine must soon be, if it is not now, one of the recognized principles of psychic science.

It will thus be seen that healing by mesmerism is a process clearly distinct from healing by hypnotism. The latter depends for its effects wholly upon oral suggestion and the unaided power of the subjective mind of the patient over the functions and conditions of his body; whereas the mesmeric healer exerts a positive force of great potentiality upon the body of the patient, filling it with vitality, in addition to the oral suggestion of the hypnotist. Not only so, but when purely mesmeric methods are employed, — that is, when the mesmerist is in subjective rapport with his patient, as fully explained in a former chapter, — he is in a condition to convey suggestions telepathically with as much certainty and potency as he could orally. In point of fact, telepathic suggestions by a genuine mesmerist are often far more efficacious than the oral suggestions of a hypnotist, for the simple reason that the mesmerist, being in a partially subjective condition himself, is able to perceive by intuition the true condition of the patient. In other words, the intuitive, or subjective, diagnosis of an intelligent mesmerist, supposing always the true mesmeric conditions to be present, is far more likely to be correct than the objective diagnosis of the hypnotist. For, be it known, it is just as necessary for the mental healer, whatever may be his processes or his theory, to be able to make a correct diagnosis of a case as it is for the allopathic physician. The reason is the same in both cases. The efforts of the healer must necessarily be exerted in the right direction, or they will be futile. Hence it is that, other things being equal, the most intelligent mental healer is always the most successful.

Taking it for granted, then, that there is a fluidic emanation, or effluence, proceeding from the mesmerist and impinging upon the patient, it follows that there is a positive dynamic force exerted upon the patient, either for good or evil, by the employment of mesmeric methods. That its effects are salutary when properly used for therapeutic purposes is proved by the concurrent testimony of all who have intelligently made the experiment, from the days of Paracelsus down to the present time.

From this it would appear that mesmerism must be the most powerful, in its immediate effects, of any of the known methods of mental healing. It combines oral suggestion with mental suggestion, and employs in addition that mysterious psycho-physical force, or effluence, popularly known as animal magnetism.

Before leaving this branch of the subject, a few remarks will be in order regarding the relative value of the different systems of mental healing now in vogue. It has frequently been charged that healing by hypnotism and mesmerism is not lasting in its effects, — that no permanent cure is ever made by these methods. It must be admitted that there is some ground for these statements, although so sweeping a charge is by no means justifiable. It is true that in many instances patients who have been cured by hypnotism and mesmerism have suffered a relapse, and in some cases the relapse has been worse than was the original sickness. This of itself constitutes no valid objection to the means of cure ; for it must be admitted that under no system of treatment is a patient free from the danger of a relapse or of a recurrence of the disease at some future time. There is, however, this to be said in regard to hypnotic or mesmeric treatment which does not apply with the same force to healing by medicines. The success of mental methods of treatment depending, as it does, upon the mental condition of the patient and upon the mental impressions made upon him, it follows that if the mental impressions are not permanent, the cure may not be permanent. Hence it often happens that a patient, elated by the success of hypnotic treatment in his case, relates the circumstances to his friends, especially to his sceptical associates, only to meet with a storm of ridicule, or at least with expressions of incredulity or doubt. In such a mental environment his subjective mind inevitably takes hold of the adverse suggestions, and without being objectively conscious of it, he has lost faith, the citadel of his defence is broken down, and if his disease had a mental origin, he is open to another attack more severe and serious perhaps than the first. That Christ was fully alive to this danger is shown by the fact that when he healed a person in private, he rarely failed to place the solemn injunction upon him, "See thou tell no man." No recorded words that the Master ever uttered display a more profound knowledge of the underlying principles of mental healing than these. Modern healers are not so modest, nor do they seem to understand the prime necessity for seeing to it that their patients are kept in a proper frame of mind in reference to their disease and the means employed to cure them. The general principle of auto-suggestion is recognized by all scientific hypnotists of the present day ; but they fail to recognize its extreme importance as a therapeutic agent. Properly understood and applied, auto-suggestion supplies a means of enabling every one to heal himself, or at least to hold himself in the proper mental attitude to make permanent the good effects of hypnotic treatment by others. Many of the pains and ills to which the average man is subject can be cured by this means, and it should be the first care of every hypnotist to instruct his patients in this branch of the science. In this respect the Christian scientists are far in advance of the hypnotists and mesmerists. They teach their patients how to help themselves. They organize them into classes, deliver lectures, and give minute instructions how to treat themselves, as well as how to treat others. Without knowing it, they in effect teach their patients the methods of autosuggestion. Without having the remotest conception of the real principles which underlie their so-called "science," they have somehow stumbled upon the machinery of mental therapeutics. To do them full justice, it must be said that they employ the machinery to good purpose. They do much good and little harm, and the little harm they do, generally arises from over confidence in the universal efficacy of their methods.

CHAPTER XIII.

A NEW SYSTEM OF MENTAL THERAPEUTICS.

Telepathy the Normal Means of Communication between Subjective
Minds. — Perfect Passivity required for Therapeutic Suggestions.
— Natural Sleep the most Perfect State of Passivity. — Hypnotic
Sleep and Natural Sleep identical. — Phenomena of Dreams. —
Subjective Mind controllable by Suggestion during Natural Sleep.
— Illustrative Incidents. — Passivity a Necessity on the Part of the
Operator. — The Subjective Mind can be caused to convey Tele-
pathic Messages during Sleep. — Illustrative Experiments.

THE science of psycho-therapeutics is yet in its infancy.
Thus far just enough has been learned to stimulate
research. It has been demonstrated that there is a psychic
power inherent in man which can be employed for the
amelioration of his own physical condition, as well as that
of his fellows. When this is said, nearly all the ground
covered by present knowledge has been embraced. It is
true that many wonderful cures have been effected, many
marvellous phenomena developed. Nevertheless, all are
groping in the dark, with only an occasional glimmering of
distant light shed upon the subject; and this light serves
principally to show how little is now known, compared with
what there is yet to learn.

In one view of the situation, however, it may be said
that much has already been accomplished. In the conflict
of theoretical discussion, and by means of the various and
seemingly conflicting methods of operation, certain laws
have been discovered which may serve as a basis for new
experiments and new discoveries. It is the province of
science to collate those laws and to classify the facts where-

ever found, and from them to try to reason up to the general principles involved. When this is done, fearlessly and conscientiously, a decided step in advance will have been made. Some new law may then be discovered, or at least some new method of operation may be developed, which shall add to the general stock of knowledge of the science, and enlarge its field of usefulness.

It is the object of the writer to offer a few observations in this chapter, in a direction believed to be substantially new, and briefly to present some conclusions at which he has arrived from a careful examination of premises which seem to have been well established by the experiments of others. Before doing so it will be necessary first to state the premises upon which the conclusions are based ; and in doing this, care will be taken not to travel outside of well-authenticated experiments.

The first proposition is, that there is inherent in mankind the power to communicate thoughts to others independently of objective means of communication. The truth of this general proposition has been so thoroughly demonstrated by the experiments of members of the London Society for Psychical Research that time and space will not be wasted in its further elucidation. For a full treatment of the subject the reader is referred to "Phantasms of the Living," in which the results of the researches of that Society are ably set forth by Messrs. Edmund Gurney, F. W. H. Myers, and Frank Podmore. It is hardly necessary to remind the intelligent reader that the methods of investigation employed by these able and indefatigable laborers in the field of psychical research are purely scientific, and their works are singularly free from manifestations of prejudice or of unreasoning scepticism on the one hand, and of credulity on the other. It is confidently assumed, therefore, that the power of telepathic communication is as thoroughly established as any fact in nature.

Now, telepathy is primarily the communion of subjective minds, or rather it is the normal means of communication between subjective minds. The reason of the apparent

rarity of its manifestation is that it requires exceptional conditions to bring its results above the threshold of consciousness. There is every reason to believe that the souls, or
subjective minds, of men can and do habitually hold communion with one another when not the remotest perception
of the fact is communicated to the objective intelligence.
It may be that such communion is not general among men;
but it is certain that it is held between those who, from any
cause, are *en rapport*. The facts recorded by the Society
for Psychical Research demonstrate that proposition. Thus,
near relatives are oftenest found to be in communion, as is
shown by the comparative frequency of telepathic communications between relatives, giving warning of sickness
or of death. Next in frequency are communications between intimate friends. Communications of this character
between comparative strangers are apparently rare. Of
course the only means we have of judging of these things
is by the record of those cases in which the communications
have been brought to the objective consciousness of the
percipients. From these cases it seems fair to infer that
the subjective minds of those who are deeply interested in
one another are in habitual communion, especially when the
personal interest or welfare of either agent or percipient is
at stake. Be this as it may, it is certain that telepathic
communication can be established at will by the conscious
effort of one or both of the parties, even between strangers.
The experiments of the Society above named have demonstrated this fact. It will be assumed, therefore, for the purposes of this argument that telepathic communion can be
established between two subjective minds at the will of
either. The fact may not be perceived by the subject, for
it may not rise above the threshold of his objective consciousness. But for therapeutic purposes it is not necessary
that the patient should know, objectively, that anything
is being done for him. Indeed, it is often better that he
should not know it, for reasons set forth in a former chapter.

The second proposition is that a state of perfect passivity
on the part of the percipient is the most favorable con-

dition for the reception of telepathic impressions or communications. It needs no argument to establish the truth of this proposition. It is universally known to be true, by all who have given the slightest attention to psychological science, that passivity on the part of the subject is the primary condition necessary for the production of any psychic phenomenon. Passivity simply means the suspension of the functions of the objective mind for the time being, for the purpose of allowing the subjective mind to receive impressions and to act upon them. The more perfectly the objective intelligence can be held in abeyance, the more perfectly will the subjective mind perform its functions. This is why a state of profound hypnotism is the most favorable for the reception of suggestions, either oral or mental. That this is more especially true of mental suggestions is shown by all experiments in mesmerism. It may, therefore, be safely assumed that the most favorable condition in which a patient can be placed for the reception of telepathic suggestions for therapeutic purposes is the condition wherein the functions of his objective intelligence are, for the time being, entirely suspended.

The third proposition is that *there is nothing to differentiate hypnotic sleep from natural sleep.* Startling as this proposition may appear to the superficial observer, it is fully concurred in both by M. Liébault and Professor Bernheim.

"There is no fundamental difference," says the latter,[1] "between spontaneous and induced sleep. M. Liébault has very wisely established this fact. The spontaneous sleeper is in relationship with himself alone; the idea which occupies his mind just before going to sleep, the impressions which the sensitive and sensorial nerves of the periphery continue to transmit to the brain, and the stimuli coming from the viscera, become the point of departure for the incoherent images and impressions which constitute dreams. Have those who deny the psychical phenomena of hypnotism, or who only admit them in cases of diseased nervous temperament, ever reflected upon what occurs in normal sleep, in which the best-balanced mind is carried

[1] Suggestive Therapeutics, pp. 140, 141.

by the current, in which the faculties are dissociated, in which the most singular ideas and the most fantastic conceptions obtrude? Poor human reason is carried away, the proudest mind yields to hallucinations, and during this sleep — that is to say, during a quarter of its existence — becomes the plaything of the dreams which imagination calls forth.

"In induced sleep the subject's mind retains the memory of the person who has put him to sleep, whence the hypnotizer's power of playing upon his imagination, of suggesting dreams, and of directing the acts which are no longer controlled by the weakened or absent will."

There are, in fact, many analogies between the phenomena of normal sleep and the phenomena of hypnotism. For instance, it is well known that the recollection of what occurred during hypnotic sleep is in exact inverse proportion to the depth of the sleep. If the sleep is light, the remembrance of the subject is perfect. If the sleep is profound, he remembers nothing, no matter what the character of the scenes he may have passed through. The same is true of dreams. We remember only those dreams which occur during the period when we are just going to sleep or are just awakening. Profound sleep is dreamless, so far as the recollection of the sleeper informs him. Nevertheless, it is certain that we dream continuously during sleep. The subjective mind is ever awake during the sleep of the body, and always active. Our dreams are often incoherent and absurd, for the reason that they are generally invoked by peripheral impressions. These impressions constitute suggestions which the subjective mind, in obedience to the universal law, accepts as true ; and it always deduces the legitimate conclusions therefrom. For instance, it is probably within the experience of every reader that an accidental removal of the bed-clothing during a cold night will cause the sleeper to dream of wading through snow, or of sleigh-riding. And the dream will be pleasant or otherwise just in accordance with the character of the other attendant peripheral impressions. If the dreamer is in good health he will dream of pleasant winter scenes and experiences. If his stomach is out of order, or overloaded, he will have a nightmare, with a winter setting of ice and snow and all that is disagreeable, dank, and dismal.

As we have seen in the preceding chapters, the subjective mind reasons deductively only from premises that are suggested to it, whether the suggestions are imparted to it by its physical environment, as in sleep, or by oral suggestion, as in hypnotism, or telepathically, as in the higher forms of mesmerism. Its deductions are always logical, whether the premises are true or false. Hence the absurdity of many of our dreams; they are merely deductions from false premises. The suggestions or impressions imparted to us during sleep being the result of accidental surroundings and stimuli, modified by the state of our health, our mental work during the day, and a thousand other things of which we can have no knowledge, and which are beyond our control, are necessarily of a heterogeneous character; and the deductions from such premises must of necessity be incoherent and fantastic to the last degree.

It is obvious, therefore, that the subjective mind is amenable to control by suggestion during natural sleep just the same as it is during hypnotic, or induced, sleep. It might not be unprofitable in this connection to enter into a general inquiry as to how far it would be possible to control our dreams by auto-suggestion, and thus obviate the discomforts incident to unpleasant nocturnal hallucinations. But as we are now engaged in a specific inquiry into the question of how far the subjective mind can be influenced for therapeutic purposes, the general field of speculation must be left for others. It is sufficient for present purposes to establish the proposition that the subjective mind is controllable by the power of suggestion during natural sleep.

Recurring in this connection to the preceding proposition, that "a state of perfect passivity on the part of the patient is the most favorable condition for the reception of telepathic impressions or communications for therapeutic purposes," the conclusion is obvious that the condition of natural sleep, being the most perfectly passive condition imaginable, must of necessity be the most favorable condition for the reception of telepathic suggestions for therapeutic purposes. It is especially adapted for the conveyance of therapeutic suggestions, for the reason that for such purposes it is not necessary that the suggestions or impressions should rise above the threshold of the patient's consciousness. Indeed, as we have before observed, it is better that they should not. The object being merely the restoration of health, it is not necessary that the objective mind should feel, or be conscious of, the impressions or suggestions made. It is precisely as it is in hypnotism ; the suggestions, whether oral or telepathic, are made to the subjective intelligence ; and, in case of profound hypnotic sleep, the objective mind retains no recollection of the suggestions. In either case the subjective mind is the one addressed ; and that, being the central power in control of the functions and conditions of the body, accepts the suggestions and acts accordingly.

There are not wanting facts which show clearly that the power exists to convey telepathic messages to sleeping persons, causing them to dream of the things that the agent desires. As long ago as 1819, Councillor H. M. Wesermann, of Düsseldorf, recorded, in the " Archiv für den thierischen Magnetismus," [1] a few experiments of his own which show this to be true. The following items are reproduced in " Phantasms of the Living," [2] from the original article above mentioned : —

" *First Experiment, at a Distance of Five Miles.* — I endeavored to acquaint my friend, the Hofkammerrath G. (whom I had not seen, with whom I had not spoken, and to whom I had not written for thirteen years), with the fact of my intended visit, by presenting my form to him in his sleep, through the force of my will. When I unexpectedly went to him on the following evening, he evinced his astonishment at having seen me in a dream on the preceding night.

" *Second Experiment, at a Distance of Three Miles.* — Madame W., in her sleep, was to hear a conversation between

---

[1] Vol. vi. pp. 136–139. [2] Vol. i. pp. 101, 102.

me and two other persons, relating to a certain secret; and when I visited her on the third day, she told me all that had been said, and showed her astonishment at this remarkable dream.

"*Third Experiment, at a Distance of One Mile.* — An aged person in G—— was to see in a dream the funeral procession of my deceased friend S.; and when I visited her on the next day, her first words were that she had in her sleep seen a funeral procession, and on inquiry had learned that I was the corpse. Here there was a slight error.

"*Fourth Experiment, at a Distance of One-Eighth of a Mile.* — Herr Doctor B. desired a trial to convince him, whereupon I represented to him a nocturnal street-brawl. He saw it in a dream, to his great astonishment. (This means, presumably, that he was astonished when he found that the actual subject of his dream was what Wesermann had been endeavoring to impress on him.)"

It would thus seem to be reasonably well established that the state of natural sleep is the best possible condition for the reception of telepathic suggestions for therapeutic purposes.

The next inquiry in order is, therefore, as to what is the best means of conveying telepathic suggestion to the sleeping patient. In a previous chapter it has been shown that a successful mesmerizer must necessarily be in a partially subjective condition himself in order to produce the higher phenomena of mesmerism. It may, it is thought, be safely assumed that the phenomenon of thought-transference cannot be produced under any other conditions. Indeed, it stands to reason that, inasmuch as it is the subjective mind of the percipient that is impressed, the message must proceed from the subjective mind of the agent. In other words, it is reasonable to suppose that, the subjective or passive condition being a necessity on the part of the percipient or subject, an analogous condition is a necessity on the part of the agent or operator. This fact is shown, not only in mesmerism, but in the methods of Christian scientists. The mesmerist, as we have seen, quietly fixes his gaze upon the subject and concentrates

his mind and will upon the work in hand, and thus, un-
knowingly, it may be, partially hypnotizes himself. The
Christian scientist sits quietly by the patient and concentrates his mind, in like manner, upon the central idea of
curing the patient. And, in either case, just in proportion to the ability of the operator to get himself into the
subjective condition will he succeed in accomplishing his
object, whether it is the production of the higher phenomena of mesmerism, or the healing of the sick by telepathic
suggestion.

If, then, the passive, or subjective, condition of the agent
is necessary for the successful transmission of telepathic
suggestions or communications, or if it is the *best* condition for such a purpose, it follows that the more perfectly
that condition is attained, the more successful will be the
experiment. As before observed, the condition of natural
sleep is manifestly the most perfectly passive condition attainable. It is necessarily perfect, for all the objective
senses are locked in slumber, and the subjective mind is
free to act in accordance with the laws which govern it.
Those laws are, it is true, at present but little understood ;
but this much has been demonstrated, namely, that the
subjective mind is controllable by the mysterious power of
suggestion, and is always most active during sleep.

Theoretically, then, we find that the most perfect condition either for the conveyance or the reception of telepathic impressions or communications is that of natural sleep.
The only question that remains to be settled is whether it
is possible for the agent or operator so to control his own
subjective mind during his bodily sleep as to compel or
induce it to convey the desired message to the sub-con-
sciousness of the patient. To settle this question, we must
again have recourse to the record of the labors and researches of the London Society for Psychical Research. It
might well be inferred that this power must necessarily be
possessed, when we take into consideration the general law
of suggestion, coupled with the fact that the subjective
mind is perfectly amenable to control by auto-suggestion.

If the law of suggestion is valid and universal, the conclusion is irresistible that this power is inherent in man, even without one experimental fact to sustain it. Fortunately, we are not left to conjecture in regard to this important question. The literature of psychical experiment is full of facts which are demonstrative. Some of the experiments recorded in "Phantasms of the Living" show that a vastly greater power exists in this direction than would be required to convey a simple therapeutic suggestion to a sleeping patient. The following experiments are recorded in "Phantasms of the Living."[1] In the first case, the Rev. W. Stainton Moses was the percipient, and he corroborates the following account, written by the agent : —

"One evening I resolved to appear to Z at some miles' distance. I did not inform him beforehand of the intended experiment, but retired to rest shortly before midnight with thoughts intently fixed on Z, with whose room and surroundings I was quite unacquainted. I soon fell asleep, and awoke next morning unconscious of anything having taken place. On seeing Z, a few days afterwards, I inquired, 'Did anything happen at your rooms on Saturday night?' 'Yes,' replied he, 'a great deal happened. I had been sitting over the fire with M, smoking and chatting. About 12.30 he rose to leave, and I let him out myself. I returned to the fire to finish my pipe, when I saw you sitting in the chair just vacated by him. I looked intently at you, and then took up a newspaper to assure myself I was not dreaming; but on laying it down I saw you still there. While I gazed, without speaking, you faded away.'"

The next case was recorded by the agent, Mr. S. H. B., at the time of the occurrence, and his account of it is duly verified by the percipients. It is as follows : —

On a certain Sunday evening in November, 1881, having been reading of the great power which the human will is capable of exercising, I determined, with the whole force of my being, that I would be present in spirit in the front bed-room on the second floor of a house situated at 22 Hogarth Road, Kensington, in which room slept two ladies of my acquaintance, —

[1] Vol. i. pp. 103-109.

namely, Miss L. S. V. and Miss E. C. V., aged respectively twenty-five and eleven years. I was living at this time at 23 Kildare Gardens, a distance of about three miles from Hogarth Road; and I had not mentioned in any way my intention of trying this experiment to either of the above ladies, for the simple reason that it was only on retiring to rest upon this Sunday night that I made up my mind to do so. The time at which I determined I would be there was one o'clock in the morning; and I also had a strong intention of making my presence perceptible. On the following Thursday I went to see the ladies in question, and, in the course of conversation (without any allusion to the subject on my part), the elder one told me that on the previous Sunday night she had been much terrified by perceiving me standing by her bedside, and that she screamed when the apparition advanced towards her, and awoke her little sister, who saw me also.

I asked her if she was awake at the time, and she replied most decidedly in the affirmative; and upon my inquiring the time of the occurrence, she replied, "About one o'clock in the morning."

This lady, at my request, wrote down a statement of the event, and signed it.

This was the first occasion upon which I tried an experiment of this kind, and its complete success startled me very much. Besides exercising my power of volition very strongly, I put forth an effort which I cannot find words to describe. I was conscious of a mysterious influence of some sort permeating in my body, and had a distinct impression that I was exercising some force with which I had been hitherto unacquainted, but which I can now at certain times set in motion at will.   S. H. B.

The next case of Mr. S. H. B.'s is different in this respect, that the percipient was not consciously present to the agent's mind on the night that he made his attempt: —

On Friday, Dec. 1, 1882, at 9.30 P. M., I went into a room alone and sat by the fireside, and endeavored so strongly to fix my mind upon the interior of a house at Kew (namely, Clarence Road), in which resided Miss V. and her two sisters, that I seemed to be actually in the house.

During this experiment I must have fallen into a mesmeric sleep, for although I was conscious, I could not move my limbs. I did not seem to have lost the power of moving them.

but I could not make the effort to do so; and my hands, which lay loosely on my knees, about six inches apart, felt involuntarily drawn together, and seemed to meet, although I was conscious that they did not move.

At 10 P. M. I regained my normal state by an effort of the will, and then took a pencil and wrote down on a sheet of note-paper the foregoing statements.

When I went to bed on this same night I determined that I would be in the front bed-room of the above-mentioned house at 12 P. M., and remain there until I had made my spiritual presence perceptible to the inmates of that room.

On the next day (Saturday) I went to Kew to spend the evening, and met there a married sister of Miss V. (namely, Mrs. L.). This lady I had only met once before, and then it was at a ball two years previous to the above date. We were both in fancy dress at the time, and as we did not exchange more than half-a-dozen words, this lady would naturally have lost any vivid recollection of my appearance, even if she had remarked it.

In the course of conversation (although I did not think for a moment of asking her any questions on such a subject) she told me that on the previous night she had seen me distinctly upon two occasions. She had spent the night at Clarence Road, and had slept in the front bed-room. At about 9.30 she had seen me in the passage, going from one room to another; and at 12 P. M., when she was wide awake, she had seen me enter the bedroom and walk round to where she was sleeping, and take her hair (which is very long) into my hand. She also told me that the apparition took hold of her hand and gazed intently into it, whereupon she spoke, saying, "You need not look at the lines, for I have never had any trouble." She then awoke her sister, Miss V., who was sleeping with her, and told her about it. After hearing this account, I took the statement which I had written down on the previous evening from my pocket and showed it to some of the persons present, who were much astonished, although incredulous.

I asked Mrs. L. if she was not dreaming at the time of the latter experience; but this she stoutly denied, and stated that she had forgotten what I was like, but seeing me so distinctly, she recognized me at once.

Mrs. L. is a lady of highly imaginative temperament, and told me that she had been subject since childhood to psychological fancies, etc.; but the wonderful coincidence of the time (which was exact) convinced me that what she told me was more than a flight of the imagination. At my request she wrote a brief account of her impressions, and signed it.

S. H. B.

One of the authors of " Phantasms of the Living " (Mr. Gurney) on one occasion requested Mr. B. to send him a note on the night that he intended to make his next experiment of the kind, whereupon the following correspondence ensued : —

March 22, 1884.

DEAR MR. GURNEY, — I am going to try the experiment to-night of making my presence perceptible at 44 Morland Square, at 12 P. M. I will let you know the result in a few days.

Yours very sincerely,   S. H. B.

The next letter was received in the course of the following week : —

April 3, 1884.

DEAR MR. GURNEY, — I have a strange statement to show you respecting my experiment, which was tried at your suggestion, and under the test conditions which you imposed. Having quite forgotten which night it was on which I attempted the projection, I cannot say whether the result is a brilliant success, or only a slight one, until I see the letter which I posted you on the evening of the experiment. Having sent you that letter, I did not deem it necessary to make a note in my diary, and consequently have let the exact date slip my memory. If the dates correspond, the success is complete in every detail, and I have an account signed and witnessed to show you.

I saw the lady (who was the subject) for the first time last night, since the experiment, and she made a voluntary statement to me, which I wrote down at her dictation, and to which she has attached her signature. The date and time of the apparition are specified in this statement, and it will be for you to decide whether they are identical with those given in my letter to you. I have completely forgotten, but yet I fancy that they are the same.

S. H. B.

This is the statement : —

44 Morland Square, W.

On Saturday night, March 22, 1884, at about midnight, I had a distinct impression that Mr. S. H. B. was present in my room, and I distinctly saw him whilst I was quite wide awake. He came towards me and stroked my hair. I *voluntarily* gave him this information when he called to see me on Wednesday, April 2, telling him the time and the circumstances of the apparition, without any suggestion on his part. The appearance in my room was most vivid, and quite unmistakable.

L. S. VERITY.

Miss A. S. Verity corroborates as follows : —

I remember my sister telling me that she had seen S. H. B., and that he had touched her hair, *before* he came to see us on April 2. A. S. V.

Mr. B.'s own account is as follows : —

On Saturday, March 22, I determined to make my presence perceptible to Miss V. at 44 Morland Square, Notting Hill, at twelve, midnight; and as I had previously arranged with Mr. Gurney that I should post him a letter on the evening on which I tried my next experiment (stating the time and other particulars), I sent a note to acquaint him with the above facts.

About ten days afterwards I called upon Miss V., and she voluntarily told me that on March 22, at twelve o'clock, midnight, she had seen me so vividly in her room (whilst widely awake) that her nerves had been much shaken, and she had been obliged to send for a doctor in the morning.

S. H. B.

Mr. Gurney adds : —

" It will be observed that in all these instances the conditions were the same, — *the agent concentrating his thoughts on the object in view before going to sleep.* Mr. B. has never succeeded in producing a similar effect when he has been awake."

The foregoing instances have been quoted merely for the purpose of showing that the power exists in mankind to cause telepathic impressions to be conveyed from one to another, not only when the percipient is awake and the agent is asleep, but when both are asleep. It is true that they do not demonstrate the proposition that the power can be employed for therapeutic purposes when both are asleep; but the inference is irresistible that such is the case. They do, however, demonstrate the existence of a power far greater than one would naturally suppose would be required to convey a therapeutic suggestion. In the cases cited, the impressions were brought above the threshold of the consciousness of the percipients. It may well be inferred that a power sufficiently great to cause the percipient, in his waking moments, to see the image or apparition of the agent, or even to dream of him when asleep so vividly as to remember the dream, must be easily capable of imparting any thought, impression, or suggestion which is not required to be raised above the threshold of consciousness.

All that would seem to be required is that the agent, before going to sleep, should strongly will, desire, and direct his subjective entity to convey the necessary therapeutic suggestions, influence, or impressions to the sleeping patient.

CHAPTER XIV.

A NEW SYSTEM OF MENTAL THERAPEUTICS (*continued*).

Recapitulation of Propositions. — Natural Sleep the Best Condition attainable both for Healer and Patient. — Demonstrative Experiments. — Healing at a Distance of One Thousand Miles. — Distance no Obstacle. — Space does not exist for the Subjective Mind. — Objective Habits of Thought the only Adverse Factor. — Diseases treated. — Strabismus Cured. — Mode of Operation. — Not a Good Money-making Scheme. — It Promotes the Health of the Healer. — A Method of Universal Utility. — Self-healing its Most Important Function. — The Power absolute. — Within the Reach of all. — Method of Self-healing. — The Patient's Credulity not overtaxed. — The Example of Christ. — Material Remedies not to be ignored. — Advice to Christian Scientists. — The Control of Dreams. — Practical Conclusions.

IT is thought that the following propositions have now been, at least provisionally, established : —

1. There is, inherent in man, a power which enables him to communicate his thoughts to others, independently of objective means of communication.

2. A state of perfect passivity on the part of the percipient is the most favorable condition for the reception of telepathic impressions or communications.

3. There is nothing to differentiate natural sleep from induced sleep.

4. The subjective mind is amenable to control by suggestion during natural sleep just the same as it is during induced sleep.

5. The condition of natural sleep, being the most perfect passive condition attainable, is the best condition for the reception of telepathic impressions by the subjective mind.

6. The most perfect condition for the conveyance of telepathic impressions is that of natural sleep.

7. The subjective mind of the agent can be compelled
to communicate telepathic impressions to a sleeping percipient by strongly willing it to do so just previous to going
to sleep.

The chain of reasoning embraced in the foregoing propositions seems to be perfect ; and it is thought that sufficient
facts have been adduced to sustain each proposition which
is not self-evident, or confirmed by the common experience
of mankind. The conclusion is irresistible that *the best
possible condition for the conveyance of therapeutic suggestions from the healer to the patient is attained when both
are in a state of natural sleep ; and that such suggestions
can be so communicated by an effort of will on the part of
the healer just before going to sleep.*

It is not proposed herein to detail the many experiments
which have been made with a view of testing the correctness
of this theory, my present object being to advance the
hypothesis tentatively, in order to induce others to experiment as I have done. It must suffice for the present to
state that over one hundred experiments have been made
by the writer and one or two others to whom he has confided his theory, without a single failure. Some very striking cures have been effected, — cures that would take rank
with the most marvellous instances of healing recorded in
the annals of modern psycho-therapeutics. It is obvious
that details of names and dates could not properly be
given, for the reason that the cures have been effected
without any knowledge on the part of the patients that they
were being made the subjects of experiment. I do not feel
at liberty, therefore, to drag their names before the public
without their consent. Besides, if they were now made
acquainted with the facts, their recollection of the circumstances of their recovery would in many instances be indistinct ; and, as a matter of course, all of them have attributed
their sudden recovery to other causes.

I have taken care, however, in many instances to acquaint

third persons with intended experiments, and to request them to watch the results; so that I have the means at hand to verify my statements if necessary.

The first case was that of a relative who had for many years been afflicted with nervous trouble, accompanied by rheumatism of the most terrible character. He was subject to the most excruciating spasms during his nervous attacks of rheumatic trouble, and was frequently brought to the verge of the grave. He had been under the care of many of the ablest physicians of this country and of Europe, finding only occasional temporary relief. An idea of the suffering which he endured may be imagined from the fact that one of his hips had been drawn out of joint, by which the leg had been shortened about two inches. This, however, had been partially restored by physical appliances before the psychic treatment began. In short, he was a hopeless invalid, with nothing to look to for relief from his sufferings but death.

The treatment began on the 15th of May, 1890. Two persons were informed of the proposed experiment, and were requested to note the time when the treatment began. They were pledged to profound secrecy, and to this day the patient is not aware that he was made the subject of an experiment in psycho-therapeutics. After the lapse of a few months, one of the persons intrusted with the secret met the invalid, and learned, to her surprise and delight, that he was comparatively well. When asked when he began to improve, his reply was, "About the middle of May." Since then he has been able at all times to attend to the duties of his profession, — that of journalist and magazine-writer, — and has had no recurrence of his old trouble.

Of course, this may have been a coincidence; and had it stood as a solitary instance, that would have been the most rational way of accounting for it. But a hundred such coincidences do not happen in succession without a single break; and more than a hundred experiments have been made by this process by myself and two other persons, and not a single failure has thus far been experienced, where the proper conditions have been observed. In two cases the

patients have not been perceptibly benefited; but in both
of those they were notified of the intended experiments, and
were profoundly sceptical. But these failures cannot be
charged to the account of this method of treatment, for the
simple reason that the fundamental principle of the system
was deliberately violated. That is to say, the best conditions were not observed, — in that the patient was informed
beforehand of what was intended. In such cases the healer
is handicapped by probable adverse auto-suggestion, as has
been fully explained in former chapters. The principle cannot be too strongly enforced that neither the patient nor
any of his immediate family should ever be informed beforehand of the intended experiment. Failure does not
necessarily follow the imparting of such information; but
when the patient or his immediate friends are aware of the
effort being made in his behalf, there is always danger of
adverse auto-suggestion on the part of the patient, or of
adverse suggestion being made orally or telepathically by
his sceptical friends. The conditions are then no better
and no worse than the conditions ordinarily encountered by
those who employ other methods of mental healing. I have
successfully treated patients after informing them of my in-
tentions; but it was because I first succeeded in impressing them favorably, and their mental environment was not
antagonistic.

One fact of peculiar significance connected with the case
of rheumatism above mentioned must not be omitted; and
this is that the patient was a thousand miles distant when
the cure was performed. Others have been successfully
treated at distances varying from one to three hundred
miles. The truth is, as has been before remarked, space
does not seem to exist for the subjective mind. Experimental telepathy demonstrates this fact. Cases of thought-
transference are recorded where the percipient was at the
antipodes. The only thing that operates to prevent successful telepathy between persons at great distances from
each other is our habit of thinking. We are accustomed
to regard space as an obstacle which necessarily prevents

successful communication between persons. It is difficult
to realize that space is merely a mode of objective thought,
so to speak, and that it does not exist as an obstacle in the
way of subjective transmission of impressions. We are,
therefore, handicapped by a want of faith in our ability in
that direction. In other words, our faith is in inverse proportion to the distance involved. When we can once realize the fact that distance does not exist for the soul, we
shall find that a patient can be treated as successfully by
telepathic suggestion in one part of the world as another.
The only exception to the rule will be when the patient
is at the antipodes; for then the healer and the patient
will not ordinarily both be asleep at the same time. But
space, or distance between the agent and the percipient,
does not enter *per se* as an adverse element to modify the
effects of telepathic suggestion.

The diseases thus far successfully treated by this process
have been rheumatism, neuralgia, dyspepsia, bowel com-
plaint, sick headache, torpidity of the liver, chronic bron-
chitis, partial paralysis, pen paralysis, and strabismus. The
last-named case was not treated by myself, and I very
seriously doubt whether I could have commanded sufficient
confidence to be successful. But a lady, whom I had instructed in the process, asked me if I thought there was any
use in her trying to cure a bad case of strabismus, her little
niece, about ten years of age, having been thus afflicted
from her birth. I unhesitatingly assured her that there
was no doubt of her ability to effect a cure. Full of confidence, she commenced the treatment, and kept it up for
about three months, at the end of which time the cure was
complete. In this case the best conditions were rigidly
adhered to, no one but myself having been informed of
the intended experiment. A volume could be filled with
the details of the experiments which have been made; but
as it is foreign to the purpose of this book to treat exhaus-
tively any one phase of psychological phenomena, but rather
to develop a working hypothesis applicable to all branches
of the subject, the foregoing must suffice.

Little need be said regarding the mode of operation, as it is apparent from what has been said that the method is as simple as it is effective. All that is required on the part of the operator is that he shall be possessed of an earnest desire to cure the patient; that he shall concentrate his mind, just before going to sleep, upon the work in hand, and direct his subjective mind to occupy itself during the night in conveying therapeutic suggestions to the patient. To that end the operator must accustom himself to the assumption that his subjective mind is a distinct entity; that it must be treated as such, and guided and directed in the work to be done. The work is possibly more effective if the operator knows the character of the disease with which the patient is afflicted, as he would then be able to give his directions more specifically. But much may be left to instinct, of which the subjective mind is the source. It seems reasonable to suppose, however, that if that instinct is educated by objective training it will be all the better. This is, however, a question which must be left for future experimental solution, not enough being now positively known to warrant a statement as to how far the healing power of the subjective mind is, or may be, modified by the objective knowledge or training of the healer.

Be this as it may, the fact remains that all men possess the power to alleviate human suffering, to a greater or less degree, by the method developed in the foregoing pages. For obvious reasons it is not a method by which money can be made. But it is pre-eminently a means of laying up treasures where neither moth nor rust can corrupt, nor thieves break through and steal. Each one has it in his power to alleviate the sufferings of his neighbor, his friend, or the stranger within his gates; but his compensation must consist in the consciousness of doing good, and in the hope of that reward promised by the Master to those who do their alms in secret. There is, nevertheless, a practical and immediate reward accompanying every effort to heal the sick by the method herein indicated. In consists in this, — that every earnest effort to convey therapeutic impressions to a patient during sleep is inevitably followed by a dreamless sleep on the part of the healer. It would seem that the subjective mind, following the command or suggestions of the healer, occupies itself with the work it is directed to do, to the exclusion of all else; and hence the physical environment of the sleeper fails to produce peripheral impressions strong enough to cause the dreams which ordinarily result from such impressions. Following the universal law, it obeys the suggestions of the objective mind, and persists in following the line indicated until it is recalled by the awakening of the bodily senses.

Moreover, therapeutic suggestions imparted during sleep inevitably react favorably upon the healer; and thus his own health is promoted by the act which conduces to the health of the patient. And thus it is that therapeutic suggestion may be likened to the "quality of mercy" which "is not strained, it droppeth as the gentle rain from heaven upon the place beneath; it is twice blessed: it blesseth him that gives, and him that takes."

It is easy to foresee that when the world once understands and appreciates the wonderful therapeutic powers inherent in the human soul, a great change will be the result. When it is once understood that the power exists in every human organism to alleviate physical suffering by a method at once so simple, so effective, and so mutually beneficial, it cannot be doubted that a large proportion of the ills to which flesh is heir will exist only in history.

The most important branch of psycho-therapeutics is, however, yet to be discussed. It has been shown in this and former chapters that auto-suggestion plays its subtle *rôle* in every psychological experiment. It has been shown that the subjective mind of an individual is constantly controlled by the suggestion of his own objective mind. This is the normal relation of the two minds; and when that control ceases, the person is insane just in proportion to the degree in which the objective mind has abdicated its functions. This control is ordinarily exercised unconsciously to the individual. That is to say, we do not ordinarily recognize the operations of the two minds, for the simple reason that we do not stop to philosophize upon the subject of their mutual relations. But when we once recognize the fact, we have not only arrived at the principle which lies at the foundation of all true psychological science, but we are prepared to accept the subsidiary proposition which underlies the science of mental self-healing. That proposition is, that man can control by suggestion the operations of his own subjective mind, even though the suggestion be in direct contravention to his own objective belief. This is unqualifiedly true, even though the suggestion may be contrary to reason, experience, or the evidence of the senses. A moment's reflection will convince any one of the truth of this proposition. It is auto-suggestion that fills our asylums with monomaniacs. That long-continued and persistent dwelling upon a single idea often results in chronic hallucination, is a fact within the knowledge of every student of mental science. That it often happens that a monomaniac identifies himself with some great personage, even with the Deity, is a fact within common knowledge. What gives rise to such hallucinations is not so well known ; but every student of the pathology of insanity will verify the statement that auto-suggestion is the primary factor in every case. The patient, who is usually a monumental egotist to start with, begins by imagining himself to be a great man ; and by long-continued dwelling upon the one thought he ends by identifying himself with some great historical character whom he specially admires. If he is afflicted with some nervous disorder which causes him to pass easily and habitually into the subjective condition, the process of fastening the hallucination upon his mind is easy and rapid, and he is soon a fit subject for a lunatic asylum. But, whatever physical condition may be a necessary factor in producing such hallucinations, the fact remains that auto-suggestion is the primary cause.

The subject is introduced here merely to illustrate the power and potency of auto-suggestion, even when the suggestion is against the evidence of reason and sense. It must not be forgotten that an auto-suggestion which produces a hallucination such as has been described, operates on the lines of strongest resistance in nature. If, therefore, such results can be produced when opposed by the strongest instincts of our nature, how much easier must it be to produce equally wonderful results when operating in harmony with those instincts, and, hence, on the lines of least resistance.

It is self-evident, therefore, that auto-suggestion can be employed to great advantage for therapeutic purposes. Indeed, the power of self-help is the most important part of mental therapeutics. Without it the science is of comparatively little value or benefit to mankind. With it goes the power to resist disease, — to prevent sickness, as well as to cure it. The old axiom, that "an ounce of prevention is worth a pound of cure," holds good in psycho-therapeutics as well as in material remedies, and he who obtains the power to hold himself in the mental attitude which enables him to resist the encroachments of disease has mastered the great secret of mental medicine. That it can be done by any one of ordinary intelligence, is a fact which has been demonstrated beyond question. The best workers in the field of Christian science give more attention to teaching their pupils and patients how to help themselves than they do to instructing them how to help others. And this is the secret of the permanence of their cures, as has been fully explained in other chapters of this book. The process by which it can be done is as simple as are the laws which govern the subject-matter.

The patient should bear in mind the fundamental principles which lie at the foundation of mental therapeutics, —

1. The subjective mind exercises complete control over the functions and sensations of the body.

2. The subjective mind is constantly amenable to control by the suggestions of the objective mind.

3. These two propositions being true, the conclusion is obvious, that the functions and sensations of the body can be controlled by suggestions of the objective mind.

The whole science of psycho-therapeutics is embraced in
the foregoing propositions. They contain all that a patient,
who undertakes to heal himself or to ward off the encroachments of disease, needs to know. The process of making
a particular application of these principles is equally simple,
and must be obvious to the intelligent reader. At the risk
of repetition, a few general directions will be given.

We will take, for illustration, a simple case of nervous
headache, and suppose that the patient resolves to cure
himself. He must, first of all, remember that the subjective mind is to be treated precisely as though it were a
separate and distinct entity. The suggestion must first be
made that the headache is about to cease; then, that it is
already ceasing; and, finally, that it has ceased. These
suggestions should be made in the form of spoken words,
and they should be steadily persisted in until the desired
effect is produced. A constant reiteration of the declaration that the head is better will inevitably produce the
desired result; and, when the effect is distinctly felt, the
declaration should be boldly made that the pain has entirely ceased. If any remnants of the pain are felt, the fact
should be ignored, and the suggestion persisted in that it
has ceased. This should be followed by the declaration
that there will be no return of the symptoms; and this
should be made with an air, tone, and feeling of perfect
confidence.

The only practical difficulty and obstacle in the way of
success with a beginner lies in the fact that at first he lacks
confidence. The education of his whole life has been such
as to cause him to look with distrust upon any but material
remedies, and there is a disinclination to persist in his
efforts. But he should remember that it is the suggestions
conveyed by this very education that he is now called upon
to combat, neutralize, and overcome by a stronger and more
emphatic counter-suggestion. If he has the strength of
will to persist until he is cured, he will find that the next
time he tries it there will be much less resistance to overcome. Having once triumphed, the reasoning of his

objective mind no longer interposes itself as an obstruction, but concurs in the truth of his suggestions. He then possesses both objective and subjective faith in his powers, and he finds himself operating on a line of no resistance whatever. When he has attained this point, the rest is easy ; and he will eventually be able to effect an instantaneous cure of his headache, or any other pain, the moment he finds himself threatened with one. These remarks apply, of course, to every disease amenable to control by mental processes.

It will be observed that in the process of applying the principles of auto-suggestion to the cure of disease the patient is not called upon to tax his own credulity by any assertion that is not a demonstrable scientific truth. He is not called upon to deny the existence of matter, nor does he find it necessary to deny the reality of the disease which affects him. In short, he is not called upon to deny the evidence of his senses, to assert a manifest impossibility, nor to maintain an exasperating absurdity as a condition precedent to his recovery. The fact that cures can be made and are constantly being made by those who instruct their patients that a denial of the existence of matter and of the reality of disease is a necessary condition to their recovery, is the strongest possible evidence of the truth of the proposition that the subjective mind is constantly amenable to control by the power of suggestion. For it is a fundamental truth in psycho-therapeutics that no cure ever was, or ever can be, effected by mental processes until the subjective mind of the patient is impressed with a belief in the efficacy of the means employed. It is obvious, however, that it is more difficult to impress a manifest absurdity upon the subjective mind of a man of common-sense than it is to impress him with a belief in a demonstrable scientific truth. Hence it is that, by methods now in vogue, both healer and patient are handicapped just in proportion to the tax laid upon their credulity. The point is, that in impressing a patient with a new scientific truth we should seek to make it as simple as possible, and avoid anything which will shock his common-sense. Christ enjoined upon his followers the simple scientific fact that faith on their part was a condition precedent to their reception of the benefits of his healing power; and he compelled them to believe, by publicly demonstrating that power. He would have had little success among the people with whom he had to deal if he had begun his treatment by telling them that they had no disease; that leprosy is a figment of the imagination, and has no existence except in the mind; or that blindness is merely blindness of the mind, and not of the body; and that the body itself has no existence except as a form of belief. He even resorted to material remedies, as in the case of the blind man, when "He spat on the ground, and made clay of the spittle, and he anointed the eyes of the blind man with the clay, and said unto him, Go, wash in the Pool of Siloam. He went his way therefore, and washed, and came seeing."[1]

The Christian scientist would doubtless say that the clay and the subsequent washing in the Pool of Siloam did no good, except as they acted through the mind. This may be true; but in either case it teaches a valuable lesson, which it would be well for all classes of mental healers to remember. If the clay had a curative effect, it shows that the Master did not disdain to employ material remedies as an auxiliary to his healing power. If, on the other hand, it possessed no curative power, it shows that the Great Healer did not hesitate to employ any legitimate means at hand to confirm and increase the faith of the patient.

But this is a digression which pertains rather to the general subject of mental healing than to that of self-healing, which we are discussing. It is believed that the few simple rules herein laid down will enable any one of ordinary intelligence to become proficient, by a little practice, in the science of self-healing. It is not a mere theory, without practice, which has been here developed. It has been demonstrated over and over again to be eminently practical, not only as a means of healing disease, but as a means of

---

[1] John ix. 6.

warding off its encroachments. Indeed, its chief value will eventually be found to consist in the almost unlimited power which it gives one to protect himself from contracting disease. To do that it is only necessary to hold one's self in the mental attitude of denying the power of disease to obtain the mastery over him. When the patient recognizes the first symptoms of approaching illness, he should at once commence a vigorous course of therapeutic autosuggestion. He will find prevention much easier than cure; and by persistently following such a course he will soon discover that he possesses a perfect mastery over his own health. In this connection it must not be forgotten that the method of healing during sleep is as applicable to self-healing as it is to healing others. Indeed, perfect rest and recuperative slumber can be obtained under almost any circumstances at the word of command. Dreams can be controlled in this way. If one is troubled by distressing or harassing dreams, from whatever cause, he can change their current, or prevent them altogether, by energetically commanding his subjective mind to do so. It is especially efficacious for this purpose to direct his subjective mind to employ itself in healing some sick friend. If one habitually does this at the time of going to sleep, he will not only be certain to obtain recuperative sleep for himself, but he will procure that contentment and peace of mind which always result from a consciousness of doing good to his fellow-creatures. The exercise of the power to heal in this way is never a tax upon the vital energies of the healer, but always redounds to his own benefit as well as to that of the patient. The reason of this is obvious. The normal condition of the subjective mind during the sleep of the body and the quiescence of the objective faculties is that of constant activity. This activity, under ordinary conditions, entails no loss of vital power on the part of the sleeper. On the contrary, that is the period of his rest and the means of his recuperation. If the activities of his subjective mind are directed into pleasant channels, his bodily rest is perfect, and his recuperation complete.

It is for this reason that the method of healing during sleep is better for all concerned than any other system of mental healing yet discovered. It follows the lines of nature, in that it employs the subjective powers at a time when they are normally active; and it employs them in such a way that the ordinary peripheral impressions, which often disturb the sleeper and produce unpleasant dreams, are overcome by a more potent suggestion. Any other method of mental healing, where the subjective powers of the healer are called into action, entails a certain loss of vital power on his part, for the simple reason that subjective activity during waking moments is abnormal. It is true that when the work is not carried to excess the physical exhaustion may not be perceptible; but any Christian scientist will testify that any great amount of effort in the line of his work produces great physical exhaustion. And it is noticeable that this exhaustion ensues in exact proportion to the success of his treatment. This success being in proportion to the subjective power exerted, it is reasonable to infer that subjective activity during waking hours and physical exhaustion bear to each other the relation of cause and effect.

CHAPTER XV.

THE PHENOMENA OF SPIRITISM.

If a Man die, shall he live again? — The Problem not solved by Spiritistic Phenomena. — The Phenomena admitted. — Their Supernatural Origin denied. — Explained by the Hypothesis. — Subsidiary Hypothesis. — An Intelligent Dynamic Force. — Its Characteristics. — Limited by Medium's Intelligence. — It is controlled by Suggestion. — Phenomena fail in Presence of Scepticism. — Reasons. — Mediumistic Frauds. — The Primary Lesson in Spiritistic Investigation. — Mediums not necessarily dishonest. — Their Honest Belief in the Phenomena. — Suggestion explains all. — Illustrations from Hypnotism. — Convincing Character of Alleged Communications. — Telepathic Explanations. — General Conclusions.

THE next subject which claims our attention in connection with the hypothesis under consideration is that of modern spiritism. It is approached with much diffidence and some misgivings, not because of any doubt as to the applicability of the hypothesis to the vast range of so-called spiritual phenomena, but because of the transcendent interest and importance of the subject to all mankind. It cannot be forgotten that millions of human beings base their hopes of a life beyond the grave upon their belief that in the phenomena of spiritism they have tangible evidence of the immortality of the soul, and that by means of such phenomena they can be put into communication with the spirits of the loved ones who have gone before. The fact cannot be ignored that there are millions of stricken hearts whose wounds have been healed by the consolation afforded by that conviction. The great question, "If a man die, shall he live again?" has been by these phenomena satisfactorily answered for many whom revealed religion failed to satisfy, for many whose reasoning powers have failed to grasp the logic of the theologian. It were an unwelcome task to throw a shade of doubt upon the validity of evidence which to many seems to be " confirmation strong as proofs of Holy Writ; " and if in the perusal of the following pages such doubt arises, the reader is begged to discriminate between the question of the validity of evidence and the question of fact. For, be it remembered, I shall not undertake to prove that the souls of men do not live after the death of the body. That question stands just where it has always stood. It is a problem which, outside of revelation, is no nearer a solution than it was when Job propounded the momentous question. Neither will I undertake to say that the spirits of the dead do not and cannot communicate with the living. I do not know. But I do undertake to say, and will attempt to prove, that the phenomena of spiritism, so-called, do not constitute valid evidence of the ability of spirits of the dead to hold intercourse with the living. In doing so, no attempt will be made to deny the phenomena of spiritism. On the contrary, I shall not only admit the possibility of every phenomenon alleged by any respectable number of reputable witnesses to have occurred, but I shall also assume the substantial accuracy of the general statements made by spiritists regarding the leading phenomena of spiritism. But I shall attempt to explain their origin on other grounds than the supposition that they are caused by the spirits of the dead. In other words, I admit the alleged phenomena, but deny the alleged cause.

I will not waste time, however, by attempting to prove by experiments of my own, or of others, that such phenomena do occur. It is too late for that. The facts are too well known to the civilized world to require proofs at this time. The man who denies the phenomena of spiritism to-day is not entitled to be called a sceptic, he is simply ignorant ; and it would be a hopeless task to attempt to enlighten him. I shall indulge in the hope, however, that by explaining the origin of the phenomena on rational principles, and thus removing them from the realm of the supernatural, those who now assume to be sceptical may be induced to investigate for themselves. It is easy to deny the existence of that for which we cannot account by reference to known laws, and it is easy to believe in that which can be thus explained. This is especially true in regard to phenomena which are popularly attributed to a supernatural origin. Modern scientists have an easy way of treating such phenomena, which consists in denying their existence and refusing to investigate. Such men would plug their own ears and deny the phenomenon of thunder if they could not account for it by reference to laws with which they are familiar. And such a proceeding would be no more senseless than, at this day, to deny the phenomena of spiritism.

In justice, however, to those scientists who have sought to investigate the subject, and have failed to witness the phenomena promised, it must be said that in many instances their failure is attributable, not to any fault of their own, or lack of earnest purpose on their part, but to a want of knowledge of the fundamental laws which pertain to the production of such phenomena. The reasons for the frequent failure to produce psychic phenomena in presence of avowed sceptics has been fully discussed in a previous chapter of this book, to which the reader is referred. But at the risk of repetition they will be restated in their proper place in this chapter, as they pertain to the subject of so-called spirit phenomena.

The laws which govern the production of the phenomena under consideration are precisely the same as those which pertain to all the other phenomena which have been discussed ; and the fundamental propositions of our hypothesis apply with equal force to them all. Again, the reader is asked to recall those propositions, in order that their force and logical sequence may remain clear to his mind in this connection. They are : —

1. The mind of man is dual in its nature, — objective and subjective.

2. The subjective mind is constantly controlled by suggestion.

These two propositions would seem to have been so well established as to need no further elucidation at this time. The subsidiary proposition, which applies to the phenomena under consideration, is that, —

3. The subjective mind, or entity, possesses physical power; that is, the power to make itself heard and felt, and to move ponderable objects.

This may seem at first glance to be begging the question; but its truth must be assumed provisionally, for the sake of the argument which follows. It will readily be seen that if those three propositions can be established, all the physical phenomena of spiritism can be accounted for on the ground that living man possesses inherently the power to produce them. And this is the position which we must assume, for it appears to be the truth.

It must be acknowledged by all who have witnessed, under test conditions, any of the physical phenomena, that there is a dynamic force residing somewhere that is capable of moving ponderable objects without physical contact, and that this force, whatever it is, or from whatever source it emanates, possesses intelligence, oftentimes to a remarkable degree. Now, this intelligent force either emanates from the spirits of the dead, or it does not. If it does not, it necessarily follows that it emanates from the living. That this last supposition is the true one is evidenced by many of the characteristics of the intelligence which it manifests, among which the following are prominent : —

It is essentially a human intelligence, and neither rises above nor sinks below the ordinary intelligence of humanity.

The intelligence is always on a level with that of the medium through whom it manifests itself. That is, it never rises so far above that of the medium as to preclude the possibility of its having its origin in the medium's subjective mind. That it often rises above the medium's known objective intelligence, is well known and admitted. But we have already seen what remarkable powers the subjective mind possesses in certain lines of intellectual activity, and with what limitations it is hedged about; and we find that the intellectual feats of mediums possess all the characteristics belonging to subjective intelligence, — the same wonderful powers, and the same limitations. That so-called spirit communications always correspond to the nature of the medium's mind and character, and are limited by his capacity, is admitted by all the ablest writers on spiritism; and their greatest ingenuity is taxed to account for the fact. Alleged communications from the greatest philosophers who have gone before, amount to the merest twaddle when filtered through an ignorant medium.

Again, we find that the intelligence is controllable by the power of suggestion. This is shown in the readiness with which "spirits" can be made to respond to calls made upon them, whether they have any real existence or not. It is well known that any one can as readily obtain a communication from an imaginary person as from a real one, from a living person as from the dead, providing the medium does not happen to know the facts. The writer has had frequent and very affectionate communications from an imaginary dead sister, and has occasionally had a very touching communication from himself, the medium believing the name to represent a dead brother. The fact that he never had either brother or sister made the communication all the more convincing.

This perfect amenability to control by suggestion is evinced in another most remarkable way. It is well known to every person who has been in the habit of attending spiritual séances how necessary it is that "harmonious conditions" should prevail. The very presence of an avowed sceptic will often prevent any manifestations. It frequently happens that some one present remarks, in a despairing tone, that he does not expect any manifestations, "because it always happens that when I am present no communications can be had." When such a remark is made, the chances are ten to one that the "spirits" will refuse to respond. Why this happens, spiritists have laboriously attempted to explain, but never satisfactorily, except to themselves. The fact that a spirit, possessing sufficient power to move a table, raise a piano to the ceiling, or levitate the medium, should be paralyzed in presence of one who does not believe in spirits, is simply inexplicable, except upon the one hypothesis, namely, that the power evoked is that of the subjective mind of the medium, which is amenable to control by the mysterious power of suggestion. It is inconceivable that the spirit of Napoleon Bonaparte, who, when living, swayed the destinies of nations, used kings and popes as his puppets, and led his hosts to successful battle against the combined armies of Europe, should, when dead, shrink, abashed and powerless, in presence of some one man who happens not to believe in spiritism. But it can be readily understood how a séance should prove a failure when we assume that the power that moves the table or writes the communications is exercised by the subjective intelligence of the medium, and that the presence of an avowed sceptic operates as an ever-present and all-potent suggestion that the promised manifestations are impossible in his presence. It is in strict accordance with the universal law of suggestion that such should be the result. It is this constant amenability to control by suggestion which always hampers mediums when they are giving test séances in the presence of sceptical investigators ; and I undertake to say that no medium ever was, or ever can be, powerful enough to produce his phenomena under test conditions in presence of a hostile and aggressively sceptical investigating committee. It is no fault of the medium that this is the case, and it is no test whatever of the genuineness of his phenomena. But it is presumptive, if not conclusive, evidence that the source of his phenomena resides within himself, and hence is amenable to the universal law which governs the action of all subjective intelligence and power. Neither is it any reflection upon the sincerity of the investigator that he fails to witness the phenomena that have been promised. His ignorance of the law which governs the subject-matter, together with his desire to be frank and honest enough with the medium to put him in possession of a knowledge of his sentiments and prejudices, leads him unwittingly to place an insuperable barrier in the way of success. It unfortunately happens that many professional mediums, despairing of success in producing the genuine phenomena, and more than ordinarily anxious to earn the reward of success, will, under such circumstances, resort to fraud and legerdemain. The temptation to do so is great when he reflects upon how much is at stake, the immediate monetary reward promised being the least consideration. His professional pride, his love of approbation, his hope of future fame and emolument in case he succeeds in convincing a sceptical scientific investigator, — all operate to constitute a temptation too great to be always successfully withstood. Besides, he knows that, under favorable conditions, he can produce the genuine phenomena, that he has produced them again and again, and he quiets his conscience by reflecting that it can do no harm to resort to legerdemain to simulate that which he knows to have a genuine existence.

In this connection it may be well to state what must already be obvious to the intelligent reader ; namely, that the only way to secure the production of genuine phenomena is, first, to secure the confidence of the medium by assuming to be in hearty sympathy with him, and by giving him to understand that you thoroughly believe in his honesty and his power to produce genuine phenomena. Give him all the time he wants, and assure him that you are in no hurry ; remembering always that quiet passivity and undisturbed serenity of mind on the part of a medium is an indispensable prerequisite to success, not only in producing the phenomena, but in entering the subjective condition. It is precisely the same in this respect as it is in hypnotism. The condition of the medium, when in a trance or partial trance, is precisely the condition of a hypnotized person, and he is subject to the same laws, and the same conditions are necessary and indispensable to his success. Every hypnotist knows that it would be madness to antagonize a hypnotic subject by suggesting to him in advance that he is an impostor, or that hypnotic phenomena are mere humbug, and then expect to hypnotize him and produce the phenomena. When investigators realize this one fact they will have taken the primary lesson in spiritistic investigation. Every one who understands the first principles of hypnotism knows what folly it would be to subject the science to the test of allowing a sceptical investigator to take a subject in hand and begin the operation of trying to hypnotize him by assuring him that hypnotism is imposture, and all subjects are mere pretenders. And yet one who investigates hypnotism in that way does, in effect, precisely what the sceptical investigator of spiritistic phenomena does when he avows his scepticism to the medium in advance. If investigators would observe the rule here suggested, and always endeavor to put the medium at his ease and accede to all the conditions prescribed by him, instead of insisting upon test conditions of their own devising, they would soon find that they would witness all the phenomena desired, and under conditions that preclude the possibility of fraud or legerdemain. Any other course almost of necessity defeats the object sought.

It will be seen, therefore, that a failure to produce phenomena at a given time does not necessarily indicate fraud on the part of the medium; and in strict justice to professional mediums, who as a class have been brought into disrepute by the fraudulent practices of some of their number, it must be said that the detection of a medium in fraudulent practices does not *per se* prove that he was consciously guilty; for it is an undoubted fact that when a medium is unconscious, and his subjective mind is in control, it often acts capriciously, and presumably fraudulent practices might be indulged in without the objective knowledge or consent of the medium. Therefore, until the laws governing the subject-matter are better understood, we should extend the broadest charity over the professional medium, except in cases where it is discovered that the paraphernalia necessary for the perpetration of fraud have been prepared by the medium in advance.

At this point the question will naturally be asked, " How can a medium, professional or otherwise, be entitled to credit for honesty, who represents himself as being able to hold communion with the spirits of the dead, or to be an instrument through which communications from spirits of the dead can be obtained, if, in point of fact, such communications have their origin wholly within his own personality? "

This is perhaps the most pertinent and the most far-reaching question that could be formulated in regard to the hypothesis under consideration. If it could not be fairly answered from a purely scientific standpoint, our hypothesis would not be worthy of further discussion ; for it is simply impossible to presuppose that all the immense number of mediums, professional and private, who may be found in all ranks of society throughout the civilized world, are deliberately and consciously perpetrating a fraud upon mankind. On the contrary, I here take occasion to say that there is no system of religious belief which is so thoroughly fortified by facts as that of spiritism, when its phenomena are viewed from the standpoint of the investigator who is unacquainted with the latest scientific discoveries in the domain of experimental psychology. But with that knowledge in possession, the evidential value of the phenomena of spiritism is vastly depreciated, and the high character of the medium for truth and sincerity loses all its weight as a factor in the case.

The intelligent reader has already anticipated the answer to the foregoing question. It is simply this : that the subjective mind of the medium, being controlled by suggestion, believes itself to be the spirit of any deceased person whose name is suggested. It has been educated to that belief through the objective education and environment of the individual. It is, by the laws of its being, absolutely controlled by the objective belief of the medium, and the suggestions embraced in that belief. It is true that it often acts capriciously and independently, but it is always in pursuance of the auto-suggestion or belief of the medium that it is an extraneous and, therefore, an independent power.

No one who has witnessed even the stage exhibitions of the phenomena of hypnotism will doubt the substantial truth of this proposition. An intelligent subject can be made to assume any number of characters, diverse as the antipodes, and in each one he will imitate the original in thought, word, and action with perfect fidelity, so far as he knows the character, habits, and idiosyncrasies of the individual personated, firmly believing himself to be the individual he represents. He may, with the same facility, be transformed into an angel or a devil or an animal; and he will never doubt the truth of the suggestion, or fail to act the character suggested, so far as it is physically possible. These facts are well known to all hypnotists, as well as to all who witness the common stage exhibitions of the phenomena. Some stage hypnotists have much difficulty in preventing their subjects from exhibiting spiritistic phenomena on the platform. This was a common experience of Professor Cadwell, an American performer, who was himself a spiritist. When it became known to his audiences and subjects that the latter were liable to be "controlled by spirits," the trouble became very marked, and the professor was greatly annoyed by the frequency with which his subjects were seized upon by "passing spirits," and made to receive communications and perform other antics in the name of the spirits of their dead acquaintances. The phenomena exhibited through these subjects were identical with those shown through ordinary mediums, and indeed some of his best subjects afterwards became successful professional mediums. That the liability of the professor's subjects to lapse into mediumship was the result of suggestion is shown by the fact that Professor Carpenter, who was Cadwell's pupil, and operated by his methods, and was in every sense his peer as an operator, never had any trouble with mediumistic phenomena, for the simple reason that he was careful to avoid suggesting the idea to his subjects that such a thing was possible. In point of fact it is well known to many hypnotists that all the phenomena of spiritism can be reproduced through their subjects by simply suggesting to them that they are under the control of spirits. Of course it may be said that the spirits do actually take possession of a hypnotic subject when permitted to do so, and that it is the genuine control of spirits after all. The answer to this is that it is also just as easy to obtain communications from a living person through a hypnotic subject as from a dead one, and from an imaginary person as from a real one, by merely making the proper suggestion. The same is true of any medium, for that matter, as will presently be shown.

It is obvious, therefore, that the universal law of suggestion operates upon the subjective mind of a medium with the same force and certainty as upon all others. He is in the subjective, or hypnotic, condition. The suggestion that he is about to be controlled by the spirits of the dead is ever present to his mind, and is all potent. It is a part of his education. It is his religious belief. No other explanation of the mysterious phenomena is known to him. He knows only that he is moved by a power, an intelligence, over which he exerts no conscious control. It gives utterance to thoughts beyond his comprehension, and possesses knowledge of matters of which he consciously knows nothing. His conclusion is, first that the intelligence is something extraneous to his personality, and secondly that it must be that of an inhabitant of another world. From his standpoint it is the only rational conclusion. His hereditary belief in the immortality of the soul confirms it. His reading of the Bible sanctions the belief in the power of spirits to hold communion with the living. His hope of a life beyond the grave, and his longing to hold communion with the loved and lost, combine to give his conclusions a welcome reception in the chambers of his mind.

A more potent suggestion was never forced upon the subjective mind of man than this; and in obedience to the universal law, it must be believed by the medium's subjective mind, and acted upon accordingly. And the subjective mind *does* believe the suggestion most implicitly. If it did

not, the law of suggestion would have no place in experimental psychology, and all the conclusions deducible therefrom would have to be revised. So believing, it follows that,
when questioned, it will unhesitatingly affirm that it is the
spirit of whatever person is suggested; and so far as the
medium knows the character or antecedents of the spirit
invoked, that spirit will be personated with all the preternatural acumen characteristic of subjective mental
activity.

If the chain of reasoning by which the medium and his
friends have arrived at the conclusion that the phenomena
must proceed from disembodied spirits seems to them to be
perfect, their conviction rises to the dignity of a certainty,
in their estimation, when the supposed spirit begins to forward alleged communications from the hypothetical border-
land of another world. They find that his alleged "control"
is able to tell them secrets which they supposed to be safe
in their own custody, or perhaps only known to themselves
and the deceased whose spirit has been invoked. He will
describe the character and personal appearance of deceased
persons whom it was impossible that he should have known
in life, sometimes even giving their names and ages; he will
tell of incidents in their career known only to the person
for whose benefit the communication is given.

If the sitter is sceptical, and has learned something of
telepathy, his ready objection is that all this is "mind-
reading." But presently the medium will describe some
one of whom the sitter has not thought for years, who was
utterly unknown to the medium, and of whom he never
heard. It is then that the sitter is confounded. His telepathic explanation is exploded, for he "was not thinking
of the deceased at all; it could not, therefore, be mind-
reading," he declares, with all the enthusiasm of a new
convert whose last objection has been answered.

There is no more common or popular explanation of certain phases of spiritistic phenomena than attributing them
to mind-reading. When a medium relates to you incidents
of your life of which you know he has no previous knowl-

edge, the most obvious explanation is that he reads your mind, — that is, if you do not believe that he is controlled by spirits ; and you are undoubtedly right. But when he tells you of things that you had forgotten, and describes persons of whom you are not thinking, you jump to the conclusion that thought-reading does not explain that particular phenomenon. And it is just here that you make a mistake, for the reason that you do not understand the first principles of mind-reading. But when it is once understood that mind-reading is the communion of two subjective minds, and that the objective or conscious thoughts of the sitter have no necessary effect upon the character of the communications, it will be seen that the fact that the sitter was not consciously thinking of the person described, or had forgotten the incident recalled, has no evidential value whatever. The sitter may or may not be thinking consciously of the subject of the communication ; he may even be endeavoring to cause the medium to speak of some particular one with whom he earnestly desires to communicate. It makes no difference whatever, for it is the uppermost thought of the subjective mind that is read, and of that the sitter has neither knowledge nor conscious control. That the medium relates incidents of the sitter's life which he had forgotten until reminded of them, is not at all strange or unaccountable, when we remember that the memory of the subjective mind is perfect. Neither is there any evidential value in the fact that the sitter cannot remember an incident related by the medium ; for he must remember that objective memory retains little, comparatively, of the incidents of life, while the subjective mind retains all.

It will thus be seen that in order to explain the phenomena of spiritism on the hypothesis that it has its origin wholly within the sub-conscious mind of the medium, it is not necessary to presuppose that he is dishonest or insincere when he attributes it to disembodied spirits. In the absence of knowledge on his part of the recent discoveries in psychological science, he has the best of reasons for so believing, for up to the present time no other hypothesis has been advanced which will account for all the phenomena on any other rational supposition. But the two great laws — duality of mind and suggestion — clear away the greatest stumbling-block in the way of scientific investigation of this, the greatest problem of the ages. It is now no longer necessary to deny the phenomena, since they can all be accounted for on scientific principles, outside the domain of the supernatural. It is no longer necessary to consider the spiritual medium either a fool or an impostor, since the phenomena are genuine, and their explanation on scientific principles is impossible, except in the light of very recent discoveries in psychic science.

Having set forth the fundamental principles underlying the production of so-called spirit phenomena, we will now proceed briefly to examine their various phases and leading characteristics, and to show how the hypothesis under consideration applies to each of them with the same force and pertinency as in the case of the other psychic phenomena which have been considered.

CHAPTER XVI.

THE PHENOMENA OF SPIRITISM (*continued*).

THERE are several ways by which the operations of the subjective mind can be brought above the threshold of consciousness. When this is done by any one of the various methods, a phenomenon is produced. Each of these phenomena has been, at some time in the history of mankind, attributed to the agency of disembodied spirits.

The leading phenomena above alluded to are clairvoyance, clairaudience, telepathy, mesmerism, or hypnotism, automatic writing, percussive sounds (spirit-rapping), movement of ponderable bodies (table-tipping), and phantasmic appearances.

Of these, clairvoyance, telepathy, and hypnotism have generally ceased to be regarded as proceeding from supernatural agencies. They are now recognized as powers inherent in mankind, and, as will be seen, are largely employed to explain other phenomena.

. Of clairvoyance little will be said, for the reason that it is still an open question among scientists who have been, and are still, investigating the subject, whether independent clairvoyance exists as a power of the human mind. Sufficient evidence has not been brought to my attention to demonstrate its existence. Certainly the great bulk of phenomena which are popularly regarded as evincing clairvoyant power must now be referred to telepathy. It must be said, however, that many phenomena have been produced which cannot at present be accounted for on any other hypothesis than that of independent clairvoyance. Yet it is not impossible that, when the laws of telepathy are better understood, all so-called clairvoyant phenomena may be referred to that agency. For the purposes of our argument, however, it is not specially important that the distinction should be clearly drawn between the two, inasmuch as telepathy, which is an undoubted power of the subjective mind, sufficiently explains all the so-called spiritistic phenomena involving the perception by the medium of facts not within his own experience or his previous knowledge. I will therefore first treat of those phenomena the mysteries of which are directly and primarily referable to telepathy.

A very simple experiment will enable almost any one to demonstrate telepathic power. Let a person be securely blindfolded, by taking a pair of kid gloves, folding them into pads, placing them over his eyes, and binding them on by means of a handkerchief. Then let a circle be formed by a few persons, with their hands joined, the percipient forming one of the circle. Let a card be selected at random from a pack, taking care that no one sees any other card of the pack, even for an instant, until the experiment is over. Then place the card in plain sight of all but the percipient, and let them fix their minds and gaze upon the card, and in silence await the result. In the mean time the percipient should be and remain in a perfectly passive and tranquil frame of mind, and simply watch for visions. He will soon begin to see indistinct objects floating in the darkness, and these objects will presently begin to form themselves into shapes more distinct. They may be evanescent, and disappear at intervals; but they will soon return in still more definite form, and will eventually assume some shape that will suggest the card selected. It may be that a vision of the whole card will be presented, exactly as it is, or it may be that there will be a sort of allegorical representation of it. For instance, in an experiment tried in presence of the author the ten of diamonds had been selected. Instead of seeing a vision of the card, there was an appearance of ten real diamonds, arranged in rows corresponding to the rows of spots on the card, each one sending forth rays of light and scintillations of color. As it was the first experiment the percipient had ever tried, he was at a loss to know the meaning, if it had any, of the vision; but as it persisted in coming, he finally ventured to remark, hesitatingly, that he had an " impression of the ten of diamonds." The applause which followed told him that his subjective mind had conveyed to his consciousness by means of an allegorical vision the information it had telepathically received. It may here be remarked parenthetically that the subjective mind of man appears to be fond of allegory as a means of conveying its thoughts or information above the threshold of consciousness. The history of mankind is full of illustrations of this fact.

When the next card was selected, the percipient saw the vision of a single heart spot floating in the darkness, unattached to anything like a card; whereupon he ventured to name the ace of hearts, which was correct. In all, five cards were selected at this sitting, and each one was named correctly, with the exception of the last, which was the five of spades. The five of clubs was named; but the percipient explained his mistake by saying that one-half of each spot was concealed from his view, namely, the points of the spade spots, which appeared to be thrust into the darkness, so to speak, leaving only the handle end of the spades exposed to view. As that half of the spade spot corresponds exactly to the corresponding half of a club spot, the mistake was natural, and was really of as great, if not greater, evidential value than if the card had been correctly named.

Others of the company tried the same experiment, generally without physical contact with any one else, and each one was able to name some of the cards correctly. But no one was able to name correctly a card which was not seen by some one else, — which showed clearly that the power to see the card resulted from telepathy, and not from independent clairvoyance. It should be here stated that there were six in the company, each one of whom tried the experiment, and each scored a sufficient number of successes to remove the result from the domain of coincidence.

These experiments were as simple as could well be devised, and to the unreflecting mind may seem trifling. But I shall endeavor to show that they possess unmeasured significance.

Before proceeding to do so, it may be well to state that visions resulting from telepathic communion are as varied as is the character of the communicants or the subjects of the messages. They are often seen by the percipient as plainly as the objective reality could be seen; and events are depicted by means of visions that re-enact the scenes, with all the characters and actors represented, as perfectly as the reality itself.[1]

It now remains to show how this faculty of reading the minds of others is unconsciously employed by spirit mediums to impart to their clients information regarding persons and events of which the medium has no previous knowledge.

We will consider, for this purpose, the case of a medium who develops no physical phenomena, but who simply receives his visitor, tells him of the events of his past life, describes his spirit-friends, conveys oral communications from them, and occasionally drops into prophecy. The visitor may or may not be a professed believer in spirit-

---

[1] See "Phantasms of the Living," and the Proceedings of the London Society for Psychical Research, for full confirmation of this statement.

ism; but the fact that he is there to consult a medium shows a faith sufficient for the purpose in view, and propinquity places his subjective mind *en rapport* with that of the medium. We will suppose that this is the first time that the two have met, and that the medium is entirely unacquainted with the character, the antecedents, or the deceased friends of the sitter. The first thing that the medium does is to become wholly or partially self-hypnotized. He may go into the state only partially, and appear to the visitor to be in his normal condition. He may, and probably does, believe that his "control" takes possession of his body and talks through him; he has, as we have already seen, every reason for this belief. He is taken possession of by some unseen force, is guided by some unseen intelligence which possesses powers and attributes of which he is not conscious in his normal condition. He has no other hypothesis to account for the extraordinary manifestations of which that intelligence is the source. To make assurance doubly sure, the intelligence tells him that it is the spirit of some deceased person, and gives him a detailed and very plausible account of itself. He is forced to believe the statements of his subjective entity, for he knows no reason for believing otherwise, and it, in turn, is compelled by the laws of its being to believe itself to be what it represents; for the suggestion has been made to it that it is the spirit of a deceased person. That suggestion having been made in a general way, to begin with, his subjective mind will proceed to fill in the details in some way with marvellous acumen, and with such logical circumstantiality of detail as to deceive "the very elect." It is just as it is in the case of a hypnotized person, who, in pursuance of a post-hypnotic suggestion, having done some absurd act, when questioned as to why he did it, will, on the instant, invent some reason so plausible that the act will seem perfectly natural to one who does not know its origin.

Again, the subjective mind of the sitter is also controlled by a suggestion, more or less strong, that spirits of the dead are about to be invoked; and it is also ready with its logical deductions from the premises suggested, and will perform its part in the séance with the same alacrity and acumen. Here, then, we have two subjective minds *en rapport*, and the telepathic conditions for a successful séance are established. The shrewd and successful medium usually begins by making some very complimentary remarks concerning the character and mental attributes of the sitter. This puts the latter at his ease, and gives him an exalted opinion of the good sense and judgment of the medium. Some incidents of the sitter's life may then be related, and his occupation indicated. It will generally be done in terms such as indicate the fact that the medium obtains his impressions by means of visions. For instance, the writer once heard a medium in New York city describe the occupation of an examiner in the United States Patent Office. The two had never met before, and did not know of each other's existence ten minutes before the séance. Even the name of the sitter had been withheld from the medium, for the purpose of testing her telepathic powers, and for the further purpose of convincing one of those present that spirits of the dead had nothing to do with the manifestations. The members of the party introduced each other by fictitious names, and talked spiritism to the medium until " harmonious conditions " were established, when the séance began. " I see an immense building," she began, " with a great number of rooms in it. In one of these rooms I see you, seated at a large desk, with a great many papers upon it. I see drawings, apparently of machinery, spread out upon the desk before you. It seems to me that you must have something to do with patent rights." She was informed that her conjecture was thus far correct. It should here be remembered that a medium should always be encouraged by a frank acknowledgment when he is correct. It encourages him, puts him at his ease, and constitutes a suggestion that he is able to perceive the truth in reference to that particular person; and, consequently, helps him to proceed correctly with other manifestations.

" But," continued the lady, "this is not your only occupation. I see you in your library at home, surrounded
by books and manuscripts. You appear to be writing a
book."

She then went on to describe correctly all the bookcases
and other furniture in the room, and then said, —

" I see the pathway by which you have arrived at your
present conclusion in reference to the subject of your book.
It is all strewn with rubbish and weeds, all of which you
have thrown aside. But you see a great light ahead, and
are pursuing that with perfect confidence and steadiness of
purpose."

" Am I in the right path ? " inquired the examiner.

" I cannot tell, for I cannot perceive the subject on which
you are writing. I think you are, however, for the light ahead
seems so clear."

After a pause she added, —

" You are making one mistake. You think that you are
doing it all yourself. But you are not. You are constantly
guided by a great spirit."

" Who is he ? " was asked, with all the greater interest
because the gentleman *was* writing a book, and, like every
other author, felt that he had perceived " a great light ; "
moreover, if he was sure of anything connected with it, he
was sure that he was doing it himself, without the aid of any
spirit or spirits. " Give me the name of my spirit friend and
guide," he added.

" I cannot do that to-day," she replied, with the true com-
mercial instinct of the professional medium ; " come to-morrow, and I will try to give you the name."

Accordingly, the same party visited her the next day,
when she made every effort to obtain the name, but without
success. It should be stated here that the lady was a
slate-writing medium. Communication after communication was written, but without signature, and all efforts to
obtain the name were futile. Finally the gentleman said,
in an aside apparently not intended for the ears of the
medium, " I think I know who it is. It must be either

A B [naming a living friend in Washington], or my brother, C D [giving his own name]," for he had no brother, living or dead. Immediately a communication was written out, signed by the supposed spirit brother, announcing the fact that he, and he alone, was the inspiring power in charge of the literary work named, that he was the "guardian spirit" of the gentleman, over whom he was "constantly watching," etc.

The emotions created by the affecting terms of the communication can be imagined when it is stated that all present, save the medium, knew that the name was that of the sitter, and that he never had a brother. But these emotions quickly gave place to wonder and admiration when it was discovered that the signature was an almost exact reproduction of his own, with all its salient peculiarities faithfully reproduced.

Comment upon this wonderful admixture of genuine telepathic power and conscious or unconscious fraud will not be indulged in, save to remark that the first day's proceedings exhibited marvellous telepathic power under the most perfect test conditions. As to the second day's performance, it need only be said that if the communication had been from a genuine spirit, struggling in vain to remember his own name, it shows that even spirits are controlled by the subtle power of suggestion; for he had no hesitation in assuming the name of the sitter when that name was suggested, and he so completely identified himself with that person as to reproduce his signature with marvellous accuracy. It may be said that a fraud was perpetrated upon the medium. To this the plea of guilty must be entered, together with a plea of extenuating circumstances, in that it was done in pursuit of scientific truth. Whether the interests of truth were subserved, the reader must judge for himself. To that end he must ask himself the question whether it is not more probable that this manifestation was of the subjective entity of the medium rather than of an independent, disembodied spirit. Conceding the inherent power in mankind to convey and receive telepathic communications, it must be evident that telepathy is a sufficient explanation of what occurred the first day. It is true that the medium thought that the information thus obtained was conveyed to her by disembodied spirits. But that does not change the facts ; and when a phenomenon is explicable by reference to known natural laws, we have neither occasion nor logical right to seek an explanation in the realm of the supernatural. The second day's performance is as easily explicable under the well-known laws of hypnotism. The medium was in a partially hypnotic state, her subjective mind was active and in control of her physical powers, and was necessarily perfectly amenable to control by suggestion from any source. In obedience to the law of auto-suggestion, it believed itself to be a disembodied spirit. It acted in that capacity far enough to write communications of the standard, indefinite character common to such productions, but could give no name, for the simple reason that there was no name to give, and none had been suggested. But the instant a name was suggested it seized upon it, and, in pursuance of the suggestion that it represented the sitter's brother, wrote just such a communication as the logic of the situation dictated, believing, without a doubt, that it was actually the spirit of the deceased brother of the sitter. It may be asked why, if the medium was possessed of such wonderful telepathic power, did she not perceive the fact that she was being imposed upon, that the sitter was not sincere in his professions of a belief in spiritism, and that he had not a brother in the spirit-land. Simply because she was controlled by the universal law of suggestion, and the oral suggestions had been made that he was a believer, and that he had a brother deceased. If she had disbelieved the statement, it would have constituted an exception to the operation of a natural and universal law, — a suspension, in fact, of the laws of nature.

On the other hand, if we are to discard the foregoing explanation and hold that it was actually a disembodied spirit controlling the medium, we must presuppose a spirit without a name, or without sufficient intelligence to remember his name. Either supposition, if it does no violence to common-sense, is contrary to all the teachings of spiritists, who have led us to believe that the law of spirit-life is that of eternal progress; that all truth stands revealed to the perception of the disembodied soul. It would cause one to lose confidence in his guardian angels if he were forced to believe that a short residence in the spirit-land could reduce the immortal mind to such a state of imbecility.

This digression is indulged in for the purpose of illustrating the fact that one of the means by which telepathic impressions are conveyed from one to another is by visions. The percipient sees a vision representing the incident sought to be communicated by the agent. He sees the image of the object or person which the agent desires him to see. Thus, when a person consults a medium he generally expects and desires to learn something of his deceased friends. The medium goes into the subjective condition for that purpose. The visitor's mind is full of anticipation and hope that he will be put into direct communication with the loved and lost. Presently the medium sees a vision of some person. He believes that he sees a spirit. He describes it, and it is found to correspond with one of the visitor's deceased friends. The visitor recognizes the description, and says so. He asks for the name, and it is given. Then the medium sees a vision representing some incident known only to the visitor and the deceased. He describes the incident, not, perhaps, as a vision which he sees, but as a statement of fact imparted to him by the spirit. The visitor very likely knows that the medium knew nothing of him or of the deceased before that hour. He is convinced that the medium has seen and conversed with the spirit of his dead friend, and he is a convert to spiritism from that moment. Now, has the medium actually seen a spirit, or has he merely read the sitter's subjective mind? Is there any more reason for supposing that he has seen a spirit of a dead man than there is for supposing that a mind-reader sees the spirit of the Jack of clubs when the image of that card is telepathed to him? Obviously not. The conditions are precisely the same in both cases. The percipient sees the image of that which is in the mind of the agent. In the one case, it is a card; in the other it is an individual. If it is the spirit of the individual that is seen in the one case, it is the spirit of the card that is seen in the other. In the case of the New York medium, did she see the spirit of the Patent Office, the spirits of the papers, the drawings, the desks, and the spirit of the examiner seated at the spirit of one of the desks, examining the spirits of the drawings and of the specifications?

I repeat it, the percipient sees the image of that which is in the mind of the agent, and he never sees more than that. It often happens that the image of some one is seen, of whom the agent is not consciously thinking at the moment. This has been already explained, on the obvious ground that it is the subjective, or unconscious, mind of the agent that is read. It sometimes happens that some fact is related, some scene described, which the sitter cannot recall to mind, and he conscientiously declares that he never knew the fact related, nor witnessed the incident depicted. But when it is remembered that the subjective mind of man retains all that he has ever seen, heard, or read, and that he retains comparatively little in his objective recollection, it is extremely unsafe for him to declare that any one fact has never been known to him. It is merely negative evidence at best, and amounts only to a declaration that he does not recall the fact. When we consider how little we retain, in our objective recollection, of what we have seen, heard, or read, we may well wonder that it does not oftener happen that so-called spirits tell us of circumstances which we do not remember. On the whole, it may be safely assumed that no medium has ever yet been able to impart any information that is not known either to the medium or to some living person with whom he is *en rapport.* There is certainly nothing but the merest negative evidence, such as has been described, that such a thing ever happened. On the other hand, there is the strongest possible evidence to the contrary, in the fact that there is room for a doubt on that question. It is self-evident that if facts, known neither to the medium nor those surrounding him, — that is, facts not known to him nor obtainable by means of telepathy, — can be perceived or obtained by him from independent sources, the evidence of that fact would be thrust upon us from ten thousand different sources every hour. This is also negative evidence, it is true, but it is all but conclusive. Thus, the question of spirit identity has given spiritists no end of trouble. Their ablest writers have sought in vain for a solution of the question why it is that spirits constantly fail to give conclusive evidence of their identity by means which could not be referred to the knowledge of the medium or to telepathy.

On this subject Allan Kardec, one of the ablest writers on the subject, discourses as follows : —

"The identity of contemporaneous spirits is much more easily proved, — those whose character and habits are known ; for it is precisely these habits, which they have not yet had time to throw aside, by which they can be recognized."[1]

This may be true ; but it is also true that where the "character and habits" of a supposed spirit are known to the medium, or to those who are in telepathic rapport with him, simulation of that character and those habits is perfectly easy to the expert medium. The more generally the character and habits are known, the less evidential value is to be attached to their reproduction.

Our author then proceeds : —

"Without doubt the spirit can give the proofs if asked, but he does not always do so, unless it is agreeable to him, and generally the asking wounds him ; for this reason it should be avoided. In leaving his body the spirit has not laid aside his susceptibility ; he is wounded by any question tending to put him to the proof. *It is such questions as one would not dare to propose to him, were he living,* for fear of overstepping the bounds of propriety ; why, then, should there be less regard after his death ? Should a man enter a drawing-room and de-

---

[1] Book on Mediums, pp 331-2

cline to give his name, should we insist, at all hazards, that he should prove his identity by exhibiting his titles, under the pretext that there are impostors? Would he not, assuredly, have the right to remind his interrogator of the rules of good breeding? This is what the spirits do, either by not replying or by withdrawing. Let us make a comparison. Suppose the astronomer Arago during his life had presented himself in a house where no one knew him, and he had been thus addressed: 'You say you are Arago; but as we do not know you, please prove it by answering our questions: solve this astronomical problem; tell us your name, your Christian name, those of your children, what you did such and such a day, at such an hour, etc.' What would he have answered? Well, as a spirit he will do just what he would have done during his lifetime; and other spirits do the same."

The above is considered the best reason that can be given for the fact that spirits whose character and habits in life are not generally known, or not known to the medium or to those surrounding him, invariably refuse to give proofs of their identity. But is his comparison pertinent? I think not. It might be considered impertinent, nay, the very height of ill-breeding, if one should insist on proofs of identity when a stranger is casually introduced, or introduces himself, in a drawing-room. But let us make another comparison. Suppose a stranger — we, too, will say Arago the astronomer — calls us up by telephone, and makes a statement of the most transcendent interest and importance to us, — a statement which, if true, will change the whole course of our lives and our habits of thought. He states that his special mission is to make this portentous announcement to us, and that his name is Arago, the astronomer. We know Arago the astronomer by reputation, but have never had the honor of his personal acquaintance. We know enough of him, however, to be certain that he would tell us the exact truth as he understood it; and we would stake our dearest interests upon a statement of his regarding that about which he professed to have positive personal knowledge. Under such circumstances would it be likely to wound his feelings or shock his sense of propriety if we should reply through the telephone something like this : —

"Sir, your message is of portentous import to us, and we cannot hesitate to believe it if we can be assured that you are Arago the astronomer, as you represent. We can hear you, but we cannot see you, and you are not vouched for by any one we know. Please give us some proof of your identity."

Would Arago the astronomer, or any other sensible man, wrap himself in the mantle of offended dignity and treat us with silent contempt, or remind us of "the rules of good-breeding"? Certainly not, especially if the object of his existence was to make the communication, not only for our individual benefit, but for the purpose of giving to all mankind that direct and positive assurance, that tangible evidence, for which all humanity has sought in vain since the dawn of creation.

Our author then continues : —

"While spirits refuse to answer puerile and impertinent questions which a person would have hesitated to ask during their lives, they often spontaneously give irrefutable proofs of their identity by their character, revealed in their language, by the use of words that were familiar to them, by citing certain facts, — particularities of their life sometimes unknown to the assistants, and whose truth has been verified. Proofs of identity will spring up in many unforeseen ways, which do not present themselves at first sight, but in the course of conversations. It is better, then, to wait for them, without calling for them, observing with care all that may flow from the nature of the communications. (See the fact given, No. 70.)"

Turning now to page 82 of the volume, we find the statement above alluded to, and it reads as follows : —

"On a vessel of the Imperial French navy, stationed in the Chinese seas, the whole crew, from the sailors up to the staff-major, were occupied in making tables talk. They hit upon the idea of invoking the spirit of a lieutenant of this same vessel, some two years dead. He came, and after various communications, which astonished every one, he said, by rapping, what follows : 'I pray you instantly to pay the captain the sum of (he mentioned the sum), which I owe him, and which I regret not having been able to repay before my death.' No one knew the fact; the captain himself had forgotten the debt, — a very small one; but on looking over his accounts, he found there the lieutenant's debt, the sum indicated being perfectly correct. We ask, of whose thought could this be the reflection?"

Here, then, we find the supreme test applied, — the best conditions possible, as prescribed by one of the ablest and most thoughtful writers on the subject. It will be observed that he is not blind to the possibilities of telepathy, and counts it as a factor in the case. "Of whose thought could this be the reflection?" he asks triumphantly. "No one knew the fact; the captain himself had forgotten the debt." It must be admitted that if this test is conclusive, their case has been proved a thousand times over. But in view of what is now known of the laws of telepathy, it is self-evident that it proves nothing. Telepathy, as we have again and again repeated, is the communion of two or more subjective minds. It is not that of which we are consciously thinking that the subjective mind of the medium perceives. Doubtless the captain had forgotten, objectively, all about the loan. It was a very small amount, and the lieutenant had been dead two years. But the subjective mind of the captain, which remembers all things, great and small, could not forget it, and it was telepathed to the subjective mind of the medium. Besides, there was another very potent agency at work to bring this loan into prominence. We have already seen, in former chapters, that the normal function of the subjective mind is to watch over and protect the life of the individual. It is the strongest instinct of all animate nature. The protection of the material interests of the individual is as much a part of the function of the subjective mind as the protection of his life. Indeed, the promotion of the one is but a means to secure the other. It was, therefore, simple obedience to the first law of nature that prompted the subjective mind of the captain to thrust this loan upon the attention of those present and thus secure its payment.

It may be said, however, that there was no evidence that the captain was present at the séance; and it may be assumed by some that telepathic communion with his mind was impossible in his absence from the circle. The former supposition is possibly correct, but the latter is not probable, in view of the well-known facts of telepathy. But assuming both to be true, — that the captain was absent from the immediate circle, and that the circumstance would prevent telepathic communion with his mind, — there still remain two or three other ways of accounting for the phenomenon. In the first place, it is extremely probable that the captain's accounts were kept by a subordinate, who was present, and who, subjectively at least, remembered the account. It is distinctly stated that all the subordinates were present, "from the sailors up to the staff-major." This would necessarily include the one whose duty it was to keep the books. His subjective mind would be just as available as that of the captain for the production of what, in those days, was considered a test case. Again, supposing that the entry of the account was made by the captain's hand, it is extremely probable that some one else had access to the books; and however superficially the knowledge was impressed upon his consciousness, it was forever fixed upon the tablets of his subjective memory, and was instantly available for use when a test case was needed. To those who regard independent clairvoyance as an established principle, or faculty, of the human mind, the explanation is easy; for there would be no difficulty in supposing the mind of the independent clairvoyant to be capable of taking cognizance of all that was to be found in the ship's records.

It is extremely improbable, however, that any third party figured in the transaction, or that it is necessary to assume that any third party knew of the loan. It is sufficient to know that the captain was aboard the ship, and that everyone on the vessel was necessarily *en rapport* with him. Besides, if any one in the circle was in telepathic rapport with the captain, it would be an all-sufficient explanation of the phenomenon; for it is well known that specific information, not known to any one in the circle, can be obtained from some one having the knowledge who happens to be *in rapport* with any person in the circle.

Thus it will be seen that there are at least four ways of accounting for the phenomenon, on well-established principles, without the necessity of resorting to the assumption of supernatural agencies.

The subtle *rôle* which telepathy plays in so-called spirit manifestations must now be apparent. It is not only in the class of phenomena to which we have alluded that its power is manifest, but it reappears in all classes and phases of phenomena popularly attributed to spirits. The greater part of the mystery which surrounds these manifestations, aside from the purely physical phenomena, is directly traceable to telepathy; and it explains that which, without its aid, would be inexplicable on any other hypothesis than that the manifestations proceed from disembodied spirits.

In concluding the discussion of this branch of the subject, I desire distinctly to impress upon the mind of the reader an important proposition which seems to have been lost sight of by many who are otherwise inclined to give full credit to telepathy as a means of explaining many so-called spirit phenomena. It is this : —

It is not necessary that any member of a circle should be in possession of objective knowledge of a fact in order to be able to communicate it telepathically to the medium.

The reason will be obvious, after a moment's reflection, to any one who admits the existence of the power of telepathy. If the power is possessed by A to communicate a telepathic message to B, it follows that B can communicate the same message to C, and C can convey it to D, and so on, *ad infinitum*. This proposition will not be gainsaid by any one who admits that A can convey a telepathic message to B. D may have no objective knowledge of A or of B, but is *en rapport* with C. Now, we will suppose that a disaster happens to A. He is missing; he is drowned; but no one possesses any objective knowledge of the fact, and his friends institute a vain search, no one having the remotest idea of what has happened to him. B, his mother, receives a telepathic message, conveyed by A at the moment of his death to her subjective mind, informing her of the sad accident. But not being sensitive to subjective impressions, it is impossible for her subjective mind to convey the message above the threshold of her consciousness. She is, therefore, objectively ignorant of the fact, although her subjective mind is fully cognizant of all its sad details. In the mean time, C, a sympathetic neighbor, *en rapport* with B, subjectively perceives that which is so strongly impressed upon the subjective mind of the mother. C is also unable to elevate the knowledge above the threshold of her consciousness; but she is a believer in spiritism, and volunteers to visit a neighboring city and consult a medium. She does so; and the moment she becomes *en rapport* with the medium, the telepathic message is delivered, and the medium perceives, objectively as well as subjectively, the details of the disaster which befell A. He describes the whole transaction, and locates the exact spot where the body may be found. Subsequent investigation demonstrates the exact knowledge possessed by the medium, for the whole environment is found to be exactly as described, and the body is found in the very spot indicated.

Now, the spiritists say that this occurrence cannot be explained by reference to telepathy, for the reason that D was not *en rapport* with A, nor with B. Nor was C *en rapport* with A, for the latter was dead before C could have become cognizant of the facts. The obvious answer to this is, as before indicated, that if the power exists in man to convey a telepathic message to his fellow-man, it presupposes the existence of the power in the percipient to repeat the message to a third person, and so on indefinitely, until some one receives it who has the power to elevate the information above the threshold of his consciousness, and thus convey it to the objective intelligence of the world. Nor is the element of time necessarily an adverse factor in the case; for there is no reason to suppose that such messages may not be transmitted from one to another for generations. Thus, the particulars of a tragedy might be revealed many years after the event, and in such a way as to render it difficult, if not impossible, to trace the line through which the intelligence was transmitted. For the spiritist the easy and ever-ready explanation of such a phenomenon is to ascribe it to the intervention of spirits of the dead. But to those who have kept pace with the developments of modern scientific investigation, and who are able to draw the legitimate and necessary conclusions from the facts discovered, the explanation is obvious, without the necessity of entering the domain of the supernatural.

CHAPTER XVII.

THE PHENOMENA OF SPIRITISM *(continued)*.

THERE is another class of phenomena which has attracted a great deal of public attention, and which
demands a passing notice in this connection. It is that
class which has received an exhaustive treatment in the
work of the late Professor Denton, entitled " The Souls of
Things." It has been denominated " psychometry," which
may be defined as the supposed power of the human mind
to discern the history of inanimate objects by clairvoyance.
Many wonderful stories are related of the exercise of this
supposed faculty, under the strictest test conditions, as test
conditions were then understood. Professor Denton made
a long series of experiments with his sister, his wife, and
some others who were supposed to possess that power in a
remarkable degree. The powers of his wife and sister were
indeed wonderful ; but, as we shall see, not in the line in
which the experiments were directed. It must be pre-

mised that the professor was a very learned man, not only in his specialty, which was geology, but in all branches of human knowledge. His wife and sister were also highly cultivated women, and were specially interested in those branches of learning in which the gifted professor excelled. Thus the conditions were extremely favorable for the production of extraordinary results in whatever branch of occult science they might jointly engage.

It was the habit of the professor to select some geological specimen, or a fragment of some historical structure, and submit it to his percipient for her version of its history. She would readily enter a partially subjective condition, place the relic on her head, and at once give a very plausible, and oftentimes a most wonderfully accurate, history of the scenes which had been enacted within its former environment. Thus, if the object happened to be a geological specimen, she would launch out into a glowing description of its surroundings when found, and going back into its history before the earth's crust was formed, trace it down through the different geological changes until she landed it in the professor's cabinet. Again, a piece of mortar from the dwelling of Cicero would be handed to her, and she would give a vivid description of the domestic life of those who had occupied the mansion, and describe historic events which "might have been seen" from the ancient habitat of the piece of mortar. It is easy to see how all this might be accomplished, and all the known facts stated with accuracy, regarding the geological environment of the piece of stone in her hands, when her own geological learning was taken into consideration. But the professor was not unmindful of so obvious an explanation of her power. To eliminate that element was his first care. To that end he would wrap the specimen in a piece of paper, and carefully conceal its character from her objective knowledge. The result was always the same. She would read the history of the specimen with the same apparent accuracy as before. The professor, however, did not forget the possibility that telepathy was an element necessary to be eliminated. The possibility that she might read what was in his own mind must, therefore, be provided against. To that end he wrapped a large number of specimens in packages as nearly alike as possible, and mixed them together so that it was impossible for him to know them apart. One specimen after another would then be handed her, and each one would be described with the same accuracy as before. This was considered the supreme test, and the doctrine that " things," in common with men, have " souls," was thought to be demonstrated. The Orientalists would say that he had demonstrated that the history of all things is " recorded in the astral light," whatever that may be. The spiritist would say that the spirits of dead men had given her the information.

The true explanation is obvious to those who are acquainted with the facts of telepathy. The professor was an eminent geologist and a classical scholar. In his subjective mind was the history of every geological specimen in his possession, pictured clearly and vividly, according to the theories of the best geologists of his generation. His imagination carried him back to the time when chaos reigned supreme. He followed the fragment of rock down through all the changes which took place in the earth's structure, until it became a part of the solid mass of rock from which it was taken. In the ever-changing environment of that fragment, since the time when it was a part of a vast mass of molten matter, there was material for pictures of the sublimest scenes incident to the formation of a world. Those pictures, to the imagination of every geologist worthy of the title, are ever present and intensely vivid. A fragment of rock to him is an open book, in which are recorded the history of the sublimest works of Omnipotence, and his imagination supplies the panoramic illustrations. In experiments such as have been described, these pictures are necessarily presented to the subjective mind of the percipient in a form so clear and vivid that she would be insensate indeed if she failed to describe them in appropriate terms. And when we consider the fact that the percipients employed in these experiments were exceptionally cultivated women, especially interested in the subjects of the professor's research, it will be seen that successful telepathic experiments were to them exceptionally easy.

The successful reading of the history of the specimens submitted to the percipients is therefore easily accounted for where the professor had conscious knowledge of the contents of the packages. It remains only to explain the reason of success when he sought to eliminate that element by submitting a large number of similar packages, not consciously knowing one from the other. This also is easy to understand when the extraordinary acumen of the subjective mind is considered. It is a common hypnotic experiment to draw a blank card from a package, hand it to a subject, and suggest that it contains a picture of some person. The card is then marked on the back and shuffled with fifty or more others. A good subject will, in nine cases out of ten, indicate the marked card as the one containing the suggested picture, and that without the possibility of seeing the mark on the other side. It is obviously a much easier feat to remember the differences in packages than in blank cards. Of the former, no two could possibly be alike. Of the latter, no two would ordinarily be sufficiently unlike to enable one to determine the difference by the unaided senses. But to the subjective mind the feat of remembering each package and its contents would be very easy, compared with thousands of recorded instances to be found in the literature of psychic phenomena.

It will be observed that we have refrained from invoking the aid of clairvoyance to account for the phenomena of psychometry. It would be a much simpler solution of the problem to assume that the power of independent clairvoyance exists, and that the percipients simply saw the contents of the packages. But inasmuch as the known facts of telepathy afford a perfect solution, we are not logically justified in entering a domain which is in the slightest degree overshadowed by doubt. By this remark it is not

16

meant to imply that there is any doubt of the existence of a
power which is generally known as clairvoyance, but that
its limitations are as yet undecided. That is to say, the
boundary line between clairvoyance and telepathy is not at
present clearly drawn. The field of clairvoyance is constantly narrowing its boundaries. Thus, a few years ago
every perception of a fact not cognizable by the senses
was attributed either to clairvoyance or to spirits. Sceptics
on the latter subject were wont to explain certain phenomena
by attributing them to the former. The phenomena which
could not thus be explained were relegated to the domain
of fraud and legerdemain. When the phenomena of telepathy became better understood, the field of clairvoyance
was greatly narrowed, as it was found that most of the phenomena before explained by clairvoyance were really due to
telepathic communion. But the powers and limitations of
telepathy are not yet clearly marked ; and it is found that
every step in advance in the knowledge of its principles by
just so much narrows the field of clairvoyance. No better
illustration of this fact could be given than the phenomena
of psychometry, which we have just been considering. The
power to read the history of a geological specimen with a
plausible show of accuracy was first attributed to clairvoyance. As telepathic powers began to be understood, it was
thought that possibly the percipient simply related what
was read in the mind of the agent. Many experiments
were made throughout the country which demonstrated
that fact, and the recognized field of clairvoyance was
thereby curtailed. But Professor Denton determined to
eliminate the element of telepathy by so disposing of his
relics as to divest himself of all knowledge of the particular one under examination. When the percipient exhibited
the same powers of discernment under those circumstances
it was thought that the element of telepathy was eliminated, and that the power of clairvoyance was demonstrated. But as the knowledge of telepathy is increased,
and when it is understood that telepathy is the communion
of subjective minds, and that the subjective mind is endowed

with transcendent powers in certain directions, while it is hedged about with limitations in others, it is seen that the professor did not succeed, as he had supposed, in eliminating the element of telepathy. Thus the field of clairvoyance is again curtailed, and that of telepathy correspondingly enlarged. It may be assumed, therefore, that the boundary lines between the two supposed powers are still unmarked. In the mean time it is unsafe to assume any one point as the boundary, or even to assume that there is, in fact, any line at all. Judgment must be suspended until telepathy is better understood. All that can be safely said is that there are facts which cannot as yet be explained on any other hypothesis than that of independent clairvoyance. When we come across such a fact we may provisionally assume the power to exist, and await the slow progress of experimental knowledge to enable us to classify the fact in accordance with its legitimate relations. It is logically safe to do this as long as we thus avoid the necessity of wholesale denials of demonstrated facts on the one hand, and on the other refrain from entering the domain of the supernatural in search of a hypothesis.

It is thought that enough has now been said to explain the part which telepathy plays in the phenomena which have been considered, and also to enable the intelligent reader to apply the principles to all other classes of phenomena in which telepathy constitutes a possible factor. It is constantly reappearing in every phase of psychic phenomena, and constitutes a factor in every manifestation of intelligent power involving the perception of that which is beyond the reach of the senses.

CLAIRAUDIENCE.

The next subject in order is that of clairaudience, or " clear hearing." It is a faculty of the human mind much more rarely developed than that of clairvoyance, — that is, if we assume the latter to be identical with telepathy, which we may do for the purposes of this discussion.

The Century Dictionary defines clairaudience as "the supposed power of hearing in a mesmeric trance sounds which are not audible to the ear in the natural waking condition."

This, as far as it goes, is a correct definition of that faculty; but it defines a very small part of its field of operations, and that part which is of the least importance. It may be defined, broadly, to be "the power of hearing the spoken words of a human soul." In other words, it is that faculty of man's intelligence which enables his objective mind to receive communications from his own subjective mind or from that of another by means of spoken words. It is one means of bringing the operations of the subjective mind above the threshold of consciousness. The power is by no means confined to persons in a mesmeric trance, although it seems probable that one must be in a partially subjective state to enable him to hear clairaudiently. The degree of subjectivity may be very slight, so that the percipient may seem to himself and others to be in a perfectly normal condition. The sounds — if that may be called sound which does not cause atmospheric vibrations — are perfectly distinct to the consciousness of the percipient, but are not perceptible to others who may be near him and in the normal condition.

Like all other means for bringing the operations of the subjective mind above the threshold of consciousness, the sounds have from time immemorial been attributed to supernatural agencies. Socrates furnished the most notable example in ancient or modern times of a man whose subjective mind was able at any time to communicate messages to his objective mind by means of spoken words. It is well known that he supposed himself to be constantly attended by a dæmon, or guardian spirit, who watched over him and warned him of any danger that was imminent. (See Chapter X. for a fuller discussion of Socrates and his dæmon.) The biblical student will recall to mind many instances where voices were heard, conveying intelligence of the most portentous character, and a critical examination of some of the instances will not fail to reveal their true nature.

Many spiritual mediums of the present day have the faculty largely developed. Some of them are enabled to obtain the names of their sitters by hearing them spoken clairaudiently, and the names of supposed spirits are obtained in the same way. It is popularly supposed that the ordinary method of telepathic communion, when the message is not brought above the threshold of consciousness, is by mental impressions. It is, of course, impossible for us to know the processes employed in the ordinary communion of subjective minds. It seems probable, however, that it is by means of such language as is employed by the communicants in objective life. All that is or can be known is, that when the ideas are communicated to the conscious mind, it is necessarily by such means as can be understood, — that is, by means which appeal to the senses. It is true that the subjective mind is often able strongly to impress the objective mind, especially when danger to the person is imminent, or when some near relative or dear friend is in danger. Such impressions are known as premonitions. Sometimes they are so strong as to be of real service in averting danger. But they are not always reliable, for the reason that we are seldom able to distinguish a real premonition from that feeling arising from fear and anxiety regarding the welfare of those who are absent and very dear to us. Thus, a mother will often feel that she has a premonition of danger to an absent child, but will afterwards learn that her fears were groundless. Perhaps at another time a real premonition will be disregarded. It seems probable that when the laws of subjective mental action are better understood, there may be some method formulated by which a genuine premonition may be recognized. It is certain that in all cases where danger to the person is imminent, the subjective mind makes a supreme effort to give warning and avert the danger. That being its normal function, its highest activity is exercised in the effort to preserve the life of the individual. It is sometimes successful, and sometimes not ; but that the effort is always made does not admit of doubt. Sometimes it succeeds by means most extraordinary, — clairaudience not infrequently being the means of receiving the warning. Thus, a lady once confessed to the writer that she at one time, in a fit of despondency arising from ill health, attempted to commit suicide. She had raised a pistol to her head and was about to fire, when she heard an explosive sound, apparently in the same room, resembling a pistol-shot. This caused her to pause for an instant, when she heard the words, apparently spoken in her ear, " Not now ; you have two years yet ! " Surprise caused her to lower the pistol, and reflection caused her to desist, and finally to abandon the idea of suicide. As the two years have not yet expired, it is too early to know whether it is a case of prevision as well as of clairaudience.

One of the most remarkable cases of clairaudient warning against danger that has ever come under the observation of the writer occurred near Washington a short time ago. A well-known colored preacher was aboard a train on its way to the city. He was dozing in his seat a few miles out, when he was suddenly awakened by a cry of " Wreck ! wreck ! " apparently sounding in his ears. He thought for a moment that he had been dreaming ; but after he was fully awake he again heard the same words repeated three times. As he happened to be the only occupant of the car, he knew that no one was playing a trick upon him, and he instantly became panic-stricken, and rushed to the rear end of the car and jumped off, although the train was going at the rate of thirty miles an hour. He was somewhat cut and bruised, but managed to walk to the next station, where he related his adventure to my informant. Little importance was attached to the circumstance at that time, as his train passed to the city in safety. But the very next train that passed over the road in the same direction was wrecked by the falling of a large rock upon it as it passed. The rock overhung the track, and had evidently become loosened by the vibrations caused by passing trains. Subsequent investigation by my informant revealed the fact that the old preacher had leaped from the train but a short distance beyond the scene of the wreck.

Now, it may be asked, how do we connect the clairaudient warning of the old man with the wreck which did not occur to his train? It must be admitted that the circumstances do not constitute an ideally perfect case of a life saved by a clairaudient reception of warning; but it must also be held that the case is of all the greater evidential value for that very reason. It is easy to perceive how the old man's subjective mind perceived the danger, when it is once admitted that it possesses the power to see that which is not within the range of objective vision. Ever alert for the safety of the individual, it perceived the danger, no matter how. It saw the condition of the overhanging rock, and believed that that train would loosen its hold. In the mean time the old man was in that passive, somnolent condition most favorable for the reception of subjective impressions or communications. He happened also to be clairaudient, and therefore in the best possible condition for the conveyance of subjective messages above the threshold of consciousness. And the message was delivered in the most effective way possible, — in the same way in which Socrates was again and again warned of impending danger. That the catastrophe did not happen to his train proves only that the intelligence which gave the warning was finite, that its knowledge was circumscribed by the limitations of human judgment, and that it did not proceed from Omniscience.

It may be here remarked that this incident seems difficult to explain on any other hypothesis than that of independent clairvoyance. To explain it on the principle of telepathy would involve the necessity of presupposing that some person or persons knew of the dangerous situation of the rock, and that they were in telepathic rapport with the percipient. Either supposition seems improbable, although not impossible. Be this as it may, the fact remains that the subjective mind of man has some means of reaching out beyond the range of our faculties of objective perception, and of knowing when and where danger threatens the individual. That it is constantly on the alert for that purpose, is also certain.

But its efforts are not directed exclusively to the protection of the body from harm. It is also on the alert for the protection of the material interests of the individual, and for the advancement of whatever aims and objects he has in life. These objects are, of course, subsidiary to the main one, being means to the end in view, — namely, the preservation of human life. One of the most eminent lawyers in the United States informs me confidentially that he is often guided, in critical emergencies, by a voice which gives him in a single, concise sentence the key to the situation. All the years of his adult life this voice has warned him of impending danger, and guided him to the attainment of the objects of his ambition. He did not, in early life, entertain any well-defined theory on the subject of the origin of the voice, but has always been guided by its monitions, and never to his disadvantage. Of late years, however, he has become convinced of its true source, and now regards his faculty as of the most transcendent interest and scientific importance, to say nothing of its value as a personal mentor.

It seems probable that the faculty might be cultivated to an unlimited extent, provided its true source could be recognized early in life and its monitions heeded. It is also probable that most people have occasionally heard clairaudiently, though but few have paid attention to the phenomenon ; and those who have done so have either attributed it to imagination, or regarded it as a subjective hallucination. In either case the auto-suggestion would necessarily prevent the development of the faculty. It sometimes happens, however, that spirit mediums develop the faculty to a remarkable extent. As they attribute the phenomena to extraneous sources, the suggestion necessarily results in corresponding phenomena. It is needless to remark that the same law of suggestion which prevails in the production of other phenomena governs the character of clairaudient manifestations. Thus, if the suggestion is entertained that the voice proceeds from a disembodied spirit, or from the guardian angel of the percipient, the character suggested will be assumed by the subjective entity, and future communications will be conducted on that basis. It may thus be made to assume the character of an angel or of a devil, just as the suggestion happens to be made. The suggestion, in the present state of knowledge on the subject of psychic phenomena, must depend altogether upon accident, or the education and habits of thought of the individual.

Doubtless, many persons have been made insane by constantly hearing what they supposed to be spirit voices. Not knowing the true origin of the phenomenon, they endow it with whatever character happens to suggest itself, and it readily assumes to be whatever is suggested ; or it may assume a dozen different characters, if the person happens to imagine their existence. The effect can readily be conceived when one is persuaded that he is beset by supernatural beings. Insane people are often seen to be engaged in conversation with some imaginary person, and when we say of such a soliloquist, " He is talking to himself," we are wiser than we think; for that is the fact. But the individual thought he was in conversation with supernatural beings. We are accustomed to regard such conversations as symptoms of insanity, whereas they are oftentimes the cause of insanity. The patient for some reason develops the faculty of clairaudience. He imagines that the voice proceeds from some extraneous source. His superstition causes him to ascribe it to spirits. He constantly develops the faculty by practice, until he becomes a monomaniac on the subject. His subjective mind, dominated by an all-potent, but false, suggestion, gradually obtains control of the objective faculties, and Reason abdicates her throne. The man is insane, just as all men are insane who allow their subjective minds to obtain the ascendency. This is, of course, an extreme case ; but it is less rare than many suppose. Our asylums are full of men and women

who, in one way or another, are dominated by their subjec
tive minds, acting in obedience to false suggestions which
have been dwelt upon so long that reason is powerless to
combat them.

The lesson is obvious. We should learn first of all that
the subjective entity within each of us, whilst it is endowed
with transcendent powers, is also circumscribed by limitations which unfit it for control of the dual man. Having
learned this, it should be our care to keep reason in the
ascendency, and to control the subjective mind by suggestions which, while keeping it in subordination, will direct its
powers in the channel of its legitimate functions, — namely,
the preservation and perpetuation of the human species.

Clairaudient powers, like every other power which enables
man to raise the operations of the subjective mind above
the threshold of consciousness, may to one who knows the
laws which govern it, who appreciates its powers, and who
is aware of its limitations, become a source of decided advantage. But to one who does not understand those laws,
powers, and limitations, those faculties may prove to be like
the wand in the hand of the slave of the magician in the
Eastern tale. He saw his master wave his wand, and heard
him give orders to the spirits who arose at his command.
The slave stole the wand, waved it in the air, and summoned
the spirits. They came at his summons, but tore him in
pieces instead of obeying his commands. He had not observed that his master used his left hand for the purpose of
conjuration.

This tale was told for the purpose of illustrating the very
point which we have sought to make. The fate of the
magician's slave was no worse than that which may befall
any man who irregularly summons his own spirit, without
understanding the laws which enable him to control it and
make it useful instead of destructive. He is conjuring
with the most potential force of nature below that of
Omnipotence.

CHAPTER XVIII.

THE PHENOMENA OF SPIRITISM (*continued*).

The Planchette. — Modifications — Easily operated. — Automatic Writing. — Governed by the Universal Law. — The Planchette without Spirits. — The Planchette and Telepathy. — Trance. — Ancient and Modern Superstitions relating to Trance. — Religious Systems founded on Trance. — Visions. — Swedenborg. — Oriental Philosophy. — Its Slow Growth and Stupendous Proportions. — Spiritistic Philosophy. — Its Evolution. — All founded on Trance Visions in Ignorance of the Law of Suggestion. — Cahagnet's Mesmeric Seers. — Their Revelations. — Objective and Subjective Visions. — Orthodoxy and Heterodoxy. — Visions of the Holy Virgin. — The Physical and Mental Attitude of Prayer. — The Prayer of Faith. — Obsession. — Possession. — Casting out Devils. — Devils out of Fashion. — The Influence of Suggestion. — The Element of Telepathy. — Dual Personality. — Loss of Identity. — Characteristics. — The Case of Ansel Bourne. — Possible Explanation. — A Proof of the Dual Hypothesis. — Multiple Personality.

ANOTHER method of bringing the operations of the subjective mind above the threshold of consciousness is by means of an instrument called the planchette. It consists of a thin board about six inches square, resting upon two castors, the third leg consisting of a pencil, which passes through a hole in the board, its point resting upon the paper upon which the instrument is designed to write. The mode of operation consists in resting the hand lightly upon the board and allowing it to move over the paper without consciously aiding its progress. In the hands of a medium it will soon begin to write, apparently propelled by an unseen power. A modification of this apparatus is now on the market, which consists of a similar piece of thin board, approximately triangular in shape, with a plain wooden leg at each apex. Its feet, like the feet of the gods, are "shod with wool." Accompanying it is a board, say two feet square, on which the letters of the alphabet and the arabic numerals are painted. Its mode of operation is similar to that of the planchette, except that, instead of a pencil being used, one of the legs serves as a pointer, and the words are spelled out, letter by letter, as indicated by the pointer, which moves over the board in the same mysterious way as the planchette. Its advantage over the planchette consists in the fact that a greater number of persons can operate it satisfactorily. Otherwise, the planchette is preferable, inasmuch as it writes continuously, instead of spelling the words letter by letter. In almost every family some one will be found who can, with a little practice, obtain communications by this means from his own subjective mind. This is the simplest way by which so-called spirit communications can be obtained.

Automatic writing is a cognate method, and consists in holding a pencil in the hand and letting it write. The subjective mind assumes control of the muscles and nerves of the arm and hand, and propels the pencil, the objective mind meantime being perfectly quiescent, and often totally oblivious of what is being written. A smaller number of persons can acquire this faculty than either of the others.

We assume, of course, that it is the subjective mind of the medium that directs the pencil. The same laws govern the manifestations, and the intelligence is hedged about by the same limitations. Suggestion plays the same subtle *rôle*, and the knowledge of the subjects of the communications are limited by that of the medium and those with whom he is in telepathic rapport. The entity that guides the pencil almost invariably assumes to be a spirit, and its communications necessarily conform to the character assumed. The reason of this is obvious when we consider the fact that automatic writing has always been associated with the idea of spirit communion. The universality of this idea constitutes an all-potent suggestion which cannot easily be overcome. Even though the medium may profess to be a sceptic on the subject of spirit intercourse, nevertheless he is dominated by that suggestion, in the absence of any definite counter-suggestion. Obviously, a counter-suggestion which could overcome the hypothesis of spirit intercourse must be in the form of a theory which appeals more strongly to the reason of the medium than the suggestion of spirit intercourse. In the present state of popular opinion on the subject of spiritism it would be difficult to find a medium whose subjective mind would not be dominated by the popular hypothesis. Nevertheless, instances have been known where the popular idea did not prevail. One case that is now recalled is reported in the " Proceedings of the Society for Psychical Research," April, 1891 (page 23). The medium, or, more properly speaking, the automatist, was a young lady, aged fifteen. "She had not previously heard of planchette," says the author, " and spiritualism was to her a mere name." This was a very desirable condition of mind for the purpose, and as rare as desirable. " She never knew what she had written till it was looked at," continues the author, " and there was often some slight difficulty in deciphering it. Thus, the first question, 'Who are you that write ?' produced what at first I took to be mere scrawling, and C (the automatist) shortly after left the room. After she had done so, I took another look at this scrawl, and then at once perceived that it was legible, and that the name written in answer to the question was 'Henry Morton.' I at once followed C upstairs, and asked her if she had ever heard the name ; and she replied that it was that of a character in a Christmas play she had acted in, more than a year previously."

This is a most remarkable case in more ways than one. It shows, first, that when the automatist knows nothing of spiritism, and there is consequently no suggestion of the spirits having any part in the performance, the subjective mind will not assume that it is a spirit that writes; secondly, that the bare fact that the question, "Who are you that write?" is asked, amounts to a suggestion that some third person is writing, and that the automatist is dominated by the inference drawn, just the same as if the suggestion had been a positive statement. The most remarkable part of it, however, is the persistency with which her subjective mind clung to the suggestion that she was "Henry Morton." She had assumed that character more than a year before, in a Christmas play, and her subjective mind still identified itself with the imaginary personage, and believed the truth of the suggestion as firmly as it would have believed the suggestion that it was a disembodied spirit, had that suggestion been made. The author shows an intelligent appreciation of this fact when he adds: "Had the name been, as it easily might have been, that of some deceased friend, it is obvious what inference would have been drawn." It is also obvious that it would have been that of some deceased person, had the young lady been acquainted with the planchette and the spiritistic hypothesis.

Another instance of automatic writing where the spiritistic hypothesis was ignored, is reported in the "Proceedings of the Society for Psychical Research," vol. iii. pages 8-23. Space can be given to a brief extract only. The experiments were tried by the Rev. P. H. Newnham and his wife, the latter acting as the automatist. The primary object of these experiments was to test the power of thought-transference. This was very successfully done, as the answers, though not always correct, referred to the questions. It appears, incidentally, that they entertained a different hypothesis from the usual one, as will appear from the answers which we quote. The questions were written down by Mr. Newnham, and no hint was given to the operator as to their character or subject. The following are fair samples: —

"*Q.* Is it the operator's brain, or some external force, that moves the planchette? Answer 'brain,' or 'force.'
A. Will.

Q. Is it the will of a living person, or of an immaterial spirit distinct from that person? Answer 'person' or 'spirit.'

A. Wife.

Q. Give first the wife's Christian name; then my favorite name for her.

A. (This was accurately done.)

Q. What is your own name?

A. Only you.

Q. We are not quite sure of the meaning of the answer. Explain.

A. Wife."

At a subsequent sitting the following questions and answers were given : —

" *Q.* Who are you that write?

A. Wife.

Q. But does no one tell wife what to write? If so, who?

A. Spirit.

Q. Whose spirit?

A. Wife's brain.

Q. But how does wife's brain know (certain) secrets?

A. Wife's spirit unconsciously guides."

At a subsequent séance the following dialogue occurred :

" *Q.* By what means are (unknown) secrets conveyed to wife's brain?

A. What you call mesmeric influence.

Q. What do you mean by ' what you call '? What do *you* call it?

A. Electro-biology.

Q. By whom, or by what, is the electro-biologic force set in motion?

A. I told you you could not know more than you did.

Q. Can wife answer a question the reply to which I do not know?

A. Why do you try to make me say what I won't?

Q. Simply because I desire knowledge. *Why* will you not tell?

A. Wife could tell if some one else, with a very strong will, in the room knew."

These two cases clearly demonstrate the proposition that where an operator can be found who is not dominated by the suggestion embraced in the spiritistic hypothesis, he will not assume to be a spirit. If he does entertain the spirit hypothesis, he *will* assume that he is a spirit, and answer accordingly. The mental and physical phenomena are the same in the one case as in the other. The logical conclusion is this: the fact that the intelligence which operates the pencil in the one case claims that it is a disembodied spirit does not constitute valid evidence that it is a spirit. We must look, therefore, to other sources for evidence of spirit origin of the phenomena. Obviously the only test by which that question can be settled is by the character of the communications. When that test is applied, it is found that all that is mysterious about them can be explained on the hypothesis of telepathy or clairvoyance. In the mean time, the fact that the power that writes is always amenable to control by suggestion, constitutes the strongest presumptive evidence that it is the subjective mind of the operator. This is the explanation which is afforded by a knowledge of some of the laws governing the action of the subjective mind. The *onus probandi* rests with those who claim a supernatural origin for the phenomenon.

TRANCE.

Under the general head of trance may be grouped all that class of cases in which the objective faculties are, for the time being, held in practically complete abeyance, and the subjective mind becomes correspondingly active. Various names have been applied to this condition, such as somnambulism, hypnosis, mesmeric trance, ecstasy, catalepsy, obsession, etc., many of the names implying a theory of causation rather than distinctive features of condition. The condition varies in accordance with the idiosyncrasies of the individual as much as from the causes which induce it. The leading characteristics are, however, the same in all cases. These are, first, the partial or complete abeyance of the objective mind; second, the activity of the subjective mind; and, third, the perfect amenability of the latter to control by the power of suggestion. Many remarkable mental phenomena are developed in these states, but this discussion will be confined to the supposed power of persons in the condition of trance to hold intercourse with the spiritual world.

This power has been held to exist from time immemorial; the ancient and modern mystical literature is filled with the most interesting, not to say startling, accounts of interviews held by these persons with the inhabitants of the spirit-land. Vast systems of religion have been founded upon the supposed revelations of persons in a trance, and untold millions of the human race base their hopes of a life in a future world upon the dreams of ecstatics. The whole vast fabric of Oriental philosophy and religion is based upon the revelations of persons in a trance. The Swedenborgian philosophy in the Western world is founded upon the dreams of a person who, in a condition of a trance, believed himself to be able to hold familiar converse with the inhabitants of heaven and of hell. Some of these systems of spiritual philosophy are of such vast and complicated structure that the mind is wrapped in wonder and admiration of their magnitude and perfection. The Oriental philosophy, in particular, is so symmetrical, so pervaded by grand and noble conceptions, so permeated with lofty precepts of morality, humanity, and religion, that we are wont to lose sight of the fact that the whole structure is built up by a process of deductive reasoning from premises that have no better foundation than the dreams of ecstatics. But we are told that it has stood the test of thousands of years of thought and investigation, and that no fact in physical science can be adduced to disprove its fundamental principles. Doubtless this is true. The adepts have steered clear of propositions in physical science which could be disproved by the learning of the schoolboy. In this they have avoided those errors of the Bible of the Christians, which, though unimportant in themselves, having no bearing upon the real philosophy of the Christian religion, have proved a stumbling-block to superficial minds. But does it follow that because a proposition regarding the condition of affairs in the spirit-world cannot be controverted by the science of the physical world, the proposition must necessarily be true? Clearly not. Again, does it follow that because a system of philosophy, the alleged facts of which are necessarily undemonstrable, has stood the test of thousands of years of investigation, it is necessarily correct? By no means. Time has effected for the Oriental philosophy that which has not been effected for the Western spiritual philosophy, simply for the want of time; it has perfected it as a system. The lapse of time has enabled the system to be evolved by the gradual but constant accretions of human thought, from generation to generation, until it has grown, from the first vague hope of the human soul for a life beyond the grave, to its present stupendous proportions. The processes of its growth can readily be seen and understood by a glance at the evolution of our own spiritistic philosophy within the memory of men now living. It is true that modern spiritism found a philosophy ready made to its hand in the writings of Emanuel Swedenborg. His descriptions of the spirit-world were in the main confirmed by the earlier mediums who were acquainted with his writings. His was essentially a material heaven. "As on earth, so in heaven," was his highest conception of the beauties and glories of the land of "spirits of just men made perfect." But he believed in hell, and he found one. He was inimical to certain Christian sects, and he found that all who belonged to those sects were condemned to everlasting punishment. When modern spiritism became a belief, it found its most enthusiastic followers among those who were outside of the pale of the Church, those who were in revolt against the asceticism of the Puritan belief and practices, those who refused to believe that a God of love and mercy would condemn any portion of his creatures to everlasting fire. They found in the Rochester knockings the first evidence which appealed to their senses of a life beyond the tomb; and they consulted their mediums with perfect confidence in their ability correctly to portray the condition of the denizens of the land of spirits. They learned from those oracles that their preconceived notions of divine justice were eminently correct, that there was no such place as hell, and that all alike shared in the boon of immortality; and, by a series of progressive steps, through seven or eight concentric spheres, all at last reached the highest state of divine felicity. They found that Swedenborg was right in the main, but was a little incorrect in his information concerning hell. It would be tedious, as well as superfluous, to enumerate the steps by which the philosophy of modern spiritism has advanced from the crude notions of the earlier writers to its present status. Every intelligent reader will recognize the wide difference between the rhapsodic hodge-podge of Andrew Jackson Davis and the calm philosophy of Judge Edmonds, and will not fail to note how completely the latter is now superseded by modern writers, who are gradually engrafting upon the indigenous stem the most luxurious branches of the Oriental tree. What their philosophy will be in coming years can be conjectured only by those who observe what evolution has done for the Oriental philosophy during the thousands of years of its existence.

The process of this evolution is easy to understand. The earlier mediums adopted the doctrines of Swedenborg, with certain amendments which seemed to them to be more in accord with reason and Divine justice. Those who followed, in turn adopted the main ideas of their predecessors, with amendments of their own. Each writer in succession amended the work of his predecessors in those respects in which it seemed to him to be imperfect, and each one had authority from the spirit-world which sanctioned the amendment. And thus the system grows in magnitude and perfection, and will continue to grow as long as men believe themselves to be inspired by extramundane intelligences.

Now, the noteworthy facts connected with this evolutionary process are, first, that all believe that they obtain their authority for every statement of fact and every new idea direct from the spirits of the dead ; and secondly, that every

260   *THE LAW OF PSYCHIC PHENOMENA.*

man who evolves a new idea, or is possessed of an old one, can easily have it confirmed by consulting a spirit medium, providing the proper suggestion is made to said medium. And this is true of all classes and ranks of mediums, from the common table-tipper to the Oriental ecstatic. If the medium is possessed of ideas of his own, and no outside suggestion is made, he will obtain information from the spirit world in exact accordance with his ideas. The same is true of all trance-seers, by whatever means the trance is brought about. Thus, Cahagnet, the French mesmerist, who devoted his life to mesmerizing subjects for the sole purpose of ascertaining what was going on in heaven, once mesmerized a French peasant, and directed him to visit the abode of the blest. This he promptly did, and reported that he saw a great white throne, surrounded by a great throng of people, all dressed in the most gorgeous apparel. On the throne was seated a man who was much larger than any of the rest, and who was further distinguished by the superior cut, make, fit, and material of his clothes. The peasant was sure that he had seen the Almighty, and so reported. It is obvious that he had simply seen a vision representing a peasant's idea of heaven. Cahagnet assured him that he must be mistaken, and quoted Bible authority to show that God himself has said, " There shall no man see me, and live." This was convincing to the simple-minded peasant, and Cahagnet advised him, the next time he was entranced, to ascertain if it was not a conclave of leading spirits that he saw, who were assembled for some purpose connected with the internal economy of heaven. Accordingly, he made inquiries the next time he was entranced, and ascertained that Cahagnet was right. It is clear that Cahagnet did not understand the law of suggestion, or his book would never have been written. It is scarcely necessary to remark that his book obtained a wide circulation, was translated into several languages, and constituted a standard mesmeric text-book for many years.

I have said that the same law of suggestion governs all trance-seers. This is obviously true. If it is a law, it is

universal in its application. Yet Orientalists tell us that
their visions are veridical, "because," they say, "they are
objective visions." This, of course, is merely begging the
question. They hold that the visions and other communications obtained by Western spiritists are mere "subjective
hallucinations." It is noteworthy that the distinction which
they make between the two kinds of visions is this: those
visions which accord with their views are "objective;"
those which do not are "subjective." It is a very easy and
comforting distinction, but it forcibly reminds one of the old
definition of orthodoxy as distinguished from heterodoxy:
"Orthodoxy is my doxy, and heterodoxy is your doxy."
The Oriental adepts claim that they have learned much more
of the laws of nature than is dreamed of in Occidental philosophy. Doubtless they have, if half the stories we hear
of them are true. They have learned to produce phenomena which far transcend anything done by our spirit mediums. Moreover, they have learned the true source of the
power, and they do not ascribe it to spirits of the dead.
Said one of them, in my hearing: "I have often been asked
the question, 'What is an adept?' An adept is a spirit
medium who knows that the power to produce his phenomena resides within himself, and who possesses the intelligence and power to control and direct it." This is the
exact truth in a nutshell. But because the adepts have
acquired the knowledge of the laws which govern the production of phenomena, and are able to apply them, it does
not follow that they are able to set any law of nature at
defiance, or that they can claim exemption from the operation of a universal law of our existence. We find in the
Western world that the law of suggestion controls all subjective phenomena, of whatever name or nature, and we
are slow to believe that Eastern people are exempt from
the operations of the same law. If they are, the burden
of proof rests upon them to demonstrate it. Thus far it
has not been demonstrated.

The literature of mysticism of all ages of the world and of
all nations is full of accounts of the visions of ecstatics. The

one noteworthy fact that is observable in all is that each one sees and hears that which he expects to see or hear. The details may be unexpected, and the whole may transcend his objective conceptions, but none controvert their preconceived ideas. Catholic ecstatics will see Catholic visions, and Protestants will see Protestant visions. In short, whatever may be the belief or the philosophy of the ecstatic, confirmation of that belief will be found in his visions of, or his communications from, the other world. The history of the Catholic Church abounds in accounts of wonderful visions seen by nuns and other religious devotees of that faith. One noteworthy fact constantly reappears in that connection, which is, that they nearly always become entranced after long contemplation of the image of the Saviour or of the Virgin Mary. This fact is interesting from a purely scientific standpoint. The physical attitude which they assume in contemplation of the crucifix is the one most conducive to the induction of the hypnotic condition. The significance of this observation will be at once apparent when we remember that Dr. Braid demonstrated that fixed gazing upon an object held in such a position as to cause the eyes to be strained upward is the easiest way to induce the hypnotic condition. The attitude, both physical and mental, of prayer, is therefore the one most favorable to the induction of the hypnotic or trance condition on the one hand, and, on the other, to the production of the visions which accord with the faith and expectancy of the individual.

The fact that the physical attitude assumed in prayer has a tendency to induce the subjective condition, will account for many of the well-recognized effects of earnest supplication of Divine favor. That calm tranquillity of mind which follows the prayer of faith may be attributed, in part at least, to the physical condition resulting from partial hypnosis. The objective faculties are held in abeyance, the nerves are tranquillized, and that part of " God in us " holds communion and is harmonized with its Divine source. Thus it is that long and earnest prayer for the restoration of health is often followed by marvellous results, especially when it is inspired by perfect faith in the promises of the Master. The fact that faith constitutes a strong suggestion to the subjective mind, which in turn controls the condition of the body, does not militate against the idea of Divine agency in the result. It is the Divine essence within us which produces the effect, and it operates in strict accordance with Divine law. It confirms and explains that which Christ taught so earnestly and so persistently, namely, that we must have faith, or our prayers will avail nothing. That he understood the principle involved, goes without saying; but it was not yet time to give it to the world, for the world was not prepared to receive it. " I have many things to say unto you, but ye cannot bear them now," were his words, uttered during his last interview with his disciples previous to his crucifixion. His was the " dispensation of faith." The promised " dispensation of knowledge " has not yet been inaugurated; when it is, the wisdom which he taught will be better understood, for it will then be known that the doctrines which he enunciated regarding his power over disease, and the conditions of immortality, were but statements in strict accordance with scientific facts.

OBSESSION.

Webster defines " obsession " as " the state of a person vexed or besieged by an evil spirit, antecedent to possession." The latter term he defines as " the state of being possessed, as by an evil spirit," etc. Allan Kardec employs obsession as a generic term, to include *simple obsession*, which accords with Webster's definition of the term ; *fascination*, which is " an illusion produced by direct action on the medium's thought," paralyzing his judgment ; and *subjugation*, which completely paralyzes the will, and causes the medium to act in spite of himself. For our purpose these fine distinctions are immaterial, as they merely represent different stages or degrees of intensity of the same phenomenon. The theory of obsession is a modernizing of the old idea of being possessed of a devil, or devils, as the case might be. It consists in being dominated, to a greater or less extent, by the idea that the person is besieged or controlled by a foreign spirit, good or bad, angel or devil. It seems superfluous to remark that the same principles prevail in these cases as in all others where the idea of spirits has been suggested to the subjective mind. It matters not how the suggestion originated, the result is the same. In ancient times the idea prevailed that any one was liable at any time to be taken possession of by a devil. When that idea was in vogue it frequently happened that persons who easily entered the subjective condition found themselves possessed of one or more devils. In those times the profession of exorcist was very profitable. The priesthood generally monopolized the business, for the obvious reason that they were supposed to entertain a spirit of more or less antagonism to devils generally. Besides, devils were supposed to have a mortal fear of anything holy; they had an especial dread of the sight of a copy of the Scriptures, and of hearing the name of God pronounced. Accordingly it came to pass that, upon the command of the exorcist, the devil would often incontinently fly, leaving the patient in his normal condition. Sometimes, however, he would be more stubborn, and the patient would go into convulsions upon hearing the magic words pronounced; and then more severe measures would have to be adopted, such as employing more exorcists. But persistence was generally rewarded with success.

In later years devils have generally gone out of fashion, and their place is taken by bad spirits of dead men. And so it has come to pass that many spirit mediums are sorely afflicted with spirits, who pester them most outrageously. The exorcist is now replaced by the family doctor, who is generally scientific to the last degree, and accordingly endeavors to get rid of the spirit by means of physic or clysters. Recently, however, such cases have been treated successfully by means of hypnotism, which is the obvious remedy, in case the hypnotist realizes the power of suggestion.

It is obvious to those who have followed our argument thus far that the subjective mind of the person obsessed is dominated by the suggestion that it is a bad spirit or a devil, as the case may be ; and that, acting upon that suggestion, it will personate the spirit or devil with the same extraordinary acumen that it would personate any other character suggested. And it will assume to be one, two, or seven devils or spirits, in accordance with the suggestion, and will exhibit as many different kinds and degrees of deviltry as there are devils embraced in the suggestion.

Such cases are frequently characterized by the development of wonderful telepathic power ; and this of course adds to the mystery and confirms his friends in the idea that the patient is controlled by an extramundane agency. But, while it adds to the mystery, it does not militate against the soundness of the explanation afforded by the laws of duality and suggestion. The ceremony of exorcism by the priests in ancient times constituted a most powerful suggestive command, which could not, and did not, fail in having the desired effect. There was an interval, however, between the days of priestly exorcism and the days of modern hypnotism, during which scepticism prevailed regarding the power of any one to exorcise an offending spirit, or to cure the patient by other than material remedies. Patients were then sent to insane asylums, only to increase their maladies. But in later years the power of hypnotic suggestion has become a recognized principle in therapeutics, and little trouble is experienced in curing obsessed patients where the brain has not become diseased. The fact that the trouble is susceptible of cure by hypnotic suggestion points clearly to its mental origin, and precludes the possibility of its being attributable to supermundane causes.

DUAL PERSONALITY.

Cognate in some of its essential characteristics to the phenomenon of obsession is that of *dual personality ;* and although it has nothing to do with the question of spiritism, it may as well be noted here as elsewhere. By this term is not meant the duality of mental organization which pertains to every human being, but it refers to a specific phenomenon which has received that name from recent scientific observers. It is characterized by a complete loss of knowledge of personal identity. The patient assumes a new name, a new personality, and a new character, the last being often in marked contrast to the normal one in every essential particular. The old personality is sometimes completely forgotten, and sometimes it is remembered only as a person whom the patient has once known. In some instances the two personalities alternate at somewhat irregular intervals. In others, the phenomenon occurs only once in a lifetime. In others, several different personalities will be assumed at different times. In all these cases certain characteristics constantly reappear, the most notable appearing in the fact that the new personality is always consistent with itself; that is, it is always the same, whenever it reappears. Its moral characteristics are sometimes in marked contrast to the lifelong character developed in the normal state, but it never varies from one time to another. If a dozen different personalities should be assumed at different times, each would always be consistent with itself. The incidents occurring during the continuance of one interval of the abnormal personality will always be remembered whenever the same personality reappears, so that the existence of the new personality, when it reappears with frequency, is practically continuous; that is, the intervals of normal consciousness do not seem to be remembered. The normal personality, however, never remembers aught of what occurred during the abnormal interval. As before remarked, the abnormal personality sometimes remembers the existence of the normal one, but always as that of a third person, upon whom it often looks, and of whom it sometimes speaks, with pitying contempt. It generally happens, in case two or more abnormal personalities are assumed, that each remembers all the other abnormal characters, but regards them as third persons having no connection whatever with itself.

One of the most remarkable cases which have been reported in the United States was that of one Ansel Bourne, a Baptist clergyman, who suddenly disappeared from his home in Rhode Island a few years ago. Every effort was made to find him, but without avail. At the end of two months he returned to his home, after an experience of the strangest character. It appears, from an investigation conducted in the most careful and painstaking manner, in behalf of the London Society for Psychical Research, that Mr. Bourne lost normal consciousness soon after leaving home, and wandered around in several different towns and cities, finally reaching Norristown, Pa., where he rented a store, stocked it with small wares, and carried it on successfully for a period of six weeks, under the name of A. J. Brown. He appeared to the citizens of Norristown as a normal person, conducting his business properly, contracting no unnecessary debts, and always paying promptly. At the end of six weeks of a mercantile career he suddenly regained his normal consciousness, and remembered nothing whatever of his abnormal experience. The article in the Proceedings of the Society for Psychical Research, written by Richard Hodgson, LL.D., exhibits exhaustive research in the investigation of this case, and its entire verity cannot be doubted. It appears that Mr. Bourne had once, in early life, had a remarkable experience, which shows a tendency to abnormal psychic conditions; but nothing was developed which throws any light upon any specific cause for the particular phase of his later experience. He had never before engaged in trade, nor had he had any taste for such a life, and nothing could be remembered which could explain why it was that he assumed the name of A. J. Brown. It is stated, however, that he had once been hypnotized, when young, and made to perform many amusing antics on the stage; but no recollection was had that the name of A. J. Brown had been suggested to him at the time. It is extremely probable, however, that that name *was* suggested to him at that time, and that his subjective mind retained the memory of the name, and that the impression lasted all those years, only to reappear when he again went into a hypnotic trance. This is only a conjecture, however; but it has been shown in a previous chapter how the subjective mind of a young lady retained the impression of its identity with a certain fictitious character, which she had once assumed in a play, and with which it again identified itself in obedience to her suggestion, made when she was in the normal condition.

Again, it is a common stage experiment in hypnotism to suggest some name to the subject, and some character in which he is made to act, that of a merchant being not uncommon. When we remember how lasting are such impressions upon the subjective mind, and how prone they are to reappear at any subsequent time when the same conditions exist, we are prepared to believe that such a suggestion, made in early life, would be an ample explanation of the subsequent event. The fact that the suggestion, whatever it was and by whomsoever it was made, was made while the subject was in the hypnotic condition, and could not, therefore, be remembered objectively, explains why it is that in few, if any, of such cases can any clew be obtained as to the origin of the suggestion, or any reason assigned for the assumption of any particular personality.

The dual character of the persons thus afflicted constitutes the most indubitable evidence of the duality of man's mental organism, and it is beginning to be so recognized by European scientific observers. Some of them say, however, " If this is evidence of duality of mind, what shall we say of those who exhibit a triple personality? Is that an evidence of a trinity of mind?" The question is pertinent, and is easily answered. It is obvious that the persons exhibiting the phenomenon are in a hypnotic trance, and are, therefore, governed by the laws pertaining to hypnotism. They have an objective mind, which is the controlling power in the normal condition. In the hypnotic state the normal, or objective, faculties are in abeyance, and the person is amenable to control by the power of suggestion. Whatever name or character is then suggested is at once assumed by the subject. The suggestion may be oral, and proceed from another; or it may be an auto-suggestion, arising from something suggested in a previous hypnotization, or from some forgotten circumstance. Be that as it may, the suggested character is assumed and carried out with all the deductive logical exactitude characteristic of subjective reasoning. This is a well-known result of a common hypnotic experiment. It is also well known that the subject can be made to assume any number of characters by the same process. It is a common stage experiment to cause a versatile subject, who is easily controlled, to assume a dozen different characters in the course of an evening's performance. It is obvious, therefore, that persons who are afflicted with a second personality, which occasionally takes possession of them, are also liable to assume a third, or, indeed, any number of names and characters, if anything happens to suggest them. In fact, the power of suggestion over the subjective mind, in the line of multiplication of characters, is practically unlimited. It is not a multiplication of personalities, however, nor an evidence of a triple or a quadruple personality, but merely an exhibition of the power of the second, or subjective, personality of man to assume, in obedience to the law of suggestion, any number of real or imaginary characters. The same power is exhibited by the subjective personality of a spirit medium when it assumes the names and characters of any number of spirits of the dead, whose names are suggested.

The specific character of the mental operations of persons in whom the second personality is abnormally developed has not been recorded, so far as we are aware. It will be found, however, when observations are made in that direction, that they have practically no capacity for reasoning by the inductive process when under the control of the second personality. This will certainly be the case if the hypnosis is perfect. Otherwise it might be modified by the synchronous action of the objective mind. It is hoped

that future observers will direct their attention to this question, to the end that a series of facts may be collated which
shall assist in determining the direction and extent, as well
as the exact limitations, of subjective mental power. When
that is accomplished, the first great step will have been
taken in bringing psychology within the domain of the
exact sciences.

CHAPTER XIX.

THE PHYSICAL PHENOMENA OF SPIRITISM.

THE physical phenomena of spiritism are in more senses than one the most interesting of all the manifestations of subjective power. They require, however, but a brief treatment at our hands, for the reason that the primary object of this book is to deal with the mental powers and attributes of mankind in their relations to psychic phenomena. No attempt, therefore, will be made to prove that the alleged physical phenomena of so-called spiritism are veridical or otherwise. It would be a work of supererogation to attempt to add force or volume to the already overwhelming array of testimony going to show the wonderful physical power often displayed in connection with psychic phenomena. For our purposes it is not a matter of vital importance whether things can be made to levitate without physical contact or not. It will be assumed, therefore, that all statements made by respectable witnesses in regard to the occurrence of physical phenomena are true. We do this partly because we believe them to be true, having seen enough to *know* the reality of the leading physical phenomena, and partly because our purpose is to deal with the mental aspects of psychic phenomena, and the laws which pertain to their development. We shall leave to those who are sceptical, or who think they are sceptical rather than ignorant, the task of investigating, after the ponderous and elaborate methods of the scientists, phenomena which can be verified beyond the possible shadow of a doubt, by the exercise of a little common-sense. And we will here undertake to guarantee that if any scientific gentleman will, in good faith, follow the suggestions offered in former chapters of this book regarding the proper method of dealing with so-called mediums, and will divest himself, for the time being, of all fear of professional mediums and all prejudice against them, he will not only see enough to convince him of the truth of all that is alleged regarding physical phenomena, but he will also see that the elaborate test conditions often insisted upon by scientific investigators are superfluous, not to say absurd. These remarks are, of course, applicable to the better class of mediums, that is, those who are recognized by the great body of spiritists as possessing a high order of mediumistic power. Their moral characteristics need not count as a factor, for it is to the interest of a medium to produce genuine phenomena when he can, and he will always do so if the conditions are favorable. Mediums are always anxious to exhibit their phenomena, when genuine, under test conditions, and will do so in a way that shall satisfy the most sceptical. A further qualification of the foregoing remarks should be made in regard to "materializing" mediums. The writer has never seen anything genuine in the line of materializations. There is here more room for fraud, and more fraud is perpetrated by materializing mediums than by any other, because materialization is a rare and difficult phase of mediumship. Yet there is every reason to believe, and we shall undertake to show further on, that the production of genuine apparitions, resembling the persons they profess to represent, is a possibility within the range of psychic power.

The remarks which follow will therefore be addressed, not to those who are not yet convinced of the reality of physical phenomena, but to those who are aware of their reality, but attribute them to extramundane causes.

There is one pregnant fact connected with these manifestations which all will admit, and that is that there is an intelligence which directs and controls them. This intelligence is that of disembodied spirits, or it is not. If it is not, it must be that of embodied spirits. These propositions, if not self-evident, will at least be admitted to be true by those who believe that it proceeds from disembodied spirits of human beings. The intelligence is a human intelligence, — that is, it is characterized by human imperfections and limitations; and, as all human beings must be classified as either living or dead, we must look to one class or the other for the source of the phenomena.

The first question in order is, What are the inherent probabilities? Conceding the power to exist, it would seem to be more inherently probable that it is possessed by a soul connected with a living organism, than it is that it is possessed by a soul that has been entirely severed from all connection with the material world. Spiritists themselves unwittingly concede the truth of this proposition when they assert, as does Allan Kardec, on the authority, as he says, of " the spirit of Saint Louis," that " the spirits who produce these effects are always inferior spirits, who are not entirely disengaged from material influence." [1] Besides, the very fact that the intervention of a " medium " is necessary for the production of physical phenomena demonstrates the proposition that the elements of physical organism are essential. It requires, therefore, two things to produce the phenomena; namely, a soul and a body. In a living man the two are united and working in harmony. Is it not probable that such an organism is capable of producing all the effects attributed to the temporary union of a dead

[1] Book on Mediums, p. 87.

man's soul and a living man's body? If not, why not? Why should a dead man's spirit in abnormal union with a living man's body possess more power than a living man's spirit in normal union with his own body? Is it because the former possesses more knowledge than the latter? No, for we have seen that it is only "inferior spirits" who are capable of producing physical manifestations. Superior knowledge confers no advantage; for, as Kardec informs us, the superior spirits have no power in that direction. We have, therefore, the authority of the spiritists themselves for formulating the proposition that the more completely the spirit of a man is "disengaged from material influence," the less power he possesses to produce physical phenomena. This being true, it follows that the converse of the proposition is true, namely, that the more completely the spirit of a man is united to material elements, the greater is his power to produce such phenomena. The conclusion is irresistible that the spirit of a man in normal union with his own body possesses the power in perfection.

If, therefore, we can find in abstract reasoning no warrant for the assumption that the phenomena are produced by disembodied spirits, we must look elsewhere for evidence of their extramundane origin. The first inquiry naturally suggesting itself is, What internal evidence is contained in the character of the manifestations which would enable one to form a correct judgment regarding their probable source? We have already seen that reasoning from their physical character leads us to the conclusion that the physical power displayed must have a physical basis, and that that basis is probably the physical organism of the medium. Now, if its intellectual character leads us in the same direction, the evidence is still stronger in favor of its purely human origin. We presume that no one will dispute the proposition that the communications received through the physical phenomena are governed by the same laws as those received by means of the other methods which have been discussed. Indeed, the fact is almost self-evident. They have the same origin, and must be governed by the same laws. The remarks, therefore, which have been made concerning the character of the communications obtained by other than physical means apply with full force to those obtained through physical demonstrations. The laws of telepathy and suggestion play their subtle *rôle* in the one case the same as in the other. If possible, there is less evidence of extramundane origin in the physical manifestations than there is in the intellectual. Indeed, this might be pre-supposed, from the gross character of the former, even though the latter had a purely spiritual source. If, therefore, we find no valid evidence of extramundane origin in the higher manifestations, it is a waste of time to seek for evidence of spirit intercourse in the tipping of kitchen tables, the levitation of parlor sofas, or the convulsions of whole sets of chamber furniture.

The foregoing remarks apply to all forms and grades of physical phenomena, of which there are many. Some of them possess the most intense interest, not only on account of the wonderful psycho-physical power displayed, but because of their intellectual phases. Slate-writing, for instance, when performed by a first-class medium, gifted with a high order of telepathic power, accompanied by other necessary intellectual qualifications, is one of the most interesting of all phases of psychic power. An instance which occurred within the writer's own experience will be here related, for the reason that it fully illustrates the essential qualifications and characteristics of a first-class medium, shows both the physical and mental powers with which he is endowed, and clearly defines the limitations which hedge him about, and which point, with unerring exactitude, to the source of the phenomena.

A few years ago, a conversation which the writer had with a celebrated Union general led to an agreement to visit a prominent slate-writing medium, then sojourning in the city of Washington. Among other things, it was agreed that the general should be the sitter, and that he should be guided entirely by my suggestions relative to the course which he should pursue before and during the séance.

My object, which he fully understood and appreciated, was, first, to convince him of the genuineness of the physical phenomena, — that is, that the slate-writing was performed without corporeal contact of the medium with the pencil, and without the shadow of a possibility of the employment of legerdemain ; and, secondly, to demonstrate the utter impossibility of the phenomena being attributable to disembodied spirits.

It must be premised that the medium was in the habit of causing his sitters to write six short letters to as many different spirits. These epistles are written on separate pieces of paper about three inches square, and are addressed to the spirits by name and signed by the writer, precisely as an ordinary letter would be addressed and signed. Each letter is then rolled into a wad as small as possible, and retained in the hand of the sitter until he is requested to deposit them in a pile on the table. When this is done, the medium reaches his hand across the table and touches the wads with the tips of his fingers, the sitter meanwhile watching the proceeding closely, to prevent the possibility of fraud. After the medium has touched each bit of paper the sitter resumes possession of them and retains them for future reference. It may be here remarked that a sitter has the privilege of bringing his own slates with him, and retaining possession of them until the writing is finished. They need not leave his custody for an instant. He may place the bit of pencil between them himself, and then securely lock or tie them together, and hold them as tightly as he chooses on the top of the table, in the broad light of day, while the writing is going on.

The plan suggested to the general on this occasion, and which he carried out to the letter, was as follows : —

1. To write three letters to as many spirits of his dead acquaintances, each one couched in general terms, — such as, " Dear B., can you communicate with me to-day? If so, tell me your condition in the spirit-land." This could be answered by very general remarks, and would require no specific answer involving any knowledge of the sitter's affairs or anything else.

2. To write two similar letters to two persons known to the sitter, but unknown to the medium, to be still living in the flesh.

3. To write one letter to a deceased person, asking a specific question, the correct answer to which neither the sitter nor the medium could possibly know.

4. To place the medium at his ease, by leading him to believe that he had to deal with a sympathetic believer in the doctrine of spiritism, who had perfect faith in the medium's powers.

5. To prescribe no test conditions whatever, but let the medium have his own way in everything.

6. Under no circumstances to let the medium know the name or antecedents of the sitter.

These suggestions were carried out to the letter. The general was unknown to the medium, and was introduced by the writer under a fictitious name. The medium occupied a suite of rooms consisting of a large double parlor separated by folding-doors. The front parlor was used as a reception-room, and the back parlor as a séance-room. The latter was lighted by one large window, in front of which stood an old-fashioned square dining-table. The medium seated himself on one side of this table, and the sitter occupied a chair on the opposite side. Several slates were lying on the table, two of which the medium washed clean and then gave them into the custody of the sitter, who carefully examined them, and kept them in his possession until the séance was over, resting his arms upon them while he wrote the prescribed letters. He was particularly cautious about writing the letters, carefully guarding them so that it was impossible for the medium to see the writing with his natural eyes, and never lifted his elbows from the two slates in his custody. When the letters were all finished and rolled into wads, they were placed upon the table directly between the medium and the sitter, the latter never allowing his eyes to wander from them for an instant. The medium then touched each wad with his finger-tips, when they were again taken possession of by the sitter.

It should be stated that the séance, thus far, was not witnessed by myself; but the circumstances were afterwards detailed by the general, whose perfect trustworthiness is beyond question. At this juncture — that is, while the wads were still lying on the table — a most remarkable incident happened. The medium suddenly arose, opened the folding-doors, and invited me in to take part in the séance. After resuming his seat, he remarked to me : " There is a spirit here who refuses to communicate until you are allowed to be present. He says his name is G —— (mentioning a common Christian name). Have you any deceased friend by that name ? " I answered, No, not remembering, for the moment, any one bearing that name. The medium then handed me a pencil, and said : " Touch one of those wads with the pencil ; then open it, and you will find that it is a letter addressed to G——."

I touched one of the six wads, at random of course, and upon opening it found, to my surprise, that it was a letter addressed by the sitter to his deceased brother G——. The brother was also a very dear friend of mine ; but his exalted position in life precluded me from ever addressing him by his Christian name, and I had not been consciously thinking of him during the séance. Then the medium again addressed me, as follows : —

" Fold the letter again, place it with the others, and mix them all together. Then take the pencil and touch another wad ; and the one you touch you will find to be a letter addressed to M ——."

This was done, and the wad touched proved to be a letter addressed to the party named by the medium. A third time this feat was performed with the same result. To say that we were surprised is but feebly to express our emotions. The first success might be attributable to coincidence, supposing the medium to be in possession of the name. The chances were one to six, and it is within easy range of coincidence that I should have hit upon the right letter. In the second trial the chances were also one to six, *per se ;* but the chances that I should succeed twice in succession were largely against me; and the fact that I succeeded three times in succession in pointing out the right letter removes the matter far outside the domain of coincidence. When we take into account the telepathic power displayed by the medium, and that other power, whatever it may have been, which transformed me for the moment into an automaton, the incident will be seen to possess an extraordinary interest and importance. I should here remark that that was the first and only experience of my own in the domain of subjective automatism, and that I did not experience any sensation which could lead me to suppose that I was not in a perfectly normal condition, mentally and physically.

The most remarkable part of the performance, however, is yet to be related. The sitter meantime did not lose his presence of mind, but carefully guarded the pair of slates in his custody, never lifting his arms from them as they lay upon the table before him. Nor did he for an instant lose sight of the wads of paper which he placed upon the table. The medium touched them with his finger-tips alone, as before related; and after I had pointed out the three letters, they were taken into the custody of the sitter. This done, the medium said to the sitter: "Open the slates, and you will find a communication from G——." This was done, and the promised communication was found, addressed to the sitter by name and signed by G——, the name of the sitter's brother. In fact, it was a pertinent answer to the letter written by the sitter to his brother, addressed as the sitter had signed his name, and signed as the sitter's brother had been addressed.

The medium then became considerably agitated, and moved with convulsive rapidity. He seized two other slates, washed them, submitted them for inspection, and placed them upon the centre of the table before us, with a bit of black pencil between them. He then invited us to place our hands upon the slate with him. This we did, whereupon the writing began. We could distinctly hear the pencil move with a gentle, but rapid, scratching sound. In a few minutes three raps were heard, apparently made by the pencil between the slates. This was said to be the signal announcing the completion of the message. The slates were then separated, and several messages were found inside.

Two more slates were then seized by the medium, washed, submitted for inspection, and placed upon the table as before. Our hands were again placed upon the slates, and the writing again began. After it had progressed for a few moments, the medium announced that the spirits wanted to write in colors. He thereupon arose, walked to the mantelpiece, and produced a box of colored crayons, all in small bits, about the size of the piece of black slate-pencil with which the writing had been done. We were about to open the slates, to allow the insertion of the cray-ons, when the medium said that it was unnecessary, as " the colors could be got from the outside just as well." The box of crayons was accordingly placed beside the slate, and the writing was resumed. After a short interval the signal was given that the messages were finished. The general thereupon very carefully separated the slates, to see if there were any colored crayons concealed therein. Only the bit of black slate pencil was there, but four or five different colors had been used in writing the messages.

The results of this séance may be summed up as follows :

The contents of every letter written by the sitter were evidently known to the intelligence which wrote the replies, for every letter received an appropriate answer, save one, which will be noted further on. The answer to each letter was addressed to the name signed to the corresponding letter, and each answer was signed with the name of the person to whom the corresponding letter was addressed.

Six letters were written by the sitter, as before stated. Three of them were written to deceased friends of the sitter, and were couched in such general terms that the replies did not require any specific knowledge on the part of the intelligence which wrote the replies.

Two of the letters were written to living persons, and they were also couched in general terms, requiring no specific knowledge to enable an appropriate reply to be framed.

Each of these five letters received a reply which assumed that its writer was a denizen of the spirit-land. There was no difference in their replies so far as that was concerned.

The sixth letter was addressed to a deceased relative, and was as follows, omitting names : —

DEAR A. B., — Whom did you desire to have appointed administrator of your estate?   (Signed)   C. D.

To this letter the only reply was from the medium's "control," who reported as follows : —

" A. B. is here, but cannot communicate to-day."

The conclusions which are inevitable may be summed as follows : —

1. The slate-writing was done without physical contact with the pencil, either by the medium or any one else. It all occurred in broad daylight. The slates were not handled by the medium, except to wash them and to place his hands upon them (in all cases but one) while the writing was going on. The slates were not for an instant out of sight of the sitter during the whole séance, nor were they out of his custody during that time, after they were washed by the medium. They were then carefully inspected by the sitter, the pencil was placed between them by the sitter, they were tied together by the sitter, and opened by him after the writing was finished. In short, there was no chance for fraud or legerdemain, and there was none.

2. The power which moved the pencil, being clearly not physical, must have been occult. This occult power was either that of disembodied spirits, or that of the medium. Did it proceed from disembodied spirits? Let us see. The replies to the five letters emanated from the same source; that is to say, if the replies to any of them were from disembodied spirits, they were all from disembodied spirits. They were clearly not all from disembodied spirits, for two of the letters were addressed to

living persons, and the replies were of the same character as the others. The logical conclusion is inevitable that none of the replies were from disembodied spirits. To put it in the simple form of a syllogism, we have the following : —

The replies to the five letters were all from the same source.

Two of them were not from disembodied spirits.

Therefore, none of them were from disembodied spirits.

Again :

The power to produce the slate-writing emanated either from disembodied spirits or from the medium.

It did not emanate from disembodied spirits.

Therefore, it emanated from the medium.

Having now logically traced the phenomenon to the door of the medium, let us see what further evidence there is in support of that conclusion. And first let us inquire, Is there anything inherently improbable in the theory that he was the source of the intelligence which guided, and the power which moved, the pencil? Was there any intellectual feat performed which rendered it impossible that he should have been its author? The power to read the contents of the six letters was obviously within the domain of telepathy. He was, therefore, just as well equipped for the performance of that feat as a disembodied spirit could be. Suggestion also plays its subtle *rôle* in this class of phenomena, as in all others, and relieves the medium of all imputation of dishonesty or insincerity in attributing it to the wrong source. The probability that the power to move the pencil without physical contact resides in the medium, is as great, at least, as the probability that it resides in disembodied spirits. All these questions have, however, been fully discussed, and are mentioned here merely to complete the chain of reasoning.

There was nothing apparent in the answers to the five letters mentioned which would indicate that they emanated from any source other than the medium. They contained no information possessed exclusively by disembodied spirits, although they all purported to emanate from them. The five letters were not, however, framed for the purpose of testing the knowledge possessed by spirits, but merely to show that the replies did not emanate from that source.

The sixth letter, however, *was* framed for the express purpose of testing the knowledge possessed by the intelligence which moved the pencil. The question, "Whom did you desire to have appointed administrator of your estate?" was asked because the sitter did not know the correct answer, and he knew that the medium could not know. The knowledge was possessed by the deceased person exclusively; and it is reasonable to suppose that if he was present, as the medium declared that he was, he would have given the desired information. The intelligence which wrote the replies was in full possession of the contents of all the letters, all the names addressed, and all the signatures, including those of the sixth letter. The answers to five of them were pertinent and intelligent, no specific knowledge being required. But when the sixth was reached, the spirit "could not communicate to-day." Why? Simply because the specific knowledge required to answer the question was not in the possession of any one present, and it could not, therefore, be obtained telepathically, as the knowledge of the contents of the other letters was obtained.

This is the rock upon which all so-called spirit intercourse splits. Everything goes along swimmingly as long as the medium knows what to reply, or can obtain information by means of his telepathic or clairvoyant powers. But the moment he is confronted by a question requiring knowledge not obtainable in that way, he fails dismally.

The circumstances of this séance have been detailed for the reason that it was a typical séance. It displayed all the essential characteristics of modern spirit intercourse, so-called. The medium displayed all the essential powers and attributes of good mediumship. The physical phenomena were produced to perfection, and under the most perfect test-conditions. The telepathic powers displayed were of the most extraordinary character, and the conditions under which they were produced were also such as to preclude the possibility of fraud or legerdemain. The results were also perfect in their character, showing, as they did, both the powers of the medium and his limitations. The dual character of the human mind was also clearly manifested, and the perfect amenability of the subjective entity to control by the power of suggestion was demonstrated.

It would be interesting to pursue the subject of physical manifestations further, and to examine all their multiform characteristics; but that would be foreign to the purposes of this book. The examination of the mental characteristics of the intelligence which controls the different manifestations is our only purpose, and we have shown that the same laws prevail in all. It is believed that enough has been said to enable the conscientious investigator, who wishes to test the correctness of our hypothesis, to apply its fundamental propositions to all psychic phenomena. It is also believed that whoever so applies those propositions will arrive at the same conclusions to which I have come; namely, that there is no valid evidence, in any of the phenomena of so-called spiritism, that the spirits of the dead have any part in their production. On the contrary, as it seems to me, the evidence all points in the opposite direction. I refer, of course, solely to those phenomena which are produced through so-called spirit mediums. If there is any communication to be had with the denizens of the other shore, it is certainly not through them. I have reluctantly arrived at this conclusion. It would be pleasant to believe otherwise, but I have sought in vain for evidence which would warrant me in doing so.

In abandoning all hope of obtaining valid evidence of the ability of disembodied spirits to hold intercourse with the living through the intervention of spirit mediums, I do not for a moment yield my hope, or my convictions, of a life beyond the grave. On the contrary, the very powers which are evoked in the production of the phenomena constitute one of the strongest links in the chain of evidence going to show that man possesses within himself an entity which does not depend for its existence upon the continued life of the body. We see that this entity possesses powers which far transcend those of our physical frame; that the mental powers of the subjective mind or entity are exercised independently of our objective senses; that they grow stronger as the body grows weaker, and are strongest in the hour of death. Have we not a logical right to infer that when it is entirely freed from physical trammels, it will have reached a condition of independent existence? What that existence is, it is not for objective man to know. It is possible that if spirits could communicate as familiarly with the living as we commune with one another, they would have no language which could bring to our comprehension their true condition. It would be like teaching an infant the principles of the differential calculus. How can the caterpillar, crawling upon the ground, hold intelligent communion with the airy butterfly, or the butterfly reveal to the caterpillar the mysteries of her winged life?

The fact remains that mankind has ever hoped, and will ever hope, for a continued existence of some kind; and all the old arguments in its favor, and all the promises of the Master, still hold good. Moreover, every new development in psychic science adds strength to the arguments, and fresh proofs of his wisdom.

CHAPTER XX.

PHANTASMS OF THE DEAD.

THERE is another class of phenomena which demands a brief notice, although it does not pertain directly to the development of the hypothesis under consideration. It is that of phantasms of the dead, or ghosts. Scientific investigations of modern times have demonstrated the fact that many of the ghost-stories which have terrified the timid in all ages of the world have a real foundation in fact ; that is, it has been demonstrated that certain impalpable shapes, resembling persons deceased, do from time to time appear to the living. The world is indebted more than it can ever repay to the London Society for Psychical Research for its patient, untiring, and strictly scientific investigations of this subject. Many facts have been accumulated, but they have not yet been classified with reference to any special theory or hypothesis. It is perhaps too early to formulate any hypòthesis pertaining to the subject-matter. It is certainly too early to dogmatize. The most that can safely be done is to speculate tentatively, and to suggest a line of thought and investigation for those who are devoting their time to the work. It is my purpose to do this, and this alone, in the hope that if the suggestions seem to be worthy of consideration, the subject may be pursued on the lines indicated until their fallacy is exposed or their correctness demonstrated.

It seems to me that sufficient facts have been accumulated to establish, provisionally at least, certain definite characteristics of all phantasms, whether of the living or the dead ; and if a theory can be formulated, however startling it may be at first glance, that will harmonize with the well-established characteristics of the phenomena, it will be at least worthy of consideration. In attempting to do this, I shall not quote authorities to any extent to establish my premises, but shall state merely what seems to be well authenticated, and leave the verification of the premises, as well as the conclusions, to those who have more time, patience, and ability to devote to the work than I have.

First of all, then, it seems to be well authenticated that the subjective personality of man possesses the power to create phantasms, or visions, which in many instances are visible to the objective senses of others. The telepathic experiments recorded in " Phantasms of the Living " and in the Proceedings of the Society for Psychical Research amply demonstrate the truth of this proposition. Every vision perceived by one in telepathic rapport with another must be presumed to have been created by one or the other. It is true that some of the visions may be merely perceived subjectively, but not all. Many cases are recorded where the phantasms have been perceived by more than one person at the same time, and others have been perceived under circumstances such as to leave no doubt that the percipient was in a completely normal condition, and saw the visions objectively. Moreover, the phenomena of so-called spirit photography amply demonstrate the fact that visions can be created of such tangible character that they can be caught and fixed upon the photographic plate. In saying this I am not insensible of the fact that many frauds have been committed in this species of phenomena, as well as in all others attributed to spirits of the dead. But this does not militate against phenomena of that character which have been produced under test conditions so strict that all possibility of fraud was eliminated. In admitting this class of phenomena to be genuine, in the sense that it is sometimes produced without fraud or legerdemain, it is also admitted that, in many instances, pictures of the sitter's dead friends have been produced which were such perfect likenesses of the deceased as to be unmistakable. Of course it will be understood that whilst I admit the phenomenon, I do not admit the claim that it has its origin in the spirit-world. Like all other so-called spirit phenomena, it is, in my opinion, directly traceable to the power of the subjective mind of the medium, aided by telepathic communion with the sitter. The latter, consciously or unconsciously, thinks of one or more of his dead friends. The medium, perceiving telepathically the image created by the mind of the sitter, re-creates it in such tangible shape that it is caught by the camera. Or it may be in some instances that the image is created by the sitter himself in such palpable shape as to be caught by the camera. Indeed, in many recorded instances, where the sitter has been a powerful medium, it seems probable that he created the image himself. In point of fact there is little doubt that the power resides, to a greater or less extent, in all human beings to create such images, their strength and clearness depending, of course, upon the power of the individual to recall vividly the remembrance of the person to be photographed, together with the power to concentrate his mind for a certain length of time upon the mental picture. Indeed, experiments have been made which demonstrate the power to produce the picture of any one, living or dead, in this manner.

This being true, two conclusions are obvious ; namely, (1) That the phenomena of spirit photography are easily accounted for, without the necessity of attributing them to extramundane origin ; and (2) That the power resides in the subjective mind of man to create phantasms perceptible to the objective senses of others. Again, it seems to be well established by experiment that some persons have the power, not only to create such phantasms, but to endow them with a certain degree of intelligence and power. Thus, the experiments recorded in " Phantasms of the Living," and quoted in a preceding chapter of this book, show that the image of the agent was not only created by him in his sleep, but was projected into the presence of others at a long distance from where he slept. The image was not only perceptible to the sight, as much so as the real presence would have been, but in some instances it was even tangible. The Orientalists call this the " projection of the astral body," and it is claimed that many persons in the East have acquired the power to produce the phenomenon at will. The fact that phantasms can thus be produced being well authenticated, many old stories of such phenomena acquire a new interest and importance, and assume an air of probability. Thus, the old stories of witches, in so far as the alleged phenomena seem to have been produced under the same conditions as those which are well authenticated, are elevated into the region of possibility, if not of probability. They are at least worthy of re-examination, in the light of modern experiments. It is foreign to my purpose to enter at large into the discussion of the alleged phenomena of so-called witchcraft, and this allusion is made here for the purpose of suggesting to those who desire to pursue the subject that if they will take for granted that which has been demonstrated to be true in regard to the power of the sub-conscious mind, or personality, to project tangible phantasms or images, and will apply the doctrine of duality and suggestion to the alleged facts, the old stories of the phenomena of witchcraft will be found to possess a scientific value and importance which cannot be ignored in the study of psychology.

For the purposes of this argument it will be assumed that the power of man, under certain conditions, to project phantasms is provisionally established. The next question is, What are the conditions? If we find that the conditions are practically the same in all cases, one great step in the classification of the phenomena will have been taken.

The one condition which seems to be necessary in all cases for the production of the phenomena is that of profound sleep, either natural or artificial. The objective senses must be locked in slumber, and the more profound the sleep, the greater the power seems to be. Thus, in the cases recorded in " Phantasms of the Living," the sleep was natural, but profound. It was at least so profound that the agent had no recollection of actually doing what he had resolved to do, and it was only brought to his knowledge by the subsequent statements made by the percipients. It is said, however, that sometimes the agent retains full recollection of what he did. Be this as it may, the fact remains that the one essential condition for the successful production of the phenomena is that of sleep. Again, the Orientalists tell us the same thing. Their adepts lock themselves in their rooms, which are carefully protected against invasion, and go into a sleep so profound as to simulate death. The witches were known to employ artificial means to produce sleep. Formulæ for producing what was known as "witches' ointment" are still extant. It was composed of the most powerful narcotics, made into an ointment by the addition of some fatty substance. The body of the witch was anointed from head to foot, and she then went to bed in some place secure from observation or disturbance, and lapsed into a profound sleep. This much is known, and many wonderful phenomena are alleged to have been produced, prominent among which was the creation of various shapes, such as the image of herself, images of cats, dogs, wolves, etc., which were sent to worry and annoy her neighbors or any one against whom she had a grudge. In fact, the shapes alleged to have been produced are protean.

Another alleged phenomenon of cognate character is that of so-called spirit materialization. In the production of this phenomenon the conditions are the same. The medium goes into a trance, or hypnotic state, and projects the shapes of various persons, generally of the deceased friends of some of those present. A good medium will produce any number of visions, of any number of persons, men and women, large and small. Spiritists believe, of course, that the real spirits of their friends are present, and are thus made visible to mortal eyes, and in many instances tangible, and able to hold a brief conversation with their friends. As the intellectual part of the performance of these alleged spirits is always on a par with that of other forms of spirit manifestation, subject to the same limitations and governed by the same laws, we must come to the same conclusion as to their origin, namely, that, whatever it may be, it is not due to spirits of the dead.

The old stories of the power of magicians to conjure alleged spirits are also raised into the region of probability by these considerations. They also observed the same conditions required in all the other cases mentioned. By the performance of certain impressive ceremonies, which they were taught to believe were necessary, they were said to be able to evoke so-called spirits and to do many other wonderful things. The ceremonies and incantations, together with the impressive environment with which they surrounded themselves, the incense, the slow music, the "dim religious light," the solemn invocations, — all had a tendency to throw them into the subjective condition, and thus enable them to evoke the shapes desired. That these shapes were literal creations of the subjective personality of the magician, rather than the actual spirits invoked, there is every reason to believe. Nor are we alone in that opinion. Eliphas Levi, than whom no modern writer on the subject of magic is better informed or more honest in the expression of his real convictions, gives utterance to the following : —

" Human thought creates what it imagines; the phantoms of superstition project their real deformity in the Astral Light, and live by the very terrors they produce. They owe their being to the delusions of imagination and to the aberration of the senses, and are never produced in the presence of any one who knows and can expose the mystery of their monstrous birth." [1]

Again, on page 160, he says : —

" The evokers of the Devil must before all things belong to a religion which believes in a Devil who is the rival of God. To have recourse to a power, we must believe in it. A firm faith being therefore granted in the religion of Satan, here is the method of communicating with this pseudo-god : —

Magical Axiom.
Within the circle of its action, every Logos creates what it affirms.

Direct Consequence.
He who affirms the Devil creates the Devil."

The author then goes on to give minute directions for performing the ceremonies necessary for raising the Devil, so to speak, with which we have nothing to do at present ; these quotations being made merely for the purpose of showing that the greatest and most philosophical magician of this century was fully aware that the shapes evoked by the Magi, whether they be of angels or of demons, whether they be perceptible to the objective senses or merely subjective hallucinations, tangible or intangible, are the creations of the mind of the magician.

The phenomenon of crystal vision is another illustration of the power of the subjective mind to create visions. Ordinarily these visions are only perceptible to the operator ; but cases are recorded where they were perfectly perceptible to the bystanders. The conditions necessary for successful crystal reading are practically the same as in all other cases, although the subjective condition is not ordinarily so pronounced. This phenomenon illustrates, however, the power of the subjective mind to create phantasms, and constitutes one of the many methods of bringing the

[1] Eliphas Levi : Waite's Digest, p. 118.

operations of the subjective mind above the threshold of consciousness. It is one of the best methods known of exercising the power of telepathy, the visions being objective reproductions of what is real or perceived in the mind of the person who consults the medium. If no one is present besides the medium or operator, he sees merely what his own subjective mind creates. It is perhaps superfluous to remark that the phenomenon is governed by the same laws which pertain to all other subjective phenomena, and the intelligence displayed is hedged about by the same limitations.

I have now enumerated several different sub-classes of the phenomena which are concerned in the creation of visions. In each sub-class instances are recorded of the visions being made perceptible to the objective senses of others. As remarked in the beginning of this chapter, we do not propose to stop to verify the phenomena of each class. It is sufficient to know that the phenomena of one of the sub-classes is verified by scientific authority. For present purposes the rest must stand or fall by that. At any rate, we shall assume the right to hold that any cognate phenomenon, alleged to have been produced under the same conditions as those which have been demonstrated to be veridical, is entitled to tentative consideration and credit.

It is assumed, therefore, that the following propositions are sufficiently verified for the purpose of formulating a definite theory of proximate causation : —

1. The alleged phenomena are all produced under the same conditions.

2. The one essential condition is that of the partial or total suspension of objective consciousness.

3. The more complete the extinction of the objective consciousness, the more pronounced the success of the experiment; that is, the more tangible to the objective senses of others do the creations become.

From these facts it is fair to conclude, —

1. That the power to create phantasms resides and is inherent in the subjective mind, or personality, of man.

2. That the power becomes greater as the body approaches nearer to the condition of death; that is, as the subjective, or hypnotic, condition becomes deeper, and the subjective personality in consequence becomes stronger in its sphere of activity.

3. That at the hour of death, or when the functions of the body are entirely suspended, the power is greatest.

Hence, ghosts.

It will be understood from the foregoing that my theory is that ghosts, or phantasms of the dead, are produced exactly as phantasms of the living are produced; that is, they are creations of the subjective entity. How they are created is of course a question that may never be answered in terms comprehensible by the objective intelligence of man. It is as far beyond our finite comprehension as are the processes by which the Infinite Mind has brought the universe into being. All that we can know is the fact that phantasms are created by some power inherent in the subjective personality of man. They may be called " embodied thoughts," as man may be called the embodied thought of God. If, as the Scriptures teach us, " we are gods," that is, " sons of God " and " heirs of God and joint-heirs with Jesus Christ," it is fair to presume that that part of the Infinite which is embodied in each of us must partake, to a limited extent, of His power to create. Experimental psychology suggests to us that we have that power, and that it is thus that phantasms are produced.

To the supposition that phantasms of the dead are thus created is opposed but one other hypothesis, and that is, that the phantasms are the real spirits of the dead persons whom they represent. Granted that ghosts do exist and make themselves manifest to the living, one or the other of these hypotheses must be true, and the other false. To determine which is true, we must have recourse to the ghosts themselves; that is, we must collate the facts regarding the characteristics of these supposed dwellers on the border-land, and ask ourselves whether their known and admitted characteristics are those which would naturally belong to the real spirit of a man, or to an embodied thought of a man.

The salient characteristics which seem to belong to all ghosts, and which pertain to the question under consideration, are these : —

The ghosts which are best authenticated and which seem to possess the greatest longevity, so to speak, — that is, the greatest persistency of power and purpose, — are of those who have died violent deaths. There are exceptions to this rule, which will be noted later on.

The generally accepted theory which has been employed to account for this coincidence is that the soul, thus torn suddenly and prematurely from the body, retains more of the material elements of the body than it does when death is the result of gradual disintegration and the natural separation of the material from the immaterial. It is thought that the physical elements thus retained temporarily by the spirit enable it to make itself visible to the living, as well as to perform certain feats of physical strength attributed to some spirits. This is very plausible at first glance, and in the absence of any facts to the contrary might be accepted as the true theory. But, as before intimated, there are exceptions to the supposed rule. It is not true that all ghosts are those of persons who have died violent deaths. On the contrary, many of the best authenticated ghosts are of persons who have died at a good old age and in the due course of nature. Moreover, there is nothing to distinguish the one class of ghosts from the other, although it is true that those who have met death by violence far outnumber the others. This theory, therefore, accounts for nothing. Nevertheless, the fact that the majority of ghosts are of those who belong to a particular class must possess some significance. Now, if we can discover some state of facts which appears to accompany all, or to precede all, ghostly phenomena, a great point will be gained, and the real significance of the other facts may become apparent.

In looking the field over with this end in view, the first

fact which forces itself upon our attention, and which seems to be universal and to possess a veritable significance, is that *all phantasms of the dead are of those who have died under circumstances of great mental stress or emotion.* No one whose death was peaceful and quiet, no one who left this life with no unsatisfied longing or desire present in the mind at the time of death, ever projected a phantasm upon the living objective world.

Again, the strength, persistency, and objectivity of the phantasm seem to be in exact proportion to the intensity of the emotion experienced at the moment of death.

It will thus be apparent why it happens that ghosts of those who have died violent deaths more frequently "revisit the glimpses of the moon" than those whose deaths have been less tragic and less calculated to inspire an intense desire or emotion. The murdered man feels, at the supreme moment, an intense longing to acquaint the world with the circumstances of his "taking off;" and he conceives the thought of reproducing the scene on the spot until its significance is understood and the murderer is brought to justice. The result is a haunted house; and those whose nerves are strong enough to withstand the shock may nightly witness a realistic reproduction of the tragedy. This may continue for days, months, or even years, but invariably ceases when the object is accomplished.

The character of the manifestations is as varied as are the phases of human emotion or the objects of human desire; but when the facts of a tragedy once come to light, the phantasm is always found to be significant of their important features.

When a mother dies at a distance from her children, she is often filled with an intense longing to see them once more before she passes away. The result often is that she projects a phantasm into their presence which takes a lingering look into the faces of the loved ones, and then fades away.

Two persons agree that whichever passes away first shall show himself to the other at or soon after the hour of death.

The result often is that the agreement is carried out with startling fidelity. The object accomplished, the phantasm disappears forever.

Another salient characteristic, which seems to be universal and which possesses the utmost interest and importance in determining the true source of the phantasm, is that it possesses no general intelligence. That is to say, a ghost was never known to have more than one idea or purpose. That one idea or purpose it will follow with the greatest pertinacity, but utterly ignores everything else. In the rare instances where the phantasm has been conversed with, it manifests perfect intelligence on the one subject, but pays not the slightest attention to any question pertaining to any other, not even to cognate subjects. This characteristic pertains to every form and phase of visions which are tangible to the objective senses. Subjective hallucinations are governed by different laws, and are not taken into account in this connection.

M. Adolphe d'Assier, in his intensely interesting work entitled " Posthumous Humanity," mentions this peculiarity in a number of instances. Thus, on page 272 he says:

" The shade only talks about its personal predilections, and remains deaf to every question outside the limits it has prescribed for itself. All the colloquies that have been gathered upon this subject resemble that of Bezuel and Desfontaine (1697), reported by Dr. Brière de Boismont. They were two college comrades, two intimate friends, who had sworn to each other that the first who died should appear to the other to give him some news about himself."

Accordingly, the year following, the shade of Desfontaine appeared to Bezuel, and addressed him as follows : —

" ' I agreed with you that if I died first I should come and tell you. I was drowned in the Caen River the day before yesterday, at this same hour, in company of Such and Such;' and he related the circumstances which caused his death. . ' It was his very voice,' says Bezuel. ' He requested me, when his brother should return, to tell him certain things to be communicated to his father and mother. He gave me other commissions, then bade me farewell and disappeared. I soon learned that every, thing he had told me was but too true, and I was able to verify some details that he had given. In our conversation he refused to answer all the questions I put to him as to his actual situation, especially whether he was in heaven, in hell, or in purgatory. One would have said that he did not hear me when I put such questions, and he persisted in talking to me of that which was upon his mind about his brother, his family, or the circumstances which had preceded his death.' "

It should be stated, in this connection, that this phantom does not appear to have been seen objectively by any one, save, possibly, by Bezuel himself. Others were present, who saw Bezuel apparently engaged in conversation with some invisible being. They could hear Bezuel's words, but neither saw nor heard those of the phantom. It seems probable, therefore, that it was a case of telepathic communion pure and simple; but it illustrates our point just as well as if it had been what it appeared to Bezuel to be, — a veritable apparition, perceptible to the objective senses. Moreover, it was a case of deferred percipience, — the death having occurred two days previously, — and is therefore more strongly illustrative of our position, as will presently be seen.

A moment's reflection will show how impossible it would be for the agent, in conveying a telepathic message on a given subject, especially in a case of deferred percipience, to do anything more than convey the message. When the agent has sent the message, the transaction is ended, so far as he is concerned. When the message rises above the threshold of the consciousness of the percipient, and he begins to ask questions foreign to the subject of the message, there is no one to answer them; the agent is no longer in telepathic rapport with him. It is just the same as if one should send a telegram to another on a given subject, and then disappear. The recipient of a message might ask all the questions he chose, on that or any other subject, but he could get no reply, for the reason that the original sender is out of reach.

It might be possible, if both the agent and the percipient were in the proper mental condition at the same time, for them to hold a general conversation; but we know of no recorded case of the kind. In all reported cases the agent telepaths the message, and the percipient takes cognizance of it by means of clairaudience, or by seeing a vision illustrating it, as the case may be, and that ends it. The message is a thought of the agent projected into the consciousness of the percipient through the medium of his subjective mind. When the message has once risen into the consciousness of the percipient, he is apparently no longer in a mental condition to communicate with the agent telepathically. At least, he never does so communicate, with the result of receiving further information in reply.

In the case under consideration the agent had been dead two days when the message was received by the percipient. If it was a telepathic message projected at the hour of death by the agent, it was manifestly impossible, for the reasons before stated, for him to respond to questions foreign to the subject of the message. If, on the other hand, the apparition was the real phantom, or spirit, of the deceased, it could have conveyed any information desired. The fact that it could not do so shows conclusively that said phantom was merely the embodied thought of the deceased, projected at the supreme moment for a specific purpose.

M. d'Assier affirms that the case here related is typical of all messages delivered by ghosts; that is, that they are apparently never able to enter into a general discussion of matters outside of the one dominant idea which called them into being. The history of all phantoms, so far as our reading extends, confirms the statement.

From these premises two conclusions seem inevitable:

1. That a phantom, whether it be of the living or of the dead, whether it is perceived subjectively or objectively, is not the subjective entity, or soul, of the person it represents. If it were, it would necessarily possess all the intelligence belonging to that person, and would, conse-

quently, be able and willing to answer any and all questions propounded by the percipient. It is simply impossible to conceive any valid reason for the refusal of a friend or relative of the percipient to answer questions of vital interest and importance to all mankind.

2. The second conclusion is, that a phantom, or ghost, is nothing more or less than an intensified telepathic vision, its objectivity, power, persistency, and permanence being in exact proportion to the intensity of the emotion and desire which called it into being. It is the embodiment of an idea or thought. It is endowed with the intelligence pertaining to that one thought, and no more. Hence the astonishing limitations of the intelligence of ghosts, before noted.

The difference between a telepathic vision transmitted from one living man to another, and a phantom, or ghost, of a deceased person, is one of degree, and not of kind ; of species, but not of genus. Both are creations of the subjective mind ; both are created for the purpose of conveying intelligence to others. In each case the vision ceases the moment the object of its creation is accomplished. In telepathy between two living persons, the vision is created, and the intelligence is communicated direct to the percipient. Its mission accomplished, it fades away. It seldom displays physical power or becomes perceptible to the touch, although there are exceptions to the rule. (See the cases noted in a former chapter.) The reasons are : (1) that the emotions and desires which call it into being are seldom of great intensity, compared with the emotions of a man dying by violence ; (2) that the conditions are not so favorable in a living person, in normal health, as they are in one whose objective senses are being closed in death ; (3) that the object for which it was created being easily and quickly accomplished, and there being no further reason for its existence, it fades away, in accordance with the laws of its being.

On the other hand, the phantom of the dead is produced under the most favorable conditions. The objective senses are being closed in death. The emotions attending a death by violence are necessarily of the most intense character. The desire to acquaint the world with the circumstances attending the tragedy is overwhelming. The message is not for a single individual, but to all whom it may concern. Hence the ghost does not travel from place to place, and show itself promiscuously, but confines its operations to the locality, and generally to the room in which the death-scene occurred. There it will remain, nightly rehearsing the tragedy, for days and months and years, or until some one with nerves strong enough demands to know the object of its quest. When this is done, the information will be given, and then the phantom will fade away forever.

We have supposed two extreme cases, — one, a simple case of experimental telepathy, and one, of a death by violence. Between the two extremes there is every variety of manifestation and every grade of power. But they are all governed by the same laws and limitations.

That the posthumous phantom is not the soul, or subjective entity, of the deceased, is evidenced by many other facts, among which may be mentioned the following : —

1. It is not controllable by suggestion. This is abundantly shown by what has been said regarding its persis· tency in following the one idea which it represents, and ignoring every effort to obtain information pertaining to other matters. This peculiarity characterizes every phantasm, whether of the living or of the dead. Again, no ghost was ever laid by the power of exorcism until the object of its existence was accomplished. Obsessing spirits, so-called, can be exorcised, because the exorcist is dealing directly with the subjective mind of the obsessed, and amenability to control by suggestion is the law of its being. But a ghost is not amenable to that law; it cannot be scolded out of existence before the object of its existence has been accomplished. In this, therefore, the phantom possesses the characteristics which might be expected to distinguish an embodied thought of a soul from the soul itself.

2. If we are to suppose a phantom to be the soul of the person it represents, we must also be prepared to believe that inanimate things and animals possess souls. Ghosts, it will be remembered, are always well provided with wearing apparel. We must therefore suppose clothes to have souls, and that the soul of the dead, or dying, man provides himself with an outfit of the souls of his hat, coat, trousers, boots, etc. Moreover, ghosts are frequently seen riding in ghostly turnouts, comprising horses, carriage, harness, and all the paraphernalia of a first-class establishment. Are we to suppose that the souls of all these things are pressed into the service of the nocturnal visitant? The same is true of telepathic visions of all grades and kinds. In this, again, the vision, or phantom, possesses the characteristics which one can easily attribute to an embodied thought-creation, but not to the actual soul of a person, living or dead.

3. Another peculiarity of ghosts is that they invariably disappear, never to return, when the building which was the scene of their visitation has been destroyed. Another building may be erected on the same spot, but the ghost never reappears. There must be some valid reason for this, for it is impossible to attribute to coincidence that which so frequently and invariably happens. It would seem to be but another limitation of the power and intelligence of the embodied thought. Its mission seems to be confined, not only to conveying the one item of intelligence, but to the actual scene of the tragedy. The effect of changing the physical environment appears to have the same effect as an attempt to change the current of its thought by asking a question foreign to it. It disappears. Now, it is impossible to conceive of an intelligent entity, in full possession of all the faculties and attributes of a human soul, being so easily diverted from the pursuit of a given object.

4. M. d'Assier arrives at two conclusions regarding ghosts, neither of which can afford any satisfaction to those who seek, in their manifestations, for evidence of a happy or a continued life beyond the grave. One is that the continued existence of the shade is a burden too grievous to

be borne ; and the other is that it eventually disappears by atomic dispersion, and loses its identity. On page 270 of "Posthumous Humanity" he says : —

"Most of the manifestations by which the shades reveal themselves seem to indicate that the posthumous existence is a burden."

Again, on page 273, he says : —

"To sum up, one may say that the impression left upon the mind by the lamentations and rare replies of those shades who succeed in making themselves heard is almost always a sentiment of profound sadness."

On page 274 he has the following to say regarding the ultimate fate of posthumous man : —

"I have said that the existence of the shade is but a brief one. Its tissue disintegrates readily under the action of the physical, chemical, and atmospheric forces which constantly assail it, and it re-enters, molecule by molecule, the universal planetary medium. Occasionally, however, it resists these destructive causes, continuing its struggle for existence beyond the tomb."

M. d'Assier is undoubtedly right regarding his facts, but wrong in his interpretation of those facts, and consequently wrong in his conclusions.

It is undoubtedly true that the shade is always imbued with a sentiment of profound sadness. The circumstances under which it is produced, and the emotions and desires which call it into being, are necessarily of such a character as to project a profoundly sad thought. And this fact is another evidence of its being an embodied thought, rather than a human soul. If it were the latter, it would be subject to varying moods and emotions, modified by its environment for the time being. But, being an embodied thought, it never changes its attitude or sentiment, but goes on in its predetermined line of action, regardless of its surroundings and utterly oblivious of anything which may be said or done to divert it. Truly, "thoughts are things."

Again, M. d'Assier is right in his declaration that the shade sustains but a comparatively brief existence. Some ghosts persist for years, it is true, in haunting a given spot, but they all eventually disintegrate. Their capacity for continued existence depends upon the intensity of the emotion which produces them. Their actual longevity depends largely upon the importance of the thought or message which they personate. It depends principally, however, upon the successful performance of its mission. When that is accomplished, it disappears at once and forever. As has already been pointed out, an ordinary telepathic message between two individuals disappears at once upon its successful delivery; whereas a phantom of the dead may persist in haunting one spot for years. It will, however, eventually disintegrate and disappear, even if its mission has proved to be a failure.

If we are to consider, as M. d'Assier evidently does, the shade of a deceased person to be the soul of such person, we must arrive at the same conclusion that he has reached; namely, that posthumous existence is a burden, and that it is but a brief one at most. According to his view, the evidence of the phantom negatives the idea of a continued existence after the death of the body. According to our view, it neither proves nor disproves immortality; it leaves that question just where it found it. Like all so-called spiritual manifestations, it adds nothing to our stock of knowledge of what is in store for us beyond the grave. We must still look for immortality with the eye of faith alone, relying on the promises of the Master.

There is another alleged phenomenon connected with this general subject which deserves a passing notice. I refer to the popular belief that certain houses are pervaded by a mental atmosphere, so to speak, which corresponds to the mental condition of those who have inhabited it. There are many sensitive persons who, upon moving into a strange house or room, are influenced apparently by the mental attitude of those who previously occupied the premises. This is especially true if the former inhabitants were the victims of any great sorrow or strong emotion of any kind whatever. The influence is felt sometimes for years, and is frequently of such a character and force as to compel the victim to vacate the premises. No ghost is seen or heard, but the influence is felt, and cannot be thrown off. Doubtless many such experiences may be attributed to suggestion, — the person having been informed of some tragic event which once happened on the premises. But many cases are recorded which cannot be thus explained. Cases are numerous where the percipient knew nothing whatever of the history of the house or of its former inhabitants.

The phenomenon is explained by spiritists by referring it to the agency of spirits of the dead. Others explain it on the theory of psychometry. That the latter explanation is not the true one is evidenced by the fact that psychometry itself is explicable on the well-known principles of telepathy. That the spirit hypothesis is not the true one is evidenced by the fact that the influence is felt when there has been no death on the premises, — when all the former inhabitants of the house are still alive. Nor is the influence necessarily a bad one. Thus, a lady of my acquaintance, who is peculiarly sensitive to psychic impressions, informs me that in one house, which she occupied some years ago, she was seized with an intense longing to study art. She had passed the age at which people usually take up a new profession, and she had never been particularly interested in art. She had no acquaintances who were artists, and there was nothing in her environment specially to attract her attention to the subject. Nevertheless, her desire to become an artist grew stronger and stronger, until she felt forced to yield. She finally employed a teacher, and eventually became very proficient. It was afterwards ascertained that the tenant who occupied the house before she took possession was an enthusiastic devotee of art. He was not a particularly good artist, but his whole soul was bound up in his profession.

The same lady occupied a house some years later which

she felt obliged to leave, on account of the evil influence
which it seemed to exert upon her. It was an almost
ideal house in its appointments and in the arrangement
of its rooms; and when she first entered it she was enthusiastic in her admiration of it. But she never spent
a comfortable day in that house. Naturally of a cheerful
and happy disposition, she became gloomy and despon-
dent, without any apparent cause, and was at last forced to
yield to her feelings and vacate the premises. An inquiry
into the history of the house revealed the fact that it had
formerly been occupied by a lady whose husband had ill-
treated her, and had finally deserted her, under circumstances of peculiar atrocity, to live with a mistress. The
history of that house from the time when the afflicted lady
left it has been one of constant change of tenants. Other
houses in the same row, built upon the same plan and
owned by the same person, have no such history. No
death has ever occurred in the house, either tragic or
otherwise, and consequently it cannot be said to be
haunted in the ordinary acceptation of the term; that is,
by spirits of the dead.

But is it not haunted, nevertheless? Is it not haunted
by the thoughts engendered from the mental agony of that
poor woman whose life was blasted by the perfidy of an
unfaithful husband, — a man whose subsequent career was
one of disgrace and infamy?

I make these suggestions tentatively, and for the purpose
of directing the attention of those interested to a line of
investigation which should not be ignored by students of
the new psychology. It is cognate with the phenomenon
of haunted houses, and may yet be found to be governed
by the same laws. If it is true that a visible ghost is but
an embodied thought of a dying man, may it not be true
that any great emotion can leave its impress upon the locality in which it is experienced? It may not be visible to
the objective senses, but it may have the power to impress
the subjective minds of those who are brought within its
environment, and to create in them the same emotions as

those experienced by the former occupants of the premises. It seems to be another form of telepathy, cognate with the phantom of the dead, differing only in the strength and character of its manifestation. It may not be visible, for the reason that the thought cannot be pictured by a vision. It may be an abstract thought, idea, or emotion, which can be transmitted to others by impression only; or the emotion which created it may not have been strong enough to project a visible phantom.

Telepathy, therefore, appears to be divisible into three generic classes, differing principally in the methods or means of percipience, — the processes of projection being the same in all.

The first is a thought sent from one living person to another for the purpose of communicating information to that one individual. It is perceived by that person only, — usually by means of visions, — and it instantly fades away when its mission is accomplished.

The second is a thought sent from a dying person to the world at large to communicate some fact of portentous import. It is sometimes made visible to the objective senses, and is always confined to one locality, which it haunts till its object is accomplished.

The third partakes of the characteristics of the first and second. It is created by a living person, and is confined to one locality. It is not sent to any particular individual, but impresses whoever inhabits the house or room it haunts.

It will be understood by the intelligent reader that these three classes are not separated by any distinct lines of demarcation, but that each possesses characteristics common to the others.

In concluding this branch of the subject we have but one further remark to make concerning those hypothetical spirits which are popularly believed to be able to make themselves visible to mortal eyes. If it is true that the power exists in mankind to create phantoms, to project visions which may become visible to others, objectively or subjectively, we have the logical right to infer that all so-called spirits, such as elementals, elementaries, *et id genus omne*, are creations of the subjective minds of those who believe in their existence.

As remarked in beginning this chapter, it is written tentatively, hoping to suggest an enlargement of the field of investigation of the subject of telepathy. That power has been found to afford an explanation of so much of psychic phenomena which had before been referred to extramundane origin that it seems probable that it may be capable of still further service in that direction. The phenomena of ghosts and haunted houses seem to be the only demonstrated phenomena of which telepathy has not been shown to be at least a partial explanation; and if it can be shown that ghosts are also the creations of subjective power, there will be nothing left for superstition to fright the world withal.

CHAPTER XXI.

SUSPENDED ANIMATION AND PREMATURE BURIAL.

Facts of Startling Import. — The Case of Washington Irving Bishop. — Other Instances of Suspended Animation. — Vampirism. — Catalepsy. — East Indian Fakirs buried alive for Months. — Fundamental Errors. — Catalepsy not a Disease. — A Recuperative Agent. — The Law of Suggestion governs the Phenomena. — Subjective Insensibility impossible. — Suggestion of Death deepens the Lethargy. — The Appalling Dangers of Catalepsy. — The Proper Treatment.

THERE is another psychic phenomenon which deserves a passing notice at our hands, not only because it is governed by the same laws which have been discussed, but because it is a matter of transcendent practical interest and importance. I refer to the subject of suspended animation, and consequent premature burial.

I know of but one physician in this country who has given serious attention to this subject. Nothing in authoritative form has yet appeared from his pen, but I am credibly informed that he has collected an array of facts of veritable significance. One assertion of startling import is that in the United States an average of not less than one case a week is discovered and reported. This statement alone attests the importance of the subject, although due allowance must be made for possible exaggeration. Be that as it may, the appalling possibility of premature burial as a result of a condition so common as catalepsy, the psychic aspects of which are so little understood in this country, invests the subject with more than ordinary interest.

The following cases have been personally investigated by the writer, and serve to illustrate the dangers which menace the cataleptic subject. Names are omitted, at the request of the parties interested.

The first case is that of a young lady, near Indianapolis, who came to life after fourteen days of suspended animation. Six doctors had applied the usual tests, and pronounced her dead. Her little brother clung to her, against the opinion of the doctors and the will of the parents, and frantically declared that she was not dead. In the excitement the bandage which held her jaw in place was accidentally pushed aside. The jaw fell, and the brother fancied that he saw his sister's tongue moving slowly.

"What do you want, sister?" cried the little fellow.

"Water," was the faint answer from the supposed corpse.

Water was administered, the patient revived, and is yet living.

A lady who is now at the head of one of the largest orphan asylums of a Western city has been twice pronounced dead by the attending physicians, twice prepared for the grave, and twice resuscitated by her friends. On the last occasion extraordinary precautions were taken, in view of her former experience. All the tests known to her physicians were applied, and all doubts were set at rest. She was a second time professionally declared to be dead, and the physicians left the house. In preparing the body for burial it was accidentally pricked by a pin. Soon afterwards it was discovered that a small drop of blood marked the spot where the pin entered. This once more roused the hope of the family, and vigorous treatment soon restored her to consciousness. She is living to-day, a vigorous, useful woman. It is proper to note here that upon being restored, the lady declared that she had never for a moment lost consciousness, that she knew all that went on around her, perfectly comprehended the significance of all the tests which were applied, but felt the utmost indifference as to the result, and was neither surprised nor alarmed when it was decided that she was dead.

A few years ago, a gentleman of Harrisburg, Pa., apparently died after a long period of suffering from inflammatory rheumatism, complicated with heart trouble. Preparations were made for the funeral; but his wife refused to allow the body to be packed in ice, fearing the possibility of a premature burial, and announced her determination to keep it for at least a week. The next day her hopes were realized by finding her husband with his eyes wide open, and one of his arms out of the position in which it had been placed. She called loudly for him to arise, and with assistance he did so, and was placed in a chair. Physicians were summoned, but before their arrival he was so far recovered that their aid was unnecessary, and he soon recovered from his illness. He states that during the time of suspended animation he was perfectly cognizant of all that occurred around him, heard the lamentations of the stricken family and the preparations for burial, but was unable to move a muscle or utter a sound.

The reading public has not forgotten the death of Washington Irving Bishop, the celebrated mind-reader, which occurred under circumstances that called forth the declaration on the part of his friends and relatives that he was not dead before the surgeon's knife penetrated his brain; that on several previous occasions he had been in a cataleptic state, resembling death, for many hours at a time; and that on one of these occasions his attending physicians had pronounced him dead. The public will not soon forget the thrill of horror which was felt when it was learned with what unseemly haste an autopsy was performed upon that unfortunate man.

These are not exceptional cases, nor is the phenomenon of modern origin. It can be traced back through all the ages of which there are records preserved, until it is lost in the twilight of tradition and fable.

In all human probability the ancient belief in vampirism had its origin in discovered cases of suspended animation. It will be remembered that whenever a corpse was suspected of being a vampire, the grave was opened and the body was examined. If it showed no signs of decomposition, the fact was held to be indubitable evidence of guilt. The punishment was summary, and fully as effective as a modern autopsy; it consisted in driving a stake through the heart. This simple process effectually laid the "vampire ghost," and it no longer possessed the power to "suck the blood of the living," and thus "continue to live on in the grave," to use the language of an ancient official document defining the characteristics of a vampire.

Revolting and gross as was the superstition relating to vampirism, is it not possible that, like most legendary tales, it had a basis of truth, and that an essential part of that truth consisted, as before remarked, of the fact that the cases referred to were cases of suspended animation? Many cases are reported which appear to be well authenticated, and they all seem to sustain this theory. One case (which was officially attested) is related, where the body of a man suspected of vampirism was exhumed after it had lain in the grave three weeks. No signs of decomposition being visible, a stake was driven through the heart, "upon which," says the report, "fresh blood gushed from the mouth and ears."

Another case is mentioned of one Arnold Paul, a Hungarian, whose body was exhumed after it had been buried forty days. "His body," says the narrator, "was red; his hair, nails, and beard had grown again, and his veins were replete with fluid blood." The stake was brought into requisition, and as it pierced his heart, he "uttered a frightful shriek, as if he had been alive."

Two erroneous impressions very generally prevail regarding catalepsy, or suspended animation. One is that depriving the subject of air will cause death in a few hours. Another is that catalepsy is a disease, or is always the result of disease. Both of these hypotheses are clearly disproved by the well-known experiments of the East Indian fakirs.

One of the most clearly attested instances of the kind alluded to is the experiment of the Fakir of Lahore, who, at the instance of Runjeet Singh, suffered himself to be buried alive in an air-tight vault for a period of six weeks. This case was thoroughly authenticated by Sir Claude Wade, the then British Resident at the court of Loodhiana. The fakir's nostrils and ears were first filled with wax; he was then placed in a linen bag, then deposited in a wooden box which was securely locked, and the box was deposited in a brick vault which was carefully plastered up with mortar and sealed with the Rajah's seal. A guard of British soldiers was then detailed to watch the vault day and night. At the end of the prescribed time the vault was opened in the presence of Sir Claude and Runjeet Singh, and the fakir was restored to consciousness.

Lieutenant Boileau relates another instance where a man suffered himself to be buried for a period of ten days in a grave lined with masonry and covered with a large slab of stone, the whole strictly guarded day and night. On being restored to consciousness, the man offered to submit to burial for a year, if the lieutenant so desired.

Many other well-authenticated instances are related by British residents in India, but these must suffice. In all these cases the subjects were in perfect health when the experiments were made, and in each instance the body, when disinterred, was found to present all the characteristics indicating death, except decomposition.

Volumes might be filled with well-authenticated cases of suspended animation, varying in duration from a few hours to many months; but it would be foreign to the purpose of this chapter to cite any. Sufficient instances have been given to illustrate the points which I shall attempt to make, as well as to show the intrinsic importance of the subject and the danger to be apprehended from ignorance of the psychic principles involved.

The fundamental error into which many physicians have fallen consists in the assumption that catalepsy is, *per se*, a disease. It must be said, however, to the credit of the profession, that no one pretends to understand it. Most medical writers confess that if it is a disease, it is one of which

the pathology is but little understood by the profession, and
they aver that morbid anatomy throws no light upon it whatever.   In fact, some well-known writers have doubted its
existence, and have attributed the recorded cases to gross
imposture.   It is, however, generally held to be a functional
nervous disorder ; but the tendency of modern investigation
is in the direction of its psychic aspects, and moral means
are now largely employed in its treatment by the best
physicians.

The truth appears to be that catalepsy is not a disease in
any proper sense of the word.   The most that can be said
is that it may be considered a symptom of certain diseases.
That is to say, inasmuch as it commonly attacks those who
are suffering from certain nervous disorders, it might be said
to be a symptom indicating the presence of such disorders.
But, I repeat, it is not a disease *per se ;* and one prominent
medical authority goes so far as to admit that "in itself
catalepsy is never fatal."   He might have gone further,
and said that other diseases are rarely fatal when catalepsy
supervenes.

Catalepsy belongs exclusively to the domain of hypnotism.
I employ this term in the broadest significance of its Greek
radix ; for no matter how the condition is induced, it is
purely a sleep of the objective senses, a suspension of the
vital functions, a rest of all the vital organs.   It can be
induced in perfectly healthy persons by the hypnotic processes on the one hand, or, on the other, it may supervene
after a long period of illness or nervous exhaustion.   In
both cases the phenomenon is the same ; and when the
patient is intelligently treated, the effect is always salutary.
It is, in the highest sense of the phrase, a manifestation of
the *vis conservatrix naturæ ;* it is, of a truth, "tired nature's
sweet restorer, balmy sleep."

Catalepsy is always easily induced in a hypnotic subject
by the ordinary processes known to hypnotists, and the normal condition is as easily restored.   It is always refreshing
to the subject, especially when he is exhausted by mental or
physical labor, — far more so than is ordinary sleep of the

same duration. The same is true of the catalepsy which supervenes after a long period of illness or of nervous exhaustion. That this statement is true of the first class, we have the testimony of all who have been subjects of intelligent experiment. That it is true of the second class also, is attested by the fact that suspended animation is nearly always followed by the recovery of the patient from illness. The cataleptic condition marks the crisis in many diseases, especially those of the nerves. If the patient is properly managed during that crisis, his convalescence is assured.

Catalepsy may properly be divided into four classes, differing from one another only in the causes which induce the condition. The first is catalepsy from hypnotic suggestion; the second, epidemic catalepsy; the third, self-induced catalepsy; the fourth, catalepsy arising from disease or nervous exhaustion. Suggestion is the all-potent factor in the production of the catalepsy of the first three classes, as it is in the production of all other hypnotic phenomena. The suggestion may come, first, from an operator who purposely induces the condition as an experiment. Secondly, it may arise from the patient seeing other cataleptic subjects. In such cases, catalepsy may run through a whole school or a neighborhood, precisely as does epidemic insanity, St. Vitus's dance, and many other nervous troubles. "Imitation," or the disposition to imitate, has generally been assigned as the cause of such manifestations becoming epidemic among children. But this is a palpable error. It arises rather from the fear that each one feels — the mental suggestion that each one makes — that he or she may be the next victim. Thirdly, self-induced catalepsy is illustrated in the experiments of the East Indian fakirs, and arises from auto-suggestion. In these cases the condition is purely hypnotic, and is self-induced by simple processes, well known to all who have made an intelligent study of hypnotism as practised in the Orient.

It is not, however, with these classes that we have to deal in this chapter, but rather with cases which arise from disease or nervous exhaustion. In such cases, suggestion can hardly be considered as an initial cause, although, as we shall see further on, it is a potent factor in deepening, prolonging, and terminating the condition.

I have said that catalepsy marks the crisis in certain diseases. It is, in fact, the supreme effort of nature to give the exhausted nerves their needed rest. When this fact is once appreciated, and the patient is intelligently treated on its basis, much needless alarm will be saved, and many fatal errors will be avoided. The patient in that condition is enjoying absolute rest. All the vital processes are practically suspended. He is free from all pain, and is enjoying a refreshing sleep, — a sleep so profound that it may be truly likened to its " twin-brother, death." The depth and duration of the trance will depend upon the necessities of the case. That is to say, it will be proportioned to the severity of the patient's illness, and his consequent need of rest and recuperation.

The primary mistake which many physicians make in managing cataleptic patients consists in seeking, by heroic treatment, to hasten restoration to consciousness. No greater mistake is possible. If the attempt is successful, it causes a fearful shock to the nerves, and the effort is thwarted which nature is making to relieve the patient and give rest to his already overstrained nervous system. If it is unsuccessful, the patient is threatened with the danger of being buried alive, or of an autopsy. These dangers are ever present; and as long as physicians fail to recognize the pregnant fact that an advanced stage of decomposition is the only infallible test of death, just so long will the human race be menaced with the horrors of premature burial.

The most important branch, however, of the subject of catalepsy is that pertaining to its psychological features. I have said that catalepsy belongs to the domain of hypnotism. I mean by this, not only that the phenomenon is identical with the condition which can be produced by the ordinary hypnotic processes, but that the cataleptic patient is amenable to precisely the same psychological laws which govern the ordinary hypnotic subject.

The two fundamental propositions which bear upon this subject are the following : —

First, a patient in a case of suspended animation or catalepsy, induced by disease or nervous exhaustion, is amenable to control by suggestion precisely as he is in the ordinary hypnotic state.

Second, a patient in that condition is always conscious, subjectively, of all that happens around him. That is to say, no matter how profoundly the objective senses are locked in slumber, the subjective faculties are ever alert, and the subject recognizes, often with great acuteness, everything that goes on around him. This fact is not always recognized by hypnotists, and it is safe to say that ignorance of this one truth has been the source of more erroneous conclusions regarding the significance of hypnotic phenomena than all other causes combined. Hundreds of cases are reported where the patients noted all the preparations for burial and all that was said and done, and yet were unable to move or make the fact known that they were alive. This seems to be the universal testimony, although it is possible that the patient might not, in all cases, remember what he had experienced. In fact, it is common for hypnotic subjects to forget their experiences during the sleep ; but that does not militate against the fact that they were subjectively conscious at that time.

The conclusions derivable from these premises are as important as they are obvious. The first and most vital is that when a patient is suffering from a disease which will induce catalepsy, and begins to enter that state, the usual remarks and conversation of those at the bedside must inevitably tend to deepen and prolong the lethargy. The patient appears to be dying. The friends, by word and action, are conveying the impression that death is at hand. The physician feels the pulse, which grows fainter and fainter, until it is no longer perceptible. He examines the heart until its pulsations cease. Finally, he turns to the stricken friends, and in a solemn voice announces that all is over, — the patient is dead. Now, if it happens that it is merely a case of catalepsy, or suspended animation, the announcement by the physician that the patient is dead is an all-potent suggestion which is, and must inevitably be, seized upon by the subject and carried to its legitimate conclusion. A case of prolonged suspension of animation is the inevitable result, as the laws of hypnotism teach, if they teach anything. The patient actually believes that he is dead. The statement of this proposition seems almost ridiculous ; but when it is remembered that no suggestion seems absurd or incongruous to the hypnotic subject, the proposition is seen at once to be an absolute verity. Who has not dreamed of being dead? Few, if any, have not had this experience ; and yet the incongruity of the two ideas — of being dead and of calmly reflecting on the subject — never strikes the dreamer's subjective intelligence. Subjective impressions never seem absurd or incongruous to the subject. This principle runs through all subjective mental action, from the dreams of the healthy sleeper to the hallucinations of the monomaniac. Subjective intelligence, be it remembered, is capable of exercising but one form of reasoning, — the deductive. But it will reason deductively from any premise imparted to it, by any form of suggestion, with great acumen ; and it never arrives at a conclusion inconsistent with the premise, — that is, the suggestion. All the facts known to the individual's objective experience which are inconsistent with that premise stand for nought in presence of the one ever-present idea. That idea is the major premise, unquestioned and indisputable, of a syllogism which he will inevitably complete with logical accuracy.

It is easy to see from what has been said what an appalling, ever-present danger menaces the patient who, from any cause, becomes cataleptic, especially the one who has reached the crisis of a lingering illness, and is surrounded by physicians and friends who are ignorant of the psychological principles involved. The natural language of the emotions of the surviving friends, the wail of hopeless grief, the administration of the sacraments of the Church, and, finally, the authoritative announcement of the doctor that " He is dead ! " all tend to the one result. When to these are added the ice-pack or the embalmer's fluid, it remains only for the performance of an autopsy to give the *coup de grâce.*

I shall not attempt to apply the principles here laid down to particular cases. Those who are cognizant of the circumstances of any case, either recorded or within their own private experience, will easily recognize their signifi- cance. Nor shall I attempt to prescribe the specific course to be pursued where suspended animation is suspected, as that is the province of the physician in attendance on each particular case. My object will have been accomplished if what I have said shall be the means of directing the atten- tion of the medical profession to the psychic aspects of catalepsy, and to a more careful study of the psychology of that science which has suffered so much at the hands of charlatanism on the one hand, and prejudice on the other, — hypnotism.

Nevertheless, a few general observations regarding the proper course to be pursued may not seem impertinent. It is obvious that when catalepsy is suspected, or is pos- sible, all allusion to or suggestion of death should be avoided, especially by the physician in attendance. It should not for a moment be forgotten that, however pro- foundly the objective senses may be locked in insensibility, subjectively the patient is awake and is taking cognizance of all that occurs, and appreciates with wonderful acute- ness the significance of every word that is uttered. It should be remembered that since suggestion can induce catalepsy, it can also deepen and prolong the period of its duration. Conversely, it is the most potent means of resto- ration. Other restoratives should rarely, if ever, be resorted to. Violent means should never be employed. The essen- tial thing is a cheerful, confident demeanor in all present at the bedside. Time should always be given for the conservative forces and recuperative powers of nature to do their legitimate work, and in due season the patient, who " is not dead, but sleepeth," will awake ; or, in obedience to suggestion, will " arise and come forth," saved from the jaws of death, — rescued from the horrors of a living grave.

CHAPTER XXII.

PRACTICAL CONCLUSIONS AND SUGGESTIONS.

The Normal Relations of the Objective and Subjective Faculties. —
Their Distinctive Powers and Functions. — The Infinite Wisdom
displayed in their Distribution. — It constitutes Man a Free Moral
Agent. — Limitation of Subjective Powers and Responsibilities in
this Life. — The Kinship of the Soul to God. — The Limitation of
the Powers of the Objective Mind. — The Transcendent Powers of
the Soul. — Errors of the Old Philosophers. — The Normal Functions of the Soul in Earthly Life. — Dangers of Abnormal Exercise of Subjective Power. — Nervous Disorders, Insanity,
Imbecility, and Moral Degradation. — The Importance of a Knowledge of the Law of Suggestion. — Dangers of Mediumship. —
Trance-speakers. — Immoral Tendency of Ignorant Mediumship.
— Tendency towards Free Love. — The Causes. — The Orientalists. — Their Greater Powers and their Greater Facilities for Self-
delusion. — Practical Conclusions. — Warnings.

I HAVE now presented the propositions of my hypothesis, together with a brief outline showing its applicability to the leading psychic phenomena; and it remains
only to draw a few practical conclusions which apply to
every-day life. The first, and the most obviously important
one, relates to the exercise of subjective power, and the
normal relations of the objective and subjective faculties.
In order to do so clearly and concisely, it will be necessary
to recall the terms of the hypothesis.

The first proposition is that the mind of man is dual in
character. This proposition, as we have already stated,
has been more or less dimly recognized by many philosophers in all ages; and during the present century it has
been gradually assuming a more definite status in mental
philosophy. Assuming, therefore, this proposition to be

true, it necessarily follows that the two minds must, normally, bear a harmonious relation to each other. It follows that one of the two minds must, normally, be subordinated to the other. Otherwise there would be a conflict. Just here Liébault's discovery of the law of suggestion comes in, and shows that the subjective mind is constantly controlled by that power. It is true that Liébault and his followers have applied the law only to the elucidation of hypnotic phenomena; and in that have not always carried it to its legitimate conclusion. But it has seemed to me that if the law is applicable to one class of psychic phenomena, it must be equally applicable to all, as nature's laws admit of no exceptions. I have therefore declared, as the second proposition of my hypothesis, that the subjective mind is always controllable by suggestion.

Assuming, therefore, that these two propositions are true, it follows as a necessary consequence that there must be some distinctive line of difference between the methods of operation of the two minds. It is obvious that there is a limitation of power in the subjective mind, otherwise it could not be subordinated to the objective. Just where this line of distinction could be drawn, and how it could be formulated, was at first a perplexing question. There were no authorities on the subject who ever hinted at a possible limitation of reasoning power in either branch of the dual mind. On the contrary, those who have observed the phenomena of subjective mental activity, as seen in hypnotic subjects, in trance-speakers, and cognate exhibitions, have been so profoundly impressed with its transcendent powers that it has seemed impossible that it could be hedged about by limitations. Philosophers from time immemorial have recognized its tremendous powers of memory, and millions have sat entranced by the eloquence of subjective speakers, and noted with profound admiration their accuracy of logical deduction. So impressed has the world been by such exhibitions that the soul has been held up as the infallible guide to all that is pure and noble and good in humanity. It has been called the Ego (which it truly is), and as such it has been recognized as the inward monitor, whose monitions are always entitled to reverential consideration. It was difficult, therefore, to imagine any line of distinction between the two branches of the dual mind which would place the subjective in a subordinate position. But for the discovery of Liébault's law of suggestion that line would never have been recognized. It now becomes evident, however, that the point of its limitation of reasoning power is the starting-point. It has not the power to formulate its own premises. The subsidiary proposition of our general hypothesis is, therefore, that *the subjective mind is incapable of inductive reasoning.* It will readily be seen that it is a corollary of the law of suggestion; but the three propositions together furnish the key to the whole science of psychology.

I am aware that those who have hitherto regarded the soul as possessing all the intellectual powers, as well as all the moral attributes, will be shocked when they realize that the object of their admiration is hedged about with any limitations whatever. The first question they will ask is, "Why is it that God has given to man a soul possessing such transcendent powers in certain directions, and yet under the absolute control, in all its ideas and intellectual functions, of a finite, perishable intelligence?" The broad and comprehensive answer is, *To constitute man a free moral agent.* It needs no argument to show that if the soul were not so limited in its initiative power of reasoning, the finite, mortal man could not be held responsible for the moral status of his soul. God gave to objective man the powers of reason, inductive as well as deductive, for the purpose of enabling him successfully to struggle with his physical environment. He gave him the power to know the right from the wrong. He gave him supreme control of the initial processes of reasoning, and thus made him responsible for the moral status of his soul. The soul, in the mean time, so long as it inhabits the body, is charged with limited responsibilities. It is the life-principle of the body, and its normal functions pertain solely to the preservation of human life and the perpetuation of the human race. It possesses wonderful powers in other directions, under certain abnormal conditions of the body, it is true. But their exercise outside of those limits is always abnormal, and productive of untoward results. Those powers of which we catch occasional glimpses, and which so excite our admiration, are powers which pertain to its existence in a future world. They are powers which proclaim it as a part of God, as partaking of the nature and attributes of the Divine Mind. Its powers of perception of the fixed laws of nature demonstrate its kinship to Omniscience. It is independent of the feeble powers of inductive reasoning when it is freed from its earthly trammels; and there is not one power or attribute peculiar to the finite, objective mind that could be of any service to the soul in its eternal home. We boast of our powers of inductive reason, forgetting how little we have learned, or ever can know, compared with what there is to learn. We forget that they are the outgrowth of our physical wants and necessities, and simply enable us to grope in the dark for the means of subsistence, and to render our physical existence tolerable. The powers of the objective mind, compared with those of the subjective mind, may be likened to a man born in a cave, in which the light of the sun never entered, and supplied only with a rushlight with which to grope his way and find the means of subsistence. The light, feeble as it is, is invaluable to him; for by its means he is enabled gradually to learn his bearings, to take note of his environment, to make occasional discoveries of the necessities of life, and finally to achieve some of the comforts of existence. The more he discovers, the more he appreciates the value of his rushlight and the more he boasts of its transcendent powers of illumination. He hears vague reports of an outside world where the comforts and luxuries of life are comparatively easy to obtain, and he resolves to grope his way out. He is told that the outside world is lighted by a great luminary which will render his rushlight of no value to him except as a reminder of the limitations of his cave-life. But he is sceptical, and points with pride to his accumulations and the discoveries he has made with the aid of his "God-given illuminant," and refuses to believe that there is a possible state of existence which would be tolerable without rushlights. At length a cataclysm of nature throws him upon the outside world in the full blaze of the light of a midday sun. He then finds that he is in a world of light; that he can perceive things as they are, and observe their bearings and relations to each other, and he finds that the rays of his rushlight are no longer visible. It is obvious that this is but a feeble illustration of the difference between the powers of inductive inquiry into the laws of nature, and the powers of perception possessed by the subjective entity. When the soul is freed from its physical trammels it ascends to its native realm of truth, and, untrammelled by false suggestions arising from the imperfect knowledge of the objective mind, it "sees God as he is;" that is, it apprehends all his laws, and imbibes truth from its Eternal Source.

It must not be forgotten in this connection that the subjective mind is the soul, or spirit, and is itself an organized entity, possessing independent powers and functions; while the objective mind is merely the function of the physical brain, and possesses no powers whatever independently of the physical organization. The one possesses dynamic force independently of the body; the other does not. The one is capable of sustaining an existence independently of the body; the other dies with it. It is just here that the ancient philosophers made their greatest error; and that error has been transmitted down through all the ages. They recognized the dual character of the mind, but saw no fundamental difference in the functions of the two minds. It never occurred to them that there was, or could be, any limitation of power in either that was not common to both. They recognized man as a trinity, the three elements of which are "body, soul, and spirit." The soul, in their system of philosophy, corresponds to the objective mind, and the spirit to the subjective mind. They considered only the functions of the two minds as minds, and constantly regarded the two as possessing only co-ordinate powers. Or, if they regarded them as entities, they considered that while each was an entity, it was, some-how, inseparably joined to the other in function and des-tiny. Hence, according to their philosophy, if one survived the death of the body, both must survive it. This funda-mental error shows itself, in various forms, in every system of philosophy, from Plato down; and it will continue to breed confusion and uncertainty in the human mind until the fact is recognized that the subjective mind, or spirit, as Plato designates it, is a distinct entity, possessing indepen-dent powers and functions; whereas the objective mind, or the "soul," of the ancient philosopher, is merely the function of the physical brain. This latter proposition is demonstrated by every consideration of its powers, func-tions, and limitations. Its powers wholly depend upon the physical condition of the brain. They decline as the body weakens. They become deranged and useless as the brain becomes disorganized from physical causes. Its distinctive functions pertain solely to physical existence. It has the power of independent inductive reasoning to compensate for its total want of power to perceive by intuition. But, as I have already pointed out, inductive reasoning is merely a laborious method of inquiry, and pertains wholly to our physical existence. It would be as useless to the spirit in an existence where all truth is perceived by intuition, as a tallow-dip in the full blaze of a noonday sun. It may be set down as a maxim in spiritual philosophy that there is not one power or function of the objective mind which distinguishes it from those of the subjective entity, that could be of any service to the latter when it is freed from its earthly environment.

The peculiar functions of the physical brain are there-fore no more entitled to be considered as an immortal entity, or as any necessary part or function of an immortal entity, than are the physical functions of deglutition or digestion, or the physical power of pedal locomotion.

It is not for man to question the wisdom of God in so

ordaining the relations of the soul to the body as to subordinate the eternal to the perishable. But it is man's duty so to exercise his powers of induction as to ascertain those relations; and, having done so according to his best lights, so to order his conduct as to do his whole duty to himself and his Creator. As we find those relations exist, the whole responsibility rests upon the objective man. He is a free moral agent, and has it in his power to train his soul for weal or woe, for this life and for eternity.

It is of the relations which exist between objective and subjective man in this life that I propose to offer a few practical suggestions at this time. I have already shown that the normal functions of the subjective mind are apparently limited to the preservation of human life and the perpetuation of the human race. These functions are manifested in what are known as instincts. The first is the instinct of self-preservation; the second is the instinct of reproduction; and the third pertains to the preservation of the offspring. In the last may be included the instinctive desire to preserve human life generally. Outside of these limits all phenomenal subjective mental activity appears to be abnormal. I say *appears* to be abnormal, for the reason that we have no means of judging, except from a consensus of facts. The facts which pertain to the subject can be found in the greatest abundance in spiritistic circles, for the reason that it is there that subjective activity is greatest in modern times. I venture to say that no one of the better class of spiritists will deny the fact that most professional mediums eventually become physical wrecks; many are overtaken by mental derangement, and some by a moral degradation too loathsome to be described. Few, if any, escape serious physical trouble. This, of itself, is sufficient evidence of abnormality, and should serve as a warning against the too frequent exercise of subjective power. The majority of spiritistic mediums are more or less afflicted with nervous disorders, and many of them are hysterical to the last degree. Most of them complain of extreme nervous exhaustion after a séance, and many require days to recover from the effects of a prolonged exercise of subjective power. It may be said that I mistake the cause for the effect; that is, that it may be only weak and nervous physical organisms that are capable of exercising subjective power. I am aware that the question is not free from difficulty, and that one is liable to fall into error in discussing a subject that is so little understood. The fact remains, nevertheless, that nervous disorders and mediumship are generally associated, and that fact alone is indicative of abnormality. Whether we are to regard the exercise of subjective power as productive of abnormal physical conditions, or are to suppose that it requires an abnormal physical organism to produce subjective phenomena, matters little. The conclusion must be the same, — that the exercise of subjective power is abnormal, and should be avoided until more is known of the proper conditions of its exercise than has yet been discovered.

There is a further difficulty attending the consideration of this subject which must not be lost sight of, and that is the question how far suggestion may enter as a factor in the case. It is well known that some mesmeric healers fancy that " they take on the conditions of the patient," as they phrase it. That is, they feel the symptoms which afflict the patient. There is no question of the fact that those who enter upon the treatment of a case with that idea firmly fixed in their minds will experience the anticipated sensations, often to a marked degree. But late scientific experiments disclose the fact that such phenomena are always the effect of suggestion. The physical exhaustion which some healers feel after the treatment of a case is also largely due to suggestion. These effects may always be counteracted by a vigorous auto-suggestion; and, moreover, the same means may be effectively employed to produce exactly the opposite effects upon the operator. That is to say, the mental healer, by whatever method he does his work, may always cause his treatment of a patient to redound to his own benefit, as well as to that of the patient, by the exercise of the power of auto-suggestion. It is therefore impossible to say just how far suggestion enters as a factor in the production of untoward physical results from the exercise of mediumistic power. It is certainly traditional among the fraternity that nervous exhaustion ensues from its exercise, and the results are appalling. How far the effects may be counteracted by intelligent auto-suggestion, remains to be settled by the process of evolution. There is, however, little hope of any change for the better so long as the spiritistic medium believes himself to be under the domination of an extraneous force which is beyond his control, and the effects of which he is powerless to mitigate.

This phase of the subject is, however, of little importance compared with the mental effects produced by the too persistent exercise of the subjective faculties in the production of phenomena. Again we must draw our illustrations from spiritistic circles. It is undeniable that the tendency of mediumship is to unhinge the mind, to destroy the mental balance, and often to produce the worst forms of insanity. And it is noticeable that the more thoroughly sincere the medium is in his belief in the genuineness of his power to evoke the spirits of the dead, the greater is the tendency to insanity. The reason is obvious. If he sincerely believes himself to be under the control of an extraneous power, he yields implicit obedience to that power; especially if it assumes to be a superior mentality, as it generally does. Instead of assuming control of the power, he allows it to control him. As a matter of course, he is ignorant of the laws pertaining to it. He is ignorant of the fact that the force which controls him resides within himself, and is not a superior being commissioned from Heaven to convey a message from the Source of all knowledge. He is dazed by its wonderful exhibitions of superior intelligence, is captivated by its eloquence, and awed by its assumption of authority. In short, he knows nothing of its source, or the limitations of its powers of reasoning. The result is that he yields implicit obedience to its guidance in all things. His reason has abdicated its throne and abandoned its functions, and he is at the mercy of his subjective mind, which, in turn, is controlled by the false suggestions of his own disorganized and subjugated objective intelligence. His physical degeneracy keeps pace with his mental decline, his whole nervous system is prostrated by excessive exercise of subjective power, and too frequently the end is acute mania or drivelling imbecility.

One of the most fascinating and seductive forms of subjective mental activity is exhibited in trance, or inspirational, speaking. A medium of fair intelligence and some education, obtained, perhaps, by desultory reading of spiritistic and miscellaneous literature, develops himself into an inspirational speaker. As a sincere spiritist, he believes himself to be controlled by some great spirit who in life was celebrated for his eloquence. He ascends the rostrum and amazes his audience by his wonderful oratory, his marvellous command of the resources of his mind, and, above all, by the clearness and cogency of his reasoning. Those who have known him before and are aware of the limits of his education are the most surprised of all, and no argument can convince them that he is not inspired by some almost superhuman intelligence from another world. They know nothing of the wonders of subjective mental power; they have no knowledge of the perfection of subjective memory, which gives the speaker perfect command of all he has ever read, or of the logical exactitude of the deductive reasoning of the subjective intelligence. The speaker, on his part, finds himself in possession of such wonderful powers and resources, emanating, as he believes, from an extraneous source, abandons his old pursuits, and devotes himself to the work of his inspiration. It is an easy and pleasurable existence for the time being. He finds that there is no need of taking thought of what he is to say, for ideas, and words with which to clothe them, flow from him like a mountain torrent. He finds himself in possession of knowledge which he has no objective recollection of ever having acquired, and of ideas which were foreign to his objective intelligence. He believes, and, from his standpoint, has every reason to believe, that he is inspired by some lofty spirit whose knowledge is unlimited and whose resources are unfailing. He feels that he has no need of further reading or study, and the work of objective intellectual labor soon becomes a drudgery. The result is that his objective intellectual growth soon comes to a stand-still, and at length his objective intellect begins to deteriorate. In the mean time his subjective powers may continue to grow in brilliancy for a time, or at least they shine with a new lustre, as they are compared with the deepening dulness of his objective intellect. At length he becomes fitful, erratic, eccentric. As his objective powers deteriorate, they no longer have any semblance of control over his subjective mind. The suggestions which reason, in its best estate, may have given to his subjective mind, as a starting-point for his discourses, are no longer available, for his power to reason is failing. His friends, who follow him from place to place, begin to notice that he talks one thing at one place, and the opposite at another. They attribute the fact to the control of different spirits at different times, and for a time they are consoled. Eventually the fact is forced upon them that in his normal, or objective, condition he is growing more and more erratic, and that at times his conversation is the merest drivel. As in all the other forms of subjective development mentioned, his physical deterioration keeps pace with his mental decline. In the mean time his subjective powers appear to deteriorate. It is not true, in fact, that his subject mind, *per se,* deteriorates, for that is impossible. But as it is always controlled by suggestion, it necessarily takes its cue from the suggestions conveyed to it by the objective mind. When that ceases to develop, the subjective mind keeps on in its old rut, for the obvious reason that no new ideas are imparted to it. When the objective mind begins to deteriorate, its suggestions are no longer coherent, and the subjective mind is necessarily incoherent in exact proportion. Its deductions from a false or imbecile suggestion will be logically correct; but, as a matter of course, a false, extravagant, or imbecile premise, followed to its legitimate, logical conclusion, necessarily leads the mind into a corresponding maze of extravagance and imbecility. It is therefore no indication of a decline of subjective powers, but it is a demonstration of the universality of the law of suggestion. It goes without saying that if an inspirational speaker were aware of the source of his power, and of the laws which govern it, and would constantly keep it under the control of his reason, he could utilize it to the very best advantage. A cultured man of well-balanced intellect would then formulate his own premises according to the best lights obtainable through the processes of inductive reasoning, and " inspiration would do the rest." If his premises were correct, the subjective mind could always be depended upon to deduce the correct conclusions, and to illustrate them by drawing upon the resources of its perfect memory of all that the individual has ever seen, heard, or read bearing upon the subject. Such a man would be known as a man of " genius," in whatever direction he exercised his powers. And just in proportion to the natural powers and cultivation of his objective mind and the extent of his objective information would his subjective manifestations be brilliant and powerful.

I do not say that such an exercise of subjective power would not be abnormal and productive of untoward physical consequences. Men of genius in all ages of the world have unconsciously exercised this power. But men of genius the world over have been too often noted for abnormalities of character and conduct. Profane history furnishes but one example where a man of genius appears to have been in possession of objective and subjective powers perfectly balanced, and who was able to utilize his enormous objective advantages, resulting from constant and intimate association with the greatest minds of his generation, in the subjective production of works which must always stand pre-eminent. It is unnecessary to say that I allude to Shakspeare. So little is known of his private life that it is impossible to judge whether abnormal physical effects resulted from his labors. But his works are full of internal evidence that his subjective powers were under the constant control of a well-trained and perfectly balanced objective intellect.

It is of course impossible to say just how far subjective power might, normally, be employed in the direction indicated, in the absolute dearth of examples where it has been employed with a full knowledge of the laws which govern it. But certain it is that so long as it is exercised under the delusion that it is an extraneous and superior power, over which the objective man possesses no control, just so long will the victim of the delusion be subject to the caprice of an irresponsible power, which will eventually drive him to the horrors of insanity or leave him in the darkness of imbecility.

Of greater importance than either the physical or mental deterioration of the one who habitually exercises subjective power in the production of phenomena, is the moral aspect of the question. One may escape serious physical consequences of mediumship, or he may succeed in maintaining a sufficient outward semblance of mental equilibrium to keep out of the insane asylum ; but no well-informed spiritist of the better class will attempt to deny or weaken the force of the statement that a mephitic moral atmosphere surrounds the average spiritistic medium. I do not assert by any means that all mediums are immoral. On the contrary, there are many noble men and pure women who habitually exercise mediumistic power. Otherwise, the tendency to looseness of morals which characterizes so many of them would be difficult to account for on other than physiological grounds. Books have been written to account for this tendency, on the hypothesis that immorality is a consequence of the nervous derangement which follows the practice of mediumship. This hypothesis necessarily presupposes the invariable connection of immorality with a nervous disorder, and the latter with mediumship. The common experience of mankind may be invoked to prove that there is no invariable connection of the kind existing.

Another cause must therefore be sought for the too-frequent association of immorality with mediumship.

Those who have followed me in my brief analysis of the causes which conspire to bring about the mental deterioration of the spiritistic medium will anticipate me in what I have to say concerning the causes of the moral degradation of the same class. The medium, if he is sincere in his professions of belief in the alleged communication of spirits of the dead through him, believes himself to be under the care and control of a higher and purer mentality than his own. He believes in its lofty assumptions of mental and moral superiority, and he becomes accustomed to ask its advice in all things pertaining to his personal well-being. He frequently finds its advice to be of the best, and he gradually accustoms himself to submit to its guidance in all things. He assumes and believes that in the clearer light of the world of spirits many of the artificialities of mundane civilization are held in pitying contempt, and he frequently comes to believe that many of the restraints of human society are purely artificial, and have no foundation in true morality or religion. He generally regards himself as a reformer, having broken away from the orthodox creed, and becomes the advocate of a new religion. Like most radical reformers who find the world all wrong in one respect, he immediately assumes that it is wrong in everything; and nothing will satisfy his ambition short of destroying the whole fabric of civilized society, and instituting a new order of things more suited to his ideas of human progress and felicity. It all too frequently happens that one of the first "artificial" institutions of society which becomes the object of private attack by the spiritual medium is the marriage relation. He sees much domestic infelicity surrounding him, and is perhaps tired of the restraints which it imposes upon himself, and he consults his spirit guide as to the propriety of setting at defiance the laws of human society in that regard. Now, if his "spirit guide" were what he believed it to be, or what it assumed to be, — a pure and lofty spirit, disenthralled from the temptations and weaknesses of the flesh, and drawing inspiration from the society of just men made perfect, — there could be no doubt of the character of the advice it would give him. But, being the medium's own subjective entity, bound by the laws of its being to control by the power of suggestion, it necessarily follows the line of thought which is uppermost in the medium's objective mind, and it gives the advice most desired. Moreover, from the premises suggested by the unhallowed lusts of the medium, it will frame an argument so plausible and convincing to his willing mind that he will fancy that, in following the advice of his "control," he is obeying the holiest impulses implanted in his nature by a God of love.

I do not charge spiritists as a class with being advocates of the doctrines of free love. On the contrary, I am aware that, as a class, they hold the marriage relation in sacred regard. I cannot forget, however, that but a few years ago some of their leading advocates and mediums proclaimed the doctrine of free love in all its hideous deformity from every platform in the land. Nor do I fail to remember that the better class of spiritists everywhere repudiated the doctrine and denounced its advocates and exemplars. Nevertheless, the moral virus took effect here and there all over the country, and it is doing its deadly work in secret in many an otherwise happy home. And I charge a large and constantly growing class of professional mediums with being the leading propagandists of the doctrine of free love. They infest every community in the land, and it is well known to all men and women who are dissatisfied or unhappy in their marriage relations that they can always find sympathy by consulting the average medium, and can, moreover, find justification for illicit love by invoking the spirits of the dead through such mediums.

As before remarked, I do not charge mediums as a class with immoral practices, nor do I say that the exercise of subjective power, *per se*, has a tendency to induce immoral practices. What I do say is, that through a want of knowledge of the laws which pertain to subjective mental activity, the one who exercises that power in the form of mediumship is in constant danger of being led astray. He invokes a power that he knows nothing of, — a power which may, at any time, turn and rend him.

The man or woman whose heart is pure, in whom the principles of virtue and morality are innate, is in no danger of being corrupted by the exercise of mediumistic power. The auto-suggestions of such are constantly on the side of virtue, and a corrupt communication could not emanate from such a source. But to the young, whose characters are not formed, and to those whose notions of morality are loose, the dangers of mediumship are appalling.

I have felt obliged to draw my illustrations from spirit mediums for the reason that mediumship is the form which subjective activity takes in the Western world. Other forms, however, are being introduced from the Orient, and may soon become common in this country. The Western world is threatened with a revival of the arts of the magician, the conjurer, and the wizard. It may be true, and doubtless is, that the Eastern adepts know more of the practice of subjective arts than is dreamed of by spiritists. The fact that they denounce as dangerous to health, morals, and sanity the practice of mediumship, is a hopeful sign. That they are aware that the power which controls the medium emanates from himself, is demonstrative of their advancement in practical knowledge of the subject. But that they are reliable guides to the safe exercise of subjective power has not been demonstrated. It is certain that they are yet ignorant of the fundamental principles which underlie the science of the soul, for they have yet to learn the law of suggestion, and to appreciate the subtle *rôle* which that power plays in every psychic phenomenon. Their whole system of spiritual philosophy has been built up in ignorance of that law, and hence they are necessarily subject to the same delusions, arising from the same sources of error, that have misguided all mankind, in all the ages of the world, prior to the discovery of that law. They believe in their power to communicate with the spirits of another world, precisely the same as do the modern spiritists. The foundation of their belief is the same; namely, psychic phenomena produced by themselves, in ignorance of the fundamental laws which govern it. The only difference resides in the fact that the Orientalists have the power to produce a greater variety of startling phenomena, and hence are in possession of greater facilities for deceiving themselves. No advantage, therefore, can be gained by studying their philosophy or practising their arts, except as a means of gaining general information or for purposes of scientific experiment; and the warning against indulging in the indiscriminate practice of mediumship holds good against the too frequent exercise of subjective power in any direction, or for any purpose save that of scientific investigation or healing the sick.

It should be remembered always that the power of the subjective entity is the most potent force in nature, and when intelligently directed the most beneficent. But, like every other power in nature misdirected, its destructive force is equally potent.

In conclusion, I desire again to impress upon the reader the absolute necessity of always holding the subjective entity under the positive domination of objective reason; and I here repeat, what I have again and again sought to enforce, that insanity consists in the usurpation by the subjective mind of the throne of reason. The terrible potentialities of the subjective entity are as much to be feared as admired, and no faculty that it possesses is more to be dreaded and guarded against than its awful power and inexorable exactitude of logical deduction, when reasoning from premises that have not been demonstrated by the processes of induction.

CHAPTER XXIII.

THE PHYSICAL MANIFESTATIONS AND PHILOSOPHY OF CHRIST.

The Great Stumbling-block, Unbelief in the Physical History of
Christ. — Modern Science confirms the New Testament. — Internal Evidence of the Truth of the History of Jesus. — The Scientific Accuracy of his Statements. — The Exoteric and the Esoteric
Doctrines. — Parables. — Esoteric Doctrines Reserved for Modern
Science to discover. — The Spirit of Truth. — Jesus the first to
proclaim the Scientific Truth. — The Doctrine of Faith. — Healing
the Sick. — Natural Law. — Faith essential then as now. — Illustrative Incidents. — Jairus' Daughter. — Seven Scientific Steps.
— Secrecy enjoined. — Scientific Reasons. — Rediscovery of the
Science of Mental Therapeutics in Modern Times. — Nothing discovered that Jesus did not know. — Absent Treatment. — The
Power to heal transmitted to all Future Generations. — The Conditions. — Conclusions.

IT was no part of my original intention in writing this
book to enter upon the discussion of theological questions, or to speculate upon the possible condition of the
soul after the death of the body. Nor shall I, to any great
extent, enter upon that prolific field of discussion at this
time. Nevertheless, I cannot refrain from presenting a few
thoughts which have forced themselves upon me concerning
the relation which the hypothesis under consideration bears
to the history and doctrines of the man Jesus Christ. In
doing so I hope to offend no man's theology, and to avoid
the accusation of seeking to " open the secret of spiritual
life in the criminal court of empirical philosophy."

It has often been said that the laws which enable man
to perceive spiritual truths, or to apprehend the relation
which his spiritual nature bears to the Christ, cannot be

formulated by any known methods of finite reasoning, that spiritual truth must be approached from the spiritual side, and that it must be perceived by the eye of faith. Nevertheless, there are many who have never been able to attain that faith in the spiritual nature of Christ, for the reason that they persist in approaching him by and through the finite processes of reasoning. Their conceptions of him come through the history of his physical life, and their doubts arise through their unbelief in the verity of the history of his physical manifestations. The history of critical warfare upon Christianity will bear out the statement that this is, and has ever been, the great stumbling-block. The assaults of scepticism have always been upon the man Christ; and, being unable to reconcile the accounts of his physical history and manifestations with the laws of nature, as understood by his critics, sceptics have ignored the spiritual side of his character, and ended in total unbelief in his divine attributes.

If, therefore, the discoveries of modern science can be made to throw any light upon the history of the man Jesus; if they confirm all that has been said of the physical phenomena which characterized his career, — the first great obstacle which stands in the way of the acceptance of the essential spiritual doctrines which he promulgated will be removed.

If, in addition to that, it can be shown that the discoveries of modern science not only confirm the story of his physical manifestations, but demonstrate the essential truth of the central idea which he promulgated concerning man's immortality, show the philosophy of his mission on earth, and prove that he was, and is, as a matter of scientific truth, the Saviour of the souls of men, there will be little left upon which scepticism can hang a reasonable doubt.

I undertake to say that modern science can do all this, and more.

It has often been said that the New Testament bears internal evidence of its own truth. This is true. But it is not true in the sense in which it has been stated. It has been said that such evidence consists in the alleged fact that at the time when Christ lived, there was no one else capable of formulating the code of ethics and morals which he promulgated. That this is not true is evidenced by the writings of many who preceded him. The golden rule itself, which may be said to embody the noblest conception which has been given to mankind of man's duty to his fellow-man, is found in the writings of Confucius. The code of ethics found in the writings of the ancient Greek philosophers will compare favorably with anything found in the New Testament. It is not in this, therefore, that the internal evidence of the truth of the New Testament is to be found.

But I undertake to say that in view of the state of scientific knowledge which existed at the time when Christ appeared on earth, it was absolutely impossible that a fictitious character could have been created, embodying the salient features of the physical history and character of Christ, by any one of his day and generation. The writers of the New Testament must have had an original from which to write the history, draw the character, and state the attributes of Christ. This is especially true of his physical history and manifestations; for no one but he was at that time capable of doing his work or of formulating with scientific accuracy the secret and source of his power. Nor was any one of his day capable of conceiving the ideas which he promulgated concerning his spiritual mission on earth, or of stating, as he did, the exact conditions upon which mankind must depend for salvation and immortality. He did not formulate the scientific principles which underlie his doctrines, for the world was not ready to receive, nor capable of appreciating, them; he only stated the facts. It has been left for the discoveries of modern science to demonstrate the scientific accuracy of his statements. That he understood the principles which underlie his doctrines and constitute the secret of his power, goes without saying; but his biographers did not understand them, or, if they did, they were as reticent as he was.

Nor is it important to know whether they were or were not in possession of that knowledge. The point is, that they could not have created the character without the original to draw from, and, *a fortiori*, they could not have formulated the doctrines which, after the lapse of nineteen hundred years, prove to be scientifically correct. But it is said that they were inspired. Leaving out of consideration the theological idea of inspiration, it is certain that they were inspired in the highest and best sense of the word. They were inspired by the authoritative declarations of the Master, — by his statement of the great principles of his philosophy; by the words of him " who spake as never man spake,"— words of which he made the declaration, that, " though heaven and earth shall pass away, my words shall not pass away." With this view of the source of the inspiration of the writers of the New Testament, the internal evidence of the essential truth of the history of Jesus Christ is demonstrative.

If Jesus had formulated the scientific principles which pertain to his doctrines and his works, and had taught them to his disciples, there would have been no internal evidence whatever of the truth of his history, or that he ever existed. The reason is obvious. If his biographers had been in possession of that knowledge, no matter from what source they obtained it, it would have been possible for them to create a fictitious character possessing all the powers and attributes of Christ. A few years ago it would have been impossible for the most lively imagination to picture two men, standing a thousand miles apart, transmitting oral messages to each other over a wire stretched between them. If, however, a statement had been made by any one that he had seen the feat performed, the existence of the telephone to-day would be demonstrative evidence of the truth of his statement, however sceptical his own generation might have been. In other words, the discoveries of modern science would have developed the fact that he spoke the truth. If it were known that the man who made the statement knew absolutely nothing of the science of electricity, the internal evidence of its truth would be all the stronger; for a man well versed in the science of electricity might be supposed to be capable of imagining the possibility of such an invention, and stating its existence as a fact. But a man ignorant of electrical laws could by no possibility conceive the idea of the telephone; he must be presented with the concrete fact in order to be able to state it intelligently.

It was so with the biographers of Jesus. They knew nothing of the scientific principles involved in the performance of his wonderful works. They knew only the facts, and they recorded them. He gave to his apostles just enough information to enable them to continue his work. He stated the conditions of success, and promised the world that whosoever complied with those conditions should be able to do even greater works than he had done. He formulated the doctrine of immortality, and stated the conditions of its attainment. His biographers have recorded his words, but not his reasons, for he gave none. If, therefore, science demonstrates that the powers that he possessed are possible, that the conditions of their exercise are precisely what he declared them to be, and that they cannot be exercised without a strict compliance with those conditions, the internal evidence for the truth of his history is overwhelming. Modified by the nature of the subject, and of the proofs required, the same may be said of his spiritual doctrines.

His practical wisdom is nowhere shown more conspicuously than in his reticence. He had two very important reasons for withholding a full disclosure of the underlying principles of his philosophy, or of the laws which pertain to his physical manifestations. The first was that the world was not ready to receive the whole truth. This was said to his disciples during his last interview with them previous to his crucifixion. "I have yet many things to say unto you, but ye cannot bear them now." He had given to his followers all that it was expedient to give in that age. He had told them the conditions of salvation. He had taught them how to heal the sick. He had taught them how to employ their powers in doing good, both physically and spiritually. But he knew that the same power which he taught them how to use for the physical benefit of mankind might also, in the hands of wicked men, be employed for doing evil. He knew that the condition of its exercise for evil purposes was a full knowledge of the laws which pertain to it. He knew that in the hands of the majority of the men of his day and generation it was a dangerous power, — too dangerous to be intrusted to the world in its then stage of public and private virtue, morality, religion, and enlightenment.

There was an exoteric doctrine which he promulgated to the world, and an esoteric doctrine which he deemed it inexpedient to divulge before the world was prepared to receive it. His whole career illustrates this important fact.

His habit of speaking to the multitude in parables, together with his reasons for so doing, constitutes the strongest evidence of his determination to conceal his esoteric doctrines from the common people.

"And the disciples came, and said unto him, Why speakest thou unto them in parables?

"He answered and said unto them, Because it is given unto you to know the mysteries of the kingdom of heaven, but to them it is not given. . . .

"Therefore speak I to them in parables: because they seeing see not; and hearing they hear not, neither do they understand. . . .

"For this people's heart is waxed gross, and their ears are dull of hearing, and their eyes they have closed. . . .

"All these things spake Jesus unto the multitude in parables; and without a parable spake he not unto them:

"That it might be fulfilled which was spoken by the prophet, saying, I will open my mouth in parables; I will utter things which have been kept secret from the foundation of the world." [1]

These passages make it as clear as words can formulate a proposition that he deemed it inexpedient to divulge to

---

[1] Matthew xiii. 10, 11, 13, 15, 34, 35.

the people anything more than they could understand and assimilate. His estimate of men and his knowledge of their needs were perfect; and he gave to each class with whom he had to deal, just what was necessary to enable it to perform the work assigned to it. He taught the multitude the principles of morality and justice among men, and pointed the way to eternal life; but he did not teach them how to heal the sick. He taught his chosen ones the true method of healing the sick, and divulged the exact conditions of its exercise; but he did not teach them the scientific principles upon which his system of healing was founded. They were no more capable of understanding those principles than were the multitude capable of acquiring the power to heal the sick. He gave to each according to his needs; and, true to his spiritual mission, Christ enjoined upon all men the necessity of first seeking the kingdom of heaven, when all other needful things would be added unto them. It was not necessary for his disciples to know the esoteric science of healing, in order to enable them to heal the sick, any more than it is for us to-day. We may know how little the knowledge of true scientific principles involved in the exercise of that power has to do with success in healing, when we observe the diversity of views entertained on the subject by the successful healers of modern times. Christ gave to the world all the knowledge necessary for the successful exercise of that power in the one word *faith*. He was the first who taught that lesson to mankind; and it holds as good to-day as it did when he first proclaimed it to the multitude upon the banks of the Jordan.

The second reason for withholding a statement of the scientific principles involved in his manifestations of power and his spiritual philosophy was that he foresaw the time approaching when the world would reason it out for itself; and that when that time came, mankind would be prepared to receive it. He foresaw that in the progress of civilization and enlightenment the time would surely come when the world would not be content to rest its belief upon the doctrine of any one, whatever his claims to inspiration or authority. In other words, he foresaw the present age of materialism, and its tendency towards scepticism regarding everything which cannot be scientifically demonstrated by the inductive processes of reasoning. He knew that when that epoch should have arrived in the history of man's intellectual development, the truth of his doctrines would be all the more forcibly impressed upon mankind if they could be proved by the inexorable rules of logic. Besides, science and inductive reasoning would have been lost upon the people with whom he had to deal. That he fully realized this is shown by his implied rebuke to the nobleman of Capernaum, when he exclaimed, " Except ye see signs and wonders, ye will not believe." To have attempted to reason with them would have been like " casting pearls before swine." He appealed to them by the only logic they could understand. He offered to them the only evidence they could appreciate, — the evidence of their senses.

That Christ foresaw the time when the world would be in possession of indubitable evidence of the truth concerning him, but that he knew that the time had not yet come, is clearly shown by his remarks to his disciples in his memorable interview with them just previous to his crucifixion :

" I have yet many things to say unto you, but ye cannot bear them now." [1]

This refers to the then existing conditions. He had given them all the proofs that they were capable of appreciating of the truth of his doctrines. In the next sentence he refers to the time to come, when still more evidence would be given to the world.

" Howbeit when he, the Spirit of truth, is come, he will guide you into all truth." [2]

This clearly refers to the time, which was yet to come, when mankind should seek the truth and demand to know it. The " Spirit of truth " is a personification of that spirit in man which seeks to learn the truth for its own sake, by

[1] John xvi. 12.   [2] John xvi. 13.

the only process known to this world, — inductive reasoning. That day has come. The Spirit of truth is abroad throughout all the civilized world, and it demands reasons for the faith that is in the Christian Church.

Again Christ said : —

"But when the Comforter is come, whom I will send unto you from the Father, even the Spirit of truth, which proceedeth from the Father, he shall testify of me :

"And ye shall also bear witness, because ye have been with me from the beginning." [1]

The first verse above quoted has the same meaning as this last quotation. The second refers to the events of his life of which they were witnesses. He foresaw that the record of those events would be read by future generations, and compared with later experiments. He had left the power to heal as a heritage to all who should come after him, possessing the requisite faith; and he knew that the testimony of his disciples concerning the works that he had performed would be compared with later exhibitions of the same power. He foresaw that the "Spirit of truth" would eventually discover the laws pertaining to his doctrines and his works, and that a comparison of the testimony of his followers with the discoveries of science would demonstrate to the world the essential truth of his history and of his spiritual philosophy.

I shall now briefly point out a few of the more salient features of the history of Jesus which bear upon the subject under consideration, and shall undertake to show, first, how the discoveries of modern science confirm the accounts of his physical manifestations; and secondly, how they confirm the essential features of his spiritual philosophy.

The prominent feature of his physical manifestations consisted in healing the sick; and in the discussion of the first division of the subject I shall confine myself to the consideration of that part of his career.

[1] John xv. 26, 27.

The first proposition bearing upon the subject is, that Jesus Christ was the first who correctly formulated the exact conditions necessary and indispensable to the exercise of the power to heal the sick by psychic methods.

The second proposition is, that the conditions which he declared to be necessary to enable him to exercise that power are the same conditions which are indispensable to-day.

These propositions will be considered together.

The condition which he declared to be essential, not only in the patient, but in the healer, is embraced in the one word *faith*. That word, more than any other, expresses the whole law of human felicity and power in this world, and of salvation in the world to come. It is that attribute of mind which elevates man above the level of the brute, and gives him dominion over all the physical world. It is the essential element of success in every field of human endeavor. It constitutes the power of the human soul. When Jesus of Nazareth proclaimed its potency from the hill-tops of Palestine he gave to mankind the key to health and to heaven, and earned the title of Saviour of the World.

It would seem to be a work of supererogation to cite particular passages of the Scriptures or to employ argument to prove the correctness of the proposition that Jesus considered faith in the patient a necessary condition of his recovery. The proposition is plainly true, and it has been so understood by all intelligent readers of the New Testament until very recent times. There are those, however, who now seem to fear that Jesus will be robbed of his glory, and reduced to the common level of mankind, if it is shown that the conditions necessary to the success of the mental healer of to-day are the same as they were nineteen hundred years ago. In other words, they endeavor to show that Jesus did not operate in harmony with the laws which he proclaimed, but independently and in defiance of the very principles of nature which it was his mission to illustrate and expound. He did not pretend to establish any new law of nature, but to teach mankind that which had been in existence from the beginning, to illustrate it in his life, and to sanction it by his death. He did not teach his disciples the principles and laws involved in healing the sick, and at the same time violate himself. He taught them his methods of healing, and sent them into the world to imitate his example. When they failed, as they occasionally did fail, he reproved them for neglecting his teachings, and upbraided them for their want of faith. When the lunatic was brought to him, and he was told that his disciples had failed to cast out the devil which afflicted the patient, Jesus exclaimed: " O faithless and perverse generation, how long shall I be with you? how long shall I suffer you?" After he had cast out the devil, the disciples asked him why they could not cast him out.

" And Jesus said unto them, Because of your unbelief: for verily I say unto you, If ye have faith as a grain of mustard seed, ye shall say unto this mountain, Remove hence to yonder place; and it shall remove; and nothing shall be impossible unto you."[1]

His expression concerning their power to remove mountains doubtless had reference to the fact that ponderable bodies can be moved by subjective power, under proper conditions, as has been frequently demonstrated in later times.

Many passages might be quoted illustrating the proposition that faith was a necessary condition in the minds of the apostolic healers; but it is believed that no one will gainsay the proposition. It may be said, however, that Jesus did not require faith in himself to enable him to heal the sick, — that he healed independently of that law. The obvious answer is that he had that knowledge of his power which transcended faith; or rather, that he had the faith which came from knowledge of that power. In the sense that faith ceases where knowledge begins, he may be said not to have had faith. His disciples arrived at that point after an experimental demonstration of their power; and

[1] Matthew xvii. 20.

so may we all do likewise. As I have shown in a former
chapter, subjective faith may be acquired in direct contradiction to objective faith or belief; but after an experimental demonstration of the power of subjective faith,
objective belief no longer sets up an auto-suggestion against
it. It then becomes knowledge, and in that sense it ceases
to be faith. Nevertheless, in the sense in which it is said
that the healer must have faith to enable him to heal the
sick, he has faith. In that sense it cannot be disputed that
Jesus had faith in his power to heal the sick. It is thought,
therefore, that enough has been said to demonstrate the
proposition that faith was a requisite element in the healers
of Jesus' time. Certainly no one will dispute the proposition that it is necessary in the psychic healers of to-day.
We may consider, therefore, that two points in our argument
are established, — namely (1), that the conditions requisite
in psychic healers of this day are identical with those required in apostolic times; and (2) that Jesus was the first
to proclaim the principle and to exemplify it in his works.
The difference is not in principle, but in degree of power.

It is said, however, that Jesus did not require faith in
those whom he healed. The first answer to this proposition is that there is nothing in his recorded words to warrant the statement. He never professed to be able to heal
independently of that condition. On the contrary, all his
expressions on that subject lead to the inevitable conclusion that faith was a necessary condition of the patient's
mind to enable him to effect a cure. It may be true that
in some cases he said nothing about it; but this is only
negative evidence, and of the weakest kind, in view of what
he *did* say on the numerous occasions when circumstances
required an utterance on the subject.

A striking instance of healing, and a fair example of his
utterances on this subject, is recorded in Matthew ix. 28,
29, 30 : —

" And when he was come into the house, the blind men came
to him : and Jesus saith unto them, Believe ye that I am able
to do this? They said unto him, Yea, Lord.

" Then he touched their eyes, saying, According to your faith be it unto you.

" And their eyes were opened."

Jesus was not in the habit of uttering idle words, or words without significance. In all history there is not an example recorded of a man whose reticence was so marked. Every word he uttered conveyed some important lesson to humanity. It does not seem probable that he would question those poor blind men regarding their faith in his power, unless their faith was an important factor in the case.

The case of the ten lepers of Samaria and Galilee has been cited as an instance of his healing in the absence of faith on the part of the patients : —

" And as he entered into a certain village, there met him ten men that were lepers, which stood afar off :

" And they lifted up their voices, and said, Jesus, Master, have mercy on us.

" And when he saw them, he said unto them, Go show yourselves unto the priests. And it came to pass, that, as they went, they were cleansed.

" And one of them, when he saw that he was healed, turned back, and with a loud voice glorified God,

" And fell down on his face at his feet, giving him thanks : and he was a Samaritan.

" And Jesus answering said, Were there not ten cleansed ? but where are the nine ?

" There are not found that returned to give glory to God, save this stranger.

" And he said unto him, Arise, go thy way : thy faith hath made thee whole." [1]

It has been said that this passage shows that nine out of the ten were healed without the exercise of faith on their part, because he said to but one of them, " Thy faith hath made thee whole." The obvious answer to this is that he had no opportunity to say it to the rest. There was but one of the ten who exhibited sufficient gratitude to return and give thanks for what had been done for him. That the rest were healed in the same way is obvious. That they

[1] Luke xvii. 12–19

all had faith in his power is evidenced by the fact that they cried to him from afar off, "Jesus, Master, have mercy on us." I submit that that is not the language of doubt.

Again, it has been said that in the cases where he raised from the dead there could have been no faith on the part of the dead. This is by all odds the strongest case that could be cited in support of the theory that faith was not required. But the objection instantly vanishes when we remember that it is the faith of the subjective mind, or the soul, that is required; and that the belief of the objective mind has only a limited control, governed by circumstances.[1] When Jesus raised a person from the dead, the conditions were, in one sense of the word, the best possible to enable him to obtain complete mastery of the soul of the deceased by the power of suggestion. The objective senses were in complete abeyance, the body was dead; consequently, there was no objective auto-suggestion of doubt possible. The soul, in obedience to the universal law, was amenable to control by the mysterious power of suggestion. Jesus, possessing more subjective power than any one who has ever lived, commanded the soul of the deceased to return to its earthly tenement. He may not have employed objective language when he issued his command, but his soul, in perfect telepathic communion with that of the deceased, and dominating it as only he could dominate the souls of men, issued his mental mandate to the departing soul to return to the body and resume its functions. That command it must obey, and it did obey. There was no law of nature violated or transcended. On the contrary, the whole transaction was in perfect obedience to the laws of nature. He understood the law perfectly, as no one before him understood it; and in the plenitude of his power he applied it where the greatest good could be accomplished.

The case of Jairus' daughter is a perfect illustration of the fact that he perfectly understood the mental conditions necessary to enable him to raise her from the dead. Jairus,

[1] See the chapters on Mental Therapeutics.

one of the rulers of the synagogue, besought Jesus to come to his house and heal his daughter, who was lying at the point of death. Jesus readily complied with the request; but before they arrived, word was sent to Jairus that the damsel was dead : —

" While he yet spake, there came from the ruler of the synagogue's house certain which said, Thy daughter is dead : why troublest thou the Master any further?

" As soon as Jesus heard the word that was spoken, he saith unto the ruler of the synagogue, Be not afraid, only believe.

" And he suffered no man to follow him, save Peter, and James, and John the brother of James.

" And he cometh to the house of the ruler of the synagogue, and seeth the tumult, and them that wept and wailed greatly.

" And when he was come in, he saith unto them, Why make ye this ado, and weep? the damsel is not dead, but sleepeth.

" And they laughed him to scorn. But when he had put them all out, he taketh the father and the mother of the damsel, and them that were with him, and entereth in where the damsel was lying.

" And he took the damsel by the hand, and said unto her, *Talitha cumi;* which is, being interpreted, Damsel, I say unto thee, arise.

" And straightway the damsel arose, and walked; for she was of the age of twelve years. And they were astonished with a great astonishment.

" And he charged them straitly that no man should know it; and commanded that something should be given her to eat." [1]

There are several points embraced in the above which are deserving of serious consideration.

The first is that Christ perfectly understood the importance of securing for his patient a favorable mental environment. To that end he endeavored to quiet the fears of the father, and to impress upon him the necessity of holding his mind in the attitude of faith and confidence. The father was necessarily in telepathic rapport with the daughter, and it was important that he should not impress his doubts and fears upon her departing soul. The injunction was, therefore, laid upon him, " Be not afraid, only believe."

[1] Mark v. 35–43.

He also understood the value of a positive mental force surrounding the deceased, which would be in perfect harmony with his own force and purpose. To that end, he selected three of the most powerful of his followers, Peter, James, and John, to be present in the chamber of death, and he suffered no one else to follow him. He kept the multitude of unbelievers as far away as possible. When he came to the house and saw the tumult, and heard the weeping and wailing of the friends and relatives of the deceased, he not only put them all out of the room, but sought to quiet their fears by the only way possible, which was by assuring them that " the damsel is not dead, but sleepeth." These words possess a double meaning, a double purpose ; and some have supposed that they implied that the damsel was only in a cataleptic trance. It is probable, however, that they were uttered in the sense that the soul never dies. It will be remembered that he used the same expression in regard to Lazarus, but afterwards explained his meaning by declaring that Lazarus was really dead in the common acceptation of the term. His object in using that expression was twofold. First, he desired to quiet the fears and stop the lamentations of the friends and relatives, for the obvious reason that their hopeless wailing must operate as a strong adverse suggestion to the soul of the patient. The only way that could be accomplished was by an assurance that the damsel was not dead. Secondly, he knew the potency of such a suggestion upon the patient herself. It was the master-stroke on his part, first, to quiet the fears of the relatives, and secondly, to fill the departing soul with the subjective faith necessary to enable him successfully to command it to return to the body. That this was his object in uttering those words there can be no reasonable doubt ; more especially as it is precisely what an intelligent mental healer who thoroughly understands the law of suggestion would do to-day, in the light of recent rediscoveries in the science which Jesus taught.

Here, then, are seven separate and distinct acts which he performed, all tending in the one direction : —

1. He inspired the father with faith, because he was in telepathic rapport with his daughter.

2. He prohibited the multitude of unbelievers from approaching the house, knowing the adverse influence of an atmosphere of incredulity and doubt.

3. He took three of his most powerful apostles with him, for the purpose of surrounding the patient with an atmosphere of faith and courage.

4. He excluded the weeping friends and relatives from the sick room, for the same reason that he prevented the multitude from following him.

5. He assured them that the damsel was not dead, for the purpose of inspiring them with faith and hope in her recovery, and thus adding another favorable element to the mental environment.

6. By the same words of assurance that the damsel was not dead he conveyed to her subjective mind the most powerful suggestion possible, — indeed, the only suggestion applicable to the exigencies of the case.

7. Having thus secured the best possible conditions, he took the damsel by the hand, and, by an energetic command, restored her to life.

The sceptic will doubtless interpose the objection that the damsel could not have been dead, but that it was merely a case of suspended animation. To this the reply is, first, that it is claimed by the Eastern adepts that as long as the vital organs of the body are perfect, it is always possible to compel the soul to return to its habitation. It is certain that there are many apparently well-authenticated instances of the performance of the feat even in the Western hemisphere. The second and most pertinent reply is that the evidential value of the case is just as great, supposing it to have been a case of suspended animation. The point is that Jesus could not have taken the course he did if he had not been in full possession of the knowledge of the laws pertaining to mental therapeutics. This one case is demonstrative, first, that he perfectly understood the laws of telepathy ; and secondly, that he fully understood the law of suggestion.

Indeed, Jesus was the first discoverer of that law, for the word *faith* is an epitome of the whole law of suggestion. In short, the internal evidence of the exact truth of this narrative is demonstrative, in view of what is now known of the laws of mental healing. For, in his day, no one but he knew enough about those laws to enable him to carry out the minute details of the process; and, *a fortiori*, no one could have written the narrative in the absence of an exemplar.

There are two other points embraced in the last paragraph of the narrative which must not be overlooked.

"And he charged them straitly that no man should know it; and commanded that something should be given her to eat."

The injunction of secrecy contained in the first part of the paragraph was often laid upon those whom he healed. "See thou tell no man" was an injunction which was often repeated by him in the course of his career as a healer of the sick, and it still further illustrates his wonderful knowledge of the science of mental therapeutics. The reason for so charging his beneficiaries has only recently been discovered. It is this: When a person is suddenly healed by mental processes, it becomes a matter of the first importance that he should not talk on the subject in public, or to persons who are sceptical. The reason is that sceptical persons are apt to dispute the facts or to ridicule the idea of healing by such processes. They often say to a patient: "You have been cured by exciting your imagination, and the disease will return as soon as the excitement is over." This constitutes a suggestion which must act unfavorably, and it often causes the patient to look for the predicted return of the disease. His fears are aroused by imperceptible degrees; and if the suggestion is persisted in, the fears will eventually be realized. A person must needs be well grounded in the faith, and well versed in the science, to resist the insidious influence of an unfavorable suggestion constantly reiterated by his sceptical friends. It is, therefore, of the highest importance that the injunction of Christ should be observed. That he did not utter those words idly, and without a full knowledge of the principles involved, cannot be doubted.

"And he commanded that something should be given her to eat." These words show merely that he did not despise the ordinary means of imparting vigor to the wasted frame. As we have remarked in a former chapter, he did not hesitate to employ material remedies in connection with, and auxiliary to, his occult power. The mental healers of to-day would do well to profit by the example of the Master, especially when their patients are new to the faith, or, from any cause, refractory.

Taken as a whole, the narrative of the raising of Jairus' daughter from the dead conveys the best lesson in mental therapeutics which has ever been given to mankind. No mental healer of this day, even though he may be thoroughly versed in all the discoveries of modern science relating to mental therapeutics, could make it more complete.

Again I repeat that no man who lived in the days of Christ could have written that narrative except under the inspiration of literal truth. The scientific knowledge necessary for the production of a fictitious narrative corresponding to that did not exist in the minds of men previous to this, the last quarter of the nineteenth century. Up to this time the knowledge of the scientific principles involved was confined to one man, — Christ Jesus.

It is noteworthy, in this connection, that Jesus was in the habit of healing by what is known at this day as "absent treatment;" that is, healing when at a distance from the patient, and without his knowledge. The healing of the nobleman's son at Capernaum is a striking example of this. The nobleman met Jesus at Cana, and besought him to heal his son, who was at the point of death. Without going near the patient, Christ said to the nobleman: "Go thy way; thy son liveth." It was afterwards ascertained that at the same hour the fever left the young man, and he recovered. The principles involved in absent treatment have been fully explained in another chapter, and will not be repeated here ; I may remark, however, that the most perfect faith that can be obtained for therapeutic purposes is that which arises from a telepathic suggestion to the subjective mind of the patient, when he is objectively ignorant of the fact that anything is being done for him. It is evident that Jesus fully understood this law, as he did all the laws of mental therapeutics. The patient in this case was objectively ignorant of the effort made to heal him ; he was, therefore, objectively passive, and no adverse auto-suggestion was possible. The father also was full of faith, or he would not have entreated Jesus in such earnest and pathetic terms to save his son. The conditions were therefore as perfect as possible for successful absent treatment.

The healing of the centurion's servant was a parallel case. It was on this occasion that Jesus declared, "I have not found so great faith, no, not in Israel."

It is needless to multiply instances to illustrate the fact that Jesus healed by the same law which prevails at this day,—the law of faith. It seems like arguing a self-evident proposition to show that he required that condition on the part of the patient to enable him to heal the sick or to do any mighty work. He never pretended to be able to dispense with that condition, or to be superior to the law which he proclaimed to the world. When he said anything about it he always gave the patients to understand that it was through faith that they were made whole. The New Testament is full of such expressions as : " Thy faith hath made thee whole ; " " According to your faith be it unto you ; " " If thou canst believe, all things are possible to him that believeth ; " " Said I not unto thee that if thou wouldst believe, thou shouldst see the glory of God ? " These were neither idle nor untruthful expressions.

On the other hand, it was said of him that at his own home he failed to do many mighty works, " because of their unbelief." The condition was absent there, because the people had known him from boyhood, and could not believe that the " carpenter's son " could do any mighty works.

Besides, as Jesus himself remarked, "a prophet is not without honor save in his own country."

Faith was the essential prerequisite to the exercise of all the power that he possessed, and it was the condition precedent to its inheritance by those who were to come after him.

"And these signs shall follow them that believe; In my name shall they cast out devils; they shall speak with new tongues;

"They shall take up serpents; and if they drink any deadly thing, it shall not hurt them; they shall lay hands on the sick, and they shall recover."[1]

Again, —

"Verily, verily, I say unto you, He that believeth on me, the works that I do shall he do also; and greater works than these shall he do; because I go unto my Father."[2]

Christ transmitted his power as a sacred heritage to all mankind. He had taught his followers, by precept and example, the conditions necessary to its exercise. Those conditions were expressed in the one word, *faith*. He never intimated to them that he healed by any other method than that which he transmitted to them. His example would have been lost to mankind if it were not illustrative of his precepts. It would be valueless to the world if it did not illustrate the principles of the science which he taught. To seek to cast a shade of doubt upon the verity of his teachings, to intimate a want of harmony between his practice and his precepts, is to attempt to rob him of the glory and honor due to one who was able to divine the fundamental laws of our being, nineteen hundred years before his teachings could be verified by the inductive process of science, and to destroy the force of the strongest internal evidence of the truth of sacred history.

[1] Mark xvi. 17, 18.   [2] John. xiv. 12.

CHAPTER XXIV.

THE PHYSICAL MANIFESTATIONS OF CHRIST (*continuea*).

The Word *Faith* in its Application to Psychic Phenomena. — Its
Definition. — An Epitome of the Law of Suggestion. — Subjective
Faith only required. — Illustrative Incident. — The " Spoken
Word." — Jesus knew the Law, and always acted within its Limi-
tations. — Intuitive Perception of the Laws of the Soul. — His
Manhood and its Limitations. — Our Warranty of Title as Sons
of God. — Christ constantly controlled by Reason. — His Subjec-
tive Powers subservient. — The Three Temptations illustrative.
— The Great Lesson to Mankind. — The Normal Exercise of
Subjective Power. — Simon the Sorcerer. — Miracle not a Neces-
sary Explanation of the Power of Christ. — Conclusions.

IN proceeding to make a more direct application of our
hypothesis to the doctrines of Jesus, it will be necessary
first to consider the meaning of the word *faith* as it was
employed by him, and as it must be understood in its
application to all psychic phenomena.

In the common acceptation of the term, faith is " belief ;
the assent of the mind to the truth of what is declared by
another, resting solely and implicitly on his authority and
veracity ; reliance on testimony." [1]   " The faith of the
gospel is that emotion of the mind which is called ' trust,'
or ' confidence,' exercised towards the moral character of
God, and particularly of the Saviour." [2]

It is obvious that neither of these definitions properly
characterizes that emotion of the mind, called *faith*, which
is the necessary prerequisite condition of the mind of a

[1] Webster.   [2] Dwight.

person to enable him to confer or to receive the benefits of psychic power.

It has been shown in a former chapter that the faith necessary to enable a person to be healed by mental processes is subjective faith ; that is, the faith of the subjective mind, or soul. It has been shown that this faith may be entertained by the subjective mind in positive opposition to the faith, or belief, of the objective mind, — that it may be forced upon the subjective mind in defiance of objective reason or the evidence of the objective senses. It is not deemed necessary, therefore, to enter at this time into a full discussion of this branch of the subject, and the reader is referred to the chapters on psycho-therapeutics. In this view of the question it is obvious that the definition of the word *faith* must be revised if we would understand it as Christ understood it, and make it conform to the facts demonstrated by modern science. In other words, we must define that particular kind of faith which pertains to the development and exercise of psychic power, — that faith of which Christ was the first to proclaim the necessity and define the attributes.

Faith, therefore, in the sense in which Jesus employed it, may be defined as the assent of the soul, or subjective mind, to the truth of what is declared to be true.

In other words, faith is that emotion of the human soul which consists in the unhesitating acceptance and belief in the absolute verity of a suggestion.

As has been frequently stated before, the belief of the subjective mind in the verity of a suggestion made to it is the essential and never-failing law of its being. If the suggestion made to it is not counteracted by an auto-suggestion proceeding from the objective mind of the individual, it will always be unhesitatingly accepted. If it is controverted by auto-suggestion, the strongest suggestion must prevail. This law is universal. It frequently happens that a therapeutic suggestion is counteracted by auto-suggestion. The latter may arise from intense prejudice, or from natural scepticism regarding phenomena not understood. It is, however, comparatively easy to overcome an auto-suggestion, in the treatment of disease, for the patient is generally anxious to be cured, and is willing to assume a passive state of mind; and this is generally all that is necessary. Moreover, the subjective mind, ever on the alert for any means of preserving the life or health of the individual, will readily accept a therapeutic suggestion if there is no active counter auto-suggestion. If the healer understands the law of auto-suggestion, and advises his patient that he can overcome the effect of objective unbelief by a simple assertion of belief, salutary results all the more readily follow.

A remarkable instance illustrating this principle occurred in the history of Jesus. It was in the case of the man who brought his son to be healed, who was afflicted with a "dumb spirit." He had gone to Jesus' disciples, who failed to effect a cure. In despair, he appealed to the Master, saying:—

"If thou canst do any thing, have compassion on us, and help us.

"Jesus said unto him, If thou canst believe, all things are possible to him that believeth.

"And straightway the father of the child cried out, and said with tears, Lord, I believe; help thou mine unbelief."[1]

Whereupon Jesus rebuked the foul spirit and commanded it to come out of the boy, "and enter no more into him." And the boy was instantly healed.

Now, the whole circumstances surrounding this case were calculated to render the father sceptical concerning the power of Jesus to heal his son. He had gone to the disciples, and they had failed. When he appealed to Jesus he said: "If thou canst do any thing, have compassion on us, and help us." This expression plainly implied a doubt. After Jesus had explained that belief was a necessary condition of success, the father cried out: "Lord, I believe; help *thou* mine unbelief." This expression plainly indicated a want of objective faith. But he spoke the words, "I

[1] Mark ix. 22-24.

believe," and then intimated to Jesus that his real belief depended upon him. He uttered the words "I believe" in pursuance of an earnest desire to comply with the conditions imposed, and that was sufficient. These words constituted an auto-suggestion from his objective mind to his subjective mind; and Jesus was satisfied with that compliance with his demand for faith, and he instantly healed the sufferer. He knew the law, and was fully aware that any lingering objective doubt remaining in the father's objective mind could not prevail against the "spoken word" of faith.

This case is also illustrative of the principle discussed in the previous chapter; namely, the desirability of having a favorable mental environment, especially in cases where the objective mind of the patient could not be appealed to. The boy was in a state of complete objective insensibility. The father was the only one present who was in telepathic rapport with him. Hence the importance of impressing the father's subjective mind with faith, to the end that his mental condition might be impressed upon the subjective mind of the son, and by that means exert a favorable influence upon the latter by telepathic suggestion. In this case the father's spoken word of belief was a more potent suggestion than his objective doubts, and the son's subjective mind, ever alert, seized upon the suggestion; and Jesus, by means of a suggestion uttered in a solemn tone of supreme authority, healed him instantly.

I do not mean to say that Jesus could not heal in such cases where the mental environment was unfavorable; but the fact that he took infinite pains, wherever practicable, to secure the best conditions, shows that he understood the law and worked within its limitations.

Certain it is that he never performed any of his wonderful works outside the laws which he proclaimed, nor did he ever intimate that he could do so. It is true that his biographers did not always relate the details of the transactions recorded; but it must be remembered that they wrote at a later day, and may not have been in possession of all the details. It is, however, a marvellous fact, and one which constitutes indubitable evidence of the truth of his history, that in no instance do they relate a single act performed or word spoken by him, relating to the healing of the sick, that does not reveal his perfect knowledge of and compliance with the laws which pertain to mental therapeutics as they are revealed in modern times through experiment and the processes of inductive reasoning.

There is but one legitimate conclusion, and that is that the discoveries of modern science demonstrate the essential truth of the history of the physical manifestations of Jesus.

The next question is, How did it happen that Jesus came into possession of the knowledge of the true science of mental therapeutics, when no one else in all the world at that time knew its rudiments? It may be true, and doubtless it is true, that there were mental healers before his time, who, by various methods, performed wonderful works in psycho-therapeutics. But it must be conceded that he was the first who evinced a true knowledge of the underlying principles of the science. He it was who first divined the very essence of that science, and proclaimed it to the world in the one word *faith*. That word embraced all that it was necessary for the world to know at that time. Faith, and the means of acquiring it, is the substance of all that he taught to his disciples concerning the means of healing the sick; and it was all that was necessary to enable them to imitate his example and to transmit the power to those who should come after them. To use his own language, it was all that they could bear. It was the exoteric science of mental healing. The esoteric doctrine he reserved for the time when mankind, inspired by the "Spirit of truth," which he promised, should be able to discover it for themselves. His was the "dispensation of faith." The "dispensation of knowledge" was yet to come. That he was in possession of the knowledge of the underlying principles of the whole science of mental healing is all but self-evident. No man without that knowledge could have done what he did to secure the most favorable conditions for the exercise of his power. It required a full

comprehension of the law of suggestion, a thorough knowledge of the law of telepathy, a complete realization of the
dual nature of the mind of man, and the power of the soul
over the functions of the body, to enable him to take the
seven steps preparatory to the raising of Jairus' daughter
from the dead. If he had failed in that attempt, his preparatory steps to that end would nevertheless have demonstrated his knowledge of the laws which pertain to healing
by psychic power.

The theologian will find a ready-made answer to the
question, How did Jesus come into possession of knowledge which it has taken nineteen hundred years of scientific research to verify? His answer will be : " By direct
inspiration from God ; by virtue of his being the Son of
God, — one with the Father." I shall not attempt to gainsay this proposition, but shall endeavor to show that it is
true in the highest and best sense of the expression. In
doing so I shall not discuss the question of his miraculous
birth ; I leave that to the theologian. I desire simply to
show that, whatever may have been the conditions of his
birth, he took upon himself the nature and attributes of
humanity, and subjected himself to its physical conditions
and limitations. In other words, his wondrous works were
performed within the domain of the same natural laws
which limit the powers of all mankind. He was a man,
and merely a man, in his physical life and manifestations,
and differed from other men only in the degree of his
faculties and in the possession of the intuitive power of
perception of the laws of the soul in its relations to the
physical world and to God.

I have shown that Jesus did not find it necessary to go
outside the pale of natural law for the power to perform his
mighty works, that he not only operated within the domain of natural law, but even avowed and proclaimed the
fact to the world. It remains for me to show that his
knowledge of those laws was obtained through the operation
of natural law, and without the necessity of our invoking
the aid of miraculous power.

It will be remembered that in a former chapter of this book it was shown that the subjective mind, or soul, of man possesses the inherent power to *perceive*, under certain exceptional conditions not clearly defined, those operations of nature which are governed by fixed laws. It was by means of this power of instantaneous perception of the laws of numbers that Zerah Colburn, before his objective education was sufficient to enable him to understand the power of the nine digits, was enabled instantly to state the cube root of any number that was given him. He could never give any explanation of the means by which the result was accomplished. It was beyond his own objective powers of comprehension. He simply perceived the truth.

It was this power that enabled Blind Tom to perceive the laws of the harmony of sounds. He was without objective education, and devoid of the capacity to acquire one ; but from the moment when he discovered an old piano in an unused room of his master's mansion, he was able to improvise beautiful melodies, and to reproduce with remarkable accuracy a piece of music after once hearing it played.

This is a power which transcends reason, and is independent of induction. Instances of its development might be multiplied indefinitely, but it is not necessary in this connection to enlarge upon a fact which will receive the instant assent of the intelligent reader when his attention is called to it. In this objective existence of ours, trammelled as is the human soul by its fleshly tabernacle, it is comparatively rare that conditions are favorable to the development of the phenomena. But enough is known to warrant the conclusion that when the soul is released from its objective environment it will be enabled to perceive all the laws of its being, to " see God as he is," by the perception of the laws which he has instituted. It is the knowledge of this power which demonstrates our true relationship to God, which confers the warranty of our right to the title of " sons of God," and confirms our inheritance of our rightful share of his attributes and powers, — our heirship of God, our joint heirship with Jesus Christ.

It was this power of perception of truth without the necessity of resorting to the slow and laborious processes of induction that enabled Christ to divine the whole law of mental therapeutics. Science, after nineteen hundred years of induction, has demonstrated the fact that he perceived the whole law and applied it with scientific accuracy. The most marvellous part of it all is that the account of it has been preserved and transmitted with such fidelity of scientific detail.

Leaving out of consideration the question of the alleged miraculous conception and birth of Christ, it is certain that he was exceptionally endowed, morally, physically, and mentally. No man ever before possessed the subjective power that he did. And yet, unlike most of those of modern times who are exceptionally endowed with that power, his objective faculties and his subjective powers seem to have been harmoniously balanced and developed. This is shown by his perfect moral character and attributes. It is demonstrated by the fact that his subjective mind was always under the perfect control of his reason. In these respects he presents a most striking contrast to the great majority of persons, especially of the present day, who are in possession of great subjective powers. Not clearly understanding the relationship between their objective and subjective faculties, they allow the latter to usurp control. They realize the wonderful powers and attributes of the human soul, but they fail to understand its equally wonderful, but necessary, limitations. They realize that the soul is "God in us," and naturally conclude that it is endowed with all godlike attributes. They fail to realize that while it is imprisoned in the body, it must be limited and controlled by its objective environment. They cannot understand that the soul, as long as it is amenable to control by the power of suggestion, must necessarily be limited in its powers of reasoning. Most important of all, they fail to understand that the soul is the seat of all human passion and emotion; that, uncontrolled by objective reason, it runs riot at the bidding of every immoral suggestion; that his objective powers of reason were given to man to enable him to train the soul for eternity, — to work out his own salvation.

The whole life of Christ is an illustration of the fact that he knew the law, and, knowing it, employed his subjective powers in their legitimate domain, and never suffered himself to be tempted to allow them to usurp the throne of reason.

The account of his temptations in the wilderness is a striking illustration of this fact, and it teaches a lesson to humanity of the utmost practical importance. Like all the recorded events of his life, it is intended to illustrate a great principle. It is not a mere literal history of an episode in his career, in which a personal devil figured at a disadvantage. To suppose that he could be tempted by such a devil as has been pictured by some, would be to degrade him below the level of common humanity. But to interpret the story as a symbolical vision appearing to Christ after his forty days' fast in the wilderness, is to find in it one of the most important lessons ever conveyed to humanity.

He was just entering upon his ministry. He had shut himself out from the world for forty days, preparatory to entering upon his work. He employed his time in silent contemplation and earnest prayer for strength and power and Divine guidance. He fasted all this time, as a physical preparation necessary to the attainment of the full powers of the soul. At the end of that time, conscious of the full possession of subjective power such as no man ever before attained, contemplating the career upon which he was about to enter, realizing all its possibilities for good and all its opportunities for the attainment of personal power and aggrandizement, the temptation came. His subjective mind was the tempter. Reasoning deductively from the consciousness of transcendent power, and selfishly, in obedience to the laws of its being, it pictured to the imagination of Jesus all the possibilities in store for him if he chose to exercise his power for selfish ends. The first temptation appealed to his sense of personal necessity. He was poor. "He had not where to lay his head" at night. He was dependent upon the bounty of his friends for his daily food.

In the pursuit of his mission he had the prospect before him of being often thrown among strangers hostile to his faith; and his immediate necessities, after his forty days' fast, gave intensity to the temptation and suggested its concrete form. It came in the words: " If thou be the Son of God, command that these stones be made bread." Jesus understood the vision, not only as pertaining to his present necessities, but, in its broader sense, as a temptation to the exercise of his power for selfish personal ends, for the promotion of his individual ease and comfort.

It was then that his objective power of reason asserted itself, and he refused to allow his subjective mind to usurp control. He knew that his mission on earth could not be promoted by the employment of his subjective powers for the purpose of ministering to his own selfish wants. Therefore he spurned a temptation which, if yielded to, would weaken the altruistic sentiment which was regnant in him.

His next temptation followed the first in deductive logical sequence. It came in the form of a symbolical vision, in which he saw himself placed upon a pinnacle of the temple, and a voice said: " If thou be the Son of God, cast thyself down : for it is written, He shall give his angels charge concerning thee : and in their hands they shall bear thee up, lest at any time thou dash thy foot against a stone." This suggestion was a sequence to the other, for it was as much as to say : " If you wish to heal the sick, exhibit your power in public, where all men can see and know that you have the power to preserve your own life. Then will you receive the plaudits of the multitude, and their faith in you will be made strong."

His answer to this, " Thou shalt not tempt the Lord thy God," conveys, in one brief sentence, a valuable and important lesson pertaining to the exercise of subjective power, — a lesson the importance of which, in its application to the science of mental therapeutics, cannot be overestimated. In its general sense it means that subjective power should never be exercised for purposes of mere display. The tempter appealed to his love of approbation, his pride of power, his desire for the plaudits of the multitude, tempered by the insidious suggestion that, by the public exhibition of his power, he could all the more readily secure the confidence of the people and promote the object of his mission. He had refused to exercise his power for the purpose of securing his own ease and comfort, for the reason that his mission, in part, was to relieve the sufferings of others ; and now he was tempted to promote that object by a public display in the presence of an admiring multitude. There was nothing morally wrong in either suggestion. It is not wrong, *per se*, to produce bread, or to take measures to secure our own comfort. Nor is it wrong, in itself, to give a public exhibition for a good purpose ; but from the standpoint from which he viewed it, both were wrong in principle and practice. The first would interfere with, and endanger the success of, his mission ; the second would be trifling with the gift of God. It would be a wanton exercise of a power which is given, not for idle display, but for the promotion of the highest good of mankind, when exercised within its legitimate sphere.

But there was another and a more potent reason still for his refusal to exercise his power for purposes of display. It is a reason which the world is just beginning to appreciate. It is a reason which finds its justification in the fundamental principles pertaining to the exercise of psychic power. As in all the words and deeds of Christ, there was a scientific principle underlying the sententious expression employed in his rejection of the second temptation. This principle applies with special force to the employment of psychic power to the healing of the sick.

It has been shown in a former chapter that the normal functions of the subjective entity consist in the performance of those acts which tend to the preservation and perpetuation of the human race. It has also been shown that all exercise of subjective power outside that domain is abnormal, and, consequently, injurious. As this subject has been sufficiently enlarged upon elsewhere, it need only be mentioned here. It was this principle which Christ desired to illustrate and enforce, and he never neglected an opportunity to do so by precept or example. As before remarked, it applies with special force to the exercise of that power for the purpose of healing, and it teaches a most important and salutary lesson both to healer and patient.   It is this : that no one should ever presume to violate the laws of health for the mere purpose of showing to himself or to others that he has the psychic power to heal himself. A necessary or an unavoidable act may be performed which is ordinarily injurious to health, or even dangerous to life, and psychic power may be invoked to avert the natural consequences ; but when one wantonly violates the laws of health for the mere purposes of display, he is apt to find that the power to avert the consequences has deserted him.   He has violated the commandment uttered by the Saviour on that occasion : " Thou shalt not tempt the Lord thy God."   He has violated a law of nature, a law of psycho-therapeutics, which Christ thus sententiously formulated for the guidance of all who should come after him.   Like all the other laws which he revealed to mankind, it applies with equal force now as it did when he first promulgated it nineteen hundred years ago ; and it may safely be said that there is no one act of his life that more clearly discloses his perfect knowledge of the laws which pertain to the normal exercise of subjective power than his rejection of the three temptations.

His next temptation came in the form of a symbolical vision, in which he saw himself, figuratively, upon the top of " an exceeding high mountain," from which he could view " the kingdoms of the world, and the glory of them."

The other temptations attacked his usefulness as a man. The third was directed against his spiritual mission also. It came in a more insidious form than either the first or second, for its promises included both.   It was equivalent to saying : " You see the wide world before you, with all its comforts, its honors and glory, its wealth and splendor and power.   All these can you acquire by the exercise of that potent force with which you have been invested."

" Then saith Jesus unto him, Get thee hence, Satan: for it is written, Thou shalt worship the Lord thy God, and him only shalt thou serve."

Again had reason triumphed over the natural, instinctive suggestions of his human nature. Again had he refused to employ the power with which he had been invested, outside the limits of its legitimate domain. Again had he taught a lesson to humanity by illustrating the normal relations between the objective and subjective faculties, — between reason and instinct. In his rejection of the last temptation he did more, — he exhibited his entire devotion to the objects of his spiritual mission. He had come into the world, taking upon himself the yoke and burden of common humanity. He was circumscribed by the limitations of its laws, municipal, ecclesiastical, and natural. He willingly obeyed them all. His lot was cast among a poor and humble people. He must mingle familiarly with them if he would impress them with the grand and awful simplicity of his philosophy. If he placed himself above the laws of the land, he would be proscribed. If he transcended or violated the laws of nature, his example would be lost to common humanity. If he sought the worldly wealth and secular power which was within his grasp, he would be feared, but not loved, by the people whose destiny it was to be the first recipients of his teachings, the beneficiaries of his power, the witnesses of his example, the recorders of his testament.

This digression from the main point of our present argument seemed necessary in order to show how perfectly the subjective mind of Jesus was under the control of his objective reason. Besides, there is no one act of his life that more clearly discloses his perfect knowledge of the laws which pertain to the normal exercise of subjective power, and his firm determination never to exercise that power outside of its legitimate domain, or for purposes of private advantage or emolument, than his rejection of the three temptations. That these principles actuated him is shown by his every act and word. That he taught them in their purity to his apostles is shown in the indignant reply of Peter to Simon the sorcerer, who offered a money consideration to Peter to purchase the secret of his power. Knowing that Simon was a professional magician, and suspecting that he desired only to add to his *répertoire* of stock exhibitions of occult powers, the apostle rebuked him in these memorable words : —

"Thy money perish with thee, because thou hast thought that the gift of God may be purchased with money. Thou hast neither part nor lot in this matter: for thy heart is not right in the sight of God."[1]

I now recur to the main question under discussion : How did Jesus obtain the scientifically accurate and exclusive knowledge of the laws pertaining to the exercise of subjective power, of which every act and word of his demonstrates his possession?

The ready and easy answer of unreasoning faith is, "Miracle." But is it necessary in this case to invoke the aid of such an explanation? Clearly not. Without entering upon the discussion of the vexed question of the possible existence of the power to work a miracle, it must be held as a self-evident proposition that we should never convert an event into a miracle when there is a satisfactory explanation within the known laws of nature.

In this case the necessity does not exist to presuppose a miraculous intervention of Divine power, since God has given to every human soul the inherent power, under certain conditions, to *perceive* and comprehend the fixed laws of nature. What those conditions are, we may never know. That they exist, the events within common knowledge amply demonstrate. That they are exceptional, goes without saying. No one man has ever been able to perceive all the laws during his objective existence. One perceives the law of numbers, another that of the harmony of sounds, another that of the harmony of colors, and so on.

Jesus Christ perceived spiritual law.

That his intuitions were scientifically exact, so far as they pertained to the subject of his physical manifestations in healing the sick, is amply demonstrated by comparison of what he did and said with the discoveries of modern science within this, the last quarter of the nineteenth century.

[1] **Acts viii. 20, 21.**

I have purposely refrained from commenting on the accounts of his physical manifestations other than those of healing the sick, for the reason that science in the Western world as yet furnishes little or no data for comparison. I cannot refrain, however, from calling the attention of the reader to the fact that a few years ago sceptics were just as incredulous regarding the biblical accounts of Christ's healing the sick as they still are regarding his feeding of the multitude on the five loaves and the two fishes. It must be remembered that experimental knowledge of the occult sciences is still in its infancy in the Western world, and that what is regarded as a miracle to-day may be known to be a scientific fact to-morrow. In the mean time enough is known to the scientific world to-day to demonstrate the essential truth of the physical history of Jesus of Nazareth. It remains to show what light the scientific discoveries of the nineteenth century shed upon his spiritual philosophy.

CHAPTER XXV.

THE SPIRITUAL PHILOSOPHY OF CHRIST.

Even now, after eighteen centuries of Christianity, we may be involved in some enormous error, of which the Christianity of the future will make us ashamed. — VINET.

The Necessity of Signs and Wonders. — Christ's Work was for all Time. — His Consummate Wisdom. — Signs and Wonders as Evidence. — His Perception of Spiritual Laws. — The Perceptive Powers of the Soul. — Propositions. — Presumptive Evidence of his Knowledge of Spiritual Laws. — Condition precedent to Immortality. — Faith the Essential Condition. — The Declarations of Christ. — He meant just what He said. — The Doctrines of the Church. — Literal Extinction of the Soul through Unbelief — Belief essential to Salvation. — Belief will not avert the Consequences of Sin. — Inherent Probabilities. — The Conscious Existence of the Soul. — The Law of Suggestion applied. — Scepticism constitutes a Fatal Suggestion. — Phenomena of Hypnotism illustrative. — Souls of Animals have no Conscious Existence ; hence not Immortal. — Christ as a Saviour of Souls. — His Doctrine new to the World, but scientifically correct.

WHEN Jesus said to the nobleman of Capernaum, "Except ye see signs and wonders, ye will not believe," he not only correctly summarized the then existing attitude of the public mind in reference to the doctrines which he proclaimed, but he declared with prophetic exactitude that which is as true to-day as it was when he uttered it in Galilee. He said it, not reproachfully, but as a statement of a condition inevitable from the nature of things, which must be recognized and dealt with in a practical manner. The wisdom shown in yielding to the demand for "signs and wonders" in that day is obvious. Without it the people could not believe ; with it they could not doubt. To them it was the power of God, working through miracle. It was to them a sign and symbol of puissance and authority. To doubt the word of one who was able to work such wonders was to doubt the evidence of their senses. Without that evidence the spiritual doctrines of Jesus would have been to them without sanction of authority. Logic and reason would have been wasted on the people of that age. Their belief that the signs and wonders were wrought in defiance of natural law was the only circumstance that could command their respect. Their idea was that the only way in which God could manifest his power was by some signal violation of his own laws. To attempt to show them that Christ healed the sick by a strict observance of natural law would have been as futile as to attempt to teach a new-born babe the principles of the differential calculus. To convince them of the fact would be to destroy their faith in the power of God. Jesus taught them all that they could understand, — all that it would benefit the world to know in that era of civilization. He was working, not only for the people of his own time, but for all future generations. He laid his foundations broad and deep, and with the most consummate wisdom. He not only conferred the benefits of his power upon the people of his own race and country, but he left indubitable evidences of the truth of his history and of his doctrines for all future generations.

Conceding, for the sake of the argument, that Jesus possessed the power to work a miracle, — that is, to work outside of the domain of natural law and in defiance of it, — his consummate wisdom in refraining from the exercise of that power is now manifest. If he had wrought his wonders by miracle, only the eye-witnesses of his works would have been benefited; for there would have been no means provided by which future generations could verify his history. But if he performed his works by and through the operations of natural law, it only remains for science to rediscover that law, in order to demonstrate the truth of his history. His consummate wisdom is, therefore, manifest in that he did leave a record, told with such accuracy of detail, that the science of this generation can verify its truth.

The immediate necessity for showing signs and wonders to his people was what he declared it to be, — namely, "that they might believe" in him; that they might be convinced of his power, and have faith in his declaration.

But he had a grander and a nobler object still than the conversion of the few people of his own race and country. He foresaw the time when mankind would not be content to rest its faith upon the dictum of a history written by obscure and unknown men; when the world would refuse to believe in the possibility of miracles, and demand a reason for faith in him, in his works, and in his spiritual doctrines. We have already seen how amply the truth of the history of his physical manifestations has been vindicated by the discoveries of modern science.

But he had a more far-reaching wisdom still. It would avail the world little, simply to know the truth of his physical history, if by that means he could not demonstrate the truth of his spiritual doctrines and philosophy. And it is just here that his utterance to the nobleman of Capernaum applies with equal force to the people of the present day, "Except ye see signs and wonders, ye will not believe." It is now apparent that those signs and wonders were as necessary for the confirmation of the faith of the scientific investigator of to-day as they were to convince the people of his day that he was invested with power and authority. Without them there would have been no means by which we could prove even his probable existence. With them we are put into possession of data which, by comparison with the known facts of contemporary science, enable us to predicate with moral certainty his existence and the essential truth of his history.

They do more. They enable us to know with scientific certainty that he was in possession of an accurate knowledge of the laws which pertain to his physical manifestations; and they logically justify us in the conclusion that by the same means he obtained possession of a knowledge of the laws which pertain to the conditions of immortal life. The subject-matter is the same. His physical manifestations were exhibitions of the powers of the soul. The philosophy of his psychic power is the philosophy of the soul in its relations to the physical man. The philosophy of immortality is the philosophy of the soul in its relations to God. A change in its environment does not change the nature or attributes of the soul; and hence we may infer with irresistible logic that Jesus was as correct in his inferences or knowledge concerning the life beyond as he was scientifically accurate in his knowledge of the laws of the soul in its relation to its physical environment.

In discussing the above proposition, the question as to how it was possible for Jesus to obtain a knowledge of the condition of the soul after the death of the body will first be considered. It has already been shown that under certain conditions the soul perceives with absolute accuracy the fixed laws of nature. It has also been shown that the soul does not possess during its sojourn in the flesh the power of inductive reasoning, but that its powers of reasoning deductively from any suggested premise are marvellous. I have ventured to use the expression in that connection, that "the subjective mind reasons deductively with extraordinary acumen." I have not ventured the assertion that its deductions are infallible, though there is good reason to believe that under certain conditions the assertion would be substantially correct. The instances cited of mathematical prodigies would seem to bear out that assertion. The power of perception in them must be perfect, or there would be nothing to distinguish them from other mathematicians. Their answers to mathematical problems, to be remarkable, must be correct. That they are correct would seem to give us warrant for the inference that under favorable conditions the powers of the soul for correct deductive reasoning, or perception of fixed laws, are perfect. If it is true in mathematics, it must be true in all other matters governed by fixed laws, especially since all the forces of nature are correlated, and all are governed by mathematical laws.

It has also been shown that the deductions of the subjective mind are always logically accurate, even though the premises may be false. Any one who has had experience in dealing with persons in a hypnotic trance will bear me out in that statement.

The question now arises, What are the conditions necessary to give us assurance of infallible deductions from given premises? Before proceeding to discuss that matter, it is proper to premise that it is difficult, in dealing with the subtle forces of the subjective mind, to draw a distinct line between its powers of perception of fixed laws and its powers of deduction from given premises. Its perceptions seem to be instantaneous, and to preclude the idea of the employment of any such processes of reasoning as are known to the logic of objective education.

The distinction seems to be this: If the premises are given from an extraneous source, in the form of a suggestion, the processes of deductive reasoning are employed. If the premises are the result of intuitive perception, the conclusion is also perceived simultaneously. In such a case the whole law pertaining to the subject-matter is perceived at once; and it is inconceivable to the finite mind how any processes of reasoning have been employed. Thus, in the case of Zerah Colburn, his answers to mathematical problems of the most intricate character were given instantaneously, and he was never conscious of employing any process of calculation whatever. Moreover, his answers were always correct.

Now, whether the processes of deductive reasoning employed by the subjective mind lead to infallible results, it is not my purpose to discuss. It is certain that they are marvellously accurate, whether the premises are true or false; but whether they may be relied upon as always correct when the premises are true, I am not prepared to say from the data before me; nor is it important, for my present purpose, to know.

It is certain, however, that where the powers of perception are employed, under proper conditions, the conclusions are infallible.

We have now a starting-point from which we may form a correct estimate of the scientific accuracy of the spiritual philosophy of Jesus.

If we are to concede that his doctrines are true, it is obvious that we must demonstrate the correctness of the following propositions : —

1. That Jesus was endowed with the power to obtain a perfect knowledge of spiritual law by perception or intuition.

2. To demonstrate this we must show, (*a*) that his knowledge of spiritual law was scientifically accurate ; and (*b*) that it could not have been obtained by the ordinary processes of objective education.

3. To show that his knowledge was accurate, it must be demonstrated that the conclusions arrived at by the inductive processes of modern science are identical with the doctrines that he proclaimed.

It has already been shown that, as far as his physical manifestations are concerned, each of the statements embraced in the foregoing propositions is true. It has been shown that he must have had an intuitive perception of the law of healing by subjective power, for the reasons, first, that in the state of occult knowledge existing in his day, it was impossible that he could have obtained his knowledge by means of objective education ; and, secondly, that his knowledge of the law of healing was scientifically accurate, as shown by the fact (*a*) that he proclaimed and constantly reiterated the essential condition of the exercise of the power of healing precisely as it is known at the present day ; (*b*) that he constantly practised by the methods known at the present day to be the best ; (*c*) that he surrounded himself and his patients with the best attainable aids to the exercise of his powers, — precisely such aids, the utility of which has been demonstrated by modern practice ; and (*d*) that he constantly sought to secure the mental environment which is now known to be of the first importance, if not absolutely essential, to successful mental healing. In short, it has been shown that he must have understood every principle and every law of mental therapeutics, the rediscovery of which has distinguished the present century.

Reasoning, therefore, from the premises which have thus been established, we have the logical right to infer that he understood all the laws which pertain to the soul. If he understood the laws which govern it in its relations to its physical environment, it is fair to presume that he knew the laws which pertain to its continued existence after it is freed from the trammels of the flesh. Without any further proofs, therefore, we have the logical right to consider the one as presumptive evidence of the other.

If I stopped right here, I might reasonably claim to have established the fact that the religion of Christ is founded upon a purely scientific basis. But I do not intend to rest content with mere presumptive evidence. I propose to show that his knowledge of the law of immortality did not rest upon inferential deductions from the facts known by him regarding the relations of the soul to its physical environment. I propose to show that the world is now in possession of facts from which we can reason inductively up to the same conclusions which he proclaimed, *ex cathedra*, as the law of immortality.

Before proceeding to do so, we must first inquire just what he taught. In doing so I intend to confine myself to the one essential proposition which he made regarding the condition essential to the soul's salvation; for I do not propose to be led into a discussion of the great fabric of doctrinal religion which has been built up since he ascended to the Father. I leave that to the theologian. What I intend to show is, that, viewed from a purely scientific standpoint, the declaration which he made regarding the condition precedent to the salvation of the soul is necessarily true.

The first question, therefore, is, What did Jesus declare to be the one essential condition necessary to the attainment of immortal life? When I say, "necessary to the *attainment* of immortal life," I mean literally what I say; for I hold that

if there is one principle laid down by the Master that is
more clearly defined than any other, it is contained in his
declaration, so often repeated, that faith — *belief* — is the
one essential condition precedent to the continued life of
the soul after the death of the body ; and that, in the absence of belief in immortality, the soul itself will necessarily
perish. That this was his doctrine, literally interpreted, no
one will deny. That he meant exactly what he said, I shall
attempt to show. That his declarations to that effect were
statements of a scientific truth, I shall attempt to demonstrate by the process of inductive reasoning from facts
known to modern science.

Before proceeding with the main argument, I hasten to
say that the doctrine of future rewards and punishments
will be left untouched. That question will stand just where
it has always stood, — for each one to decide for himself
according to his own interpretation of the Scriptures on
that point, or his own sense of Divine Justice. I shall not
even attempt to destroy the comfort and consolation which
many good persons seem to derive from their belief in eternal fire. My only object is to show, from a purely scientific
standpoint, that the history and essential doctrines of Jesus
are confirmed by the facts and necessary inductions of
modern science, and, incidentally, to harmonize certain
passages of the New Testament which, through misinter-
pretation, have seemed to be at variance.

According to the Gospel of Saint John, the first declaration by Jesus of his doctrine of immortality was made to
Nicodemus in the following words : —

"And as Moses lifted up the serpent in the wilderness, even
so must the Son of Man be lifted up :

" That whosoever believeth in him should not perish, but
have eternal life.

" For God so loved the world, that he gave his only begotten
Son, that whosoever believeth in him should not perish, but
have everlasting life." [1]

[1] John iii. 14–16.

Again, in John vi. 40, 47, he makes the same declaration in the following clear-cut sentences : —

" And this is the will of him that sent me, that every one which seeth the Son, and believeth on him, may have everlasting life. . . .

" Verily, verily, I say unto you, He that believeth on me hath everlasting life."

Again : —

" Verily, verily, I say unto you, He that heareth my word, and believeth on him that sent me, hath everlasting life, and shall not come into condemnation, but is passed from death unto life." [1]

" I am the resurrection, and the life : he that believeth in me, though he were dead, yet shall he live :

" And whosoever liveth and believeth in me shall never die." [2]

Other passages might be quoted to the same effect, but these must suffice.

The question now is, Did Jesus mean just what he said ; or were these idle words, having no significance taken in their literal sense? Jesus was not in the habit of uttering idle words, or of making statements that did not contain the elements of eternal truth. If these are exceptions, they are the only ones recorded in his history. I hold that they are not exceptions, but that they are authoritative statements of a literal scientific truth.

I have already shown that in formulating the doctrine of faith as the essential condition prerequisite to successful healing, he gave utterance to a scientific principle which it has taken nineteen hundred years for the world to understand and appreciate. It is equally true that, in formulating the proposition that *belief* is the essential prerequisite to the attainment of immortality, he gave words to a scientific principle of far greater importance than the other.

I am aware that one portion of the Christian Church believes that by the words " eternal life " Jesus meant that reward in heaven which is promised to the just, and that by

---

[1] John v. 24.   [2] John xi. 25, 26.

" eternal death " he simply meant the punishment which the wicked must undergo for their sins. On the other hand, there are those of the Church who hold that the literal death of the soul is the punishment meted out to all who die in their sins, while " eternal life " is the reward promised to all who are good. Neither of these sects has, however, satisfactorily explained to unbelievers why it is that belief or unbelief enters as a factor in the case, since man is not supposed to be able to command his belief.

It is to the reconciliation of these conflicting theories that I shall now address myself.

The first proposition of my theory is that the death, or practical extinction, of the soul as a conscious entity is the necessary result of unbelief in immortality.

The second proposition is that the soul, having attained immortality through belief, is then subject to the law of rewards and punishments " according to the deeds done in the body."

The same propositions are more sententiously expressed in Romans ii. 12 : " For as many as have sinned without law shall also perish without law : and as many as have sinned in the law shall be judged by the law."

In other words, the condition precedent to the attainment of immortality, or salvation, — that is, the saving of the soul from death, — is *belief.* The condition precedent to the attainment of eternal bliss and the avoidance of the punishments incident to sin, is righteousness.

It will thus be seen that if it can be shown that these two propositions are necessarily true, we shall avoid, on the one hand, the incongruous idea that *belief* will atone for all sin ; and, on the other, the equally incongruous idea that the extinction of the soul is the necessary consequence of all sin.

In discussing the first proposition we shall first inquire what are the inherent probabilities regarding the meaning which Christ attached to the words which are quoted above. Is it probable, or even possible, that he could have taught that *belief* alone was a sufficient atonement for the sins of the wicked? Knowing, as all must know who have followed his career and noted his sayings, his utter abhorrence of all wickedness; reading, as all may read, his sublime code of ethics and morals, together with the awful maledictions pronounced upon all violations of that code, and the punishments which he held before the world as a consequence of sin,— it is simply impossible rationally to conceive the idea that he taught that all consequences of a life of sin could be avoided by *belief*. It is a self-evident proposition that a man may believe in Christ, may believe in immortality, and at the same time be steeped in all manner of wickedness and crime. No more devout believers can be found in all Christendom than those of an unfortunate race in America who are proverbial alike for their devoted piety and for their propensity to steal on their way home from prayer-meeting; unless we except the bandits of Italy, who are as noted for their strict observance of the forms of the Church as they are for the fact that they live by the perpetration of murder and robbery. Unfortunately, our illustrations cannot be drawn exclusively from any one race or nation. In every Christian society there are all too many devout believers who live in constant violation of every law, human and Divine. It is an insult to the intelligence of Christ and of humanity to hold the monstrous doctrine that the belief of these men can shield them from the punishment due to infamy, or that they can be adequately punished, "according to their deeds," by annihilation.

On the other hand, it is impossible to believe that Christ summarized all the virtues, human and Divine, in the one word *belief*, or that by the employment of that word he simply meant that all who live pure and virtuous lives before God and man will be entitled to the rewards of heaven. If this was all that he meant, he taught nothing new, either to the Jewish nation or to any other civilized nation then in existence; for the Hebrews had been taught the doctrine of future rewards and punishments, of heaven and of hell, long before the appearance of the Messiah. It is true that Moses did not teach the Israelites any doctrine of the future world, and very vague mention is made of it in the later books of the Old Testament. It is a historical fact, nevertheless, that before the advent of Jesus the Jews had become imbued with the Greek doctrine of Hades, which was an intermediate waiting station between this life and the judgment. In this were situated both Paradise and Gehenna, the one on the right and the other on the left, and into these two compartments the spirits of the dead were separated, according to their deserts. Jesus found this doctrine already in existence, and in enforcing his moral precepts and in his parables he employed the symbols which the people understood, neither denying nor affirming their literal verity. I remark, therefore, that in simply teaching the doctrine of future rewards and punishments he taught nothing new ; and, in that sense, he is no more entitled to be considered the Saviour of mankind than would be any other successful teacher of the same doctrine.

We are, therefore, forced back to a literal interpretation of the statements under consideration. In this sense they can have but one meaning, and that is, that *in the absence of belief in immortality, the soul cannot have a conscious existence.* Reasoning from known facts, there is no other rational conclusion. In explanation of the meaning of " conscious existence " in the sense in which I have employed that phrase, it is only necessary to direct the attention of the intelligent reader to the accepted definition and doctrine of consciousness. " In taking a comprehensive survey of the mental phenomena," says Sir William Hamilton, " these all seem to comprise one essential element, or to be possible only under one necessary condition. This element or condition is consciousness, or the knowledge that I — that the ego exists, in some determinate state." [1] Again, he compares consciousness to " an internal light, by means of which, and which alone, what passes in the mind is rendered visible." [2]

The existence of a man without the knowledge of sensations or of mental operations would be one without con-

[1] **Metaphysics, p. 126.**   [2] **Ibid.**

sciousness, and would constitute a purely vegetative existence as long as it continued. One can readily understand this condition in the objective mind from the observation of physical phenomena. It is equally comprehensible how the subjective mind, or soul, may be deprived of a conscious existence when we remember the fundamental law of its being, the law of suggestion. We have already seen how the law of suggestion operates upon the soul in cases of cataleptic trance, where the suggestion is made that the patient is dead. In that case the suggestion was believed implicitly, and the preparations for the funeral did not disturb the equanimity of the patient in the least. Nor did the incongruity of the situation suggest itself to the patient; namely, the idea of being dead and of thinking of being dead at the same time.

The suggestion to the patient's subjective mind that he was dead, rendered that mind unconscious of its own mental operations, and he was, to all intents and purposes, dead.

This is, obviously, but a feeble illustration of the principle involved. It is, however, sufficient to show how the soul may be deprived of a conscious existence. A life-long scepticism regarding the existence of the soul, and a consequent disbelief in immortality, constitute a suggestion that must operate to deprive the soul of a conscious existence, if the law of suggestion is universal in its operations.

The phenomena of experimental hypnotism also demonstrate the truth of the proposition. Every hypnotist knows that a suggestion to a deeply hypnotized subject that he is dead will produce a condition of such profound lethargy or catalepsy as closely to simulate death, and were the impression not removed, it would doubtless end in death. When the subject remembers what has passed, he testifies that he believed himself dead, and saw no incongruity in the situation. A settled belief that the death of the body ends all, and the absence of any belief or knowledge of the subject, must each operate to the same end.

It is this principle which constitutes the difference between men and animals, and which gives the one the power

and potency of immortality, and leaves the other to perish.
Animals, in common with men, are possessed of a duality
of mind ; the subjective in the former being proportionately
stronger than in the latter, as is shown in their stronger instincts. Objective reason being weak, and the power of
speech being absent, there is no possibility of the idea or
suggestion of immortality being imparted to the animal.
Hence its soul can have no conscious existence after the
death of the body. It has the instinct of self-preservation
in common with man, but it is the preservation of the life
of the body. If the animal has any definite idea regarding life and death, it all pertains to the body. An animal
certainly can have no idea of the possession of a soul,
much less of its immortality.

When, therefore, Jesus proclaimed the law that belief was
a condition precedent to immortal life, he formulated a
scientific proposition then new to the world, and at the
same time proclaimed himself master of the science of the
soul. He had declared the law of faith as it applied to
the power of the soul to heal the sick, and he knew that
the same law governed the soul in its relations to eternal
life. He did not formulate his propositions in the terms
demanded by the science of the nineteenth century, nor
did he give such reasons for his conclusions as inductive
processes require. The time for that had not yet come.
Reasons would not have been appreciated in his day and
generation. Nor was it necessary for the accomplishment
of his mission — which was to proclaim the law of immortality — to show that the man whose soul has not been
aroused to consciousness dies as the brute dieth. This
was his mission ; and in so far as he has accomplished that
mission is he entitled to be called the Saviour of the souls
of mankind. He preached no new doctrine other than this.
His code of ethics was sublime and godlike in its purity and
simplicity, but it was not new. He taught the doctrine of
future rewards and punishments ; but the symbols which he
employed to describe the condition of the soul after death —
the rewards bestowed and the punishments inflicted — were

those which were current among the people with whom his earthly lot was cast; nor does this fact argue for or against his omniscience. It would, obviously, have been impossible for him to convey to the world any adequate idea of the modes of spiritual existence in terms which could be understood. He used the current coin of expression to convey to mankind the broad idea that the soul that is "saved" to immortal life through "belief" will then be punished or rewarded according to the deeds done in the body. It would, obviously, have been useless and confusing to his hearers had he attempted to employ any new symbols, or any language to which they were not accustomed, to convey that idea.

His mission, therefore, as the Saviour of the souls of men was accomplished when he revealed to the world the essential condition of immortal life. His mission as a moral teacher was secondary in importance. The one doctrine was new, the other old. The one was a scientific fact, the other a code of ethics. The one was essential to the attainment of man's ultimate destiny as an immortal entity, the other a standard of right and justice in this world, and a condition of felicity in the world to come.

It is said that when Hillel, who flourished in the century preceding Christ, was asked whether he could give the whole Jewish law in one sentence, he answered: "Yes, perfectly well. What you do not want anybody to do to you, do not you to them. That is the whole law; everything else is only commentary."

The same may be truly said of the New Testament doctrines and the law of faith. The only thing wholly new was the doctrine of faith. That is the whole law; everything else is commentary.

CHAPTER XXVI.

THE MISSION OF CHRIST; FUTURE REWARDS AND PUNISHMENTS.

The Success of Christ's Mission. — Chaotic State of Spiritual Philosophy in His Time. — The Various Doctrines in Vogue. — Jesus the first to simplify the Doctrine of Immortality. — He gave it a Definite Status in Philosophy. — The Doctrine of Future Rewards and Punishments. — God will "render to every Man according to His Deeds." — Spiritual Penalties for Violations of Spiritual Law. — The Sin against the Holy Ghost. — The Sin of Unbelief. — The Status of a Lost Soul. — Possible Reincarnation. — The Means of Punishment for Sin. — Affections. — Conscience. — Memory. — General Conclusions. — Scientific Basis of Christianity.

IT is often charged by the sceptical world that the mission of Jesus has thus far proved a failure, for that only about one third of the inhabitants of the earth have ever heard the name of Christ; that of Christian nations but a limited proportion of the inhabitants belong to the Christian Church; and that of the church membership there is but a limited number who so live as to entitle them to the rewards of heaven. Measured by the common idea of what constitutes salvation, there may be good ground for that criticism. But measured by the number of those who believe in the immortality of the soul; by the number who have a hope of a life beyond the grave; by the number who have a consciousness of the existence within them of the transcendental ego; or by the number of those who have risen, directly or indirectly, through the teachings of Christ so far above the level of the brute creation as to have a consciousness of the possibility of immortal life, and a consequent hope and subjective belief in immortality, — his mission has proved the grandest success recorded in the history of missionary effort.

It must be remembered that when he came into the world the doctrine of immortal life held a very vague and uncertain place in the philosophy of civilized mankind. I do not say that the doctrine of immortal life was unknown, but it was undefined, and so tinctured with finite conceptions, and limited by the uncertain boundaries of a hundred different systems of fantastic philosophy, that it did not, and could not, form a basis of rational hope or intelligent promise.

Thus, among the Chinese of that day (1), the doctrines of Confucius held the most prominent place. His was a system which might be called a parent-worship, in which virtue was rewarded and vice punished in the individuals, or in their posterity, on earth, no promise of immortality being held out. (2) The sect of Rationalists, founded by Lautsz in the sixth century before Christ, taught the emanation of all good beings from the Bosom of Reason, and their absorption thither for an eternal existence, while the bad were doomed to successive births and many sorrows. (3) Another sect held that the principle of all things is but a vacuum, — nothing, — from which all things have sprung, and to which all must return.

The Hindoo doctrine was substantially the same as it is now; and it is so well known as not to require a particular statement, further than to say that its disciples believe in successive incarnations of the soul, and its final absorption into the incorporeal nature of Brahm.

The Persians believed in the doctrine of hell for the wicked, and of paradise for the good; but held that all the wicked would eventually be purified by fire. It was thought that the fires were hot enough to purify the most abominable soul in about three days.

Herodotus tells us that the Egyptians were the first to defend the doctrine of the immortality of the soul, and he says that they believed in its transmigration through various animal bodies for a period of three thousand years before its return to a human body

Of the Grecian schools, the Pythagoreans held that the soul is eternal, — that is, uncreated and indestructible; that no real entity is either made or destroyed. The Eleatics held practically the same doctrine. The Ionics taught that the soul was reabsorbed into the Divine reason. The Stoics believed in the periodical destruction of all things by fire, when the good will be absorbed and the wicked perish. The Epicurean faith was well described by Paul in the phrase, "Let us eat and drink, for tomorrow we die." The Pyrrhonists were the sceptics of the age, and doubted everything. Socrates taught the doctrine of immortality for the good, the virtuous, and the wise. The incurably bad are "hurled into Tartarus, whence they never come forth;" whilst those who can be cured are subjected to needful punishments before being admitted into the mansions of the blest. Plato was a Pythagorean, with certain bizarre notions of his own, such as the migration of souls through various brute and human forms; and he believed that even the duration of divine work is limited.

It will thus be seen that when Jesus appeared on earth he found the philosophy of the soul in a very chaotic state. It was his mission to bring order out of chaos, and to proclaim the true philosophy; to declare the conditions of immortality, and point the way to eternal happiness. That he simplified the doctrine of immortality into a system so plain that "the wayfaring man, though a fool, need not err therein," no one will deny. Its grand simplicity, when placed in contrast with the complicated doctrines of all other systems of religious philosophy, ancient or modern, places upon it the stamp of inherent probability; for scientific truth is always simple and free from complication. It was Jesus who gave the doctrine of immortality a distinct and definite form and a permanent place in the philosophy of the civilized world. It was he who first proclaimed the fundamental law underlying the science of the soul. It was from his words, spoken to a few humble followers in an obscure corner of the earth, that the doctrine has spread throughout all the civilized world. From the centres of civilization the Church has sent its missionaries, its representatives of the Master, among all peoples, civilized and savage, preaching the gospel of immortality to all mankind. Its influence is not confined to those who believe in the tenets of the Christian Church, nor even to those who have heard the name of Christ. It has spread, through some subtle, unseen power and potency, until it permeates every fibre of human society, and constitutes the promise of every religion, the hope of all humanity.

I have, in other chapters, pointed out some of the proofs which science affords of the doctrine of immortality, and of the verity of the history of Jesus of Nazareth. I have shown that every known fact which bears upon the subject points to the continued life of the soul after the death of the body. I have shown that the discoveries of modern science demonstrate the fact that Jesus was in possession of a complete knowledge of the science of the soul in its relations to its physical environment. I have shown that all known facts bearing upon the subject go to prove that he also had a knowledge of its laws in its relations to a purely spiritual existence.

We have then, *first*, an array of demonstrable facts which irresistibly lead to the conclusion that the soul survives the body; *secondly*, another array of facts which prove that it was possible for an exceptionally endowed person to perceive the laws of the soul; *thirdly*, an array of facts which demonstrate that Jesus did understand those laws as far as they pertain to the soul's relations to the physical man; *fourthly*, we have facts which show that he understood the laws of the soul in its relations to the spiritual world, and the essential conditions of its conscious existence after the death of the body; and *fifthly*, we have in the New Testament a record of the acts which demonstrated his knowledge of the subject, as well as of his solemn and repeated declarations of the laws which pertain to that subject.

When we consider together all these cumulative proofs, it may safely be said that there are few principles of nature that are more clearly established by inductive processes of reasoning than is the principle of immortality.

Having established this proposition, it remains only to consider Christ's doctrine of future rewards and punishments. Obviously, this is a more difficult question to handle, for the reason that there are necessarily few facts known to mankind which can be considered scientifically demonstrative of any proposition which has been made by any one on that subject. Nevertheless, if there is one known fact which confirms his declarations on that question, and at the same time satisfies the demands of human reason and the common sense of Divine Justice, we may safely conclude that the Christian religion rests upon a purely scientific basis.

The first important fact which confronts us in considering this branch of the subject is, that Jesus said very little on the subject. It was obviously impossible for him to convey to the human mind any adequate knowledge or idea of the actual conditions of a spiritual existence. He was hedged about by the limitations of human speech and the finite understanding of his followers. His descriptions, therefore, of the places of future rewards and punishments were necessarily limited to material conceptions. He could effectively employ no other symbolism than that with which his hearers were familiar and which they could appreciate. He had taught them in plain and unmistakable terms the conditions upon which the soul could attain a conscious existence ; and having done that, his mission was thenceforth a moral one. Having taught them how to attain eternal life, he taught them so to conduct their lives in this world as to entitle them to the joys of that life. It was no part of his mission to reconstruct the accepted geography of the world of spirits, for it could only add confusion to their crude conceptions. His parables were drawn from the objects and incidents of their every-day life, and were necessarily limited in their application to a spiritual existence. His only object was to enforce a code of morals founded upon the eternal principles of right and justice, simple in terms, and adapted to their comprehension, but

grand in its simplicity, and adapted to the varying conditions of human society for all time.

The question now is, What is to be considered the doctrine of future rewards and punishments to be gathered
from the New Testament? It is clear that we must reject
all material conceptions of both heaven and hell. It follows that the punishment must be a moral one, since there
is no material entity to be dealt with. The sense of justice
inherent in all mankind would seem to indicate that the
punishment shall be commensurate with the offence. It
must be assumed, therefore, that the true doctrine is expressed in Romans ii. 6, where it is said that God will
" render to every man according to his deeds."

This satisfies the finite sense of justice, and perfectly accords with the highest human conceptions of the character
of a God of love, mercy, and justice. The good man would
ask nothing more, the bad could expect nothing less. Reasoning from analogy would lead to the same conclusion. We
know from daily experience that every violation of the laws
of our physical nature is followed inevitably by its adequate
punishment. We have a right to suppose, therefore, that
every violation of moral and spiritual law will be followed
by its appropriate penalty. We know, indeed, from what
we have seen of the teachings of Christ, that spiritual
penalties follow a violation of spiritual law. In other
words, the law of suggestion follows the soul across the
boundaries of eternity. Spiritual death is the inevitable
result of spiritual unbelief. It is not a vindictive punishment, it is the fundamental law of spiritual life. Just as
the spirit quickens the flesh, so does faith quicken the
spirit.

Again, we find a spiritual penalty following a violation of
spiritual law in what Christ taught regarding the sin against
the Holy Ghost. Just what that sin consists of, never has
been satisfactorily defined. We are told that it is a sin which
cannot be forgiven. It must, therefore, consist of a violation of some fundamental law of the soul's existence, the
penalty for which is inevitable according to the fixed laws

of God. It cannot be a moral offence, consisting simply in wrong-doing, for such sins can be atoned for. A moral offence so gross that a God of infinite mercy and love cannot forgive it, and, if the Scriptures are to be believed, does not stand ready to forgive it when proper atonement is made, cannot be conceived. Nor has it been mentioned in Holy Writ. We are therefore forced to the conclusion that, as before remarked, the sin against the Holy Ghost must consist of a violation of the fundamental law of the soul's existence. It must, therefore, be the sin of unbelief, and consist of a blasphemous denial of the existence of the soul and its Father, God. This would be in strict accordance with the fundamental law of suggestion, as it has been scientifically demonstrated to exist. The emphatic and persistent denial of the soul's existence must eventually prove to be a suggestion so strong as to overcome its instinctive belief in its own existence, and thus neutralize its instinctive desire for immortal life. It would, therefore, have the same effect as unbelief arising from a want of knowledge, or a lack of the intellectual power to conceive the idea of immortality. The soul, in either case, could not have a consciousness of its own existence or individuality.

It may be asked, What becomes of the soul when deprived of a conscious existence? Does it actually die, disintegrate, and return to its original elements? Is it possible that a human soul, created by God and endowed with the power and potency of immortal life, can fail of accomplishing its mission, and become extinct? Can a segregated portion of the Divine essence, once individualized, ever perish or lose its identity? All these questions, and more, will be asked. I do not know. Perhaps it is reincarnated. I do not know anything about reincarnation. I know as much about it, however, as any one else knows. I mean by this that no one can be said to know anything about the truth of any proposition that has not underlying it a substratum of demonstrable fact. The theory of reincarnation has no such basis; and I shall not, therefore, indulge in speculation on the subject further than to say that it is possibly true that reincarnation is the process of the soul's evolution. If so, reasoning from analogy, I should say that the process ceases when the soul reaches the status of a conscious existence. In the physical world we see that the process of evolution has gone forward progressively from the lowest form of animal life up to man. There the process ceases. All further progress is in the line of improvement in the human race. No higher type of animal life is developed, and in our pride of manhood we believe that there never can be any higher animal existence. It may, therefore, be true that the progress of a soul is through reincarnation from the lower animal life to the higher, until it reaches the human; and that it may still go on in the lower grades of human organisms until it reaches the dignity of a conscious human soul. Having reached that point, the law of progress will expend its force in carrying it forward to its ultimate destiny. Considered as the process of the soul's evolution, the necessity for further reincarnation apparently no longer exists after the soul has attained the power and potency of a conscious, self-existent entity.

I throw out this suggestion for the benefit of those spiritistic mediums and other trance-seers who have found out so much more than Jesus knew about the internal economy of the spiritual world and the laws which pertain to spiritual existence. But this is a digression into the forbidden field of speculation without facts.

The common experience of mankind demonstrates the proposition that appropriate physical penalties are the necessary result of a violation of physical laws; and it has been shown from the teachings of Jesus, confirmed by the inductions of science, that the violation of the laws of spiritual existence is followed by inevitable spiritual penalties. It now remains to be considered what facts are known to science which will confirm the doctrine that moral punishment will follow the infraction of moral laws, in exact accordance "with the deeds done in the body." In order to do so intelligently, we must first briefly consider the question

as to what the nature of the punishments and rewards must
be. It being manifestly impossible for us to know, affir-
matively, the particular modes of spiritual existence, we
can arrive at a conclusion only by the method of exclusion.
We must, therefore, begin by excluding all idea of material
penalties or rewards. All such conceptions of spiritual life
must be relegated to the dark ages of human intelligence,
when man was able to conceive of no joy apart from physical pleasure, and no punishment other than physical suffering. Our conceptions must, therefore, be limited by what
we know of the nature and attributes of the soul, as exhibited through phenomena. The first question, then, is,
What do we know of the attributes of the soul?

We know, first, that it is the seat of the emotions. It is
therefore capable of being rewarded or punished through
the natural affections.

Secondly, we know that it possesses the inherent power
of perception of the laws of nature and of God, including
the eternal, God-ordained principles of right and wrong.
It will, therefore, after its release from the body, be able to
estimate the value of every good deed, and realize the inherent infamy of every wrong one, as weighed in the scales
of Eternal Justice.

Thirdly and lastly, we know of one attribute and power
of the human soul more pregnant with weal or woe, with
joy or sorrow, than all the others combined; and that is its
perfect memory.

These are the essential things that we know of the soul
from the observation of phenomena. Our conceptions
of it, therefore, are limited to its intellectual, moral, and
emotional attributes. We know it only as an intellectual
entity, and our conceptions of the rewards and punishments adequate to the ends of Divine Justice must be
limited accordingly.

Little need be said in explanation of the trend of this
brief summary. The conclusions are obvious. We have
before us an intellectual entity capable of experiencing all
the natural emotions of humanity, of joy and sorrow, of

love and friendship; endowed with a perfect perception
of the principles of right and wrong, and consequently in
possession of an awakened conscience more keenly alive
and active than the objective mind can conceive, and possessing a memory so perfect that every good and every bad
deed of its whole earthly existence is constantly before it
like a vast panorama. What greater reward could such a
being ask or experience than would be found in the contemplation of a well-spent life? What greater punishment
than the remorse of conscience arising from the ever-per-
sistent memory of a life of wickedness and crime?

It is obvious that both rewards and punishments are adequate and exact, and that God will "render to every man
according to his deeds," by and through the operation of
his immutable, unchanging laws.

I have now summarized enough of the leading points in
the history of Jesus of Nazareth and of his doctrines, and
compared them with known phenomena with sufficient par-
ticularity to show that the inductions of modern science
demonstrate the essential truth of the history of his physical
manifestations, and to prove, as far as inductive reasoning
from known phenomena can prove anything not physically
demonstrable, the truth of every essential doctrine of his
spiritual philosophy. I have by no means exhausted the
subject, for the New Testament is full of passages confirmatory of the view I have taken. It is true that I have interpreted the passages relating to the conditions precedent to
the attainment of immortal life in a way in which they have
never before been interpreted; but in doing so I have harmonized that which has heretofore seemed incongruous, and
have thus removed a stumbling-block from the pathway of
scepticism. I have no fear that even prejudice will find
fault with my interpretation; for it not only leaves the essential doctrines relating to rewards and punishments uncon-
tradicted, but it affords strong confirmation of their essential
truth. Moreover, my interpretation is confirmed by the facts
of modern science, and must, therefore, shed a new lustre
upon the name and attributes of Jesus, demonstrating, as

it does, the accuracy of his knowledge of the laws of the soul.

It has been but a few years since the researches of science began to furnish facts confirmatory of the history and doctrines of Christ ; but it has come to pass that every new fact discovered, and every new principle evolved, weakens the foundation of every other religious superstructure, and adds strength and harmony of proportions to that erected by the man of Nazareth.

It may, therefore, be now confidently asserted that Christianity possesses that to which no other system of religion can lay a valid claim ; namely, a sound scientific basis.

CHAPTER XXVII.

DEDUCTIONS FROM VARIOUS ATTRIBUTES OF THE SOUL.

IT has often been said that no proposition is worthy of belief that is not verified by phenomena. Whilst I do not commit myself to a maxim so broad in its terms, I have thus far religiously refrained from advancing an idea that is t so verified. In other words, the primary object of this ok is to interpret phenomena, and not to advance new eas, except those which are thrust upon me as necessary deductions from the terms of my hypothesis. Sincerely believing that the fundamental propositions of that hypothesis are true, I have not hesitated to follow them into whatever field they might lead, and to accept every legitimate nclusion. In pursuance of such deductions I have been led reluctantly to the conclusion that none of the phenomena commonly attributed to supermundane agencies afford tangible evidence of the continued existence of the soul after the death of the body. I have, however, been more than compensated by the discovery, in pursuance of the same hypothesis, that in the inherent powers and attributes of the soul is to be found indubitable evidence of its immortality. This evidence is based on phenomena which have been, and may be, produced by experiment. Many of these phenomena have been already pointed out, but others remain to be considered which have an important bearing upon the question under immediate consideration; namely, the immortality of the soul, and its relations to the Supreme Being.

There are still other attributes and powers of the soul which have been considered, from which further conclusions may be drawn which may assist us in forming correct conclusions regarding its status in a future life. The first of these attributes which I purpose briefly to discuss is that of memory, and its relations to the question of spirit identity.

The question as to whether the soul of man retains its identity after the death of the body, is second only in interest and importance to the question of immortality. There are many who hold that the soul is necessarily reabsorbed into the Divine essence, and finds its compensation for the ills of earthly life in becoming an integral part of God, and, as such, a participator in his power and glory. This presupposes a loss of identity, and to most minds would be considered equivalent to annihilation; by others it is regarded as the highest conception of eternal felicity. Thus far no one, as far as I am aware, has attempted to offer any scientific reasons for believing one way or the other. It seems to me that there is abundant evidence in phenomena observable in this life to demonstrate, as far as such a proposition is demonstrable, that the soul does retain its identity in a more pronounced degree, if possible, than we can retain it in this objective existence. In what does identity consist, or, more properly speaking, how is it retained? The answer is, through our consciousness and memory. It is obvious that if either is lost, identity is lost. It is equally obvious that if both are retained, identity is retained. Now, the phenomena alluded to which bear upon the question relate to the perfect memory of the subjective mind, or soul. This faculty of subjective memory is implanted in the human soul for some purpose. It certainly does not pertain to this life, for, as we have seen, it is only under abnormal conditions that the phenomenon is observable. It must, therefore, be a part of the Divine economy pertaining to the future existence of the soul. It has no use here, for objective recollection is all-sufficient for objective existence and purposes. The conclusion is irresistible that it is for the purpose, amongst other things, of enabling the soul to retain its identity. Its bearing upon the question of future rewards and punishments has already been commented upon; nevertheless, at the risk of repetition, a further remark will be ventured. It is obvious that if the soul did not retain a conscious memory of its earthly life, no adequate or just reward or punishment could be meted out to it. Even human justice would revolt against, and human laws would prevent, the infliction of the penalty for a capital crime, if it were clearly proved that the criminal had so far lost his mind as to have no recollection of the events of his past life, or, in other words, had lost conscious identity. Besides, it must not be forgotten that the soul is the seat of the emotions, as well as the storehouse of memory. It is obvious that it is only through the emotions and the memory that rewards can be conferred, or punishments inflicted, upon the immaterial soul.

Another question which has been incidentally alluded to deserves a more extended notice, for the reason that it bears directly upon the question of future rewards and punishments, and is also illustrative of the general hypothesis under consideration; it is the question of conscience. Metaphysicians are divided in opinion on this question, one school holding that conscience is innate and instinctive, and the other that it is the result of experience and education. My hypothesis leads to the conclusion that each school is partly right and partly wrong. Granted that the eternal principles of right and wrong are a part of the fixed and immutable laws of God, it follows that the soul of man will, under favorable conditions, have a clear perception of those laws. Those conditions may or may not be present during the life of the body. They certainly will be present when the soul is freed from the clogs of the flesh, and is able to perceive all the fixed laws of nature. In the mean time, while it is an inhabitant of the body it is amenable to control by the power of objective suggestion, and hence is dependent upon the objective education of the individual for its standard of right and wrong. This standard may be high or low in any individual case. There will be one standard in one community, and another in another, all depending upon education and social environment; but in each case the subjective mind will follow the suggestions imparted to it by objective education. If the standard is high in any individual case, the sentiment will gradually become instinctive, so that the subjective impulses and emotions will play an important part. If the standard is low, the instinctive emotions will only be conspicuous for their absence.

Man stands in his relation to the principles of right and wrong in just the same position that he occupies in his relation to the laws of electricity or any other natural law. He is struggling to ascertain the laws in each case for the purpose of placing himself in harmony with them. His knowledge is of slow growth, but each century finds the general standard of right and wrong higher than it was the century before. If the soul possessed, in the normal condition of man, an instinctive knowledge of those laws, he would not have to await the slow process of evolution to develop them.

History records the name of but one man in whom the eternal principles of right and wrong were instinctive. That man was Jesus Christ. He perceived those laws, as he perceived all spiritual laws, while yet in the flesh. We may profit by his example and his precepts, but otherwise we must work out our own salvation, knowing that, when the soul reaches its final home, it will be in possession of the eternal standard by which to measure the guilt or innocence of every deed done in the body.

The only remaining psychic phenomena which I propose to discuss are those connected with that emotion of the human soul which finds its expression in the worship of the Supreme Being. This feeling is so widespread that no system of philosophy is complete that does not take it into account. Like every other emotion, it has its normal mode of expression, and its abnormal manifestations. The difference between the two modes of expression is so great that their identity of origin has been, to a great extent, lost sight of.

The abnormal manifestation of this emotion now occurs principally among the uncultivated classes of religious worshippers, and the feeling has been somewhat contemptuously designated as " emotional religion." It is conspicuous in the revival meetings of certain religious sects, where in former years its manifestations were so violent and unseemly that it was looked upon as reprehensible ; but these exhibitions have been, of late years, generally repressed, except among the lower orders of the people. Scientists have tried to account for it on the ground that it is the result of mesmeric power consciously or unconsciously exerted by the preachers over their congregations, resulting in an ecstatic emotion wholly abnormal and entirely unconnected with true religion. The fact that it sometimes results in a cataleptic condition, and sometimes in a trance undistinguishable from that produced by hypnotic processes, lent color to the theory, and has gradually brought the educated classes to regard the feeling of religious emotion with distrust. The result is that what used to be known as " vital religion " is gradually becoming a thing of the past, and is giving place to a cold, self-contained, unemotional sentiment, which is as unlike true religious worship as the other, and as abnormal.

It is true that the abnormal manifestations of the emotion are governed by the same laws, and are produced by the same causes, as other subjective phenomena. Suggestion plays its part in these as in other things pertaining to the attributes of the soul ; and in these, as in all others, a wrong, extravagant, or misdirected suggestion produces abnormal results. But this does not argue that the emotion is abnormal. There is no emotion of the human soul that has not its abnormal manifestations when not directed and controlled by reason. The common experience of every-day life demonstrates this proposition. One of the most sacred and praiseworthy of all the human emotions is that of love between the sexes. But the fact that our jails are filled with those who have indulged in its abnormal manifestations does not argue that the institution of marriage is abnormal.

The sentiment of worship is as widespread as the senti· ment of love ; and that very fact shows that it must be taken into account in the diagnosis of the human entity, if we would arrive at correct conclusions. That this sentiment is universal, and is repressed only by an effort of will, no one will deny. It is its abnormal manifestations merely that are to be guarded against. Like every other emotion of the soul, its normal indulgence is in the highest degree healthful and exalting. The normal expression of the emotion of earthly love brings us into harmonious relations with our fellow-beings. The normal expression of the emotion of worship brings the soul into harmonious relations with its Creator. Every form and act of worship is an expression of this emotion. It is experienced by all races of the human family, from the fetich worshipper to the Christian. Each stands in awe and reverence before some superior power, external to himself, and capable of controlling his destiny. In proportion to his intelligence will his conceptions of that power be exalted ; and in proportion to the exaltation of his conceptions will be the intensity of his emotions of awe, reverence, love, worship.

The conclusions which necessarily follow are of the most important character. The first and most important — for it includes all the rest — is that the fact of the existence of the emotion of worship is demonstrative of the existence of a Supreme Being.

And right here I wish to make an important distinction. The standard theological argument in favor of the immortality of the soul is based upon the following syllogism :

1. There is a universal desire for immortality.

2. The mind of man cannot conceive an object of desire the means for the attainment of which are not somewhere in existence.

Conclusion : Man is necessarily immortal.

Now, if these premises were demonstrably correct, we might safely rely upon the conclusion. But they are not correct. The first may be assumed to be practically true, for the sake of the argument ; but the desire for continued life beyond the grave may be explained upon other grounds, namely, upon the instinctive desire to prolong life. This instinct is shared with man by all the animal creation, and pertains, primarily, to the preservation of animal existence. Man soon learns that continued animal existence is impossible. He sees that all must die ; but, as " hope springs eternal in the human breast," he conceives the hope that he may, somehow, live after the death of the body. The existence of the desire for immortality is, therefore, traceable directly to the purely animal instinct of self-preservation.

The second premise is intrinsically absurd. It is obvious that the brain of man may conceive of many objects of desire which are manifestly impossible of realization, as well as non-existent. In the Christian mythology of Milton the idea is developed of a rival power — Satan — in heaven almost, but not quite, equal to God. In the struggle which ensued from a rebellion of Satan he was cast out, and set up a kingdom of his own on this earth. Now, a strictly orthodox person might say that this was merely an allegorical representation of an existent fact. But suppose the poet had gone a step further, and had represented Satan as going outside the universe and setting up a rival universe of his own. Would that conception have proved that an outside universe is possible or existent? [1]

Again, the existence of a Supreme Being is thought to have been demonstrated by the argument of Socrates wherein he confuted Aristodemus the atheist, and used the statues of Polycletus and the pictures of Zeuxis to illustrate the idea that, as the structure of the universe shows evidence of design, therefore there must have been a designer. Theology has never improved upon this argument, and Paley makes the same use of the watch for an illustration as Socrates did of the statues and pictures. It is a strong argument, but it does not reach the point which the human heart desires to have demonstrated. Nor does it add force to, but rather weakens, the argument which is found by all reflecting minds in every tree, leaf, bud, or flower. It simply proves the existence of a force, which all admit.

What the human heart desires, and what the human mind seeks, are proofs of the existence of a God, not of mere intelligence and potentiality, but such a God as Jesus characterized, — a God of love and benevolence, a God who sustains the relation of Father to all humanity.

It seems to me that in seeking within the realm of human desire for an argument in proof either of immortality or the existence of a Supreme Being, theologians have failed to make a necessary distinction between desires which may or may not be universal and inherent, and desires which have their source in the affectional emotions. It is upon the latter only that an argument can be logically predicated.

[1] One of the most eminent and fair-minded theologians in the United States, who has kindly read the manuscript of this work and indulgently criticised its contents, suggests that I have not treated the standard theological argument quite fairly, in that I should have stated the second proposition less broadly: that the desire referred to is *instinctive desire*, and should have been so limited. I freely admit that as careful and candid a reasoner as he would naturally so limit the statement of the proposition. But not all theologians are as candid and logical. However, I provisionally accept his limitation, and reply that the answer to the amended second proposition is embraced in the answer to the first.

And I may go further, and say that an argument logically predicated upon the affectional emotions, is demonstrative. It is true that some of the emotions of the soul seem to pertain exclusively to this life ; but not all. The emotion of religious worship pertains solely to that invisible power which we call God. Nevertheless, we may employ the others for illustration. Let us see how this doctrine applies to the subject under consideration. Putting it in syllogistic form, we have the following : —

1. The affectional emotions are universal attributes of every normally developed human mind.

2. No affectional emotion can have an existence in the normally developed human mind in the absence of an object of affection capable of reciprocal feeling.

Therefore, when a normally developed human being experiences the emotion of love or affection, there is necessarily existent an object of love or affection normally capable of reciprocal emotion.

Thus, the emotion of friendship presupposes the friendly relation existing between man and his fellow-man.

The emotion of sexual love presupposes the sexual relation and the existence of persons of the opposite sex normally capable of reciprocal emotion.

The emotion of parental love presupposes the relation of parent and child, each normally capable of reciprocal attachment.

It follows that *the emotion of religious worship presupposes the existence of an object of worship capable of reciprocal emotion.*

If this is not the correct interpretation of the universal sentiment of worship which is inherent in the breast of every normal human being, then there is an exception to the laws which govern every other human emotion. As there are no exceptions in the operation of nature's laws, the conclusion is inevitable, not only that the emotion of religious worship is normal, but that it is the one phenomenal attribute of the soul which gives to man indubitable evidence of his Divine origin, and demonstrates the existence of a God of love. It is the connecting link between man and his Creator. It is the instinctive manifestation of filial affection which proclaims our Divine pedigree, and demonstrates the universal brotherhood of man and the Fatherhood of God.

" Thou hast made us for Thyself, and our hearts are restless till they rest in Thee."

THE END.

A SCIENTIFIC DEMONSTRATION *of the* FUTURE LIFE

By THOMSON J. HUDSON, LL.D.

THE success that " The Law of Psychic Phenomena " met with induced the author to prepare and publish the present volume, for the purpose of carrying to their legitimate conclusions some of the principles laid down in his former one. Dr. Hudson, in pursuing his inquiry, has endeavored to follow the strictest rules of scientific induction, taking nothing for·granted that is not axiomatic, and holding that there is nothing worthy of belief that is not sustained by a solid basis of well-authenticated facts.— *The New York Times.*

12mo. $1.50

A. C. McCLURG & COMPANY
PUBLISHERS · CHICAGO, ILLINOIS

FIFTH EDITION

THE DIVINE PEDIGREE
OF MAN

*Or, The Testimony of Evolution and
Psychology to the Fatherhood of God*

By THOMSON J. HUDSON, LL.D.

AN original conception of evolution which is worked out with the same avoidance of vague theory, and the same adherence to a basis of well-authenticated facts and to cogent and logical reasoning, which characterize Dr. Hudson's former works. It presents an original and convincing interpretation of the facts which have been accumulated by the labors of scientists such as Hæckel, Darwin, and Spencer; and constitutes an attempt to establish thereby the belief in Christian Theism. It shows that the god-like powers of man exist potentially in the lowest forms of animal life known to us; and advances a powerfully eloquent argument against the atheistic attitude which so many evolutionists have assumed.

The book reveals much study and research, and its optimism is sure to bring much cheer to those who can accept its theories. — *Chicago Tribune.*

An interesting and valuable contribution to the discussion of a great problem.— *The Sunday-School Times.*

12mo. $1.50

A. C. McCLURG & COMPANY
PUBLISHERS · CHICAGO, ILLINOIS

THE LAW OF MENTAL MEDICINE

The Correlation of the Facts of Psychology and Histology in their Relation to Mental Therapeutics

By THOMSON J. HUDSON, LL.D.

The book is one to read studiously, and will appeal to a large class of modern thinkers who have caught a theoretical glimpse of an existence free from the misery of disease. Dr. Hudson's celebrated work, "The Law of Psychic Phenomena," has paved the way for the student of psychic lore to receive and digest his later works.— *New York Tribune.*

His theories are scientific in method, and soundly based, as well as sufficiently untechnical for the general reader.— *San Francisco Argonaut.*

There is no denying the interest the book holds for the thinking, earnest student of mental phenomena, and even those who scoff and sneer at " faith cure " in its various branches will find much in this volume that will start a serious train of thought.— *Nashville American.*

There is nothing of the quack about Dr. Hudson. His book is eminently practical, and is quite free from "the falsehood of extremes." Nobody can be hurt by reading it, and it will help many to correct erroneous prepossessions and misunderstandings.— *Charleston News and Courier.*

"The Law of Mental Medicine" is the title of an interesting book from the pen of Thomson Jay Hudson, in which he points out a simple system of practice depending for its efficacy on natural laws.— *Detroit Free Press.*

12mo. $1.50

A. C. McCLURG & COMPANY

PUBLISHERS · CHICAGO, ILLINOIS

THE EVOLUTION OF THE SOUL

AND OTHER ESSAYS

By THOMSON J. HUDSON, LL.D.

AFTER the death of Dr. Hudson in 1903, enough material was found among his papers for one more book from his bold and original pen. It consists of a number of lectures delivered at various times, and all dealing with the subject on which he is now an acknowledged authority. This collection of scattered papers supplements most admirably his previous books,— particularly "The Law of Mental Medicine" and "The Law of Psychic Phenomena," —and will, in a way, help to complete the work most deplorably interrupted by his untimely death. To say that these essays are in Dr. Hudson's characteristic and illuminating style is all that is needed to convince his thousands of admirers that this posthumous volume is one of the most absorbing interest. The addition of the portrait and biographical sketch will also be much appreciated.

With portrait, $1.50

A. C. McCLURG & COMPANY

PUBLISHERS · CHICAGO, ILLINOIS